COMMUNITY

PURSUING THE DREAM, LIVING THE REALITY

SUZANNE KELLER

PRINCETON UNIVERSITY PRESS
PRINCETON AND OXFORD

COPYRIGHT © 2003 BY PRINCETON UNIVERSITY PRESS
Published by
Princeton University Press,
41 William Street,
Princeton, New Jersey 08540

In the United Kingdom:
Princeton University Press,
3 Market Place,
Woodstock, Oxfordshire OX20 1SY

Library of Congress Cataloging-in-Publication Data

Keller, Suzanne.
Community : pursuing the dream, living the reality / Suzanne Keller.
p. cm. — (Princeton studies in cultural sociology)
Includes bibliographical references and index.
ISBN 0-691-09564-7 (alk. paper)
1. Community. 2. Community life — Case studies. 3. Community life — New
Jersey — Case studies. I. Title. II. Series.

HM756 .k44 2002
307 — dc21   2002072253

British Library Cataloging-in-Publication Data is available

This book has been composed in Sabon with Futura display

Printed on acid-free paper. ∞

www.pupress.princeton.edu

Printed in the United States of America

10 9 8 7 6 5 4 3 2

FOR CHARLES

"My true love hath my heart . . ."

CONTENTS

TABLES

PREFACE

Why does one write a book? It is a question I have often asked myself during the past few years. Specifically, why *this* book? There are two answers, one short and one long.

The short answer takes me back to a dinner party. I had just joined Princeton University's sociology department following a four-year stay in Greece. As is customary on such occasions, there was the usual exchange of pleasantries around the table during the first course. By the second, I discovered that the diner on my right was a developer who had just completed a "new community." When I told him of my work at the Athens Center of Ekistics headed by the charismatic architect-planner, C. A. Doxiadis, he seemed more than politely interested. As I elaborated on my research on Athen's neighborhoods, he sat up and said "Why don't you take a look at the community I have just put together?" Little did I know that this invitation from Herbert Kendall, the developer along with Gerald Finn of Twin Rivers, would affect my future for decades.

The long answer to the question is that this book reflects my abiding interest in an endangered species called community. It reflects my deep conviction that modern life suffers from both an excess and a deficiency: too much emphasis on "the great big I," as the Shakers termed it, and too little on community. Why this gap?

Well, modernity, for one. Modernity altered the basic conditions of life in the society-in-the-making along with extensive mobility, urbanization, and an accent on achievement and self-determination. The new society, it seemed, had no need of community.

This would have stunned the citizens of ancient Greece or medieval Florence who appreciated individual excellence, but assumed the indispensability of community.

What the ancients did grapple with was how to make communities more vital and just, so as to enable human beings to live together cooperatively and harmoniously.

That ideal still beckons, but in a subdued way, overshadowed by an overriding focus on personal success and well-being. This liberating thrust tends to undervalue the human need for security, fellowship, and, most significantly, meaningful participation in a totality greater than one's self. We do acknowledge the need for community for the uprooted or the culturally adrift, but even those on top of the survival chain have need of it. Privilege does not shield one from the question that the French writer Albert Camus called the most painful, the most heartbreaking, question of our time — "Where can I be at home?"

This is a question that resonates in many quarters today — for the native born no less than for immigrants — as they search for home in community or community as home.

We tend to confine the idea of home to the small, domestic nest, which has placed burdens on the family that the family was not designed to meet. But historically, home was blended with community — as in such place names as Birmingham, Nottingham, Framingham — where one had roots, ancestors, collective memories, shared experiences.

The radius of human connections expanded with the advent of industrialism and the machine age, and the guiding image became the individual who strove and succeeded — the "self-made man" ascendant. When the mores of the metropolis displaced the mores of main street, the new watchwords became autonomy, independence, self-realization — wonderful qualities if within a wider context.

As modern life unfolded, however, the virtues extolled early on lost their luster for many. Privacy became isolation. Anonymity imperiled one's sense of identity. The self, severed from traditional moorings, stood apart from community.

Gradually, moderns became so adept at the pursuit of self-interest that they ignored their dependence on others — on the people, resources, traditions, and ideas on which human survival ultimately rests.

But the tide would turn as early as the nineteenth century, when the theme of community lost was sounded in literature and in life. A century later, the theme persists as people realize that their choices may be too narrowly self-centered and too disconnected from broad social goals.

Our ample cultural and material resources notwithstanding, the Tower of Babel (noncommunication) and the Tragedy of the Commons (noncaring) cast their shadows behind the scene and moved our gaze to community once again.

Several questions have impelled this book. How does a sense of community take hold? How, at critical junctures, can we become each other's keepers? And where might one best study the conditions under which community can grow?

I found the opportunity to explore these questions at close range when I accepted the invitation to take a look at the living texture of a community in the making. This permitted me to test ideas I had explored in the classroom. It was a laborious, arduous, yet also fascinating undertaking.

I began my research with the goal of discovering how a "new, planned" community comes to life once the physical infrastructure is in place. After two years of studying the charter of Twin Rivers, interviewing residents, formally assessing the architecture and design, and monitoring the settling-in phase, a more fundamental question not unrelated to the first, emerged: What are the characteristics of community that the planned design intended to foster? How do we identify them? Who needs community most? How does a plan come to life?

So my questions evolved as I watched a community evolve. Human beings and their creations are so complex that no one-shot survey would suffice. To study the genesis of a community requires time and deep acquaintance to distill wheat from chaff, the enduring from the ephemeral.

The book is divided into three parts. Part I, *Community As Image and Ideal* (chapters 1–3) reviews classic and contemporary theories of community. Part II, *A Community Is Launched*, presents the empirical analysis of a community in process of formation, including the nature of a planned unit development (PUD) (chapter 4); the residents responses to house, space, place and people (chapters 5, 7, 8, and 9); the struggle for self-government (chapter 6); private and public obligations (chapter 10); governance and leadership (chapters 11 and 12); and sources of unity and division (chapter 13).

Part III, *Old Imperatives, New Directions* (chapters 14 and 15) reflects on the meanings of the empirical analysis and the vicissitudes and vagaries of this collective experiment over time.

A single study, even if it takes a long and in-depth view, cannot be definitive of course. Hopefully, it will inspire future studies to enrich our understanding of how to create vital and fulfilling communities.

I should also add that I see the local, territorial community not as an alternative to the modern megalopolis but as a companion to it. Nor do I have any illusions about the dangers of bigotry and Babbitry in small circumferences. But I do argue for the community as a counterforce to the TV-directed lonely crowd in the mass society of the twenty-first century. To ignore the need for community is to invite its reactionary manifestations in a lockstep mass conformity that feeds on the potential for hatred and destructiveness behind the intricate façade of contemporary society.

COMMUNITY

PART I
COMMUNITY AS IMAGE AND IDEAL

CHAPTER 1

COMMUNITY: THE PASSIONATE QUEST

All of us carry within us more love and above all more longing than
. . . society is able to satisfy.

—Karl Mannheim

When I asked the undergraduates in my Princeton University seminars
on ideal communities what, if anything, they would want to change
about their Princeton experience, their answers startled me. Most of the
hundred or so students wished there were more of a sense of community. But why? I probed. The number of undergraduates is small, the
university merits its reputation for its commitment that students be amply supplied with a great variety of activities and opportunities for social contacts and a social life beyond the classroom, and privacy when
desired. What more could one possibly want? The replies of the students
varied, of course, but the underlying themes were almost unanimous.

They mentioned the fragmentation and the lack of a unifying principle that would help to bridge distances across departments and help
them integrate the exciting intellectual fare offered. This unifying princi-

ple would assist them in sorting out relevant from irrelevant, essential from trivial, information. They wanted to locate some basis for choosing one subject over another, other than the expansion of intellectual horizons, a star professor, or delight in learning, important as these obviously were.

They acknowledged also feelings of isolation amid all the lavish resources and sought to overcome these in various ways: Some turned to religion, others threw themselves into social life, volunteer work, or more intensive studies, while others sought romantic partners to cling to. Choosing a major resolved the smaller question of focus and identity but left hanging the larger question of purpose and meaning — what to work toward.

The accelerated tempo of their lives was another recurrent theme. Their packed days and evenings left little time for reflection.

Some also suggested that the lack of community may have helped lead to the unintended — and often deplored — segregation of students by race, regional origins, wealth, or religious affiliation. Instead of informal social contacts across groups, black students ate at one table, Hispanics at another, Asians at a third. Other tables were separated by prep school or major — engineering, for example. Some of this may be desirable for bonding, but much of it is antithetical to pluralism — a defensive banding together for solace through group affiliation.

As I listened to these young, bright students privileged in the opportunities offered by a great university, I was struck by how their concerns reflected the often-cited complaints about modernity: specialization, a sense of aimlessness, loneliness amid multitudes, the lack of a center and a grounded self. In a word, the missing community.

This must come as a surprise to those who consider community as superfluous for the most modern sectors of contemporary societies — the young, highly educated, technologically sophisticated, success-bent — which these students obviously are.

Of course, community is a chameleon term that is used in many, often contradictory, ways. It might be helpful to begin this inquiry with two prevalent perspectives.

One is that community is akin to an organism where the whole is more important than individual members. This organic model is historically the oldest. It is also all-embracing, hence less well suited to modern circumstances, though it continues to prevail as a nostalgic fantasy of a lost Eden.

A more recent model, which developed in the West in response to revolutionary political and economic developments in the seventeenth and eighteenth centuries, the "atomistic/contractarian" model, is based on the idea of a social contract that binds "free persons" who have consented to live together.

Both models are present in the world today but to differing degrees. Sir Henry Maine (1864) saw a historic evolution from the organic to the contractarian model or, in his words, from status *to* contract, as in the technologically developed societies. On a world scale, however, the majority of people continue to live in relatively bounded communities that function as organisms rooted in tradition and precedent. Each conception has strengths and weaknesses. The organic conception gives too much power to the community and threatens to leave too little room for individual freedom, though this need not be so. Wylie's portrait of the Vaucluse (1974) or Colette's of Saint-Saveur en Puisaye (1953) portray communities where people were rich in individuality and tolerant of diversity, yet mindful of their interdependence and their need for one another.

The social contract model of community, most forcefully articulated by John Locke and Adam Smith, following, yet sharply divergent from Hobbes, stresses self-determination and autonomy, delimited government, and the self-regulating market. But the freedom and opportunities it exalts are double-edged, favoring those with personal and social resources and neglecting the economically and socially disadvantaged for whom freedom may mean poverty and social inferiority.

Each model also accords a different place to the common good and collective requirements. The organic model defines and structures the common good via divine or secular authorities. The contract model leaves it to the invisible hand or ignores it altogether unless prompted by an enlightened public or protesting minorities.

When Plato wrote *The Republic* he did not question the idea of community but assumed its indispensability, if only for lack of meaningful alternatives. What he wrestled with was how to obtain and preserve the just community within which humanity could live productively and peacefully imbued with a strong sense of interdependence and empathy.

In the several hundred years of the modem era, however, the questions have shifted and community has become problematic. A threatened species whose demise some welcome and others deplore, it is alternately longed for or ignored as passé, as people struggle with Camus's question "Where can I feel at home?" It is a question that surfaces not only for the wanderers, the exiled, the homeless but also for their more settled confreres in cities and suburbs at the top of the survival chain. One way this question resonates now is in the search for community — how to find it, nurture it, and keep it.

Given the profusion of definitions of community, one is often at a loss as to how to separate the essential from the superfluous, especially since there are always exceptions to the general rule. For example, most scholars define community as rooted in territorial/spatial and generational togetherness. But for the Christian Gnostics, the root of community rested on the emancipation of human beings from earth, blood ties, and place, and linked by universal aspirations.

In short, the term "community" is an all-encompassing one. The territorial connotation of community is surely the most familiar and, in my view, the most basic. But there is also community considered rhetorically, as in reference to the academic community, the sailing community, or the bohemian community. Hence there is the danger of attaching the term "community" somewhat indiscriminately to all human aggregates.

Community may be used in a philosophical sense, as a reference to a moral or spiritual entity, engendering communion with one's fellows and a fate that is shared, or as a term to designate distinct units of territorial and social organization, such as hamlets, villages, towns — all the typical places in which people maintain their homes, raise families, and establish roots.

Despite this profusion of emphases, some basic agreements do exist, and the following themes recur repeatedly.

Community as Place, Turf, Territory

The idea of a bounded, identifiable territory is taken for granted by virtually every serious commentator until we get to cyberspace in the late twentieth and early twenty-first century, which we shall discuss later.

Community is the antithesis of Gertrude Stein's description of Los Angeles: "There's no there, there." With few exceptions, community always denotes a there. The territory that encloses a community offers a proximity and density conducive to other kinds of closeness. No matter in which container — village, town, suburb — community as captured, delimited space shapes the scale of collective life and the patterns of life created therein.

Community as Shared Ideals and Expectations

The focus here is on a life in common, resulting in shared emotional stakes and strong sentimental attachments toward those who share one's life space. These are the "habits of the heart" in de Tocqueville's memorable phrase; they are states of mind that generate reciprocity, a sense of duty, and the moral sentiments that forge collective coherence and endurance.

Community as a Network of Social Ties and Allegiances

Of the ninety-four definitions of community identified by Hillery (1955), social bonds and social interaction were cited in two-thirds of them. But social interaction does not operate alone. It reflects and reinforces additional dimensions — a given scale, shared goals and sentiments that bind people to their common enterprise.

When directed toward common goals — let us say, support for schools or recreational programs — social interaction can become a source of unity. And unity is a central component of the word "community," which is a combination of two Latin terms with opposite meanings: *com*, with or together; and *unus*, the number one. Hence community is a union of many elements.

Community as a Collective Framework

Here community defines, names, encloses, organizes aggregate activities and projects, and encompasses the institutions and rules that guide the collectivity, including:

- Legitimate governance, authority, and leadership during emergencies and crises
- Ideologies that justify collective arrangements and goals and
- Values that sustain social solidarity and commitments

Collective frameworks interpenetrate with the physical shell and the cultural mold to create unique community configurations.

What Community Is Not

To arrive at a definitional shorthand for community, it may be useful to pause for a moment to consider what community is not.

Interpersonal intimacy is often considered antithetical to community. Gossiping across a fence, sharing secrets, joining to do battle for a common cause do not by themselves suffice for community. Such closeness needs structural, cultural, and sentimental supports as well as an altruistic outreach of affection and empathy to bind a totality.

The same might be argued for formal organizational membership. If organizations are joined to pursue personal interests, they are too limited for community: "With such egoism, there is no love of others for their sakes, no identification of their good as one's own . . . no tie that binds" (Mary Rousseau 1991, p. 52). For community to exist, individuals must not only be close to one another but moving toward collective goals as well.

Nor are group affiliation or social categorization on the basis of race, class, gender, nationality, or generation automatically insignias of community. These have community potential only if individuals consider them significant bases for a shared identity. To qualify for community, social categorization must be translated into a consciousness of kind, a sense of belonging, and a shared destiny, past or future.

Then there is *communitarianism*, often confused with community. Beyond their linguistic kinship, the two terms are only tangentially related. Community is concrete and rooted in place. Communitarianism is abstract, emphasizing a set of moral and philosophical principles — social justice, civic responsibility, cooperation — for citizens to strive for wherever they reside. Communitarians, as represented in key works by Pocock (1975), MacIntyre (1980), Sandel (1982), Walzer (1983), Sullivan (1982), Gutmann (1985), and Etzioni (1993), oppose the impersonality of bureaucracies and advocate decentralization and a human scale infused with traditional human values.

But while communitarians do not deal with actual communities, they have been a critical force for drawing attention to the idea of community in the public dialogue. In essence, their message is that the culture of individualism, the laissez-faire market society of consumerism, and self-advancement have been carried too far. A return to the basics — civic commitment, social solidarity, public participation, and devotion to the common good — is urgently called for. Nothing less than human survival is at stake.

Their impressive body of work notwithstanding, there is one question that communitarians do not raise and therefore cannot answer, namely, how their high ideals can be realized. How can one move from moral exhortation to being just, cooperative, responsive, and responsible to the living test and concrete texture of community?

That question is at the heart of this book, which seeks to separate the term "community" from all-encompassing generalizations, grasp its significant dimensions, and study its evolution over time. The course of this evolution remains largely uncharted, since most studies, mired in static description, focus on a single moment in time, thus missing the long-range view. This is where the study of a new community is crucial. Unlike established communities that have grown in unplanned, piecemeal fashion, the secret of their births well hidden from view, a community in the making permits one to monitor its often tortuous gestation. This can tell us much about how a community comes to life, who makes it happen, the high and low points of this development, and at what point the "newborn" can look forward to a long and productive life.

These issues and others are explored in this book using the genesis of Twin Rivers, the first planned unit development in the state of New Jersey. This longitudinal excursion over several decades reveals the deeper forces that build up and tear down the tissue of community. It also provides a context for addressing questions about the possibility of community that have preoccupied thinkers for thousands of years.

So far, then, we can say that community is both archetype and elusive ideal. Even in our time, when communities are being envisaged for outer space as well as for cyberspace, there are always two recurrent questions: How can self be linked to community and how can community be linked to society?

De Tocqueville was one of many to underscore that linkage, especially in his volumes on nineteenth-century America (1990, vols. 1, 2). He saw collective responsibility, civic concern, and a morally sound private life as parts of a whole. The investment of one's energies and passions in the community gave shape and direction to one's personal life, which in turn fed back into community.

By contrast, contemporary individualism, with its accent on privacy and separateness makes community problematic. For those who consider community essential for human existence, the loss of community means the loss of a central part of human identity, a "signal of a humanity gone astray" (Lasch 1991). In the same vein, Bellah (1991) describes contemporary Americans as "suspended in glorious isolation." Though they may not be aware of it, they are missing one language, while being too fluent in the other—the language of individualism, where people are separate and competitive. The missing language is the language of community, where individuals are seen as organically connected to each other (ibid.). This second language is much more difficult to learn given the individualistic bent of modern societies where striving for the common good while pursuing one's own interests becomes inherently contradictory.

Still, community continues to have a magical ring. Modernity, for all its technological wonders, has not managed to dispel the need for it. Never a simple matter, this need has become vastly more complex. Always somewhat mysterious and enigmatic, community cannot simply be grafted onto the huge bureaucracies of modern life. This trivializes the concept of community (Bender 1978, pp. 143–44). For, "no large-scale organization," writes Nisbet, "can really meet the psychic demands of individuals because by its very nature it is too large, too complex, too bureaucratized and altogether too aloof from the residual meanings by which humans live." Individuals need "communities small in scale but solid in structure" that will offer them a sense of security and fulfillment (Nisbet 1960, p. 82).

Thus, those who predicted that industrialization would cause the death of community need to reconsider their conclusion, as the continued salience of community defies its premature burial.

Modernity, to be sure, promised much, but it also took much away. In the past, community represented a total web of life. There was a perceived order guiding the cosmos, and life, though not secure, was somehow predictable. To be expelled from one's community was akin to death.

With industrial urbanism, the taken-for-granted-world collapsed and the "disrupted transcendence" and "great feeling of meaninglessness" led to an often intense search for "one unifying thing" (Luckman 1970, pp. 585–86). For many, the newly won freedoms spelled rootlessness. It was harder to fit the pieces of one's life together. This might work well for mobile cosmopolites seeking adventure and opportunity, but it left the more traditionally minded emotionally stranded. In time, the desire for stability and security propelled many to search for ethnic, racial, or religious roots in a move to "escape from freedom" (Fromm 1969). To them, community beckoned as the nucleus of human connectedness and solidarity in a world of huge Kafka-esque institutions — corporations, city halls, suburban malls, government bureaucracies.

An interesting historic example of this struggle stems from Boimondau, a French factory producing watch cases in Valence, France. When the employees turned the factory into a cooperative venture they were at first exhilarated by the liberation from the hierarchy of the workplace. But, to their surprise, it soon became evident that too much freedom resulted in a kind of chaotic anarchy that was as destructive to achieving their goals as excessive control and the suppression of spontaneity had been. After considerable soul searching, the workers realized their need for some kind of binding force and a shared ethical basis. Hence, in trial-and-error fashion they went on to reestablish rules and work toward a balance of freedom and discipline embodied in a lawful community.

The cry for freedom and the need for order has a universal cadence, one deeply linked to the nature of community. Banish or suppress the communal impulse, and it will come back with a vengeance. Sometimes it does so in relatively benign form, as it did in the utopian experiments that proliferated during the nineteenth century, but it can also emerge brutally, as it has in various forms of ethnic- and racially based genocide.

Misconceptions about Community

A common misconception is that community must result in the suppression, even the extinction, of individuality. As always, this depends in part on the definition employed. If individualism is seen as directly related to community, then community and individualism are and have been compatible in many traditional and preliterate societies (Diamond 1981).

In contrast, contemporary individualism, with its accent on anonymity and separation from others, emphasizes the individual, not in relation to a community, but as uniquely different from it. The two are constructed as antagonists, which makes them incompatible.

Another misconception speaks of society and community interchangeably. This effaces the distinctiveness of each.

Society might be thought of as an overarching system of social, political, and cultural arrangements that encompass the totality. Its practices are formalized and abstract; its scale is superpersonal.

By contrast, community is tangible, proximate, based on direct contact, mutual awareness, and a sense of empathy with those with whom one shares one's life in a definite place. In community, self and terrain are intertwined.

Without communal underpinnings, society tends to become rigid, ritualistic, lifeless. People may go through the required motions but they do so amid distrust, indifference, apathy. Hence we must make room in our thinking for the "little community" (Redfield 1960, p. 41) to nourish the great society, not as its antithesis but as its complement.

One fact attested to over and over again is how fragile communities actually are and how easily they become undone. Calamities are thought to strengthen communities but the contrary is often the case.

In the Buffalo Creek calamity, analyzed by Erikson (1976), for example, a seventeen-mile-long coal-mining area was deluged by 132 million gallons of water when the dam collapsed. In a minute, everything — houses, livestock, vehicles, and people — was swept away, leaving 80 percent of the five thousand residents homeless. In the aftermath of the silence, numbness, and shock, the integuments of community were laid bare. The community was destroyed, not only physically but culturally and symbolically.

Before the flood, Buffalo Creek had been homogeneous both materially and culturally. Its people worked, married, raised children, and lived by similar rules and values. Community was "the envelope in which they lived." Families, neighbors, and friends formed a series of concentric circles that linked strangers and intimates in a shared round of life. Where the wider society extolled the separate, self-propelled individual, each an island unto him- or herself, Buffalo Creek drew its boundaries around whole groups. Neighbor would reach out to neighbor, and the fate of one affected all. "Like when somebody was hurt, everybody was hurt" (ibid.).

In seeking to grasp the essence of community for the shell-shocked survivors, Erikson singled out the "networks of understandings," and a "constant readiness to look after one's neighbors, or, rather, to know without being asked what needed to be done." In contrast to the individualistic ethos of the society at large, here the community was the key actor, and emotions generally ascribed to individuals were ascribed to the community: "It is the community that cushions pain, the community that provides a context for intimacy, the community that represents morality." This confirmed Erikson's conclusion that the loss and despair community members experienced was a reaction not only to the disaster itself but also to the destruction of the web of community. "There's a part of us all missing somewhere" (ibid., pp. 189, 193–194, 196). It was the end of the world, a wound that would never heal.

In the aftermath of the deluge, two developments proved surprising. One was the absence of the community outreach and empathy that often accompanies such catastrophes and gathers the survivors into a "community of sufferers," a "democracy of distress," or a "post-disaster Utopia" (ibid., p. 200). Trauma does, at times, strengthen community, as shared pain mobilizes latent energies to repair the damaged texture of collective life. That did not happen in Buffalo Creek, perhaps because the ubiquity of the disaster left its victims disconnected. There was no remnant intact or strong enough on which to rebuild and regenerate.

The other development was a surge of immorality that accompanied the ensuing depression and demoralization. Thefts, delinquencies, alcoholism, and indifference multiplied, as "the boundaries of moral space began to collapse." Long-term marriages fell apart, friendships faded. When the moral and material framework of the community was destroyed, so were the inner supports it had sustained. In the long run perhaps, muses Erikson, "morality is a form of community participation." People's health deteriorated as well with ailments that no medical diagnosis could explain. "Health has something to do with feeling whole and in harmony" with the larger totality, which suggests that the health of the individual is dependent on the state of communal health. When the community is intact, it can provide a protective layer of insulation and a reassuring camouflage of real life, since "one of the crucial jobs of a culture is to edit reality in such a way that it seems manageable" (ibid., pp. 205, 209, 226, 240). All of that was lost in Buffalo Creek.

Eventually, the people of Buffalo Creek would win $13.5 billion from the coal company that was responsible for the collapse of the dam, but they would never recover their sense of community, of meaning, of wholeness.

Ironically, the help extended by outside agencies, in this case by HUD (Federal Department of Housing and Urban Development), inadvertently reinforced the community's breakdown. HUD focused on individuals, dispensing material resources on a first-come, first-served basis, regardless of the neighborhood in which people had lived or how much they had lost. Well-meaning and helpful to individual victims as this may have been, it left the victimized community unattended. By ignoring the community context of the disaster, it froze the residents in their isolation.

This is a good illustration of the collision between two different social orders, the one personal, rooted, emotionally coherent, the other impersonal, categorical, and based on individual interest. Much of what was lost could not be retrieved because it rested on things unspoken and tacitly understood. Neighborly rituals and relations, for example, could not simply be transplanted. Once disrupted, one cannot carry them into new situations "like negotiable emotional currency" (ibid., p. 191).

Traumatized communities differ from an assemblage of traumatized persons because a collective trauma affects all simultaneously. Collective trauma, by damaging the "bonds attaching people" to one another, erodes the core, the heart, of the afflicted communities and precipitates their deaths.

Abiding Questions

The nature of community has engaged thinkers from ancient times to the present. Plato, Aristotle, Hobbes, de Tocqueville, Marx, Tönnies, and others posed the central questions that absorb us still. Among them are:

- How are communities created and maintained over time?
- How is a "spirit of community" generated?
- How are human differences bridged for the sake of the common good?

In ancient times, and for centuries until the modern age, there may have been too much community, as community stifled individuals under the yoke of collective demands. Today, there may be too little community and the longing for community is displaced into substitute or illusory forms. From time to time, the need bursts through in frantic, excessive, and at times, explosive ways sweeping order and reason aside in favor of a passionate but disruptive collective frenzy. One thinks of postsoccer mayhem, mass revelries, inflagrations of hate, or worshipful throngs teetering on the edge of hysteria. It is especially at such times that questions about community — or the lack thereof — come to the fore. But what also becomes painfully apparent is how little we understand about such mass phenomena or the lack of community that permits collective anonymous violence to surface.

This book is several books — a literal account of a community in formation; an ongoing tale of the trials and tribulations of the common life; a report of how plans and programs become living realities — but principally it is a book about people and their struggle to fashion unity and community.

The big social questions yield their answers but slowly. The explorer who wishes to penetrate them requires time, patience, and persistence. The nature and genesis of community is such a question. If it is true that the "little community" is seen as "something to be made good" and as "something through which to make the great society good" (Redfield 1960, p. 154), it deserves careful and sustained study, which I have endeavored to do.

By studying one community in depth, I hope also to illumine questions about communities in general. Many forces are at work here, both local and global, historic and contemporary, internal and external, ideal and real.

Chapters 2–3 of Part I, Community as Image and Ideal, examine guiding theories, historic prototypes, and core concepts of community as background for the substantive analysis of the in-depth exploration of a new community in the making.

Part II, A Community Is Launched, monitors the course of community formation for a middle-class American population.

Part A, Creating Roots, spells out the launching of Twin Rivers, New Jersey, a planned development — its physical setting; the social characteristics of its first inhabitants (chapter 4); and the residents' reactions to their neighbors, houses, and facilities (chapter 5) as they move toward self-governance (chapter 6).

Part B, Creating a Collective Self, discusses the extent of community participation (chapter 7) and the nature of friendships and social relations (chapter 8).

Part C, Building the Foundations, focuses on the role of space and design (chapter 9); private and public rights and responsibilities (chapter 10); the first collective undertaking, the lawsuit (chapter 11); the critical role of leaders (chapter 12); and the forces for unity and division (chapter 13).

Part III, Old Imperatives, New Directions, reflects on key themes and issues for communities in the future (chapter 14) and on the import of key findings (chapter 15). An epilogue on community in cyberspace concludes the book.

CHAPTER 2
HISTORIC MODELS OF COMMUNITY

Utopias strive to turn over a new page.

— Lewis Mumford

In the quest to distill some essential properties of community that are instructive for our own day, I have chosen four historic prototypes: the Greek polis of the fifth century B.C.E., the monastic community of Western Christianity, the Puritan towns of seventeenth-century New England, and the Utopian communities of the nineteenth and twentieth centuries.

Each of the four prototypes had a moment in the sun only to be displaced by newer, later models better suited to the changing times. Each had unique features and each was exemplary in important respects. All have something to teach us about the forces that build, and the forces that erode, community.

The Greek Polis

"Protagoras, as described by Plato, recapitulates the condition of humanity before they had devised a binding social order. At first, he says, there were no cities and people lived a scattered life. And so the wild beasts destroyed them. They lacked the political skill to live in concert — and they fought amongst themselves. Zeus then moved to preserve the human race and sent Hermes to bring *aidos* (*mutual respect*) and *dike* (*justice*) to mortals so as to promote social order and social bonds." Indeed these were to be *shared* goods, shared skills; those who lack these were proof not of personal deficiencies but of collective defects. (Arthur Adkins, 1972, pp. 103–104)

The polis of ancient Greece offers us a model of community in a civilization very different from ours. As a first effort at democracy — one discussed, criticized, and admired for thousands of years — it continues to merit careful scrutiny. The usual translation of *polis* as "city-state" is misleading, because the polis was not a city and, at the same time, it was "much more than a State" (Kitto 1959, p. 65).

The earliest poleis were geographic units, small in size and population, economically sustained by agriculture, and centralized with respect to political, religious, and military functions (Starr 1991, p. 37). Originating around the eighth century B.C.E. and lasting for several hundred years, the poleis seem to have amalgamated historic tribal allegiances into larger territorial settlements, challenging the hereditary aristocratic social organization that was fueled by military glory, hierarchy, and status. In its historic resonance, however, the polis refers not to an actual community but to the *ideal* of community that emphasized lawful self-government by all citizens within a small area demarcated by clear, often natural, boundaries that fostered the spiritual and religious unity of the inhabitants. Held together by "religion, by pride, by life" (ibid.), the bonds of the polis were psychological and spiritual, not physical, and continual emphasis was placed on creating such bonds by celebrating community festivals, emphasizing legendary tales, building temples, and making sacrifices to the gods.

The *polis*, which originally meant citadel, as in Acropolis, was the center of public life. Its aim was the attainment of a just society able to reconcile the contradictory tensions between individual ambition and collective goals.

Above all, the polis was a symbol of unity in a fragmented and fractured age. Though autonomous, each polis was also part of a wider cultural terrain — of Hellas, or Greek civilization generally — that prevailed despite continuous warfare. Hellas pulled the Greeks together with a common language, shared myths, and a special worldview.

Nonetheless, there were patent contradictions in the polis, often unrecognized by scholars enamored of its ideals. The democracy it embodied was confined to a small segment of the population: Only adult men of birth and status could become citizens. This meant that democracy extended to one-tenth of the population and excluded nine-tenths. Yet it was inclusive, in principle at least, for it extended democratic participation to all qualified citizens, who were encouraged — indeed expected — to debate, challenge, and deliberate in open assembly on basic questions of social policy and law.

Whatever its shortcomings, the idea of the polis as the civic *community* that tied all citizens to one another and to common projects and purposes was a stunning intellectual achievement for its time. Though it always remained more ideal than real, it also moved humanity a huge step forward by preparing citizens for self-government based on informed deliberation and public participation. And although democracy was available only to one stratum of the population, the general atmosphere of these small, autonomous, self-contained units was conducive to a spirit of community as geographic and economic characteristics combined to encourage a "communal predisposition and character" (Kitto 1959). Size and scale were able to strengthen the sense of community despite sharp class and status divisions. Citizens knew one another by sight through frequent encounters in shops, streets, public squares, and places of amusement. Familiarity and reciprocity encouraged a sense of shared existence.

Indeed every Greek could know the polis in a way today's citizens cannot know, hence grasp, the society in which they live. Less divided into separate subworlds, citizens could experience the interconnectedness of society directly. If the crops failed, the citizens "could see the fields" that gave them sustenance; they could see "how agriculture, trade, and industry dovetailed into one another"; they knew "the frontiers where they were strong and where weak"; they could "discern shifts in public opinion." At bottom, it was the "small scale of things" that permitted the ancient Greeks to perceive and grasp "the entire life of the polis, and the relation between its parts" (ibid., p. 72).

Public affairs had an "immediacy and concreteness which they cannot possibly have for us." "Duty" was not an idle word but an unquestioned call to action, concrete and direct. Instead of paying taxes, for example, the rich Athenian was responsible for certain "liturgies" — keeping a warship for a given period of time or financing plays for the great festivals. Although the obligations were burdensome, those who undertook them were admired, and this made the connection between individual citizen and the polis vivid and immediate. By a continuous process of interaction, the polis kept ideals of citizenship aloft. Where the modern attitude emphasizes the state "as a piece of machinery, for the production of safety and convenience," the polis was a living force always in the process of creation, the sum total of "the whole communal life of the people, political, cultural, moral — even economic" (ibid.).

Plato, Socrates, Aristotle, and the great poets and playwrights we revere to this day were all deeply a part of the polis. Aeschylus depicted it as "the very crown and summit of things" (ibid., p. 75). Aristotle defined man as "a creature who lives in a polis" and only within it could he attain humanity (Bosanquet 1895, p. 27). The polis and its religion, art, games, and debates were "necessary" in a way that voluntary associations of like-minded people are not. "Vivid and comprehensible," the polis was one with the hills and sea, with the acropolis and the market, with one's self and one's world, a living community.

Though ancient Athens scarcely represented the model of the "face-to-face" society that many have claimed, attributes of a local community, were clearly in evidence: Close interaction with known others provided the feeling of community, and the crossing of social boundaries via the exercise of citizenship provided its substance. If in the classical fifth-century B.O.E. Athens had evolved into a "an imagined community" run by an elite (Ober 1989, pp. 31, 33), at a deeper level, it drew on a common ethnic heritage, ancestral ties to Attic soil, and a common political and ecological framework.

At its height, the polis was complemented by elaborate public buildings. These included an acropolis, protective walls, the agora, temples, a theater, and gymnasia. Public assembly, rotation of office, and periodic election of officeholders characterized its governance. Citizens were expected to help shape public policy directly, in contrast to modern political democracies with their representative institutions that make government seem distant and remote. Without a polis, one had no home and faced permanent exile. At its noblest, polis meant freedom, security, connectedness, and the good life (MacIntyre 1980, p. 127).

Not unlike two thousand years later, however, another prominent theme vied with the polis to create familiar and stressful contradictions: the theme of individual glory, as exemplified by the victors in athletic contests. These victors were a source of pride, since they brought honor to the entire polis, and they were celebrated in song and story. Yet the contests also encouraged a self-aggrandizement and self-centeredness inimical to the sense of community. Eventually, the "fierce competition for public honor and a raw, undisguised drive for riches scarcely ever again equaled in ancient times" came close to destroying the spiritual unity of the polis.

Yet another familiar and continuous source of tension and disappointment in the ancient polis was public indifference to the obligations of citizenship. Citizens did not always live up to their duties or appreciate the rights granted them. The ideals of public duty, self-governance, and commitment were often elusive, undermined by fractious civil strife and social indifference. Still, the structure — the framework — was in place. It stood as a testament to the brilliance of Greek civilization and the inspiration it offered in the centuries to follow.

It was the Greeks who were the first in Western civilization to work out the complex links between the individual and the community: The community expressed the "common mind," one reflected in every individual; but in turn, the individual needed the community for full humanity (Bosanquet 1895).

The polis was the framework within which every citizen was expected to take part and join with others to address common concerns. As a forum it would enable the citizens to deliberate as a body; as a court, it would judge wrongs done to citizens.

A modern person forced to choose between family and country might well choose family. Such a choice would have been inconceivable to the ancients. Whoever would pose such a choice obviously was a "citizen of nowhere, an internal exile wherever he lived." Hence a barbarian lacked a polis and the political relationships based on freedom and negotiation among sovereign subjects (ibid., p. 146).

Although remote in historic time, the Greeks suffered from some very modern ills that would eventually bring down the society of which the polis was a prime creation. Warring city-states, internal factionalism, and a narrow conception of community and citizenship that excluded a majority of the people would seriously undermine the body politic (Gouldner 1965, p. 166).

The promise of full citizenship in ancient Greece was a bit like the promise of equality in the modern United States. It was an ideal deeply embedded in institutions and belief systems, a theory available to all, yet reality fell short. Such cultural inconsistencies, then as now, are not without serious psychic and political consequences.

While the actual poleis of the ancient Greeks have all perished, the ideal remains alive, not only because of its salience in the written legacy of the greatest minds of the day but because of the grandeur of its vision of a just and vital community.

Socrates, Plato, and Aristotle, each in a somewhat different way, sought to anchor community "independently of society" since society was in the process of institutional and moral breakdown; hence each stressed the importance of the moral underpinnings of community. For Plato, especially, social disunity was viewed as the greatest evil, reflecting a breakdown of social hierarchies and a lack of consensus on basic values and standards. Indeed, in *The Republic*, the guardians upon reaching the age of fifty were, above all, to reflect on the nature of community. Toward this aim, group goals and loyalty to the totality were to be put above individual striving for wealth and fame. The highest honors were accorded to those who put the common good above individual gain.

Like a well-functioning organism, the good community would be maintained by sound laws, shared values, leadership by a moral and disciplined elite of philosopher-kings, and citizens valuing a life of reason, justice, and moral probity.

The community Plato and his teacher Socrates envisioned rested on a view of human nature that differed sharply from that of today. The exemplary citizens of *The Republic* practiced self-constraint, took the long-range perspective, and deferred gratification. They aspired to virtue, not happiness, and virtue was rooted in communal well-being.

It is not that the ancient Greeks abjured self-interest, which focuses individuals on their own well-being. They understood its lures only too well. What they urged was that it become enlightened self-interest, which rests on people's awareness that they need others and have a stake in each other's lives. Therefore, the good life depends on the realization that it involves everyone's participation and effective leadership. Corrupt leaders could spell disaster for a community. Such ideas, notes MacIntyre, are alien to the "modern liberal individualist world" where there is "no conception of such a form of community" (MacIntyre 1980, p. 46).

While Plato and Aristotle agreed on the necessity for a vital, cohesive, self-governing community, they differed strongly on how such a community was to be attained. For Plato, the cohesion and integrity of the polis rested fundamentally on the creation of a special elite—the guardians or philosopher-kings—who would be selected at birth and reared communally in order to fulfill their great obligations. They would know neither private property nor the private family, presumably to eliminate the strongest sources of vested group- and self-interest. Their education would stress an abstemious style of life, immersion in heroic ideals, and the readiness to defend the community in case of attack and to sacrifice their lives for its sake.

Voegelin speaks of "the somatic unity of the Polis," an observation that stems from the communal mating scheme Plato devised for the elite guardians. Why, he asks, was Plato not content to strive for a spiritual unity achieved by a sharing of ideals and commitments? This was, after all, the historic "solution" to the problem of forming communities beyond real or fictitious family relationships (Voegelin 1991, p. 118). The answer lies in Plato's belief in the inseparability of body and psyche; according to him, community has to become organically merged with its constituents.

Aristotle also focused on the leadership of the ideal polis, but he felt that the aim should be to educate all the citizens so that they would be capable of electing their own rulers. Plato, by contrast, endeavored to fuse his "guardians" into a separate entity that would enact the public interest for the community.

The use of the pronoun "mine" illustrates the difference clearly. "Mine" for Aristotle refers to the sum of each individual's stake in the common interest. "Mine" for Plato means a collective designation, in which the individual is effaced. In Aristotle's view, this confounds self and society, the personal and the political.

Instead of abolishing private property, as did Plato, Aristotle would extend property ownership widely, for he believed that it is out of such personal interest and attachments that a common interest might emerge. The *philia* or friendships that get translated into shared goals and ideals are *not* the result of "the communization of their property" (ibid., p. 39). The reverse is true: Friendships grow out of shared experiences. No superimposed guardian elite can achieve the proper goals of the polis. Only education for excellence among citizens able and willing to build a community can achieve them.

It appears, then, that Plato and Aristotle each aimed for unity in the polis, but they entertained quite different conceptions of unity. For Plato, unity was for the like-minded; Aristotle believed that there was unity in interdependence. For both thinkers, furthermore, unity in the polis was linked to size. Plato opted for 5,040 citizens (which would total some 20,000 people if families, servants, foreigners, and slaves were included), a number he thought small enough to be addressed by a single orator. Aristotle advocated limits of size consistent with familiarity so that citizens could "get to know one another personally," which would then enable them to "judge one another's suitability for high office" (Ober 1989, p. 33). It was above all the spirit of connectedness that the polis was to encourage and sustain (Voegelin 1991, p. 247).

Since the good community requires citizens of virtue, breadth, and commitment to a moral framework guided by philosopher-kings, attention must be paid to both education for citizenship and education for leadership. Plato focused more on leadership than did Aristotle, but both looked to the polis to save the world the Greeks knew and loved.

The Monastic Community

Quite a contrast to the polis is the monastic community, a community that eschews diversity and worldliness in favor of a quiet, isolated, contemplative existence. Those who would join are chosen for their suitability to this way of life. As a voluntary community, those who choose to remain must abide by a set of distinctive values and goals that reinforce its mission on an ongoing basis. Though marked by an intense spirituality, the monastery is similar to other kinds of communities in its reliance on a number of essential integrative mechanisms. In addition to selective recruitment and voluntary participation, there is a characteristic spatial pattern with clear-cut physical boundaries, an ethos of mutual aid, shared beliefs and rituals, and the authoritative guidance of the abbot. Hillery's careful in-depth analysis (1992) of Trappist monasteries — which have a history that dates back to the early Christian communities — depicts a way of life dedicated to the communal ideal. Indeed Hillery proposes that men come to the monastery "ultimately because of a need for love" (p. 34), and that the "search for love becomes a search in community."

But the love sought and inspired is not as the world outside defines it. The love generated there is "unselfish, universalistic, and inclusive," a diffuse, benign feeling that unites the members into one devout congregation. Unlike *eros*, or romantic love, which is possessive and self-centered, *agapic* love requires detachment and unselfish devotion to all the members. Where *eros* divides and is antithetical to community, *agape* helps to solidify community. *Agape* is fostered in numerous ways — by spiritual readings and prayer, common worship, gatherings for the common daily meal, and the rule of celibacy — all of which help diffuse sentimental attachments throughout the community.

The entire social organization of the monastery is geared to realize this ideal. To achieve it, however, requires enormous effort involving a continuous struggle against contrary impulses and often "unbearable tensions."

Another value central to furthering the mission of all-embracing commitment of self to community is "disciplined freedom." This contrasts with egoistic freedom, the self-interest that is incompatible with the intense communal goals of the monastery. Disciplined freedom rests on a balance between obedience to the rules, the liturgy, and the expectations of monastic life. Its freedom lies in the choice to commit one's self to the goals of monastic life (Hillery 1992, p. 209).

The abbot sets the spiritual tone of the monastery, coordinates schedules and activities, and adjudicates disagreements, making the tough decisions when necessary. Although the modern abbot does not have quite as much power as his medieval counterpart, he is a critical focus of the community. The role of the abbot is much like that of the Guardians in Plato's *Republic*; on his wisdom and integrity rests the fate of the totality. As both spiritual head and political leader, he must help the community find consensus and assure that the rules are observed (ibid., p. 125).

Given the supreme and continuous emphasis on the values required to sustain the community — *agape*, celibacy, and disciplined freedom — how successful has the monastery been in achieving its stated goals? In a series of surveys, Hillery found a "striking uniformity," along with some important dissenting views. More than nine-tenths of the monks unquestioningly supported the monastery's rituals, the authority of the abbot, and the values of caring and sacrifice. They endorsed:

- The dignity and worth of each person
- The indispensability of sharing and sacrifice
- The value of group discussion
- The leadership of the abbot, subject to the same rules as the members
- *Agapic* love and communion (ibid.)

But there were widely perceived problems as well: Ideological heterogeneity was seen to undermine value consensus and clarity of purpose. Although emotional cohesion and value consensus was strong, mistrust was there too, impeding open communication. Consensus and allegiance were further challenged by the impact of the outside world, which weakened community cohesion. The monastery, set apart and self-contained as it strove to be, was not an "isolated capsule." Some of the monks worked outside the community and outside visitors regularly appeared, so that the lures of material possessions and consumerism encroached on their ideals. These worldly temptations were not so strong, however, as to endanger the monks' commitments to their basic principles. In an important sense the monastic community is ever in process of becoming.

Perhaps the chief lesson for moderns to be learned from the monastic community has to do with its concept of love. "Love in some form," notes Hillery "is important to any communal organization," and love *can* be built into a collectivity on a "diffused, detached, inclusive, universalistic . . . and spiritual basis (ibid., pp. 212, 214).

How can *agape* be made part of less spiritually focused communities? In Hillery's view, *agape* as a principle of togetherness may not develop until humankind is compelled to it by necessity—until the end of organized social life is signaled by poverty, crime, family disintegration, and institutional corruption. But even in as closely focused a community as a Trappist monastery, the cultivation of selfless love requires constant vigilance and continuous reinforcement.

The monastic community, spiritual, selfless, and cooperative in principle, requires careful nurturing in practice. It cannot be taken for granted; nor can it be created once and for all. It is the outcome of continual and profound devotion to a way of life, of work, and of abiding ideals.

Agape maintains the monastic community (ibid., p. 212); it plays the same role as familial love in worldly communities and thus fosters human evolution.

However, Hillery takes great pains to distinguish the monastic type of community from familial institutions in secular communities. In the monastery, the monks' allegiance is not to specific others but to God and their "common mission." Also, the emphasis is on a solitary, not an interdependent, existence that is committed to collective survival and spiritual unity (ibid., p. 50).

The Puritan Commonwealth

Between 1628 and 1634, ten thousand Puritans settled in the Massachusetts Bay Colony of North America, and the colonial towns they and later immigrants created were each "a little commonwealth" and would become the model later settlers would strive to emulate. Unlike historic European communities, they had to focus on survival under pressing and urgent circumstances and create community from scratch (Powell 1965, p. xvi). Able to select their members and fashion their own laws, the Puritan communities of New England put a permanent stamp on American society.

Under the aegis of Governor John Winthrop, this "model of Christian charity . . . was to work out its common destiny under God in the community they were about to build." Winthrop gave them their assignment in these ringing words:

> We must delight in each other, make others' conditions our own, rejoice together, always having before our eyes . . . our community in the work, our community as members of the same bond. We shall be as a city upon a hill with the eyes of all people . . . upon us. (ibid., p. 6)

The community fashioned by the Puritans became the model followed by countless others, and once formed, only a nucleus of the faithful was needed to maintain it. But at the start, the crucial struggle was to develop a model that would hold the community together and preserve it from disintegration. There was no established place to run to, no "ancient walls suggesting continuity and stability amidst flux," no "market square stones worn by countless feet to give a reassuring sense of permanence." Instead, the wilderness, the hazards of fire, pestilence, and storm all reminded the inexperienced settlers of the "precarious, man-made, consciously fashioned character" of their world (Smith 1966, p. 7).

The terrors of the wilderness were not as fearful as the psychological terrors that beset the pioneers. One's sins imperiled the group, and one's dereliction of duty could hurt one's neighbors. "In such a crucible was the spirit of the covenanted community forged, wracked by anxiety and yearning, tormented by self-doubt, exalted by hope, cemented by faith" (ibid.). Their ceaseless struggle confirmed Martin Buber's concept of the true community as a "community of tribulation . . . which makes it a community of spirit" and also a community of salvation (Herberg 1956, p. 129). Indeed, a "chronic state of crisis" created anxieties that led to periodic public confessions and punishments for "delinquent saints," which mobilized the community to reaffirm its commitment to the covenant. Many a community periodically renewed this commitment in public ceremonies "of extraordinary power and solemnity" (ibid., pp. 8, 10).

In fact, it has been suggested that the early English settlers established a "more deeply rooted" communal life on American soil than the one they had left behind in Europe. Due to the disruption of their historic communities by the forces of industrialism, they brought with them a "threatened sense of community" which reinforced their "commitment to localism" when they reached these shores (Bender 1978, p. 63).

The covenanted communities of New England like the early Christian communities and later nineteenth-century communes typify community at its greatest intensity. "Its imperatives were passed on to children and grandchildren" and survived in secular variations over the centuries. "Without covenants, the pioneers would simply have recreated the European system of peasants and landlords . . . and so perpetuated the old system of ranks and authority onto the new soil" (ibid., p. 11).

By the time of the American Revolution, the covenanted communities had paved the way for unity among the original thirteen British colonies. It was in these small, local communities that future actors in the national drama were spawned. The power of collective purpose exemplified by these impassioned, inner-directed men and women was to inspire citizens to seek a common destiny under the Constitution of the United States. Although from the earliest days in the American colonies traditional communal patterns coexisted with more diversified noncommunal ones, a thread of communalism cemented a deep connection between "the community on the hill" and the new nation of 1776.

The covenant, it is generally agreed, was the distinctive feature of the New England communities of the seventeenth century, endowing these settlements with a spirit of fellowship and a divinely sanctioned mission that fused reason and emotion into an abiding whole. Still, community building was not an automatic process and the covenant did not create a mystic bond without hard effort. There was much unrest and instability in the early days, and many settlers moved from one community to another in rapid succession until they found one that suited them ideologically as well as personally.

As the population of a community increased, entire groups might split off to seek more opportune settings. But for those who remained, "the web of community drew all important social networks together" (ibid., pp. 73, 132). It was obvious to all that economic survival required everyone's cooperation and the settlers joined in building roads, planting crops, and harvesting, all of which reinforced a profound sense of "totality and unity" (Bushman 1967, p. 16).

Between 1760 and 1776, 264 new towns were established in northern New England by the General Court, which granted the rights to establish such towns to groups of settlers. The center of each colonial settlement was the meetinghouse. Always the first important building to be erected (Wright 1981, pp. 3–17), it was the center of social and public life as well as of religious worship. And by all accounts, life was tightly integrated and focused on home, worship, work, and common enterprise.

These communities became deeply rooted quite quickly, helped initially by "diffuse spiritual and emotional bonding" that stemmed from the settlers' profound experiences of migration and uprooting, their religious commitments, and their fears of the unknown. Then too, the settlers had some choice as to where to settle and could move and sample until they found a site and people they liked — which increased the potential for cohesion. Ideology was also significant, as were spatial centrality and interdependence.

Another impetus for cohesion, widely remarked upon, was the high degree of homogeneity of the Puritan community with its narrow band of occupations and a fairly even distribution of wealth. It was sustained by religious belief, a unified political vision, the interpenetration of family and community, and the merging of private and public life. Imbued with a spirit of community, the traditions they created would inform the civilization-in-the-making for generations. Like the ancient polis, the "local community was a concrete reality that was immediately seen, felt, and experienced" (Bender 1978, p. 88), whereas the larger society taking shape was remote and abstract. In numerous ways, then, eighteenth-century colonial communities were closed islands in an open society concentrating economic, political, social, and religious forces within a small compass.

In time, extensive geographic mobility would result in a two-tiered community. One tier was "an economically successful permanent group that shaped the values and direction of social life in the town," the other was a less successful, more transient population in search of opportunity elsewhere. Multiple loyalties and identities fashioned "contradictory systems of order," and eventually "two cultural systems coexisted side by side — one, local, intimate, face-to-face, and the other, abstract, formal, distant, and in the custody of an elite" (ibid., pp. 64, 77).

In the century to come, political division would increase and the community would cease to speak to the larger world with a single voice. While family, church, school, work, and government continued to find their meaning in the local community throughout the nineteenth century, it no longer reigned supreme.

Some of the flavor of the early struggles is illustrated by the story of seventeenth-century Sudbury, Massachusetts, a tale "replete with the Devil, greed, and ambition," stock themes in a "local morality play." In Powell's careful analysis, the difficulties confronting the pioneers emerge in sharp relief. The newcomers came into a wilderness without even minimal amenities—there were no taverns, shops, or markets. They had no foreknowledge of the conditions they would face, and once faced with them, any understanding of how to deal with them. No institutions were in place and each community floundered amid chaotic indecision (Powell 1965, pp. xvi, 102).

Still, within two years after settling Sudbury, a distinctive social, economic, and political life had taken hold. Every male citizen had access to some portion of land as well as to a "town-right" in the commons where the cattle could feed.

The farmer who was seen to care more about "his own selfish aims" than about the common good faced fierce reactions from his fellows. Two decades later, however, major generational cleavages surfaced. Younger sons, pitted against their elders, demanded more land, and this would threaten the "entire order of Sudbury," despite the strong "spirit of mutual cooperation" and social harmony. Contending factions multiplied (ibid., pp. 121, 123).

For some years, differences were resolved by means of negotiation and discussion until group consensus was reached, a process helped by the faithful under the guidance of outstanding town leaders. However, the "new institutions of Sudbury being hopelessly inadequate to handle the frustration and the hostility" engendered by major and growing policy differences did not fare so well (ibid., p. 142). Still, the extent of self-government between 1639 and 1655 was striking—more than one-half of the male land grantees served as selectmen and ran virtually every town function.

However, within a few decades there was trouble in paradise from several unexpected sources. One was the very nature of self-government: "The headiness of power" made citizens "arrogant and unmanageable," leading the pastor of Concord to declare that perhaps too much liberty and power had been put into the hands of the multitude (ibid., p. 152).

Generational schisms over access to land and to political office accentuated ideological cleavages between conservatives and egalitarians and pitted a rigid and exclusive old guard against radical young Turks seeking to expand access to the social hierarchy or abolish it. These issues rent the community and despoiled the "peace and comfort of our meetings both in church and town" (ibid., p. 159). Eventually, economic self-interest and governance became such contested issues that an entire group of citizens decided to found another town with quite different political institutions.

But the rebels founded a new community that was more conservative than the old. Having "learned the necessity of order," these breakaways established even stricter entrance requirements and sharper criteria of citizenship. Land grants were dependent on the extent of citizen participation and devotion to the new Sudbury. Formal commitment and service became key criteria of social rank and resource allocation. Responsibility for creating and maintaining the community became a paramount obligation, and self-governance, a respect for law, orderly processes of cooperation, and a sensitivity to social justice became primary virtues (ibid., p. 177).

Town leaders confronted critical problems in all of the pioneering communities and toiled hard to forge a basis for a life in common, joined in the tasks by groups of knowledgeable citizens. In Sudbury, some fifty-five of these elected the mayor each year, and he, along with the aldermen and burgesses, conducted "the mystery of government," some of it in secret. These ran virtually every town function. Initially, any citizen could volunteer for service, but in time a familiar division emerged between those who assumed responsibility for the town and those who were pulled along without contributing their share. Also, one must note the paradox that, if the first generation departed from their English experience, the second generation returned to it. They reintroduced English common law, levied "the King's tax" and invoked the "ultimate authority of the King." Growing pains aside, one must marvel at the ability of these small communities to create a basis for survival by means of their faith, their good will, their hard work, and their support of such key institutions as the town meeting (ibid., pp. 184, 185) in which problems were aired and resolved by means of negotiation and discussion until group consensus was reached. There was concern for every inhabitant and anyone in need could receive communal attention no matter what their economic and social rank. Leadership proved critical throughout the development of the community. The conscientious few kept the early spirit alive, standing guard and caring for the community's present and future.

One of the forces sustaining community was a common view of the future. The Puritans did not look backward to a shared past but forward to a shared future. Not to be underestimated was the sense of crisis: A chronic state of anxiety and self-blame, partially relieved by periodic public confessions and repentance, reaffirmed the covenant (Smith 1966, p. 8).

An ideology of social equality was also important to sustaining community. Despite the existence of social ranks and a social hierarchy, this ideology generated a one-for-all philosophy nurtured by bonds of "compassionate sympathy." There were persistent efforts to balance "the impulse toward individualism" with the "primacy of the common life." A local government created by periodic local elections, along with the debates and decisions taken at the town meetings, stressed government by consensus, hence a collective orientation (ibid., 118, 197, 207).

Thus, despite social diversity — by ethnic origins, time of arrival, ideology, and generation — a "fundamental uniformity" based on "legal equality, individual liberty, and republican institutions" prevailed (ibid., p. 218). Diverse loyalties, identities, and obligations along with increasing social and technical complexity rendered life more confusing but also more challenging. And in the changing cultural kaleidoscope, the private domain began to assume growing importance.

The intense focus on the collective spirit in colonial New England had not obliterated the desire for privacy. In fact, Flaherty (1972, p. 2) notes that privacy was important to the Puritans and it collided with the ever-present, watchful community. Market fairs, house-raisings, quilting bees, town meetings, gossip networks, weddings, and funerals kept a focus on community, and, given the norms of collective obligation and responsibility, privacy was not as greatly valued at first as it was to be later, but the pull between individualism and community was definitely in evidence.

In time, growing wealth, the rise of industry, and population growth would erode the pioneering focus on community. The Yankee spirit of independence, shrewdness, and desire for material gain would replace the Puritan spirit and accord an "honorable place for self-interest in the social order." Thus, in the century to follow, individualism would flower along with the economic renaissance of industrialism, but with these also came the "sorrows of rootlessness" and loneliness (ibid., pp. 287, 288).

Much of early community development rested on the shoulders of designated leaders who were expected to give their time and energies unstintingly to town affairs. In old Sudbury, for example, Peter Noyes, its founder, a member of a leading family in the small English village from which he came, was responsible for establishing the framework for the entire community. In his capacity as church elder, judge, legislator, and town selectman, his influence on the shape of the community would last hundreds of years.

The counterforces of community surfaced too, however. Competing sects and factions in religion, politics, and thought weakened the covenant and dispersed collective energies. The result was a ceaseless struggle to discover "substitutes for the primitive covenant" in a cause, a movement, a force providing a sense of unity amid change and mobility. As the nation grew, nationwide allegiances and definitions of success multiplied. The lure of the city and quick riches, the excitement of the high life, and a growing focus on self-interest and self-advancement as time passed proved irresistible to many. Rapid social change and the turnover of ideas and patterns of conduct also eroded the earlier uniformity.

But the key force against community, manifested earlier than generally realized, was the individual pursuit of material gain in the form of land speculation, division of the commons, and absentee investments. New groups vying for supremacy created social instability, endemic social conflict, and social irresponsibility as they struggled to amass and augment property. Eventually, the tide of economic advancement and social mobility would overwhelm the local community and erode ties of place. Thus, the prized ideals of individual self-reliance and acquisitiveness were also the potent forces in the dissolution of community.

In the classical view, individual self-interest and the good community were viewed as interrelated, each reinforcing the other. The prosperity of the individual depended on that of the community. By the nineteenth century, the reverse was believed: Success and prosperity, pursued individually, would ultimately lead to the success and prosperity of the community.

By the nineteenth century, therefore, two types of settlements were in evidence: "colonized" towns, which were explicitly created for like-minded ethnic, religious, or political inhabitants to realize some collective goal, many designed as experiments in communal living, and "cumulative" towns that grew without a plan or purpose except possibly that of material advantage—these were "mere collections of houses and stores, clustered around a landing, where nothing but mercantile and mechanical business is done; where the inhabitants form no connections, or habits, besides those which naturally grow out of bargain and sales . . . where beauty is disregarded, and every convenience, except that of trade is forgotten" (Smith 1966, pp. 17, 31). Notably "lacking in community structure," such towns were chaotic and lawless unless "a father-authority figure emerged" who took control to help develop community in places, such as the frontier towns of legend and late-night movies, where there were neither common traditions nor common interests.

Smith notes a sequence or phasing process here — which we shall explore in the case study of Twin Rivers — from "an inchoate and formless period" to one with a psychologically coherent community. But the price paid for the early disorder "often left permanent scars" (ibid., p. 32).

The two types of communities bore the marks of their origins long after they had coalesced into functioning communities, the one unified socially and religiously, self-restrained, anti-urban, and disdainful of the acquisitive society and its materialist excesses, the other glorying in its rugged individualism and the untrammeled pursuit of wealth.

In time, the covenanted community would become but a nostalgic memory. Although the original dream of the good community that would dispel greed, poverty, and factionalism was never entirely extinguished, it had to accommodate itself to the large-scale forces of an industrial social order that shifted the cultural spotlight to more distant horizons.

The covenant, so essential for the launching of early American communities, was a unique achievement: It put the common good ahead of individual advantage without extinguishing the significance of the individual, although individualism was far more circumscribed then than it was later.

Nineteenth-Century Utopian Communities

From the beginning, communal utopias proliferated in the United States as nowhere else. There was space and the freedom to build, and there were pioneers eager to construct brave new worlds. A utopian aura permeated the country, attracting idealists, reformers, and dreamers of every stripe. The spirit of progress, optimism, and innovation permeated nineteenth-century America as it confronted both the opportunities and dislocations of industrialism.

Some of these social experiments were short lived while others lasted for hundreds of years. Some sought salvation through spiritual regeneration while others sought a radical transformation of social institutions. All of them, however, are instructive for what they can tell us about utopian experiments in community and the sources of their successes and failures. There are many accounts available of the more than two hundred utopian communities that came into being during these formative years, alternately reflecting the desire to escape from the world or to build it anew. And whether these communities survived, as did some, or perished, as did most, they attract our attention because they pursued a dream of human togetherness that still beckons us.

The impulse to construct better worlds survives in those "intentional" communities that emphasize sharing, cooperation, and a set of ideals that put the individual in a context of collective well-being. Other communities inspired by similar ideals include the secular kibbutzim of Israel and the more short-lived urban American communes of the decades following the Second World War. Careful studies of these help shed light on such key questions as how community takes root and what are the minimal ingredients necessary for its survival.

Kanter's comparison of nine communes that lasted with twenty-one that did not yielded important insights into the sources of their success and failure. The enduring communes possessed a structure of leadership, rules of membership, and ideological justifications that the others lacked, along with identifiable physical sites; explicit criteria of membership denoting those who did and those who did not belong; a label, or name, for self-identification; and an ideology that guided members toward desired goals (equity, justice, harmony, unity) and that justified the hard work needed to get there (Kanter 1972, p. 52; Keller 1973).

Communal existence, like social life generally, is fraught with struggle and conflict. The successful communes find ways to cope with conflict so that they can stay alive; those that fail to do so do not survive. Most successful communes also develop structures of authority organized around a hierarchy of leaders, as in the case of the Shakers, or a single charismatic figure, as in the case of the Oneida community led by Humphrey Noyes. These leaders embody collective unity and help devise an acceptable framework for the group's survival beyond the euphoric and exalted expectations of the earliest days.

"Commitment mechanisms" greatly aid this process by linking self-interest to communal needs. Successful communes promote a sense of belonging and devise strategies to merge individual and communal objectives, exacting some sacrifices from their members.

For nineteenth-century communes, sacrifices might have included, as they did for the Shakers, sexual abstinence; the forgoing of alcohol, tobacco, or favorite foods; the elimination of all personal adornment. Closely allied to such personal sacrifices are investments of time, money, or labor, which give members a stake in the communal undertaking. Another commitment mechanism encourages the renunciation of personal relationships in favor of group attachments and loyalties, a trade-off that the successful communes accomplish only after a hard struggle and the unsuccessful ones fail to achieve at all (Kanter 1972, p. 93). Individuals stand to reap important benefits when they subordinate the private self to the larger totality, including a sense of belonging, a moral framework, human fellowship, and goals to strive for. Nonetheless it remains a constant struggle. The Shakers had a phrase for it: "That great big 'I,' I'll mortify."

Twentieth-Century Communes

The communal experiments of the 1960s drew some of their inspiration from the utopias of the nineteenth century, but most were propelled by the movements for civil rights, women's rights, and the antiwar protests of the period. They attracted young, college-educated idealists seeking to transform the world. Their well-intentioned efforts were far more fragile than those of their nineteenth-century predecessors, and failure rates were high. Signal deficiencies included shaky organization; inconsistent leadership; romantic, that is unrealistic, expectations; and a waning of commitment over time for both members and leaders; lack of a coherent set of principles emphasizing group values (Roberts 1971, p. 116); and ignorance of what it takes to create a viable commune on a day-to-day basis.

Above all, the enthusiastic and idealistic young people who sought to devise communes in the 1960s were not aware that freedom needs to be tempered by some controls, or that the communion they longed for required a willingness to make room for other people's needs and demands. They were not trained for the life that intellectually beckoned them, their attachments to privacy and individualism too deeply implanted. Leadership proved particularly problematic. Although communes need leaders, they rejected them on principle. Hence they lacked people who were able to convey a sense of authority and trust, to maintain a sense of purpose, and to represent the commune to the outside world. In addition, especially in such small, intense groups, leaders must be available to monitor personality conflicts that can undermine group harmony and to see to it that loves and hates do not get out of hand once the euphoria of the early days fades. But without firm direction, "the leaderless commune is doomed" (ibid., p. 147).

Despite their shortcomings, there is much to be learned from utopian experiments in living. They offer moments of freedom and human possibility and give expression to unmet needs for belonging, meaning, and participation.

Hence the words uttered by a member of the Icarian commune to Charles Nordhoff in 1878, when the commune was on the brink of breakup, are still worth heeding:

> Deal gently and cautiously with Icaria. The man who sees only
> the chaotic village and the wooden shoes, and only chronicles

those, will commit a serious error. In the village are buried fortunes, noble hopes, and the aspirations of good and great men.
(ibid., p. 140)

These brief historic examples are instructive in several respects. They
show that community is built slowly. Once like-minded individuals have
come together, their most immediate need is a physical site on which to
begin their communal existence. But even before that, the group must
fashion "a mythical existence in the minds of the would-be participants" (Hall 1995, p. 27). The myth may derive from historic or ideological precedents or it may be forged in the heady initial days of communal exuberance. An inspiring leader may coalesce the group by the
force of his or her charisma and inspire people to join. It is the myth of
community that fuels the fusion of individual wills into a force for unity.

However diverse these examples, they all attest to the immense difficulties involved in creating communities — even when small, voluntary,
and self-contained. Even successful communities are the precarious outcome of forces sustaining and forces eroding community.

The sustaining forces include:

a. A territorial base that marks the community off from the
   outside world
b. An ideology of mutual responsibility and a one-for-all and
   all-for-one philosophy that unites members across social
   ranks
c. Institutions that build for the future
d. Members giving their time, effort, and devotion to the public good
e. Symbols and rituals of community — a name, an emblem,
   community rites.

The eroding forces include:

a. Factional strife and dissension over land, wealth, goals
b. The pursuit of self-advancement
c. High membership turnover
d. Precarious leadership

Interestingly, many of these elements are spelled out in *Utopia*,
Thomas More's sixteenth-century treatise that gives the name to all
later versions of ideal societies. Aware that physical and spatial identity
was essential, More made Utopia an island whose leaders, the magis-
trates, presided in central buildings in its fifty-four cities and chief town.
In Utopia, a belief in equality and simplicity made community possible,
and community fostered cooperation in turn. In other words, a commu-

nity develops only to the extent that its members share their possessions and abjure privilege (More 1999, p. 301).

Identity, unity, and justice are central ideals for utopias past and present. And, as we shall see, they are critical for community survival to this day.

CHAPTER 3
KEY THEORIES AND CONCEPTS

There is that "subtle but invincible conviction of solidarity that knits together the loneliness of innumerable hearts which binds together all humanity—the dead to the living and the living to the unborn."
— Saul Bellow, quoting Joseph Conrad
in his Nobel Prize acceptance speech

The history of human thought is studded with inquiries into the nature and genesis of community. From Plato and Aristotle, apprehensive about the fate of the ancient polis, to Hobbes, Montesquieu, Rousseau, and Marx grappling with the chaos of the industrial revolution, thinkers have pondered the nature of collective life and how to achieve social continuity, good citizenship, and a sense of community. In this chapter we will briefly examine the reflections of several key thinkers on the subject of community.

Plato stipulated the ideal polis should be small in size (five thousand male citizens and the supporting population consisting of wives, servants, slaves, foreign workers, and, of course, children) and unified around themes of justice and unity. A ruling elite of guardians, whose virtuous character and lofty ideals were geared to the survival of the entire community, would guide the polis.

Aristotle's polis was closer to a stratified version that ranked men "naturally" higher than women, and the wealthy higher than those of modest means. Favoring unity based on diversity, Aristotle also put stress on individualism and the pursuit of self-interest as desirable goals.

Plato and Aristotle thus disagreed on how the polis should be structured, but they agreed on other aspects. Each made the face-to-face community in which citizens lived out their lives in public central to a moral and political quest. Both also agreed that community comes into being through collective effort, is spatially rooted, and can be taken in through the senses — seen, touched, and felt as part of a concrete, familiar experience. And they agreed that the polis was a crowning achievement of human effort and imagination. It rested on each citizen's giving up a part of himself but regaining it in the larger totality of the group.

Several hundred years after the ancient polis had passed into history, we find Cicero deliberating on the nature of community in his day. Projecting the image of a declining polis, Cicero shifted the basis for community from shared faith and feeling to binding laws. A "legal commonwealth" would be a sounder basis for collective life than volatile public support (Friederich 1959, p. 6).

Moving to a still later period, we come to St. Augustine, who placed community at the "very center of his thought." Drawing a contrast between *civitas Dei* and *civitas terrena*, he considered the true community to be the *civitas Dei*, which focused on the "one Supreme and true God" and united citizens of "all nations" and "pilgrims of all languages" into a "universal community of the faithful" (ibid., p. 8). This introduced a universal dimension into the discussion akin to that of the Stoics, who, having witnessed the decline of the ancient polis, proposed the "community of the wise" as more inclusive than the polis. This also moved the idea of community beyond the bounds of physical territory to a more spiritual perspective, which foreshadowed that of later Christian thinkers.

The concepts of Aristotle, Cicero, and St. Augustine characterize discussions on community through the subsequent course of Western history, alternately seeking the basis of community in law and rationality or in emotional and spiritual union.

Thomas Aquinas, infused with the notion of community as organism, an idea derived from Augustinian thought, added as an additional ingredient of community the pursuit of the common good. "If the common good is being pursued in and by a group of human beings, a community comes into existence no matter what its size." The unity created thereby is a complex blend of sentiments geared to the "common happiness" (ibid., 1959, pp. 10, 11).

The varying emphases of these thinkers introduced confusion into discussions of community that persist to this day. There is community writ small and focused on the local domain, as compared to community writ large, which may embrace the globe. Clearly different in scale, level of abstraction, and comprehensiveness, the same word, "community," when applied to both, muddies the conceptual waters. Then there is the community rooted in laws and institutions in contrast to the community rooted in love and shared faith.

This contrast is strikingly evident in the work of sixteenth-century scholar Johannes Althusius, "the political theorist of Calvinism par excellence." Drawing on the historic experience of the small republics and city-states of the Swiss Federation, he anticipated the Calvinist future with extraordinary prescience. Caught between the declining city-states and the emergent national and territorial states, he was both prophet and obituarist. (ibid.)

The *Politica Methodica Digesta* contains Althusius's key ideas on the politically organized community based on popular government — a radical idea for this time — and a common life based on shared fellowship and brotherhood. Opposed to both the masses, whom he considered "inconstant, violent, envious, frivolous and turbulent," and the idea of individual freedom, he argued for two essentials for communities: first, that the individual be submissive to the decisions of the community, the majority, the group, hence subordinating personal goals to the welfare of the whole, and second, that the community be governed by good will (*benevolentia*) and amity (*concordia*). It was the "togetherness of men in their hearts" that constituted the natural foundation of community (Althusius 1932, pp. 1, lxx, lxxii). From these flowed mutual need and reciprocity: "I need your gifts and you need mine."

In Althusius we can already discern the tension between community based on emotional union and community organized by a legally based central authority, reflecting the growing problem of social order in an expanding, diversified, increasingly urbanized society. Still, Althusius continued to put major emphasis on faith and consensus as facilitators of community. There was also the idea of a tacit compact, a compact for togetherness, familiar to him from the oath sworn by feudal lords and vassals, and fitting the doctrine of "Protestant individualism," which was a forerunner of the contractual theorists of the seventeenth and eighteenth centuries. But in his day, the individual was greatly dependent on community, though as Althusius recognized, community might increasingly have to be organized into ascending hierarchies, from villages, guilds, and towns to provinces and metaphorically to entire kingdoms. Always, however, Althusius stressed faith and feeling, empathy and reciprocity as the defining characteristics of community.

By his advocacy of people power, cooperation, and a spirit of mutual respect and affection, Althusius reveals himself as a humane and sympathetic proponent of community, even as he accepts the need for authority and command and for the submission of individuals to the collectivity.

A more formalized social-contract theory would develop with Hobbes (1588–1669), who was anti-community, and Rousseau (1712–1778), who believed that the social contract marked the "actual birth of humanity proper." Both start from highly individualistic premises and reach anti-individualistic conclusions, and both rely on a transcendent principle to unite the aggregate: the *Sovereign* for Hobbes and the *general will* for Rousseau (Louis Dumont 1986, p. 85).

It is somewhat paradoxical to include Hobbes among community theorists, since he was antagonistic to the idea of community. But Hobbes's stand has been so influential in political thought that he warrants inclusion in a company he would have disdained. Along with Locke, Bentham, Adam Smith, and de Tocqueville, Hobbes developed his theories of human association as the market society was taking shape, old institutions were toppled, and new ideals of individualism took hold.

Hobbes (1651) is remembered by the generations that followed him for his designation of the state of nature as "solitary, poor, nasty, brutish, and short." In the state of nature, fear and hostility prevail so that there is always a war of each against all. In Hobbes's view, in contrast to those of earlier thinkers, neither love nor empathy characterizes human nature. To escape the brutal conditions of the natural state, human beings voluntarily join with others in a compact binding on all. Although this curtails their freedom, it assures them the security needed to survive. This compact (or covenant) is based purely on self-interest. Neither the desire for human fellowship nor a loving concern for others plays a role in this social revolution. The totality is held together by a sovereign ruler called the Leviathan, who exacts everyone's allegiance and secures the liberty and property of all.

By the time of Rousseau, the social contract, having been debated for several centuries, was part of the common currency. There were anticipations of it in the work of Althusius and other medieval thinkers, and more explicit political formulations of it, as in Locke (1632–1704). From there, it became a cornerstone of Anglo-American political institutions. Rousseau contributed the idea of the "general will," which is reminiscent—in a benign version—of Hobbes's Leviathan, but he underscored the need for a shift from what he called the *moi seul* to the *moi commun*. This was a distinction Hobbes would have dismissed as irrelevant. All told, the social philosophers of the seventeenth and eighteenth centuries formulated a view of human nature that would render intelligible the shift from feudalism to industrialism.

For our purposes, however, it is important to stress their atomistic conception of society. Primarily motivated by self-interest, persons remained essentially isolated nomads seeking self-sufficiency and avoiding social contact and human fellowship (Kirkpatrick 1986, p. 16). In this philosophy, community was bypassed in favor of the large-scale, impersonal, formally organized society ruled by a prime mover.

The struggle between competing ideals reflecting different phases of civilization receives its most comprehensive treatment by a nineteenth-century social theorist whose paradigm continues to be used to this day.

Ferdinand Tönnies

The most influential modern treatise on community is that of Ferdinand Tönnies. In his book, *Gemeinschaft und Gesellschaft* (1887), he poses a contrast between community (*gemeinschaft*) and society (*gesellschaft*) that still stands, as do his original German terms. *Gemeinschaft*, or community, refers to a pattern of social life based on personal attachments, traditionalism, and deep interpersonal affinities rooted in holism, loyalty, shared experience, and commitment to a totality. Its countermodel, *gesellschaft*, denotes a more abstract, impersonal, formalized system of social rules, roles, and institutions marked by selective affinities, rational calculation, formal exchange, and negotiated interests and goals (Cahnman 1995, p. 81).

Between these polar opposites extends "the totality of social reality." The polarity itself seems to reach back to Aristotle's dichotomy between *philia* and *koinonia*, the first referring to intimate connectedness, the second to purposive association.

Although analytically distinct, in life there is an admixture, the extent of which must be determined empirically. That is to say, we are not here dealing with static categories admitting of no ambiguity but with dynamic and complementary processes ever in flux. "What the pure theorist isolates, the applied analyst carries back into the stream of life" (ibid.).

As a Hobbes scholar, Tönnies built on and supplemented the master, who postulated an evolutionary trend from the state of nature to a rationally organized society held together by the Leviathan or sovereign state. For Hobbes, the counterimage to *gesellschaft* was not *gemein-schaft* but chaos and breakdown. Given the dynamic and fractious English society of his time, Hobbes saw the social world in ferment as a result of civil war, the rise of modern science, the erosion of custom, and the middle classes challenging the aristocracy for power and wealth. This is where Hobbes developed his notion of society as a necessary antidote to the state of nature and the "war of all against all." To offset the "chaos of conflicting interests," Hobbes proposed a social contract whereby individuals voluntarily subjected themselves to the sovereign and a system of moral rules to guarantee social order.

Tönnies also drew on Henry Maine's pioneering analysis of a key historic shift from status to contract as the basis of collective life, the one rooted in kinship, ascriptive social status, and joint property rights, the other in social contract and individual rights (Maine 1864).

Tönnies used the entities in his dichotomy—*gemeinschaft* and *gesellschaft*—as both ideal types and analytic categories. At times, the designations reinforced one another, at other times they were treated as polar opposites, mirroring the contradictory pulls of modern society as it struggled toward unity amid fragmentation (Cahnman 1995, p. 189).

Imbued with the universalistic ideals of the eighteenth-century enlightenment as well as with later nostalgic visions of community, Tönnies endeavored to steer an intermediate course between community and society. Yet also, and somewhat confusingly, he saw *gemeinschaft* and *gesellschaft* as end points in a historic trend from one to the other. But he did grasp the essential difference between *gemeinschaft* and *gesellschaft*, noting that in *gemeinschaft* people "remain essentially united in spite of all separating factors whereas in *gesellschaft they* are essentially separated in spite of all uniting factors" (ibid.).

Virtually all the great figures of nineteenth-century social thought — de Tocqueville, Hegel, Marx, Weber, Durkheim, and others — concurred that the overriding problem of their time was the breakdown of traditional society, and each sought ways to deal with it. Tönnies, often cited, less often closely read, and rarely interpreted in accord with his professed principles and objectives, was the most persistent. Having spent six years (1881–87) on his famous treatise, he hoped that his concept would provide a base from which to invigorate social life and advance human freedom (Samples 1987, p. 66).

At the end of his life, his opposition to national socialism cost him his position at Kiel University as well as his pension, leaving him isolated and poverty-stricken. This was an ironic turn of events for one who had long argued against the indifference and impersonality of the modern Leviathan and for the human dimensions of community.

Tönnies's concepts have entered mainstream sociology, though often in a simplistic, reductionist manner he would have opposed. Many have used them to buttress ideological arguments for or against modernity, a practice he would have deplored. Others have proposed their own readings of his concepts, chiefly Talcott Parsons who elaborated them into the "pattern variables" (1954).

In addition to those who have drawn on Tönnies's work, not always explicitly crediting his ideas, there are those who seem to establish parallel dichotomies also bent on capturing historic trends away from community.

Emile Durkheim's Counterproposal

Emile Durkheim, for example, proposed two types of solidarity—mechanical and organic—that at first glance seem akin to those of Tönnies. In fact, however, they are fundamentally different. Durkheim may have been inspired by Tönnies, whose book he reviewed favorably two years after its publication (in 1889), but he drew very different, indeed opposite, distinctions. To be sure, as did many nineteenth-century thinkers following Darwin and Spencer, he spotted an evolutionary trend from simpler to more complex forms of social organization. But the "mechanical solidarity" of an earlier period refers to an externally mediated and orchestrated cohesion leading to a collective like-mindedness and lack of individuation. This is far from Tönnies's notion of *gemeinschaft*, an organic, holistic social entity rooted in a sense of personal attachment and reciprocal obligations conducive to individuation. Durkheim differed also from Tönnies in his concept of "organic solidarity," which he considered an evolutionary advance toward greater individual freedom. Tönnies was far less sanguine about modernity and the long-range prospects for human well-being. Moreover, while he did see *gesellschaft* as part of a historic trend away from *gemeinschaft*, he also viewed them as coexisting tendencies at any given time. Finally, Tönnies's concepts were more sweeping and inclusive, encompassing more than the nature of social solidarity that intrigued Durkheim.

Actually, Durkheim's conception of "the collective conscience," which he defined as the "totality of beliefs and sentiments held in common" by a group or aggregate (Durkheim 1933) is closer to Tönnies's idea of *gemeinschaft*. Both involve mutuality, attachment to, and identification with the collectivity as well as a commitment to it.

Durkheim also challenged the liberal view embedded in a profit-oriented market economy that self-interest would be able to "produce sufficient solidarity to maintain social order." He agreed that self-interested pursuits could provide links among people but that these remain superficial due to the lack of a "shared moral code and normative sanctioning of reciprocity" (Sullivan 1982, p. 35).

Both Durkheim and Tönnies owed much to Herbert Spencer's evolutionary scheme (1967), though each bent it to his own needs. Spencer's original state of society was coercive in essence, whereas Tönnies saw the primary foundation of human society as one of natural cohesion and empathic social bonds.

Max Weber, his great German contemporary, acknowledged his debt to Tönnies when he described *Gemeinschaft und Gesellschaft* as "a beautiful work" and drew on it for his own discussion of "communal and associative relationships" (Cahnman 1995, p. 117). Weber's *The Protestant Ethic and the Spirit of Capitalism* (1930) builds on the contrast drawn by Tönnies between a social order grounded in personal loyalties and impersonal calculation: deep personal bonding and commitment versus a formal, rule-based contract. According to Weber's thesis, the Protestant ethic was a means to assure divine blessings in an impersonal world via visible proofs of individual worth based on the accumulation of wealth. This became necessary in a society that had grown beyond communities where everyone could feel connected and be personally recognized, and where virtue was observable through long and deep acquaintance (George E. Gordon Catlin in Friederich 1959).

Tönnies had witnessed such a development in the social transition from a rural-agricultural to a capitalist ethos and the absorption of small towns and villages into larger urban aggregations under the centralized nation-state. Since he understood this development better than most, Tönnies was well aware that the coexistence of *gemeinschaft* and *gesellschaft* created great complications, as people had to learn to "live in distinct worlds each with its own rules and expectations." There was the small community of day-to-day family life, work, and friendships, as well as the larger, more abstract social universe. These did not mesh easily and modern citizens had to learn two different, yet intertwined repertoires (Bender 1978, pp. 136–37).

Tönnies saw *gesellschaft* as gaining in significance in people's lives without, however, eliminating *gemeinschaft*. But he was not entirely consistent on this, hence the confusion in the existing literature — between *gemeinschaft* and *gesellschaft* as ideal types; as historic trends; and as types of social relationships. The contrast between community and society, according to Tönnies, entails all three at times, but he most emphasized them as ideal types.

Community is built on:	Society features:
Group traditions	Self-interest
Faith	Skepticism

Custom, habit	Rational calculation
Feelings	Reason

It is important to view these as ideal types or central tendencies, not as descriptions of actual social conditions. Even if the contrast is not as sharp in real life as these ideal expectations decree, it helps sort out characteristic tendencies.

Contemporary Adaptations of Tönnies

The themes that Tönnies made central to his deliberations attracted the attention of virtually every major figure in nineteenth-century social thought. And the parameters of the debate on the salience of community in modern societies are with us still. Two questions capture their key elements: (1) Does community arise spontaneously if conditions are favorable, or must it be assiduously coaxed into existence? (2) Is the cornerstone of community love or law? The contrast between *gemeinschaft* and *gesellschaft* was carried over into the twentieth century by Robert Park, John Dewey, Robert MacIver, and others who considered their interplay an important source of contemporary vitality and creativity (MacIver and Page 1949).

In the twentieth century, the study of community took several turns. One path, that of MacIver (1949) and Bellah (1985), discussed below, continued to focus on the generic nature of community and its theoretical foundations.

Another path, based on the Chicago School (Park, Burgess, Hawley, etc.) featured the ecological determinants of community. A third path explored the impact of the expanding metropolis on community formation. This led to important theoretical contributions notably by Janowitz (1967), Suttles (1972), and Hunter (1974) on hybrid forms of community in urban areas.

Robert MacIver and Robert Bellah present an interesting contrast in their reflections on community. MacIver wrote from a vantage point that acknowledged urban expansion and the suburban exodus but took for granted the persistence and necessity of community. Community is home, "the permanent background of people's lives" (MacIver and Page 1949, p. 292). For the individual, community "is not an outer compulsion but an inner necessity" held together by a "we-feeling" rooted in shared traditions and common interests. This feeling reflects a concern for the fate of the totality seen as an "indivisible unity" (ibid., p. 293). The "we-feeling" is equal in importance to the structural supports of community, and in the modern world with all its social divisions and cultural permutations, the feeling must be assiduously cultivated.

Still, this is the last comprehensive treatise to put the focus on community as such, a focus that had weakened when modernism came to frame the sociological discourse. With a few important exceptions, the subject had receded from mainstream sociology, pushed aside by modern developments. However, to the surprise of many, community kept resurfacing. Apparently, noted Bender, "community . . . is more pervasive than urban theory would predict" (1982, p. 25). That could prove surprising only in light of an unstated assumption that community must decline as societies modernize. To be sure, community is not as self-contained or prominent as in earlier epochs and as bigger systems encompass it, but it did not disappear. "Moderns" noted Redfield, "no longer belong to "one inclusive community but to nearer and wider communities at the same time" (Redfield 1960, p. 113).

Still, it would take some time for the topic to regain its earlier prominence with the shift to multiculturalism and pluralism. These shifts revitalized ethnic and immigrant studies, at the center of which stood community.

As Tönnies and Durkheim anticipated, modern societies embrace *gemeinschaft* and *gesellschaft* simultaneously. These are not antitheses but "two kinds of collective living" (Bender 1978, p. 43) whose interplay may be a source of vitality and creativity. Henceforth, communal and noncommunal perspectives would enlist people's multiple loyalties to "contradictory systems of order" (Weber 1978, p. 125).

The most penetrating recent exploration of community is that of Robert N. Bellah and his colleagues, presented in two volumes: entitled *Habits of the Heart* (1985) and *The Good Society* (1991). The analysis of community was not their primary aim but a fortunate by-product of their endeavor to delineate the attainment of a more just, humane, and morally sound society in the twenty-first century.

The work of Bellah echoes a number of thoughtful observers earlier in the century, among them, John Dewey, Lewis Mumford, and Walter Lippman, who worried about the fate of democracy itself when large-scale bureaucratic organizations "grow over the heads of the citizens" and people lose a sense of connectedness with their government, corporations, and other Leviathans. How can one pay attention to the whole when the whole is out of reach?

A commitment to place and a sense of being rooted helps a people to "understand its own habitat" so that they can trace out the consequences of collective policies and decisions. This is why Bellah argues for the regeneration of the local community where mutual trust and vital connections are sustained by the cultivation of "supportive institutions" such as civic associations, churches, and family. These can mediate on behalf of the individual and uphold decentralized power, which is critical for "genuine communities to flourish" (Bellah et al., 1991, pp. 275, 282). Responsibility and accountability are learned best close to home, in active engagement with others on issues of common concern.

Noting the social fragmentation and moral decay of modern times, Bellah reminds us that the "Lockean ideal of the autonomous individual was, in the eighteenth century, embedded in a complex moral ecology" and—as was true for the ancient polis—society, economy, and polity were still "sufficiently small-scale as to be understandable to the ordinary citizen" (ibid., p. 265).

Bellah also reminds us that we need both generic and specialized conceptions of community for a world that contains many scales. Hence new models are called for to guide us through the mazes of collective life, models that manage to integrate two coexisting, though antithetical, emphases: spatial rootedness and spatial transcendence.

In recent work, all address this duality in some measure, using terms such as "the community of limited liability" (Janowitz 1967), "symbolic communities" (Hunter 1974), "defended neighborhood" (Hunter and Suttles 1972), and "enclaves," among others.

The first concept, that of "the community of limited liability," refers to the specialized nature of contemporary communities and to the division of urban areas into a "mosaic of noncoincident but overlapping communities" (ibid.). Participation in such communities is voluntary and limited by one's interests. Residents are only partially focused on the local area, hence their loyalties tend to be fragmented.

The "defended neighborhood" is typically "the smallest area which possesses a corporate identity," and "the smallest spatial unit within which co-residents assume a relative degree of security on the streets as compared to adjacent areas" (ibid., p. 57). Defended neighborhoods are sustained by symbolic boundaries, self-labeling, and social exclusiveness. Defended neighborhoods restrict access to nonmembers and so cut themselves off from others, thus becoming too small and self-focused to constitute community.

Two other concepts for the current context are the "intermittent community" proposed by Robert Redfield—one "that is dormant until an issue or crisis mobilizes it" (Redfield 1960, p. 1)—and the "imagined community" proposed by Anderson (1991) with reference to nationalism. Anderson denotes nationalism and nation as "imagined" in the sense that "the members of even the smallest nation will never know most of their fellow-members, meet them, or even hear of them, yet in the minds of each lives the image of their communion" (ibid., p. 6). He calls these "imagined communities," but that is stretching the term. For what distinguishes the local community from these "imagined" national and supranational associations is the direct, human, connectedness to a place and a people that is made palpable by experience. Thus we always come back to the local community as the foundation of more distant, complex, and abstract forms of collective association: attachment, a sense of belonging, and a deep, personalized, holistic focus. In a world that increasingly focuses on the global context, the local continues to be vital.

PART II
A COMMUNITY IS LAUNCHED

A. Creating Roots

TWIN RIVERS TIME LINE 1970-2000

May 1967	PUD enabling legislation signed into law in New Jersey.
October 1967	East Windsor Township passes the PUD ordinance unanimously.
February 1968	East Windsor Planning Board unanimously approves the PUD application.
1969	The First Charter National Bank is appointed Twin Rivers Trustee for seven years.
1970	First residents have moved in. The Trust Advisory Board is formed to link residents and the bank trustee. The Twin Rivers Homeowners Association is formed to represent residents for internal community issues.
1971	An Architectural Advisory Committee is established to maintain the design integrity of Twin Rivers.
1972	Arson destroys six townhouses. First Court Action to compel a minority of non-paying residents to pay their monthly fees.
September 1973	First lawsuit filed by the TRHA representing the residents against the developer and trustee.
December 1973	Seventy percent of the residents (2,000 by then) contribute financially to the legal fund for the lawsuit.
1974	A pet registry is started. First time drug arrests made in Twin Rivers.
1975	Four homeowners taken to court for violations of architectural and color standards.
August 1976	Power passes to the residents, 90% of whom vote for the TRHA and against the bank trustee.
1976	Appointment of first trust administrator by the Twin Rivers board of directors — out of fifty-two applicants.

1977   Twin Rivers Day is launched.

1978–1984   Formal rules and penalties established for
                    recreational usage, safety, speed limits, noise, and
                    disruptive behavior at pools and on common
                    grounds.

1979   Joseph A. Vuzzo selected trust administrator, a
                    post he will hold for eighteen years.

1982   Defeat of proposed changes to original trust
                    documents.
                    The "Year of the Library" is proclaimed.
                    Residents unite to defeat Belz Mall proposal.

1985   Defeat of a fiercely disputed proposal for a
                    park-and-ride facility.

1987   A Parking Review Committee is established.

1995   Critical election victory.

1997   Jennifer Ward succeeds Joseph A. Vuzzo as Twin
                    Rivers trust administrator.

2001   Lawsuit filed by faction challenging board of
                    directors on transparency.

CHAPTER 4

TWIN RIVERS: THE FIRST PLANNED UNIT DEVELOPMENT IN NEW JERSEY

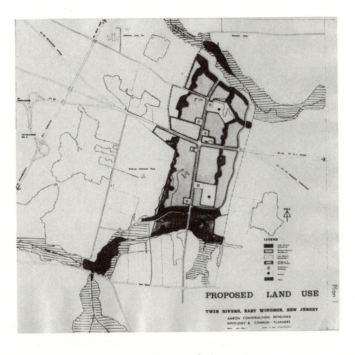

PROPOSED LAND USE

TWIN RIVERS, EAST WINDSOR, NEW JERSEY

AMRON CONSTRUCTION - DEVELOPER
WHITTLESEY & CONKLIN - PLANNERS

To plan is human, to implement, divine.

— Charles M. Haar

Place, Space, and Land

What is the fate of traditional cities, towns, and communities in the twenty-first century, the era of cyberspace? Some fear, others welcome the possibility that the electronic society will make traditional communities obsolete because instant communication permits the creation of instantaneous communities independent of any given site. This strikes me as not only premature — with potentially destructive effects on traditional communities — but based on a misreading of contemporary trends. Place, space, and territory cannot be dispensed with quite so easily. To be sure, twentieth-century humans are prone to mobility, but they still

53

need to reside somewhere. Even if their roots are not permanent, they need to establish some kind of home base between moves. Even outer-space colonies will be settlements in place.

Land has played a crucial role in the history of American communities. In colonial New England, for example, land was "a means of social fulfillment, a form of transferable property, and a promising object of speculation," and they "bought and sold, bequeathed and inherited, mortgaged and released land in a bewildering maze of transactions" (Wright 1981, p. 103).

Battles over land were stock themes in these nascent communities.

Every male citizen had access to some portion of land as well as to a "town-right" in the commons where the cattle could feed. And within two years after settling Sudbury, Massachusetts, for example, a distinctive social, economic, and political life had taken hold.

As would be true for Twin Rivers centuries later, however, generational cleavages would soon surface and most of these involved land. The demands for land pitted younger sons against their elders and threatened "the entire order of Sudbury" (Powell 1965, p. 123). Eventually, the dissatisfied young seceded to found a new community which, ironically, was to become more conservative than the parent community.

In both old and new Sudbury, however, an ethic of social responsibility was upheld. Those who were seen to care more about their "own selfish aims" than about the common good faced fierce reactions from their fellows (ibid., p. 121).

In the new Sudbury, the "pressure to pursue common over individual interests" was, if anything, more intense, with stricter entrance requirements and more stringent criteria for citizenship. Land grants were now linked to the extent of citizen participation and devotion to community undertakings.

Whether we are considering the many radical communal experiments that have been a staple of our national history or the slowly evolving small towns that we repair to in memory, the availability of land was always a prime consideration. One way of distinguishing between Utopian fantasies and more earthly developments is whether or not there is land to translate the daring visions of the mind into flesh-and-blood creations. Without land, the best visions must remain unrealized.

The Evolution of Planned Residential Communities

The Puritans connected land use to society's moral fiber. As early as 1642, John Cotton castigated New Englanders "who wanted to live apart from the meeting house, religious ordinances, and pastoral care."

He and others inveighed against "outlivers who put their souls in jeopardy for the sake of elbow room," in pursuit of "elbow room enough, and meadow enough . . . to live like lambs in a large place" (Stilgoe 1988, p. 7).

A generation later, people's "spatial requirements had mushroomed" and they were no longer content with the allotted acre per individual and twenty acres per family of the original settlers. This trend continued through the eighteenth and nineteenth centuries in an expanding society with its frontier still ahead.

In the suburban expansion following World War II, land became critical once again as reunited families sought greener climes and open spaces. Suburbia has a long history in this country, beginning in the 1870s, with the great post–Civil War suburban migration. It was fed by forces very similar to those that would feed a similar exodus less than a century later. Even the lures were similar: an environment free of the problems that beset the cities of the time. Crime, social unrest, and urban blight could, it was suggested, be avoided by moving to healthful suburbs where the chief goals of middle-class families — a home of one's own amid safe, clean, open spaces — could be realized. Then, as later, the idea of home as refuge would be featured in builders' plans along with the implicit links drawn between suburban residence, upward social mobility, and domestic contentment (Wright 1981, p. 107). The ideal was the single-family, detached house with a lawn and the proverbial picket fence. It was the American Dream, supported by existing political and financial institutions and featured in films and other media geared to shaping public tastes.

But as suburban growth accelerated, architectural, zoning, and aesthetic controls multiplied along with homeowner associations and deed restrictions. Planned residential environments, which may be traced back to nineteenth-century company towns, railroad towns, and bungalow courts, assumed new forms in the twentieth century. In the nineteenth century some fifty-two company towns were built, among which were Lowell, Massachusetts, in 1832, and Pullman, Illinois in 1867. To these must be added religious and utopian communities such as Oneida, New York, and the Harmony Society towns in Pennsylvania and Indiana. More ambitious in scale, their aims were to create healthy, happy communities. Mariemont, Ohio, was advertised as "A New Town Built to Produce Local Happiness" (ibid., p. 184).

Community, home ownership, and family formed the core of middle-class aspirations. But the house exalted was the freestanding, single-family house, which would harbor the model family and shore up morality, morale, and the virtues of community.

Important departures from the single-family house were townhouses and cluster housing. While their origins may be traced to the nineteenth century, such types of housing received special emphasis in the twentieth, when they became standard features of suburban subdivisions. In the mid-1960s, the cluster concept reemerged, fueled by a changing housing market, declining federal support, inflation, and the transformation of the middle-class American family, which was now likely to have not one but two wage earners. As had been the case in the late nineteenth century, efficiency, easy home care, economy, and good design became prominent themes.

While spatial segregation and isolation had served a nest-building generation weary of war, it was increasingly less suited to the changing demographics of job-holding wives, single parents, and self-supporting, unmarried householders. This created a demand for compact, low-maintenance dwellings with new kinds of amenities and support services such as shopping, education, and transportation. The twentieth-century version of the nineteenth-century row house became the townhouse and the condominium. The townhouse with shared walls and contiguous neighbors had the advantage of costing less than the single-family house and provided home ownership to millions who could not have afforded it otherwise. The economy of scale proved attractive to builders and potential buyers alike.

A similar economic benefit was to be realized in the creation of the planned unit development that was inaugurated in the post–World War II period. Pioneered on the West Coast, PUDs were a preplanned mix of residential, industrial, commercial, and open space intended to provide affordable, healthful, safe, and convenient living environments. They were designed to correct the flaws and deficiencies of suburbia: environmental neglect, the spatial profligacy of the single-family house that resulted in costly duplications—such as equipment for providing water and sewerage—and the political and social fragmentation of a car-dominated culture.

PUDs, envisioned as solutions for some of the more potent urban ills, were designed to allow growth with less congestion, sprawl, and pollution, and more social, political, and economic balance, than suburbs.

The British launched the movement for new towns for the modern era. A key argument initially was to find a way to defuse the population pressure of the metropolis and to recapture a more natural, a more gracious and humane way of life. The following comment summarizes a constant theme:

City lights and clamor can prove enticing, but there is a limit— when "crowds become oppressive, brightness becomes painful glare, and the sense of fellow-feeling in a community passes over into that of isolation in an anonymous mob." By contrast, the bucolic new town beckons to create a vital alternative:

The multimillion metropolis, with its layered apartment dwellers, its paucity of recreation space, divorce of workplaces from homes and of homes from green surroundings, and its mounting congestion of movement, is about as pointless and uncomfortable a fashion as humanity has every embraced. (Osborn and Whittick 1963, pp. 28, 31)

Based on the key ideas of the British new towns, a PUD is characterized by the separation of residential from commercial land uses, and the separation of vehicular from pedestrian traffic. The neighborhood unit is focused on the elementary school and local shops. The theory was that higher residential densities and compact road networks would make possible more residential land for public consumption and aesthetic enjoyment. Land that traditionally would be part of the suburban homeowner's private space would belong to the entire community.

Twin Rivers as a Planned Unit Development

Twin Rivers, in East Windsor Township, fifteen miles east of Princeton, was the first planned unit development in the state of New Jersey and served as a standard for others to emulate or improve upon. In the postconstruction evaluation of the community I am about to present, a key objective was to be attentive to the development of key institutions and a sense of community over time. A precise dating of the community's beginning permitted the construction of a baseline against which to chart its complex pattern of growth and change at various phases.

The community opened its doors to the first of a prospective ten thousand residents in 1970. The initial population mix was in most respects typical of modern suburbia. So were the motives that propelled the newcomers. Most had to do, in one way or another, with land and space: They were seeking the good life, the clean life, a home of one's own with a lawn and a backyard—a place for children to play and be safe. "These were the things most people wanted when they moved to this community" (*Periscope*, September 1975, p. 32).* As is true of PUDs generally, the plans for Twin Rivers conserved public open space for residents by means of higher housing densities, large areas of common land, and judiciously designed roadways and parking lots. These elements would not only reduce the costs of construction, but also facilitate the creation of a balance among dwellings, recreation spaces, pe-

---

*Twin Rivers community newsletters, issued under varying names and irregularly over the decades, were an important source of information. The most frequently cited in the text include *The Periscope*, from 1983–93 and *Twin Rivers Today*, 1993–2002 along with *Opus* for the 1970s and the *Windsor Heights Herald* for all three decades.

destrian access, and facilities. In keeping with the cultural preferences of most Americans, Twin Rivers was privately organized, although it gratefully accepted federal help with mortgage funding when needed.

The prime mover behind Twin Rivers (and with planned communities, there is usually a prime mover) was Gerald Finn, a visionary businessman and developer who presented the idea of a PUD to the East Windsor Planning Board in 1963. It took five years and nearly two hundred recorded meetings with authorities to make it a reality. The hurdles were many — vested interests in existing arrangements, of course, and fear of the new — in this case of a townhouse development in an essentially single-family terrain. Hence, the approval of township officials was critical. There were legal requirements, including the passage of a township PUD ordinance and state PUD enabling legislation. All of this was predicated on land assemblage and financing. These essential prerequisites are a study in themselves, showing the extraordinary interconnections of local and state politics, personal networks, business interests, and strategic actors in a variety of critical roles (Hackney 1975, p. 45). The PUD-enabling legislation was signed into law on May 23, 1967, and the East Windsor township committee unanimously passed the PUD ordinance in October 1967. By February 1968, the PUD application was unanimously approved by the East Windsor Planning Board.

Twin Rivers benefited, as did other PUDs, from the support of the Federal Housing Agency (FHA), established in 1934; the Veterans Administration (VA) mortgage guarantees, established in 1944; and the Housing Act of 1949, which offered favorable terms to builders, bankers, and developers. All of these fueled the housing boom and the American exodus from the cities to the suburbs in the post–World War II era.

Having ventured $1.25 million up front, not including the cost of the land, before construction began, Finn teamed up with a Princeton-based developer, Herbert Kendall, who invested $1 million of his own and assumed the land mortgage from Finn. Soon thereafter, American Standard bought out the partners and, in 1974, W. R. Grace bought out American Standard for $10 million. From a visionary dream it had become a marketable property wedded to the bottom line. However, hidden within the bricks and mortar was the hope of something grander and more fundamental. Twin Rivers promised to recapture something of the traditional sense of community that would have an appeal to residents beyond immediate practical interests.

The Twin Rivers Planned Unit Development, like PUDs generally, was inspired by the pioneering work of William J. Levitt whose Levittowns were to become the most widely copied mass-produced house

Table 4.1
**U.S. Home Ownership Rates, 1920–2000
(Owners As Percent of Householders)**

Date	Percent
1920	45.6
1930	46.8
1940	43.6
1950	55
1960	61.9
1970	62.9
1980	64.4
1990	66.7
2000	68

Source: Joint Center of Housing Studies, Harvard University 2001.

types in the decades that followed World War II. The Levitt houses of 1949, set on 60-by-100-foot lots, featured built-in refrigerators, washing machines, and what were truly novel then, TV sets. Public swimming pools, carports, and children's playgrounds were other innovations that linked houses and residents to more public activities. The suburbia of the 1920s was for affluent homeowners. Several decades later, home ownership came within reach of middle-class and lower-middle-class families because of the availability of long-term mortgages and low interest rates. Not surprisingly, the nation's housing inventory increased by 21 million units in the 1940s and 1950s (Sternlieb 1982, p. 29). Home ownership accordingly surged. Three-fourths of the total U.S. housing stock was built after 1940.

What New Communities Have to Offer

Although Twin Rivers was a "new" or "planned" community, its ancestry reaches back a century or more. There was Radburn, New Jersey, launched in 1928 as an offshoot of Ebenezer Howard's Garden City Movement of 1898. There were three greenbelt towns built by the Federal Resettlement Administration in the 1930s, as well as company towns to house workers for large power projects such as the TVA; Boulder Dam; and Los Alamos, New Mexico. New communities in the post–World War II era were in large part a response to the drawbacks of laissez-faire suburban settlement patterns. They were intended to counteract the problems accompanying a too rapid suburban expansion — suburban sprawl, environmental indifference, waste of space, and overall incoherence of design (Burby et al., 1976). The key goals of such communities were to plan for growth and balance, to avoid sprawl and pollution, to achieve the integration of services, transportation, work, and housing, and eventually to break bad habits of social and racial exclusion by explicitly striving for a social and housing mix. Convenience, safety, health, and an integrated mode of life were to create a more attractive and satisfying hybrid of small-scale community and large-scale urban worlds.

The direct antecedents of Twin Rivers were the Levittowns pioneered by Abraham Levitt and his sons Alfred and William, already among the largest home builders in the nation. Levittown (called Island Trees in its first version) transformed the process of building by its innovative techniques and extraordinary speed of production. The first Cape Cod boxes were rentals for postwar veterans in the main, but this changed quickly into home purchasing arrangements for middle-class families. Eventually, Levittown, with 82,000 residents in more than 17,000 houses was the "largest housing development ever put up by a single builder" (Jackson 1985, p. 235). Also, the Levitts at first insisted on certain restrictive rules as to fences, lawns, and signage. The aim was not, however, to provide community but recreational amenities along with the well-equipped houses. The Levitts offered nine swimming pools, sixty playgrounds, ten baseball diamonds, and seven village greens.

Though the critics scoffed at these mass-produced houses, the public was enthusiastic. The houses offered many novel and attractive features, including washing machines, picture windows, and later, television sets.

Though heavily criticized for spatial and aesthetic monotony, social exclusiveness, and racial segregation, Levittown was ahead of its time in extending the American Dream to millions. It was a tremendous achievement, putting homeownership, open spaces, privacy, and safety within reach of countless families.

Twin Rivers, combining features of the new community concept and of the earlier Levittowns, offered an extraordinary opportunity to explore the genesis of community by following its course, not retroactively as is so often done, but literally from the ground up, as it moved from the physical shell to a social and cultural reality.

In the vast literature of community studies there are countless portraits of communities past and present. The best of these provide rich details on how people go about creating a place, as distinct from a site, for living together more or less successfully over time. In general, these portraits remove any illusion that communities are based on some simple, readily grasped formula. In fact, the closer you look, the richer the terrain and the more intricate the web of collective life. What a great many of these studies lack, however, is a framework that would put the rich details into some order from which general principles of community could be deduced.

As a departure from traditional American ideals of private property and individual home ownership, Twin Rivers was bound to raise many fundamental questions among home builders and home buyers. It provided a unique opportunity to track the potential for community in this unfinished site; to monitor the process whereby the potential for community becomes activated, and the impediments to it; to set up timetables and stages of community formation; and to evaluate how solid, cohesive, and enduring the community would be.

One question, which becomes more critical and problematic as community becomes a matter of choice rather than inescapable legacy, is: How does an aggregate of strangers develop a sense of community, a sense that they are part of a bigger story involving numerous unknown others on whose combined actions and sentiments their destiny depends? This is the question at the heart of this book.

A planned unit development, with its shared land uses and higher population density, differs from conventional suburbs in its aim to achieve a compromise between urban concentration and suburban privacy. Households have shrunk in size because of rising rates of divorce and single parenthood, and marriage at later ages. Suburban self-containment spell isolation and loneliness for such households and others who seek to reach beyond the cocoon of family and household to a wider social terrain.

In Twin Rivers, outreach was built into the design of houses, the road network, and private as well as public spaces.

The Master Plan for Twin Rivers

The master plan for Twin Rivers, developed by the New York firm of Whittlesey and Conklin, allotted acreage as shown in table 4.2. The townhouse, in particular, linked residents physically, visually, and aurally and made every homeowner automatically a land sharer. How and whether this would translate into a sense of community was thus of considerable interest.

The houses people choose to live in tell us much about their society, their values, their status, and their opportunities. House and environment, house and community, though often discussed as separate domains, are profoundly interconnected. However, the house occupies such a central focus in individual aspirations that its links to wider insti-

62   Chapter 4

Table 4.2
Twin Rivers Land Allocation

Housing	249 acres (36%)
Light industry	198 acres (28%)
Schools, parks, open space	164 acres (23%)
Commercial	55 acres (8%)
Roads and parking	34 acres (4%)
Unassigned	19 acres (2%)
Total Acreage	719 acres

tutional spheres are often disregarded. The house is for most people a central preoccupation. Most of their free time is spent in it, the high points of the life course unfold there, and it is a prized possession of deep cultural and personal significance.

The house has also been a key impetus for technical innovations, a living laboratory for testing out central heating and cooling systems, indoor water supply, plumbing, designer kitchens, avant-garde bathrooms — marvels of "efficiency and clever design . . . with their advanced lighting, electrical wiring, laundry systems, and rubbish disposal. "In almost every respect . . . the American house is a completely appropriate capsule world, fleshing out the main principles, myths, and values of the larger cultural system" (Zelinsky 1973, pp. 93, 94).

Within this larger context, the badge of achievement and respectability is a house of one's own, certifying one's soundness of character and self-respect and providing the conditions for a proper family life — by its linkage to the central cultural values of privacy, property, independence, the distribution of wealth, as well as to patterns of work and the structure of domestic life.

The rural character of eighteenth-century Colonial America and the peasant immigrant heritage of the nineteenth century make current housing aspirations resonate backward in time and outward in space. Then as now, a house meant rootedness, contact with terra firma, a sense of permanence in a transient world.

A house also means freedom — and the right to one's own living space, to make noise, for children to play — creating a buffer thereby between one's self and the outside world.

A house is typically the largest amount of property that most Americans will ever own. It thereby binds individuals to the basic financial and legal institutions of their world.

Home ownership constitutes an abiding goal and value for most Americans. It is seen as a major primary marker of social worth, a public proof of success and ultimately of self-worth. Ex–apartment dwellers turned homeowners, for example, have been shown to experience notable boosts in morale and well-being, and home ownership lessens stress for urban residents, even at low income levels and among the unemployed. And unemployed home owners, research has shown, were "much more likely than non-owners to avoid mental strain, feelings of unhappiness, and marital strain." For them the house was a "major buffer" against economic hardship (Caplovitz 1963 pp. 176, 178), whose purchase enhanced family life, and simply fixing up the house boosted morale and family togetherness (Gans 1967, p. 255; Keller 1989).

Thus many forces combine to make home ownership a cornerstone of the American way of life. Along with the psychological quest for security or status, it reflects a desire for symbolic closure. For the house has power as a symbol of belonging and respectability apart from its provision of shelter and safety. In a mobile, fluid, modern environment, the house constitutes a rare theme of constancy for individuals ever on the move yet searching for roots.

The suburban ethos captures the twin themes of this cultural dualism for permanence and change in its standardized physical design. From the late eighteenth century onward, as many European travelers observed, suburbs expressed Americans' characteristic love of newness, nearness to nature, individualism, and competitive emulation. And the suburbs of the early nineteenth century forged a cultural pattern that endures to this day, continuing to be the place where the American Dream has best been realized.

The Townhouse

In the late 1970s, what with smaller families, two-job/career couples and high costs of home ownership, the majority of young couples began to question the suburban ideal. Two breadwinners made the length and ease of commute more critical than it had been, and access to job sites and transportation became doubly problematic.

In response, a new concept in housing reemerged in a late twentieth-century version: cluster housing. This type of housing is based on grouping houses around publicly shared open spaces as well as shopping areas, schools, walkways, and recreational facilities.

Cluster housing had its precedents. First proposed as winter housing in southern California in 1910, it was to promote social solidarity among residents along with less costly forms of shelter.

In the mid-1960s, the cluster concept reappeared, fueled by a changing housing market, declining federal supports, inflation, and changes in work and family arrangements. Suburban segregation and separatism had served a nest-building generation after World War II, as weary of war and doubling up, they sought space and privacy. A generation later, this mode of living, though still culturally idealized, seemed ever less suited to job-holding wives, single parents, and self-supporting single men and women. And so, as new cultural ideals were fashioned, a new concept of housing took hold.

Most people seem unaware of the deep connection between house form and the web of community. And yet, as indicated earlier, the culture of traditional suburbia rested heavily on ideals of privacy and separatism, which the freestanding, family-focused house encouraged.

The subsequent shift to cluster housing and the kinds of communities it spawned likewise tapped new concepts and ideals of individual as well as collective responsibilities.

Townhouses are attached houses in rows of two or more. Townhouse aggregates are managed by home-owner associations and constitute a combination of public and private arrangements in which residents own their houses and a proportionate share of the open space, common grounds, and recreation facilities (Norcross 1973).

Such aggregates represent an amalgam of private and public, retaining the ideal of individual home ownership and single family occupancy but expanding its territorial and symbolic limits. By sharing common walls, open spaces, and numerous facilities and services, a new pastiche of mine and yours is created. In the process, traditional designs for living are transformed and new cultural patterns and priorities take center stage. Townhouses, because they are attached to one or more adjacent dwellings, challenge the image of the house as one's castle and private refuge, an ideal difficult to sustain where dwellings are physically linked and involve owners in shared financial and spatial obligations.

Single-Family Houses versus Townhouses

Twin Rivers permitted an exploration of the response to townhouse living for Americans who were traditional in their orientation to family life and home ownership. Such a traditional population would have been expected to aspire to live in freestanding houses. Instead, they were pioneers for a new mode of living. And contrary to initial misgivings, the townhouse proved very successful. It satisfied the need for separateness yet also gave to residents a joint stake in each other's lives and the land they possessed in common. This gave the residents a taste of the integration of "family, house, and village" that formed the pattern of the original settlers of New England (Jackson 1985, pp. 12–13), which was lost in the transition to industrialism.

In Twin Rivers during the 1970s, home ownership was possible for as little as $100 down and ten monthly carrying charges of $255 each. This included principal, interest on thirty-year VA or FHA mortgage, estimated taxes and home-owner's insurance, and a monthly fee of $17 for lawn maintenance, snow removal, garbage collection, and membership in one of four tennis clubs and swim clubs. Those who could not afford to buy could rent an apartment.

Divided into four quads or neighborhoods, each with its own swimming pool and tennis courts, Twin Rivers had a mix of housing types arranged in rows of six to ten dwellings. Townhouses, which predominated, generally faced onto parking lots in front and common grassy areas in back. Each townhouse also had as its own private space a patio area enclosed by a five-foot-high fence in back. Residential densities ranged from four to eighteen dwelling units per acre. All told, there were three thousand dwelling units on 719 acres for a population of ten thousand. See table 4.3.

There are two antithetical views on the rise of condominium and townhouse developments. One holds that they are evidence of a propensity for stronger social and neighborhood ties because they involve the sharing of responsibilities and land. The other holds that such ties are weakened by the transience and brevity of social contacts in new developments, which precludes a deeper interdependency. The Twin Rivers data support the proposition that townhouse living can foster social and neighborhood ties, but it does not do so automatically or without considerable effort.

Townhouses, despite shared walls and common spaces, were connected in the minds of their owners, not with apartments, which they resemble somewhat, but with freestanding houses. A consistent pattern of association between housing type and life satisfaction showed the satisfaction of apartment dwellers to be low and that of townhouse residents to be high.

Table 4.3
Housing Types in Twin Rivers

Town houses	63%
Condominiums	5%
Apartments	25%
Freestanding house	7%

Here, too, land use played a significant role. The house was seen not only as a shelter but also as a provider of nearby outdoor spaces for easily supervised play space for children and a site for adults to gather for gossip or social celebrations. Even high population densities were taken in stride if they allowed for some private space and amenities close by. Thus, contrary to much expert opinion, residents of Twin Rivers were both receptive and adaptable to what was in the 1970s considered a novel form of housing in suburbia. Levittowners, by contrast, were not attracted to townhouses, leading Gans (1967) to the following conclusion: "Unless future row houses are designed to maximize privacy and can also overcome their present low-status image, they will not be very popular with the next generation of home buyers." And Zelinsky (1973, p. 93) refers to the American "aversion" to inhabiting multi-family structures. Some residents (7 to 10 percent on average) discovered almost immediately that townhouse living was not for them and left Twin Rivers as soon as they could. A larger proportion (20 percent) stayed and clung to the ideal of having a detached house some day. However, this ideal seems to have persisted in fantasy without affecting the satisfaction with the house actually inhabited. The majority of residents were more than willing to give townhouses a try.

Satisfaction seems to depend on skillful design. Design can provide the illusion of spaciousness, thereby enlarging what Becker has called "the psychological size of the house" (Becker 1977, p. 27), and can make a small house appear spacious, even luxurious, by the use of skylights, high ceilings, mirrors, and open floor plans. In our image-conscious culture, the illusion of space is at times as effective as the actual provision of space. By and large, the Twin Rivers townhouses seem to have provided both the space needed by their inhabitants and the spaciousness desired by them.

A General Profile of the First Wave of Residents

Who were these pioneers who ventured to live in this ex–potato field with grand designs for community?

In contrast to the vast majority of past communities studied — ethnic, immigrant, slum, or ghetto — this population was squarely in the middle class. They were imbued with the credo of the American Dream — of high aspirations, mobility, and self-development. They were eager to claim their birthright of opportunity. But they were also ready to take a chance on the new patterns of housing tenure and land ownership.

The first wave of residents was rather typical of New Community populations: young married couples with one to two children who had moved to a townhouse or garden apartment from New York City, Long Island, or suburban New Jersey. For the large majority, the move represented an opportunity for first-time home ownership. By comparison with the Levittowners studied by Gans (1967), they were higher on the socioeconomic scale occupationally, financially, and educationally.

Townhouse living in Twin Rivers turned out to be a positive experience for the first wave of residents. Whichever indicator was examined — the reactions to the house as a whole, the desired improvements, the need for privacy, or responses to density, noise, and neighbors — the house came out as a plus. None of the prophesied fears — from ruthless invasions of privacy to horrendous neighbors — materialized for more than a fraction of the population. This contradicts the conventional wisdom that Americans are not ready to give up the single-family house with its own front lawn and private backyard or that they experience extreme stress in doing so. Two-thirds of Twin Rivers residents liked their houses; one-third was enthusiastic, and only a minority had mixed feelings. Two percent or less, a minuscule proportion, disliked their houses.

The religious complexion of Twin Rivers was also unlike that of the Levittowns. It attracted a disproportionate number of Jewish residents at the start — estimates vary from 25 to 40 percent, a disproportion that diminished over time with the arrival of Asians, African-Americans, and a variety of other groups. Still the Jewish component far exceeded its national representation of around 3 percent, though it should be emphasized that the large majority of these Jewish in-migrants, or residents from New York City and Long Island, were secular in orientation and comparable in this respect to the Protestant and Roman Catholic residents.

The question of social mix, which will be fully discussed later, surfaced early. Some outside observers hastened, without much basis, to deplore Twin Rivers' homogeneity. A closer assessment, however, indicates considerable diversity in regard to religion and occupation; social, ethnic, and regional backgrounds; and personal aspirations and social priorities.

At the start, residents were traditional in the domestic division of labor — the men were the principal breadwinners; the women focused on house, home, and children, regardless of their high educational attainments and prior job experience. The men were employed in corporations, professions, and small businesses. The fraction of women who worked outside the home in the early years held skilled, semi-professional, and professional part-time positions as teachers, office workers, nurses, or librarians.

These pioneering twentieth-century Americans were in some respects similar to the pioneers who struggled to devise communities in the earliest years of the republic. They sought a "close-knit community that existed for the good of all its members and in which each man was his brother's keeper" (Bailyn 1986, p. 39).

Still, both sets of pioneers had only the dimmest notion of what building a community would be like and they were quite unprepared for the actual tasks of pioneering as distinct from contemplating the concept in heroic fantasies. The culture shock occasioned by this discrepancy was clearly behind the pandemonium of the earliest years in both cases. Twin Rivers was thus an extremely interesting case for questions about identity and community.

These parallels aside, however, there were important differences. Early American settlers, who tended to come in groups, were imbued with a unifying set of beliefs that made the idea of sharing more readily acceptable. There was no such overarching ideology or common culture of community for Twin Rivers. And though there was a rhetoric of common enterprise, most residents thought that community would come along with the purchase of their homes and not demand more than minimal participation.

This go-it-alone philosophy is hardly surprising given current cultural lessons and precepts emphasized in American society. Then, too, southern New Jersey is not a primeval wilderness — residents had access to alternative sites and resources via jobs, shopping, and friendships outside Twin Rivers. If they were dissatisfied, they could readily leave, as some did. But if they chose to stay, as most did, they discovered it was up to them to create the social institutions and forms of cooperation on which the developing community would rest. This required countless appeals to each resident to re-define the situation by taking the "social viewpoint" (Thomas and Znaniecki 1958, p. 1259). Most residents were not prepared for this difficult task; they assumed, or were led to believe, that the purchase of their homes was a speedy ticket to community.

The early days were filled with exhortations for residents to think in terms of community, the virtues of which were depicted in almost Biblical terms by the 1974 sales brochure:

> It all began as a dream propelled into action by men of ability and determination and is being taken forward to fruition. From it all has arisen a fine young town and the magnificent people who live there. . . . there are thousands of people from all walks of life. They work hard and live in the hectic contentment which is 1974.

Hyperbole also marked the advertisements for Levittown decades earlier, which left out a good deal along with what was featured. The dwellings were generally pictured as freestanding and surrounded by greenery and trees, when they actually were densely clustered townhouses amid parking lots and construction equipment (Baxandall and Ewen 2000, p. 137).

Unprepared for the trials ahead, and resistant to appeals for community involvement, the new residents of Twin Rivers suffered unavoidable culture shock. This was magnified by the hype of sales brochures that depicted "a community so complete, when you drive home on Friday evening, you won't want to leave until Monday morning." A 1970 sales brochure asserted:

> Until now, most people have had a dismal choice: city life, or the suburbs with their endless blocks of tract houses. The comforts and joys of city living are fast disappearing. Even survival there is becoming a daily chore, raising a family, impossible. The suburbs have their own problems: rising taxes, a limited social and economic cross-section, a certain monotonous isolation from the world.

By contrast, Twin Rivers was billed as the most desirable alternative, "a total environment."

Given that the residents were generally employed and had many contacts outside the borders of Twin Rivers, a self-contained environment was never to be realized. Still, though not self-sufficient, it was able to provide for a wide range of needs — for shelter, recreation, material goods, and sociability. Twin Rivers was thus closer at the start to what Redfield termed an "intermittent community" — where families and households remain private and separate until a crisis or issue mobilizes them (Redfield 1960).

Productive and subsistence activities, as well as religious, entertainment, and health-care resources were located outside the development, whereas elementary education, domestic life, social celebrations, and association memberships were concentrated within its boundaries, thus making Twin Rivers a composite creation, that tapped into local as well as nonlocal resources.

The Strains of Creating a New Social Code

In addition to being a PUD and a "new" community, Twin Rivers was not finished when the first residents moved in. An unfinished community—with construction equipment dotting the landscapes, houses in varying states of completion, and large tracts of empty land waiting for their complement of buildings, open spaces, and parking lots—makes enormous psychological demands on its initial residents in regard to the most elementary plane of existence. In addition to the inconveniences of dirt and noise, adjustments to new neighbors, and a house that one must strive to make one's own, is the lack of reliable guides to help orient one's behavior. Indeed, the tasks confronting the residents were huge: They needed to create viable routines of living and a shared social code virtually overnight.

This made the first decade of residence in Twin Rivers very trying. Later, when the social and physical structure of the community was in place, newcomers would still have to grapple with the dislocations of a move, but the general atmosphere had stabilized. Still, the growing pains persisted far longer than one might have expected. In addition to the reorientation needed in regard to shopping, traveling, and visiting, family life was disrupted and husband-wife as well as parent-child relations were exposed to unaccustomed strains.

A frequent response to these strains was anger—anger at the physical setting, the new neighbors, the real estate agents, the Trust Administration. One or all were blamed for the frustrations experienced. Nervous ailments were not unusual as individuals struggled to find their balance. Many couples found themselves more on edge, despite greater togetherness. An almost universal problem was spending beyond one's means as the expenses of settling in, including the purchase of new appliances, accumulated. The pressure to keep up with the Joneses fanned anxieties as well as financial indebtedness. These problems called for counseling, but no such services were available in the first years. Eventually, counselors and family therapists in surrounding towns were consulted, but this occurred years after the move and only among the most troubled or most dissatisfied residents.

Young people of both sexes faced special problems. Public officials noted a rise in juvenile delinquency and commented on its greater incidence in new communities as compared to established communities of comparable size. They believed that the children were "acting out" their parents' complaints and disappointments by petty stealing, vandalism, and, later, drug use. These family and youth problems had not been anticipated in the plans for the community, but proved to be a critical source of stress in the early years.

While the newcomers were fairly typical of Americans generally, seeking to climb up the ladder of success by investing in a home of their own and staking out a better life for their children in the safety and open spaces of suburbia, they also wanted something more. They were drawn to Twin Rivers because of the promised community.

It was community that beckoned them, though what exactly that meant to them is not clear. But since they had been reared in the individualistic ethos of contemporary American society, the critical question was, would they be able to create community? And if so, what kind of community would it be? And who would bring it into being?

Studying a Community in Progress

I began the study of Twin Rivers as a naturalist might explore the milieu and behavior of a heretofore uninvestigated species, seeking to build up a comprehensive picture of a community in progress, step by step. I hoped to avoid an all-too-common error of generalizing from evidence gathered early in the life of a community when problems loom large and transitory stresses are viewed as permanent strains. This is not to say that the formative period in a community's life is not critical for later developments. Indeed, one of my main hypotheses postulates that the first years of life of a community are the foundation for what is to follow. But the extent of their influence cannot be assumed. It can be assessed only by comparing the formative years with a later period of relatively greater stability.

It was the German sociologist Max Weber who prodded sociology to "examine a particular community" by asking the "real empirical sociological question: What motives . . . lead individuals to participate in this community?" — what caused this community to come into being in the first place and what makes it continue to exist? (Weber 1978, p. 70.) These are among the central questions we shall be pursuing.

How does a community come to life? What are the major growing pains? Who are its prime movers? What are the critical milestones? The answers should illumine the process by which thousands of strangers become bound to one another and come to realize that their individual fates are joined, their lives intertwined.

The study of the first Planned Unit Development in New Jersey had both scientific and practical aims. I hoped to add to the general knowledge and understanding of the formation and endurance of community as well as to explore questions of interest to architects, planners, and designers charged with translating principles into practice. My access to the initial plans and the key figures responsible for the establishment of Twin Rivers enabled me to be present at its creation and to chart its course from birth to maturity.

A variety of methods was used to penetrate the mysteries of such a complex — and exhilarating — transformation: direct observation of behavior, participant observation, repeated surveys of residents' attitudes and reactions, and photographic analyses of the changing landscape and physical ecology of the site.

There were three major community-wide attitude surveys. The first involved 350 in-depth interviews of the earliest wave of residents; these were the basis for two follow-up surveys in the 1980s and 1990s. Comparisons were drawn between men, women, and children; between renters and owners; and between original and later settlers. The follow-up, which rounded out the interviews, was a Gallup survey of one thousand households in the 1980s. The third, a survey conducted by Response Analysis of Princeton in 1998, tapped a random sample of another one thousand households, also followed by one hundred in-depth interviews.

A panel study of forty-four residents in the 1970s and 1980s that drew on the same respondents at two time periods a decade apart showed the constancies in the attitudes and reactions of residents to their environments.

To obtain a picture of the emerging social and political framework of Twin Rivers, an ongoing scrutiny of records, commemorations, and events was carried out via content analysis of local papers and the monthly Twin Rivers Newsletter as well as public records on governance, public participation, voting, and crime.

Of the two parallel strategies, one focused on the subjective dimension of community formation, that is, the residents' attitudes and reactions as individuals, the other on collective indicators, both physical and social.

The key physical indicators included the changing appearance of Twin Rivers, notably landscaping, grounds, and upkeep; the positive — and negative — modifications of the environment, such as the embellishment of houses and lawns and the existence of litter, vandalism, and cleanliness. Signage — mainly tracked by photographic monitoring — proved to be a very useful indicator of the emerging community's self-presentation.

Social indicators were tapped by tracking rates of voting in local and national elections and following collective responses to crises via rallies of support or protest on critical issues. These included law suits brought against the developer early on and against the Trust Administrator later; the waste disposal site issue; the opposition to a proposed factory outlet.

Also important to this study was participant observation of community-wide events such as the annual Twin Rivers Day, local holidays, local sports events, and other festivities. This involved frequenting the pizza parlor favored by teenagers; going to the library, which served as a quasi–community center; watching school events; and attending the monthly Homeowners Association meetings on a systematic basis.

Following new rules and regulations and amendments to the charter illuminated aspects of community building, as did a special analysis of the views of one hundred leading citizens, which explored some of the reasons why they were willing — when so many were not — to assume responsibilities for the collective life. It is important to know why they took on projects that most residents were too busy or apathetic to support; volunteered to serve as candidates for local offices; provided professional advice and services; served on a myriad of committees that mushroomed forth from day one; created theater groups, parent groups, newsletters, and the like; and helped to shape in countless ways collective life in the difficult early months and years.

Whenever possible, "unobtrusive measures" were used. This involved obtaining information without asking the participants directly but inferring reactions and moods by noting the turnout at festivities; the uses of local shops and facilities; street life — people walking, hanging out, pausing to talk with one another; the uses of ball fields, tennis courts, swimming pools; and the atmosphere of conviviality or aloofness generated on various occasions.

The data gathered by these varied methods revealed routine patterns of conduct as well as departures from routine, agreements as well as sources of strife and controversy. Given the longitudinal perspective of the study, it was possible to follow attitudinal stability and change as well as the community's developing sense of itself, its capacity to act on its behalf, and the growth of collective identity and social cohesion.

Interestingly, Vico, Goethe, and de Tocqueville each argued that the study of beginnings is especially instructive. Goethe called it the "initial phenomenon" and considered it "indispensable for the comprehension of the phenomena that present themselves to us in the here and now." Vico earlier contended that "we understand what happens now from beginnings [and that] doctrines or theories must begin where the matters that they treat begin" (Cahnman 1995, p. 189). De Tocqueville applied this to community. Rather than studying "communities in their latter days," he proposed going to "first occurrences" to fathom the origins of prejudice and ruling passions (de Tocqueville 1990, pp. 6–9).

By endeavoring to grasp collective moods and rhythms of Twin Rivers — from the initial euphoric fantasies to a more measured stance followed by massive disaffection, chaos, and near dissolution midway in development to a final thrust toward permanence — a model of the phases of community evolution may be devised.

Table 4.4
Summary Table

Twin Rivers	
Total Population	10,000 people
Acreage	719 acres
Total number of dwelling units	3,000
Land use—in percentages	
Residential	35%
Commercial	7%
Industrial	28%
Open space	23%
Schools	3%
Roads, parking	4%
Types of dwelling units	
Townhouses	63%
Garden apartments	25%
Condominiums	5%
Single-family houses	7%
Gross density	4.1%
Net density	18% (High)
	12% (Low)
Four quadrants	Quads I, II, III, and IV

    Studying a community in formation gave me an opportunity to witness the floundering emergence of a complex social construction. This was daunting but also exciting. It also yielded richer findings, I believe, than the more typical retrospectives, which often involve one-shot reconstructions of community that offer conclusions but reveal little of the process at work.

CHAPTER 5

THE RESIDENTS APPRAISE THEIR ENVIRONS

Beauty is in the eye of the beholder.

Can planners and builders create communities for a population whose habits and hopes they do not know? Can they rely on categorical assumptions about what young or old, rich or poor, natives or immigrants are likely to desire? All too often, when these assumptions are actually put to the test, it is too late to change course. The study of Twin Rivers sheds some light on these frequently asked questions.

Community was important to the pioneering wave of residents in the 1970s. Nearly one-half said they moved to Twin Rivers because of the PUD concept, because they liked the idea of a physically designed

setting. The large majority were intrigued by something new and different; they were attracted by the promise of a community with good facilities, pleasant neighbors, an attractive appearance, and an ambience of
safety and freedom. The fact that someone had made the effort to map
out a provisional social order geared to everyone's benefit seemed to
give them a feeling of security. True, actual conditions were far from
ideal in those early years, but the newcomers were encouraged by the
promise.

Initial Reactions to Twin Rivers Overall

> For me everything is here. I am involved with children. There is
> enough going on here to fill everyone's needs. Almost a Utopia for a
> first home for a young couple. For us it's perfect. We like to walk, go
> to the Flea Market. Pricewise it was perfect.
> —Woman, 28 years old, 1970s

> The people—they don't care, expect everything to be done for them.
> —Woman, 25 years old, 1970s

> An apathetic community—people don't care and bring their bad atti-
> tudes. Act as renters not homeowners and don't care.
> —Woman, 29 years old, 1970s

Reactions to a community are obviously complex and not easily summarized. Depending on how one asks the question, one taps different
nuances of feeling. Still, an overall pattern of likes and dislikes did
emerge very early in Twin Rivers' life.

The answers to the simple, comprehensive question, How do you
feel about Twin Rivers? show that positive feelings far outweighed negative ones:

Table 5.1
Feelings about Twin Rivers

Response	1970s	1990s
Like very much	35%	23%
Like pretty much	42%	56%
Like so-so	20%	20%
Dislike	3%	1%
	100%	100%
	N = 246	N = 450

Table 5.2
Reasons for Liking Twin Rivers (all three decades)

People, community	56%
Dwelling, construction, and financing	47%
Convenient location, schools, shopping, and community	46%
Features	34%
Scale of community	30%
Advantages for children	30%
Recreation	26%
Quietness, safety, privacy	23%
Miscellaneous	8%

Note: Composite, based on adding the first three responses given, for a total of 434 responses.

The reasons for the positive feelings were many — recreation, commuting convenience, safety for the children, and the whole complex of a new home and new patterns of living.

Not surprisingly, there were mixed feelings from the start. Two-fifths of the residents in Phase I (the 1970s) had the pleasant surprise of finding Twin Rivers better than they had expected, but an even higher proportion — two-thirds — expressed disappointment with various aspects.

The plusses generally rested on satisfaction with recreation (40%), the people (30%), commuting convenience (28%), the house (28%), and quietness/safety (26%). The negatives centered on a lack of facilities (18%), a disapproval of management (21%), and worries about self-centered people (20%).

The earliest residents represented two distinct groups: those who came to Twin Rivers because it was new and planned (45%), and because they liked the idea of a PUD design (one-sixth) and the prospective social life (one-sixth). Those who were not drawn by the community (40%) cited finances and the dwelling as prime reasons for moving there. Thus from the start, some residents were much more community-minded than others. And the expectations they harbored greatly affected how they would react to the new site. Indeed, the willingness to involve one's self in the new community rested heavily, especially at the start, on expectations and fantasies about leaving a familiar way of life for a new and different one.

The move to a pre-designed community may spur the wildest fantasies akin to winning the lottery. Then there was the house itself, typically the first one owned, that the new owners endowed with extraordinary meaning. Dreams of unparalleled family togetherness, opportunities for the children, the promise of new friendships, and an exciting social life, contributed to the fantasy of community held by many who moved in.

Table 5.3
**Reasons for Moving to the New Community
1997 Residents***

Community-related factors (Liked PUDs; wanted a "real" community; close social life)	77%
Home ownership	67%
To get out of the city	38%
Good schools for the children	29%
	N = 450

*The first two reasons were combined.

Specific appeals were designed to induce young, ambitious, well-educated couples bent on raising a family and working hard for success to uproot themselves and venture forth into new experience. The fact that Twin Rivers' residents came for both community and housing contrasts with the Levittowners studied by Gans a generation earlier, for whom the house was the prime lure and the "community . . . of secondary importance." It also challenges Gans's recommendation that "from a market point of view" the emphasis need not be on site planning or "other community innovations because when people move into a new community they do so primarily for the house" (Gans 1967, p. 41). In Twin Rivers, the community and the house were both important, but community more so, and this pattern continues into the 1990s.

Twin Rivers' residents were critical of numerous aspects of their housing—construction flaws, the poor quality of built-in features—but their true disappointments focused on insufficiencies of community: lack of community spirit, insufficient civic concern, too little concern for others. This was a constant refrain in the ensuing years.

Townhouse Living and Privacy

One source of anxiety associated with townhouse living is that privacy, that coveted nugget of well-being in an impersonal mass society, becomes endangered. High densities, as well as the visual and auditory proximity of neighbors, are assumed to affect privacy adversely.

Privacy is a top priority for Americans generally and is a cherished value for the architects, builders, and developers trying to house them. What, then, of privacy in the housing clusters spreading over the modern landscape? How adequate is one's personal space in a dense settlement in which much of the space left to individual control in conventional suburban developments is collectively shared?

Table 5.4
Ratings of Privacy in Twin Rivers by Decade: Townhouse Dwellers

Privacy in Twin Rivers is	1970s	1980s	1990s
Particularly good	32%	50%	90%
Adequate	35%	32%	10%
Bad	33%	18%	0%
Total	100%	100%	100%
	N = 167	N = 71	N = 450

As table 5.4 shows, privacy fared very well in Twin Rivers. In all three surveys of the 1970s, the 1980s, and the 1990s, the large majority of residents thought privacy was satisfactory and one-third thought it especially good. The number of people — a minority — who gave it low marks decreased over the decades, suggesting either reduced needs for privacy or habituation to the townhouse version of it.

Privacy was generally viewed positively. It was "very important" to 80 percent of the residents, and the large majority felt it was available in Twin Rivers. Privacy was also highly correlated with a strong liking for Twin Rivers (see table 5.5).

Indeed, ratings on privacy improved with residents' length of time in the community. The twice-interviewed residents, for example, gave privacy higher ratings in the 1980s, when 82 percent were satisfied with it, than in the 1970s, when only 67 percent were satisfied. This suggests that people can learn to satisfy their needs for privacy under varied conditions.

Privacy is a function not only of density but also of visibility and observability, as for example, in the parking areas of Twin Rivers. Located in front of the houses, these generate a high degree of visibility, and it is easy to see which residents go in and out of their houses frequently, who has visitors, and who gets packages, all of which makes some resi-

Table 5.5
Ratings of Privacy by Liking of Twin Rivers: Townhouse Dwellers

Rating of Privacy	% Saying They Like Twin Rivers Very Much
Particularly good	50
Adequate	32
Poor	10
Mixed, no answer	8%

$X_2 = 10.17$
$df = 4$
$sig = 0.031$

dents feel they are living in a fishbowl (O'Toole 1971, p. 10). However, while watching the daily routines of their court neighbors was initially quite fascinating to many residents, in time they lost interest in observing them, and this spontaneously generated what we might call a privacy of inattention. Thus, privacy is not a given. It is a dynamic aspect of collective life that residents adapt to their needs at different phases.

The Role of Facilities in Community Formation

A community generally must make provisions for a wide range of services to meet a variety of aggregate needs. In Twin Rivers, the details as to the kinds and numbers of such services had to be worked out from scratch. The first decade's record reveals the successes and failures, the compromises and disputes these entailed.

The traditional services communities need are police and fire protection, snow removal, garbage collection, first aid, recreation, and shopping. Some of these were the obligations of the Twin Rivers Trust for which residents paid a monthly fee. Others were dependent on the efforts and time of volunteers. Inadequacies were perceived as more stressful if they involved Trust obligations that residents felt should be mandatory as opposed to services that were considered optional, such as day-care centers. Over the decade, many problems with one or another service were worked out satisfactorily for most residents, but some difficulties remained. Police protection, for example, was problematic because of jurisdictional ambiguities. As part of the township and as taxpayers, Twin Rivers' residents had the right to police protection. The problem was how much. On the basis of its demographic concentration, Twin Rivers stood to receive less protection, but as the most congested part of the township and with more than one-half of the township population, it deserved more patrols. In addition, Twin Rivers was bisected by a major state highway, and its residents drew on a commercial center outside its borders, which created a demand for even more police attention. In the earliest years, the needs of the community seemed to exceed the readiness of the township to respond adequately. The ensuing frustration accentuated frictions between Twin Rivers and East Windsor Township.

Internally, there was a constant, if silent, altercation between residents and Trust over the use and repair of facilities. From the start, the common grounds — the swimming pools, the shopping center, the streets and roadways — being public goods, were often abused. Vandalism reached epidemic proportions at various periods resulting in exhortations by the Trust administration to regard the common property as one's own. In the1980s, for example, vandalism — broken or defaced street lamps, public phones, pool furniture, landscaping — amounting to $20,000 compelled Twin Rivers to hire off-duty police patrols. This aroused the resentment of the residents, who felt that as tax-paying citizens they were not getting the first-class treatment they deserved.

Fire protection, which also had to be negotiated with the township, proved less problematic. In January 1973, the all-volunteer E.W. Volunteer Fire Company assumed responsibility for protecting Twin Rivers. Thirteen Twin Rivers residents immediately joined the company as volunteers. Unlike the police department, the Fire Company received widespread support from residents. The sentiments expressed in the following letter were representative:

Dear Fire Company:
I want to thank you all for the help you gave me a while ago. . . . I called you about the chandelier in my kitchen . . . smoke . . . You were all so terrific in handling the situation . . . so efficient, reassuring, kind. . . . You're great — "out of the ordinary" dedicated people. I'm enclosing a donation. (*The Periscope*, January 1983)

Also appreciated was the township's rescue squad. Dependent on volunteers, it provided reassurance to residents that their emergencies would be responded to swiftly, within between three and five minutes on average. Throughout the decade there were frequent appeals for more volunteers to receive training in first aid, defensive driving, emergency childbirth, and cardiopulmonary resuscitation to which many residents responded.

The most controversial services were those under the aegis of the bank-trustee. The usual problems of quality control, efficient scheduling, cost constraints, and hard-to-please customers were magnified by the ambivalence felt toward the trust, the sole governing agency during the earliest years. Hence the vehemence of the residents' critiques must be seen within that special context.

Take snow removal, predictably likely to arouse anxiety among those expecting to drive to work. Wrote one despairing resident:

Here I sit, my car plowed under 12 feet of snow by the Trust plows, waiting for the same plows to dig it out! . . . Where are the plows when we need them? . . . What happens on Monday? Should I call in and tell my boss not to worry . . . the Trust which I pay to have my snow removed will get me out eventually. . . . when is eventually? Should I lose a day's pay because of the Trust's ludicrous routing priorities? . . . I think the Trust should review its snow removing tactics. (*The Periscope*, March 1973, p. 5)

Messages from the trust administrator to the residents shuttled back and forth each winter, with the trust manager repeating the rules and schedules and the residents complaining of services that came too late or were not up to standard.

All the larger problems of the community were played out in miniature here. When rules formulated abstractly had to be applied in concrete instances, many residents balked. Then there was the matter of priorities. In general, the common areas and shared public facilities superseded the needs of private households. In the case of snow removal, for example, the first to be plowed were the trust-owned roads, followed by emergency access lanes, parking lots, and main common walkways; and thereafter the snow plows turned to driveways and interior sidewalks. Those ignorant of the complicated structure of municipal responsibilities were likely to feel abandoned or confused because they could not remember which areas were under Trust jurisdiction and which were not. Accusations of neglect by residents vied with pleas for understanding by the trust administration: "During the week of . . . with an accumulation of . . . 13 inches of snow within three days . . . Twin Rivers crews worked for 48 hours within a four hour break." (*The Periscope*, February 1982, p. 4).

Another service that garnered more than its share of complaints was garbage removal. Rising costs and irregularity of service were the most troublesome features for residents. For the trust administrator, a continuing irritant was the residents' disregard of formally posted times for garbage pick-up and the resulting unsightly garbage bags and bins put out too early or at the wrong sites.

The shopping center was also a persistent irritant. The proposed shopping center was to contain a delicatessen, a Chinese restaurant, an Italian restaurant, a liquor store and lounge, a drugstore, barber shop, beauty shop, clothing store, a shoe store, dry cleaner, and a post office. By 1971–72 nearly all of these plus a Foodtown had opened, and the industrial park was expanding with a dental-research division, a publisher, and appliance distributors. But turnover kept things unsettled and the shopping center, seventy thousand square feet in size, went through many ups and downs as the gift, sports, lighting, fabric, and music stores went out of business soon after they opened, to be replaced by other stores, equally short-lived. Residents were urged to patronize the center, but the economics were not promising, and many turned to shops outside the community.

In 1982 the merchants and office managers of the Twin Rivers Mall made one of their repeated efforts to organize a commercial tenants association to "promote the shopping center and to act for the common good of all the merchants." The new owner of the shopping center had purchased the mall about one year earlier and hoped to double the number of tenants from the initial thirty (*Windsor-Heights Herald*, March 18, 1982, p. 22A). But residents were wary. Surveys in the 1970s and 1980s show dissatisfaction with the shopping center to have been high from the earliest days. Only 1 percent rated the shops "especially good" in the 1970s, a figure that rose to 11 percent by the 1980s. In the 1970s, in fact, 55 percent rated the shops as "bad," a figure that dropped to 38 percent a decade later, a definite improvement except that shopping still headed the list of community negatives. Frustration levels were high. By the 1990s the shopping center was revamped and was not in operation until later in the decade.

The Twin Rivers Report Card in the 1970s

What, then, can we conclude about the role of facilities and services in this developing community? Let us keep in mind that recreational facilities and activities for the children were important enticements to those who moved to Twin Rivers. Aspiring residents sought not suburban isolation but *surbanity*, a mix of tranquil lawns and greenery along with an active social and recreational life. Their expectations were deflated, especially in the early years when shopping, play spaces, and recreation were not adequate to meet their needs. It took years of effort to organize and maintain sites and facilities satisfactorily. It would not be an exaggeration to say that initially these inadequacies soured many residents on Twin Rivers. Most took them in stride but not without complaining, often bitterly, over delays and deficiencies, and this colored their feelings about the community as a whole. Consider their ratings of fifteen facilities and services in the 1970s:

Table 5.6
Percent of Residents Designating Particular Characteristics as Especially Good

Parking Facilities	66%
Noise	56%
People	53%
Household work	45%
Dust, dirt	43%
Recreation	42%
Transportation	39%
Lighting	38%
Schools	34%
Privacy	34%
Community participation	25%
Maintenance of services	20%
Prices	19%
Playgrounds	18%
Shops	7%

The rank order of approval of specific aspects of the community ranged from a high of two-thirds who praised the parking facilities to a low of 7 percent for the shops. There was variation in satisfaction among the ratings within a given decade and between decades. Overall, ratings improved between the 1970s and 1980s, but only one-half of the facilities received strong approval at both times. Recreational facilities received the highest approval ratings — two-fifths of the residents deeming them "particularly good" in the 1970s and two-thirds in the 1980s and the 1990s — and shopping received the lowest at all times (7%, 11%, and 13%, respectively).

Subjective reactions to the site, facilities, and social character of a community are all part of the substructure of community formation. The sense of well-being that stems from the satisfaction of needs for shelter, provisions, recreation, and upkeep of grounds and landscaping should not be underestimated. These are always important dimensions, but never more so than at the start, when the unsettling experience of moving combines with the unfinished nature of the site to create an atmosphere of chronic disorder and disarray. To the residents, this leaves the impression that no one cares, that they have been abandoned.

The 1970s newcomers to Twin Rivers, as was true for Levittowners thirty years earlier, found an unfinished community in an unwelcoming terrain, with debris strewn about; unoccupied houses; no trees to soften the landscape; and noise, dirt, and chaos. Most residents, but by no means all, accepted these strains as the growing pains of a "new" community and emphasized their satisfaction with their houses, recreation, and neighbors. But some types of residents turned out to be easier to please than others. Older residents, ex–apartment dwellers, ex-renters, and men were less critical of existing lacks than were younger residents, ex–home owners, and women. Teenagers were the most critical of all.

Teenagers, though very pleased with their houses — many had rooms of their own for the first time — were far more dissatisfied than their parents with the available facilities and opportunities for social life. Indeed in each decade, the young were the most discontented group, and this increased as their presence in the community increased. Very small in number in the 1970s, they became more voluble from the 1980s on. Disgruntled youth is not unusual, of course, but a new, unfinished community is especially hard on them. Being homebound, without a car, and short of money makes them more dependent on a community than are most adults or teens in more established communities. It was not long before a teen problem surfaced that would engender controversy that persists to this day, with some arguing for a special teen center reserved for the young. Since there was no easy solution, the tendency was to let problems slide. By the 1990s, however, two-thirds of the residents interviewed still thought that there was a definite teenage problem.

Given the newness of Twin Rivers, one would expect the level of criticism to be higher than in established communities because great expectations prior to the move are often followed by great disappointments thereafter. Also, a new community setting suffers from the misalignments and discordances of unfinished projects generally. There are no traditions in place and few reliable guides to behavior while there are the enormous inconveniences of constant delays and postponements of repairs and construction. All of this occurs in the general context of a community struggling to be born and trying out new identities, institutions, and relationships. Initially, the greatest distress focused on aspects of design and spatial arrangement. Housing, density, territorial boundaries, public and private property arrangements, spatial access, and spatial convenience determined moods and morale profoundly. Social divisions became salient later.

What seems to have sustained residents through these difficult times was the idea, however unformed, of community. The large majority (81 percent) indicated that the PUD concept of a compact, physically designed arrangement of houses, shops, and open spaces continued to hold great appeal for them. Despite its shortcomings, by the 1980s, Twin Rivers actually struck residents as quite close to their conception of an ideal community. On a scale from 0–100, 40 percent ranked Twin Rivers at the high end of the scale (90–100), 43 percent in the middle (60–80), and the remaining 17 percent below that. A pleasing appearance, good facilities, and a generally friendly, supportive ambience were the prime criteria of the ideal they hoped Twin Rivers would become.

But hope was not enough, as the residents learned to their dismay. Nothing seemed to have prepared them for the fact that community was not a fixed entity but part of a process of growth, a movement toward a crystallized form, a collective social construction.

The opinions of residents at that point reflected a general cultural ignorance as well as the impatience associated with the "now" generation. Many expected instant community. They envisioned some growing pains but did not expect that they would have to be a major part of the creation. They had to learn the essentials from scratch, the most difficult being:

1. the duty to help fellow residents as a basic and unreflective obligation
2. The feeling of individual responsibility for other members of the community.

These were things that would come much later, after arduous struggle and turmoil to sort out the personal from the collective domain. Until then, community in Twin Rivers was little more than a nostalgic referent, a rhetorical flourish. In time, most of the residents would become aware that community is a living entity that is born, grows, changes, and may die.

Overall, the pioneering residents were a specially hardy breed and very much in keeping with their historic ancestry in their desire for a fresh start. They looked forward to a future that would fulfill their dreams of the good life. Unlike traditional villagers, whose future was generally much like their past, moderns dream of change, of what is beyond the horizon, of the best that is yet to be, of a future that will be shiny and new.

CHAPTER 6

SECURING THE VOX POPULI:
THE STRUGGLE FOR SELF-GOVERNMENT

Community is the story of integration preserved against difficulties.
—Robert Redfield

In a democracy, the voice of the people is channeled through established political institutions. In a new development such as Twin Rivers, political institutions are not as yet available and this provides an unusual opportunity to observe the formative process in action. In Twin Rivers, as in many newly built communities, the developer-builder-planning team was the initial governing authority, deciding on all matters affecting the residents within the borders of their common life. Wider township, county, and state issues — for example schools, police, and traffic control — were negotiated by the team with outside agencies. Naturally, in a society committed to democratic selection and participation, this unusual state of affairs rankled many of the residents.

But democracy is easier on paper than in actuality. "Not many of us" writes one historian of British new towns, "have experienced such local democracy before," and "the responsibility is daunting" (Ward 1993, p. 131).

I have divided the discussion of governance into two parts: (1) as seen from the point of view of the responsible agents, and (2) from the point of view of the residents who struggled for their own "voice" in the community's affairs.

When individual home owners have to share common areas and properties, they are responsible not only for their private houses but also for developing rules for cooperative living. This has generated the home-owners association (HOA), a new political form to represent the common interests and concerns of those who live in planned communities. These occupy a curious place in American political life. They occur outside the traditional political structures, yet their tasks are standard political ones: making rules, legislating policies, levying fees, and serving as symbols for the expression of collective needs and choices.

Home-owners associations appeared in the United States in the nineteenth century but by 1962 there were only 500 such associations. Since then, however, there has been explosive growth to some 130,000. They now involve one in eight Americans or more than 30 million people (Langdon 1990, p. 87).

HOAs are generally organized in advance of housing sales so that the by-laws are in place at the time of the purchase of the house. Membership in these associations is mandatory. Residents pay monthly dues and are expected to abide by the rules and regulations, which often seem arbitrary and unreasonable to residents who believe that their powers of self-determination have been undermined (ibid., p. 89). The ensuing resentment then works against the spirit of cooperation needed at the start.

In Twin Rivers, proposed arrangements narrowed down to two types: (1) a home-owners association to manage and control the affairs of Twin Rivers with the assistance of the builder, and (2) a trust, set up apart from the home-owners association that would act as a "benevolent" dictator for the development.

The township officials and the builder favored the trust arrangements, as did the developer who needed to maintain control over the stock of houses and his front-end investment in the project. The VA and FHA, who financed the mortgages of the home-owners, favored a home-owners association.

Home-owners associations, by the management of their own affairs, in effect are forms of local governments, sharing governance with traditional municipal, state, and national authorities. Though not autonomous, they exhibit a degree of independence that is rare in the complex interdependencies of modern life.

In Twin Rivers, after much discussion and debate, the decision was made to have a trust govern for seven years and thereafter pass governance to a home-owners association. The First Charter National Bank was appointed as trustee by the Twin Rivers Holding Corporation on July 29, 1969. It was responsible for basic services such as water, sewerage, garbage collection, snow removal, and physical upkeep. Residents at that time paid monthly fees of $17 per household for these services.

The bank-trustee created a budget, set the monthly fee (or tax rate) for each dwelling unit, and paid a managing agent (the HDM Corporation) a salary not to exceed 3.5 percent of the total collected. It set community policies and made rules on the uses of the recreational facilities, the open spaces, and the services to be provided, and it paid its manager $10,000 per year for the first three years. Residents were expected to familiarize themselves with the Twin Rivers Trust Document they received at the closings and to obey the trust in the areas of its legal jurisdiction.

The private homeowners association is a form of decentralized power, along with the city and the business corporation. Such an association "enables households that have clustered their activities in a territorially defined area to enforce rules of conduct," to provide public goods, such as open space, and "to achieve other common goals not possible to achieve without some form of potentially coercive central agency." Once rare, such associations now outnumber American cities. Developers create thousands of these each year "to govern their subdivisions, condominiums, and planned communities" (Ellickson 1982, p. 1520).

In American law the city is treated as public, but the HOA is private, though the only difference between them is that membership in HOAs is entirely voluntary. The differential legal treatment results in certain anomalies. (1) The courts treat the substantive validity of rules passed by HOAs more strictly than those of cities — whereas the opposite might have been expected, since it is considered a "private" association. (2) Cities have a pattern of voting rights that home owners are forbidden to use (ibid., p. 1521). In cities, the formula is one resident per one vote. For HOAs, it is one *unit* per vote.

The HOA shares many defining features with a government, hence it is surprising that it is treated differently. An HOA rules over a territorially defined area and does not obtain its power through any form of property ownership; also, HOAs can regulate behavior (e.g., physical changes to houses, common grounds, etc.) and "tax" (i.e., assess fees and levies); and they do not need unanimous consent from members. Some, by expelling a member, even can be said to have the power of condemnation, but their scope is less comprehensive than that available to local government. Finally, they use majority rule and representative procedures when they elect a board of directors to manage association affairs. HOAs may also be said to have private "constitutions" — articles of covenants and association plus by-laws — that is, a "true social contract" (Ellickson 1982, p. 1527). These must be unanimously ratified. Judicial decisions tend to honor the principle of greater autonomy for private associations than for public ones. It would be difficult, for example, to imagine city governments making the kind of architectural and other design rules that are routinely made by HOAs without an outcry over invasion of privacy and personal freedom.

There are two models for allocating voting rights to residential communities: The first allocates voting rights to *residents*; the second allocates voting rights according to the economic stake in the community by each person, a rough index of which is the value of one person's real property in the community. In general, perhaps even universally, "voting rights in community associations tend to be apportioned according to share ownership," or economic stake. Also, in general, absentee landlords can vote in these local arrangements but tenants cannot. And the owner of multiple units can cast multiple votes, if these are allocated by units. The assumption is that a "voter's interest in the community" will be consonant with the voter's economic stake in it" (Ellickson 1982, pp. 1540, 1544).

Homeowners associations fit the definition of "intermediary association" between the individual and the state (ibid., 1982, pp. 1564–1601). John Locke likened "political society" . . . "intermediate between an anarchic state of nature and . . . a formal . . . government" (Crenson, 1983, p. 17). Some treasure, others attack this independence, part of the process of the restructuring of contemporary society. By comparison with large cities, home-owner associations are likely to be more participatory in decision making — hence more democratic.

In a commentary, Gerald E. Frug challenges Ellickson's liberal interpretation of HOAs since the original constitution of the HOA "might well be the work of a developer without the participation of a single person who becomes a resident of the community" (Ellickson 1982, p. 1590). That was not the case in Twin Rivers but the precursor of its HOA was certainly developer based and the struggle for resident control took up years of the life of Twin Rivers.

Frug points out the dilemma of the liberal position: It seeks alternately to buttress the HOA against arbitrary power or to restrain the HOA by means of such power. In point of fact, HOAs may be tyrannical or authoritarian on certain matters and less inhibited than city and state governments rooted in the democratic process. Moreover, by favoring property owners in voting, HOAs may be as "dangerous to the liberty of their residents" (ibid., 1982, p. 1591) as are other governments with a restrictive franchise.

The problems dealt with by HOAs include the management of the transitional period as control is relinquished by the developer, the confusions of new home owners turned administrators, and sheer inexperience in living in a PUD. Ignorant about most of the details of budgets and running a community, yet concerned about their investments and the kind of life they and their children will be able to enjoy, residents have to learn through trial and error, grappling with timeless questions of rule enactment and enforcement, strategies for compliance and cooperation, and the creation of public spirit and commitment.

Three typical stages in the process of communal self-government are described in the following tongue-in-cheek comment: "[A]s soon as the homeowners take over . . . they sue the developer, then they fire the manager, and then they raise the assessments" (Oser 1977, Section 8 p. 1). This fits Twin Rivers to a T.

Questions of governance loomed large from the very start in Twin Rivers despite the fact that it was a privately financed and organized undertaking. After the PUD ordinance was passed by the state legislature, the township stipulated a number of additional conditions for the construction of Twin Rivers (the details are described in chapter 4). Because the township was concerned about the possibility that Twin Rivers might become a burden, it became a matter of some urgency to decide who would manage the open spaces, operate the recreational facilities, and provide the essential services for the community.

During the first two to three years, the degree of control at first exercised by the developer and subsequently by the bank as trustee, was a cause of considerable distress for the residents of Twin Rivers. That this is not uncommon is evident in the following observation:

> Builders tend to think of an association as a means of retaining or enhancing their land values, and nothing more. While this is valid, it is hardly an adequate basis for maintaining and administering a substantial community, or encouraging maximum homeowner participation. This kind of development involves social change as well as construction problems, and a successful developer cannot be blind to the New Society he is helping to develop. (Norcross 1973, p. 37)

To provide a link between the home owners and the trust, a Trust Advisory Board (TAB) was created. It was composed of ten people, five elected at large and five serving on the Twin Rivers Homeowners Association (TRHA) board and appointed by the trustee. The views of the board were in no way binding on the trustee, however.

All of the home owners in Twin Rivers were automatically members of the Home-owners Association. To fulfill their legal obligations to the VA and the FHA, they needed a board of directors to represent them with the trust. The first board, consisting of nine men and one woman, was appointed by the Twin Rivers Holding Corporation. In 1970 a special meeting was called by the developer's staff to elect a nominating committee. Twin Rivers was broken down into four areas, and volunteers from each area put their names into the hat and were chosen at random. The resulting committee then asked for more volunteers from their areas to present themselves as candidates before the nominating committee. Nine board members were then elected by secret ballot from a pool of twenty-one candidates.

Thus the structure of governance included the developer and the trust as the rule-making body in charge of the common grounds, the collection of fees, and the management of community-wide services. Then there was an advisory board to serve as an intermediary between the residents and the trustee and to represent the interests and needs of the growing community by providing the residents with some effective voice in the management of their community property. Alongside the TAB there emerged the board of directors of the Twin Rivers Home-owners Association representing the residents for internal community issues. This association was supported by a modest fee of three dollars per year per homeowner. Its chief objectives were first, communication, and second, recreation. Communication involved keeping the residents informed about happenings within Twin Rivers and without, via radio announcements on the local station, the monthly open board meeting, and the articles in *The Periscope*. In addition, the board sponsored recreational activities of many kinds: sports and tournaments, bowling and baseball leagues, teen and adult dances, theater trips and bridge clubs.

As 1976 approached and the term of the trustee (Heritage Bank North) was due to expire, controversy and debate intensified. Township officials feared the potential power of the homeowners association as a second government and had all along insisted that a bank control the Twin Rivers trust. Their fears were increasingly voiced as the time for restructuring the governance of Twin Rivers drew near. The assumption of control by the homeowners would, in the view of township officials, result in a rise in the measure of unreality as well as a loss of political control. Homeowners associations, it was observed, had, in other developments, threatened to stop repairing streets or disposing of garbage, and by law, the township would then be legally required to perform these services. Or, if the trust were to declare bankruptcy, the township would have to maintain the open spaces and community facilities at huge expenses to local taxpayers. In 1975, these costs were borne by Twin Rivers homeowners to the tune of $650,000 per year. Not surprisingly, township officials therefore favored the status quo. Indeed, if ever the township were to get another PUD, according to one local official, the council would write in an eventual take-over clause for the municipality (*The Periscope*, 22 August 1976, p. 12).

In contrast to the township, the VA and FHA supported the passing of control over the internal operations of Twin Rivers from the trust to the residents by means of a homeowners association. The residents of Twin Rivers likewise favored self-determination and self-management via their Homeowners Association. The arguments supporting this stand emphasized the board's continuity of knowledge and leadership, its respect for democratic procedures, and its responsiveness and openness to the community. Its directors were democratically elected and all lived in Twin Rivers. On all these grounds the current trustee was found deficient.

In October 1975 the second meeting of the TRHA was attended by almost two hundred residents, and there was overwhelming agreement that they should have some kind of organization to deal with the trust and the developer, whom many thought high-handed and unresponsive.

Dramatic slogans, such as "No Taxation without Representation," reminded the residents of their powerlessness, in contrast with the trustee's, to set fees, costs, and quality of services. As the time of decision approached, residents were urged to cast their ballots for residential control in order to protect the ultimate resale value of their houses and the future social structure of Twin Rivers (Editorial, *The Periscope*, March, 1976, p. 1).

Residents were ready for the change. For years the chorus of dissatisfaction with the trust's indifference and disregard had grown in number and intensity. As early as 1972, the trust's disregard of the opinions of the trust advisory board rankled. The group had no real say, it was a mere figurehead that was given no financial accounting and not taken seriously. These charges were countered by the trust representative, who thought it "necessary to remind the Board that responsibility of decision-making rests with the Bank" (*Windsor-Heights Herald*, 13 April 1972, p. 1).

There were numerous petty complaints: Calls to the trust office after 4:00 P.M. were unanswered and the pool's closing for repairs in the summer was attributed to poor planning by the trust. The Committee for a Reasonable Pool Policy let it be known that the trust "administers the pool but it is ours, by right, not theirs. When important decisions must be made, the ultimate decision must be made by the residents" (*Opus*, 71, March–April 1971, p. 8). "Why should we be controlled by a Trust that denies us self-government; are we children?" (*The Periscope*, 10 April 1974, p. 3). Then there was a fire that raged through eight apartments and made twenty-four families homeless; it was claimed that no help was given by the development staff. Residents referred to the incident with righteous outrage long after the disaster had passed.

Thus, the first five years of life in the developing community were characterized by an intricate minuet between the nascent governing institutions decreeing, managing, and organizing the institutional framework with rules of order and continuity, and an impassioned populace seeking self-determination but ignorant about self-government and cooperative living.

The developer, seeking to protect his substantial economic investment in the community, sought control over key decisions, while the residents, resenting their lack of power, also sought control. In addition to the ever-present physical inadequacies — such as drainage and plumbing problems, untagged pets, and neglected common grounds, which we will explore more fully later — there were social problems and friction between neighbors, among children, and between renters and homeowners. Irate parents resented paying dues for basketball courts when their children were chased off by other children claiming seignorial rights. Frustrated residents protested the nonresponsiveness of the developer, and later the bank trustee, to their requests for a civic center, or for information about the size of the trust budget or increased monthly fees. Dissatisfactions with the drab appearance of the community fueled further resentment. In the end, residents went to court to get the hearing they thought they deserved. In the meantime it was a tenuous and strenuous struggle for control and authority that created distrust on both sides.

Year by year, demands for change grew louder and more vociferous, with factions taking sides for and against the existing governing mechanism, that is, the trust. Those who favored the trust's continuing beyond the first seven years, including township officials and trust-appointed residents, saw citizen protest as trouble fomented by malcontents exploiting community problems for personal reasons. In contrast, protesters saw the issue as a we/they struggle between tyranny and liberty and warned that Twin Rivers would become a second-class community unless the residents organized to defend their interests and assert their power.

In May 1976 shortly before the election was to take place, a maneuver by the trust threatened the residents' assumption of control by challenging the voting system. The trustee argued that it could not turn the trust over to the home-owners association unless more than 50 percent of all homeowners voted to do so. The TRHA replied that the winner should reflect the majority of those voting and *not* of those eligible to vote. The latter would be a victory for the bank without a single vote being cast for it. A no-vote was a pro-bank vote. The TRHA representatives were outraged and sought legal counsel (*The Periscope*, May 1976, p. 1).

In August 1976 the election for community control, pitting the TRHA against the bank trustee, took place. "Your future and the future of Twin Rivers depends on your voting." The power passed to the residents by an overwhelming vote of 90 percent.

The tension between the home-owners association and the bank-trustee has in a somewhat different context been described as the pull between "use" values and "exchange" values of place. "Use" value refers to the available resources to advance the quality of life; "exchange" value refers to an interest in economic growth generated by alliances between the business and political leaders of an area.

In the contentiousness between the trust and the HOA, the former stands for an "exchange" strategy while the HOA and the residents are aligned with "use" values aimed at increasing the quality of life and commitment to community (Logan and Molotch 1987, pp. 32, 34).

As the old witticism says, there are two tragedies in life—the first, to fail to get what one wants, and the second, to get it. Once the Twin Rivers Homeowners Association got its wish of self-determination, it not only became responsible for itself but also became a target for protests and grievances of its own malcontents. Nonetheless, the victory tasted sweet for a while.

Among the first tasks of the TRHA was to search for a trust administrator. Fifty-two candidates applied for the position, as did five management-consulting firms. The individual candidates responded to a classified advertisement in the Sunday *New York Times*. Of the original fifty-two, ten were selected to be interviewed. None were local residents. The first administrator was chosen in the fall of 1976 by a unanimous vote of the board to serve a one-year term. He was described as having experience as a builder "out West" in garden-apartment management and inspired confidence that he would be able to handle a wide variety of problems (*Windsor-Heights Herald*, 21 October 1976, p. 1). Other administrators followed. Problems multiplied. In 1979, for example, a trust administrator was arraigned for embezzlement of trust funds and forgery in the township court. At the same time, five of the nine members of the board were accused of negligence of their "fiduciary duties" for not immediately dismissing the culprit. Some residents angrily demanded the dismissal of the entire board, but this proved inadvisable as the community could not afford such a vacuum at the top (*The Periscope*, 27 September 1979, p. 1).

Finally, and fortunately, Joseph A. Vuzzo was selected the trust administrator, a position he was to occupy for eighteen years. Henceforth, the governing structure was well in place with a trust administrator well equipped by personality, skill, experience, and commitment to lead the community. In 1982 Joseph Vuzzo was reappointed to a second three-year term to the enthusiastic praise of the board of directors. "For those of us who remember the 'olden' days," the chairman of the board wrote at that time, "the difference is very striking. . . . Joe's careful investments have helped keep fees down and his expenditure of funds is always done after a lot of careful checking. No one can deny that Twin Rivers is run better and looks better today because of Joe" (*The Periscope*, December 1982, vol. II, no. 11, p. 2).

Along with a popular and effective trust administrator, in the late 1970s the remainder of the governing structure was also in place. There was a nine-member board of directors, each elected for a three-year term with one-third elected each year. Its officers — president, vice president, and secretary/treasurer — were elected by the board. These nine directors served without compensation and no "perks" and received "very little if any recognition" (*The Periscope*, December 1982, p. 2). Why, then, did they bother? Perry Shapiro, president of the TRHA explained it in October 1982: "One does this out of a sense of community spirit, a desire to help Twin Rivers be a better place, and insanity" (*The Periscope*, October 1982, vol. II, no. 9, p. 1).

Trust Responsibilities

The responsibilities of this "second government" ran a wide gamut from regulating fees to providing the services included in the residents' fees.

At the start, in the early 1970s, there was considerable frustration about issues not dealt with by the builder. Indeed it was suggested, with the humor often displayed in the pages of the Twin Rivers monthly paper, *The Periscope*, that Eric Berne's next book should be "Games Townships and Builders Play" (*The Periscope*, May 1973, p. 1).

The trust's main areas of responsibility were capital improvements and maintenance of the site, the common grounds, and the facilities. This ranged from color coding of the tennis courts to foliage control, improved illumination in the tunnel, sun shelters at the pools, road resurfacing, and plantings throughout the community.

Along with the announced scheduling for the annual spraying, plant-ing, resurfacing, pest control, front-lawn maintenance, and cleaning of streets and parking lots, came continuous instructions on the residents' responsibilities and the uses permitted in the community. "What are common grounds?" asked an article explaining the reasons for the adoption of a 1982 resolution on common grounds. "The common grounds" replied the would-be authority, "are those areas of the devel-opment that are owned by the Trust for the use of all the beneficiaries" (*The Periscope*, June 1982, p. 10). Evidently residents had difficulty keeping such definitions straight for they were repeated again and again.

Along with the instructions about procedures went instructions about rules and rights. "We must insist that no planting be done by residents on common grounds without the express permission of the Trust" (*The Periscope*, November 1984, vol. 13, no. 11, p. 1). There were also rules about conduct in the "open areas" where organized baseball, football, track, and field activities were permitted, and semi-open common grounds where unorganized activities such as catch and tag were allowed. And how were residents to know what activities could occur where? A map of each quad in the trust office was made available for their perusal.

Violations of the common rules were subject to penalties by the trust, such as letters of reprimand, revocations of recreational privileges (swimming pool, tennis courts) for a specified period, and eventually fines not to exceed $50 per violation (*The Periscope*, June 1982, p. 10). Given the bewildering array of rules, many involving complex jurisdic-tional distinctions, there was considerable resentment toward both the confusing rules and the punishments for violations.

Another area of complex rule enforcement concerned safety and speed limits; the catalogue of complaints included cars driving at unsafe speeds, not stopping for school buses, and disregarding stop signs. In part, this reflected the township's inability to enforce traffic rules on private property in the early years before the roads were turned over to the townships and became public property, and in part, a self-centered disregard of the public order.

Other rules that had to be instituted involved excessive noise, dis-ruptive behavior at the pools, and revelry out of doors. In May 1976 the Trust Advisory Board formulated rules regarding hours for pool parties (9 P.M. to 1 A.M.), with speakers to be pointed away from the populated areas of Twin Rivers. The volume of music was to be deter-mined by the pool directors, who also could designate the proper areas for food consumption at the pools. Rules for proper attire and sign-ups at the tennis courts were other areas of formal rules and publicly desig-nated penalties.

And then there was the volatile issue of pets, to which more space will be devoted later. Here we should simply note that a policy on pets proved necessary soon after the first batch of residents moved in. In 1975 a pet committee handled stray animals at the rate of more than one hundred a year — "Twin Rivers has apparently become a dumping ground for unwanted animals" — and the problem grew dangerously out of hand. By 1985 the TRHA board adopted a resolution to regulate the conduct of pets on trust land, in response to "the serious health and esthetic problems caused by the discharge of waste by pets in Trust land." Pets had to be restrained by a leash while on the common grounds and a pooper-scooper law was put in effect as well. After a decade of exhortation and hand wringing about enforcement, moreover, fines and the withholding of recreational privileges were formalized. To ascertain violations, however, proved complicated. It required a special complaint procedure whereby a resident had to submit a signed complaint in writing, followed by a committee hearing. If found guilty, a violator could appeal the decision to the entire TRHA Board. In a small community such as Twin Rivers, residents would be reluctant to file signed complaints about fellow residents (*The Periscope*, April 1985, vol. 4, p. 5).

Thus, building the consensus needed to create and abide by its basic rules so as to guide an aggregate is only one hurdle to be surmounted. Enforcing these rules is another. As early as 1972, the trust went to court to compel a minority of nonpaying residents to pay their monthly fees. In April of that year, the judgment of the county court ruled in favor of the trust saying that "the defendants' remedy for alleged nonperformance by the plaintiff does not lie in the withholding of the payments from the plaintiff" (*The Windsor-Heights Herald*, 26 October 1972, p. 4).

The Fight against Resident Apathy

The trust also had fee-setting powers and could increase the monthly trust fees if necessary. Just as the TRHA board had protested against what it perceived to be inequities in trust levies when the bank was the trustee, so individuals rose to protest when the trustee was the entire community. Any increase in "taxes" created resentment and resistance. This is a familiar reaction in such communities.

Meanwhile, an enormous uphill battle was continually being waged against apathy and indifference to civic duties. Quick to protest, residents were not equally quick to offer to help solve common problems. Again and again, the "this is your community" refrain was sounded.

Don't allow a handful of people to pick the directors. All of you have an important stake in Twin Rivers. Don't throw it away. (*The Periscope*, December 1982, vol. 11, no. 11, p. 6)

Join us for an evening *without* fun and games and meet the TRHA Board members.

Communicate with the Board. . . . they will be readily accessible. Don't confine your ideas and complaints to your neighbor or laundry man. The pure and simple fact is that it is your trust and your money to be used the way you wish. (*The Periscope*, 15 January 1975, p. 6)

"Most people do not have the desire, the drive, the confidence, or the time to be running our community" but there's no excuse for not helping choose those who do. "If you do not participate in electing the directors you have no right to complain about the outcome." (*The Periscope*, December 1982, vol. 11, no. 11, p. 10)

But these exhortations proved of no avail. As late as January 1982, only 156 of the 2,100 eligible voters cast their ballots for the incumbents of three uncontested seats on the TRHA board of directors.

Attendance at board meetings fared no better. Though residents had the right, indeed were importuned, to attend once-a-month open meetings of the board to inform themselves, voice their grievances, and make their presence felt, few took advantage of that right. They were strong on complaining but weak on taking action. It was as if they were more attached to their grievances than to possible remedies.

A dramatic illustration of the residents' apathy was their response to proposed changes in the original trust documents in the spring of 1982. By then it had become clear that the three major documents of Twin Rivers—the Trust Indenture, the Declaration of Restrictions and Easements, and the by-laws of the Twin River Homeowners Association—had become outdated and required changes. For a year and a half, a special documents change committee met to study and revise these documents and, after presenting them to the board, prepared them for the approval of the homeowners. Approval would require a 75 percent vote of all the property owners.

Among the proposed changes was a change in voting rights giving preference to homeowners even when these had leased their houses to others. "Did you know that if you are a resident of California you can sit on our Board of the TRHA and make decisions for the residents of Twin Rivers?" was one challenge. Other changes involved provisions that required that copies of the lease agreements between property owners and tenants be made available to the trust, and that the trust's purchasing title to real estate or obtaining a mortgage be restricted. The abolition of the Trust Advisory Board seemed called for once the trustee was an elected body (*The Periscope*, May 1981, vol. 10, no. 5, p. 8). All of these changes were proffered as beneficial to the majority of residents and as a desirable aspect of "home rule." Specifically, ten amendments were proposed:

1. A maximum payment of ten dollars per month for late payment of monthly maintenance charges.
2. A reduced majority (from 75 to 66 percent) approval of the current homeowners for the board of directors of TRHA to borrow money on real estate mortgages. (This figure parallels that in other planned developments.)
3. The time period within which certain additional land may be awarded by the trustee without consent of the homeowners to be extended from fifteen years to twenty-five years of the date of the trust. Such additions will also require a smaller majority of approval by homeowners — from 75 to 66 percent.
4. The trust to be permitted to collect 25 percent of the annual fee when the owner purchases a home. This is to be returned with interest when the title is transferred.
5. Those who rent out their homes will be expected to make sure that their tenants pay their fees and "understand the rules by which the community functions" and fill out a form to be kept by the trustee. In 1984 it was estimated that some 15 percent of Twin Rivers homes were being rented out, but there was no way for the trustee to have precise information.
6. The TAB (Trust Advisory Board) to become inactive. It was initially created as a liaison between the developer and the trustee (TRHA) when the development was under construction and when the trustee was not (yet) elected by residents. Once the trustee was elected by the community and the developer was gone, the TAB was redundant.
7. Legal insurance protection to be extended for board members to cover the $5,000 now deductible.
8. If fire destroys a dwelling unit, the owner has six months time to begin restoring it before the trustee declares the property abandoned — and after thirty days, if the owner does not respond to a notice to that effect, the trustee can buy and sell the property.

9. To amend the trust document will require 66 percent, not 75 percent, approval by the homeowners.
10. Before a title transfer, trustee will inspect the premises to assure that the property is consistent with the architecture of the overall community.

On February 17, 1982, the homeowners of Twin Rivers went to the polls to vote on the amendments designed to update the constitution (i.e., the trust document) that controlled the internal government of Twin Rivers. Originally there were two classes of voters in Twin Rivers. Class A voters included all homeowners and Class B voters included the vote of the developer. At the start, the developer had three votes for every unoccupied house in Twin Rivers, which gave him three votes for every homeowner vote and control over decision making until all houses were sold and his investment secure. This situation changed as homeowners outnumbered unoccupied houses.

A second anomaly of the voting arrangements divided the residents' political rights according to their economic worth. Votes were apportioned on a dollar basis and reflected the assessed value of a voter's property. Thus the owner of an $80,000 house in Twin Rivers had a vote worth twice as much as that of the owner of a $40,000 house. Renters could not vote. The owners of the apartment complexes, however, did have a vote, which again reflected the dollar value of that complex.

After a huge two-year effort by the trust, the Twin Rivers board of directors, and the document change committee, and after many instructive and detailed articles in the monthly *Periscope*, the vote was very disappointing. Voter turnout was a scant 17 percent, yet enough to defeat eight of the ten proposed changes to the charter.

The two amendments that passed were (1) a drop in the majority required to vote a change in Twin Rivers governing documents, and (2) the right of the trust to rebuild abandoned townhouses destroyed by fire or other calamities. Ironically, all amendments would have passed had the 66 percent approval rule been in effect.

The disappointment among the board of directors was keen: "The Board was sorely disappointed with the apathetic reception the Document Change Committee's efforts were received with by the Twin Rivers residents." Postmortems abounded. One key issue was the resistance of owners investing in rental properties in Twin Rivers to the proposed filing of an information sheet with the trust. Then there was the opposition of a $5 million apartment complex landlord who was angry about high taxes and rent control. To counteract his $5 million vote, $15 million beneficiary votes would have been needed. The outcry was not long in coming:

I am ashamed of my friends and neighbors. No, not ashamed . . . angry and resentful. You call yourself a community? . . . Twin Rivers screams that they don't get no respect. . . . They don't deserve respect since they don't respect themselves. . . .If the beneficiaries wanted to see [the amendments] defeated they should have done it through a vote not by apathy. (Small, *The Periscope*, March 1982, p. 3)

The recent election was a sad disappointment. So many people worked so hard to improve the community and you allowed the special interests to beat you. . . . How can this Board reach you people? We alone (the nine Directors) cannot go door to door on issues. We cannot call thousands of people. There was good local and state newspaper coverage. I cannot tell you how disappointed we all were by the vote. . . .There are some people who care very much about Twin Rivers and work hard for it. Couldn't you have gone along with the recommendations of these people (if you couldn't attend Board meetings or familiarize yourselves with the issues)? We can't just throw away this community. (Shapiro, *The Periscope*, April 1982, p. 1)

Trust administrator Vuzzo felt that too much was assumed and a reelection should pay more attention to direct communication with the voters explaining, arguing, and exchanging views on the issues.

Concerned about this public and visible proof of apathy more than a decade after the founding of Twin Rivers, the "block captain" approach resurfaced once again. This would have each housing court elect residents to serve as block representatives and act as liaisons to the board. Such suggestions were tried in the early 1970s. Perhaps, suggested then board president Bob Schwartz, "we should change the name to 'minute men' " (*The Periscope*, March 1976, p. 2).

Apathy continued to be of concern to Twin Rivers officials as they struggled to provide more adequate transportation services, maintain the physical upkeep of the grounds and plant, establish sound relations with the township, and attend to the countless day-to-day problems of Twin Rivers. It was the worm in the bucolic apple that needed all the perseverance those responsible for the community could muster to combat it.

Of course in one sense, a high degree of apathy could mean that the residents were satisfied with the way things were being managed, and this could then be taken as a general vote of confidence. While reassuring in principle, this was not convincing. A community-in-waiting such as Twin Rivers, if it is to thrive, must have volunteers, a sense of pride of place, a concern for the environment, and a general spirit of vitality and cooperation. Without these, the few will carry the burden for the many, and the temptation exists for the few to become arbitrary and self-serving. It was a temptation Twin Rivers had so far escaped, and under the genial leadership of Joseph A. Vuzzo and the board of directors, there was reason to believe it would continue to do so.

There are critical moments in the life of a community, when programs are still flexible and citizens are able to exert influence and participate in creating the governing machinery that will affect their lives. That historic moment of openness, reciprocity, and the possibility for direct contact between governors and governed passes all too soon, leaving in its wake a cynicism about the individual's power to shape the world in which he or she lives. In its wake, institutions assume a life of their own, their origins become obscure, their powers set, and citizens become in varying degrees dependents and outsiders in regard to them. The springtime of freedom will then have passed.

There are some parallels between the formation of this small community and the national society two hundred years earlier, except that the order seems to be reversed. For the era of the founding fathers of the eighteenth century, George Washington, the acknowledged leader, may be said to have created the new government by his presence as a trusted national symbol. He preceded the new constitution and made it possible — and hopefully would guide the country until "habits of authority and obedience could be established" (Wiebe 1984, p. 42). In Twin Rivers, the unifying leader came after the key structures of governance were already in place and the key battles had been fought. In that sense he was truly more of an administrator who appeared after the difficult birth to watch over its infancy and to build a common framework and purpose. Actually, the new trust administrator missed one of the key events of the 1970s, the Twin Rivers lawsuit (see chapter 13), which took shape in the years from 1972 through 1976, and whose impact extended far beyond those years. It mobilized the nascent community into a stance of protest and combat that would remain long after its origins had been forgotten.

Architectural Controls

The PUD format mandates architectural supervision by those acting on behalf of the totality under its care. Though the aim may be well intentioned, residents were not prepared to consider its implications, and architectural controls became one of the most controversial aspects of living in Twin Rivers, as they are in most such arrangements. Architectural and aesthetic controls constituted a first experience for most residents of restrictions on their freedom to do with their property as they saw fit.

The chief purpose of architectural controls is generally to assure some degree of aesthetic uniformity for the community. The restrictions therefore apply to all manifest insignias of individual tastes, including doors and windows, awnings, and exterior colors that depart too noticeably from some broad common standard established during the first decade. Residents could not change the exteriors of their houses without written permission, and all proposed spatial or aesthetic additions had to be checked with a special committee established for this purpose.

Such constraints on the freedom of the property owner are not unfamiliar historically. As early as the U.S. colonial period and despite the ready availability of land on these then sparsely settled shores, individual settlers endured stringent local controls as to the amount of land made available to them and the freedom to use it as they pleased.

Only much later in the country's history, principally under the impetus of the move westward, did opportunities for exchanging land and building upon it multiply. It is then that the laissez-faire habits of a market-oriented society took hold.

In Twin Rivers, an architectural advisory committee was established as early as 1971 to assist the community trust in the enforcement of the "Declaration of Restrictions and Reservations of Easements." The chief objective of these controls was to maintain "the design integrity of Twin Rivers" (*The Periscope*, 1 December 1972, p. 11) as well as to help homeowners to make desired improvements on their property. This goal was easier to state than to achieve. The following list of architectural violations indicates the range of vigilance needed to preserve the integrity of design for a community in progress. Residents were chastised and warned about:

- Moving court fences beyond their designated positions to obtain more privacy
- Replacing gate doors with materials out of harmony with overall community design
- Installing signs, drainpipe extensions, chain-link fences
- Putting bric-a-brac on front lawns
- Inappropriate door-trim colors, nameplates, and lighting fixtures

The purpose of these controls was to assure some degree of architectural uniformity in styles and colors. Residents, forbidden to change the exteriors of their houses without written permission, endorsed the general objectives of these regulations, but were resentful when the rules interfered with their desires to paint their houses, install storm doors, add awnings or nameplates, and otherwise display visible signatures of personal taste (O'Toole 1971, p. 119).

Throughout these early years we find continuous public exhortations for individuals to curtail personal preferences for the sake of obligations to the community. Constant reminders dot the community paper to uphold the structural and aesthetic standards that affect the appearance and the "design harmony of the community." Residents are urged to "be considerate of your neighbor's view"; to use only colors within the permitted range; and to maintain their houses, fences, gates, and landscaping so as to assure an attractive appearance for the community. Of course the community was not yet formed—which was part of the problem.

There was, from the beginning, much heated discussion around this issue. Many residents insisted they be allowed to do as they pleased with what was, after all, their own property, and they resented these infringements upon this basic freedom. Not unexpectedly, the guardians of spatial and aesthetic uniformity became the targets of a profound ambivalence in the community.

Repeatedly, features in the local papers attempted to explain the reasons for architectural controls and enlisted the support of residents for the committee entrusted with their enforcement. One notes alternately a tone of patient reasonableness and of exasperation: "Are architectural controls another step toward the 'Big Brother' society of 1984 or merely a civilized method of maintaining the harmony of design and color in the community? Do they threaten individualism and freedom of expression or protect property values?" (*The Periscope*, November 1975, p. 23). The residents were continually urged to consult the Declaration of Restrictions and Reservations of Easements that came with the house.

Part of the problem was the chaos of the pioneering years when the governing structure was not yet fully in place and when the tensions between the developer and the homeowners that would eventually culminate in a lawsuit ran high. Also, early on, especially, enforcement lacked teeth. Initially, violations were met with no more than a threatening letter or two that the violators ignored. But perhaps even more significant was the lack of aesthetic consensus among residents—yet another indication of the lack of common cultural standards. Indeed the extraordinary variety of tastes for a population with many shared interests often proved exasperating to the aesthetic guardians.

"What deep psychological need possesses someone to paint their abode pistachio or perhaps fluorescent yellow. . . . Aren't pink and lavender more suited to the bathroom than the backyard?" exclaims one desperate editorial voice, concluding with: "We must have architectural controls. They must be enforced now. . . . If there are no controls, we might as well put up the sign, 'Welcome to Twin Rivers, New Jersey's first totally psychedelic PUD'" (*The Periscope*, November 1975, p. 23).

Residents were clearly of two minds about these architectural controls. They understood their necessity in principle and approved of their application—but only for the other fellow. "They made a terrible decision at the beginning when they didn't make every house the same way re color, sidings, and everything else." Why? "Because some people have terrible taste. Some of these colors are just incredible—even though it's supposed to be controlled by the Trust" (Man, twenty-seven year resident, age fifty-seven). They balked when these controls applied to themselves, perceiving them as an unacceptable form of tyranny.

The attempt to formulate reasonable and enforceable guidelines went through innumerable stages as the general rules kept being challenged. It took more than a decade to work out the sanctions needed to induce conformity, though vigilance has to be exercised continually.

In the struggle to achieve the desired aesthetic uniformity, residents were chastised, cajoled, and threatened, alternately treated as if they were willful children who refuse to be good or adults who should know better, and always appealing to their self-interest to maintain the value of their property. Many a time, some exasperated community leader would demand to know why controls could work well in other communities but not in Twin Rivers (*The Periscope*, November 1975, p. 12).

Part of the problem stemmed from misconceptions among exurbanites about the nature of townhouse living, and part from overconfidence by well-meaning guardians of public taste in the efficacy of rational appeals to those not educated to appreciate the necessity for them.

A milestone of sorts was reached in 1975, when four homeowners were taken to court for nonconformance with the architectural and color standards of Twin Rivers. And year by year since, the list of forbidden changes has multiplied to include TV antennas on roofs, permanent awnings, flagpoles, exteriors and storm doors painted in colors unacceptable to the committee—the acceptable colors being earth tones browns, grays, gold, russet. Slowly, private taste was forced to yield to public canon. One unintended consequence of strict architectural hegemony was to heighten suspiciousness among neighbors, each watching for someone's violations as they struggled to avoid their own.

Also, while residents were willing to go along with some controls, many controls seemed arbitrary and excessive. And while most residents were probably ready to agree with Robert Schwartz, architect and former head of the Homeowners Association, that since the houses "are built very close to each other," it would lead to a community that looked "like a circus," residents nonetheless wanted more leeway and a less punitive atmosphere. Asking for permission reminded too many residents of the classrooms of their childhood. And more than one resident urged the committee to "pay more attention to the spirit of the people" and to be sensitive to their desire for individuality and diversity (*The Periscope*, 5 June 1974, p. 23).

It was, and continues to be, a hard battle for individuals raised in the belief that their homes are their property to embellish as they choose, while also remaining aware that the colors they find enchanting might repel a neighbor. In a dense townhouse community, such divergences of taste cannot remain a purely private matter, yet public norms and procedures need time and patience to be worked out to most residents' satisfaction. In the 1990s, these controls were still a sore point.

PART II
A COMMUNITY IS LAUNCHED

B. Creating a Collective Self

CHAPTER 7

JOINERS AND ORGANIZERS:
COMMUNITY PARTICIPATION

There is a world of difference between a development and a community.
— A Twin Rivers resident

New communities are distinctive for the plethora of organized groups that spring up virtually overnight. Joint activities can bring people together in a number of ways by regular face-to-face meetings that strengthen shared interests and common aims. In Twin Rivers, a wide range of groups, from baby-sitting co-ops to a chess club cropped up early on. De Tocqueville, in a widely cited passage, thought Americans particularly adept at forming organizations and thereby creating the foundation for national unity. Americans have "associations of a thousand kinds, religious, moral, serious, futile, general or restricted, enormous or diminutive" (de Tocqueville 1990, Vol. II, p. 106). In most communities, the associational web is already in place when the observer comes upon it. In a "new community" it must be created, but judging from Twin Rivers, it soon takes off.

Recreational activities were initial drawing cards for Twin Rivers.

Three years after the first residents had moved in, there existed a basketball league, a softball league, swim teams, Ping-Pong, bridge groups,
a photography club, and the Twin Rivers chess club. The local paper
frequently reminded residents of the offerings available. "Twin Rivers
has a lot to offer in the summer of 1975 — four pools . . . not to mention tennis after dark, jogging, biking, and . . . the junior softball
league" (*The Periscope*, June 1975, p. 29). By 1976 there was a soccer
league, a day and toddler camp, volleyball, basketball, jogging, and
tennis. Each of these enlisted substantial numbers of residents. For example, in the summer of 1976, 480 children and 60 women participated
in the Twin Rivers softball league. Night and summer activities expanded, as did lessons in swimming, diving, and tennis. There was a
women's summer volleyball and softball league, a men's winter basketball league, and an over-thirty softball league.

Slowly but surely, various activities became intramural. In 1975 the
Twin Rivers Torpedoes defeated the Trenton Jewish City Center (*Windsor-Heights Herald*, 24 July 1975, p. 8A). Activities for children were
organized by age — toddlers, 8- to 15-year-olds — and girls' and boys'
teams vied for medals with teams from other towns.

Recreation thus served both individual and community interests. It
was a source of enjoyment and sociability, and by creating team spirit
and intramural competition, it also helped generate group loyalties.
When the competition was within Twin Rivers, however, it could generate strong and highly partisan feelings. "We urge the players and the
parents not to heckle or abuse the umpires." admonished *The Periscope*
in May 1976.

If recreation was the key area of community-wide interest, other
interests united smaller segments of the population. "We would like to
start a Weight Watchers class in Twin Rivers . . . if at least 40 people
are interested," read a notice in *The Periscope* (10 April 1974, p. 16).

Women from various charitable organizations held annual table and
recipe-swap parties at the Twin Rivers branch library; in fact, the library became a focal point for a wide range of gatherings, commemorations, lessons, and meetings. Its offerings included Lamaze childbirth
classes, holiday-card workshops for children and adults, puppet shows
and Christmas films, story time for toddlers, free blood-pressure service,
advice on stamp collecting, and seminars on fitness and on taxes. The
residents' wish to be with others, to learn skills and hobbies, and to
make sure their children were entertained and instructed led them to
pursue causes great and small. The sum total of these varied activities
was a microcosm of the modern world with its penchant for organizations, committees, and resolutions.

There were countless parties planned around holidays, sports events, and social groupings. A meeting of the Princeton chapter of the Sweet Adelines celebrated "Husband Appreciation Night" and concluded dinner with a serenade of songs to "Mr. Wonderful" (*Periscope*, May 10, 1974). The impulse to join others with similar interests crested early in the life of the community as new organizations and clubs emerged during the next two decades. The same held true in Levittown, where the organizational impulse was strong in the first two years of the community's existence, when the majority of organizations were started (Gans 1967, p. 124), but later seemed to have died out. The organizational impulse seems to have been stronger in Twin Rivers than in Levittown, which could reflect its middle-class character.

The impressive mix of social, civic, service, and cultural associations was truly remarkable and created a texture of interconnectedness. At the same time, however, the selective affinities that emerged may have reinforced specialized interests and separate enclaves, thus strengthening private over public concerns. This is one of the unintended consequences of aggregate organizational activity.

Another consequence is that while many desire the benefits of association, only a few can be counted on to do the hard work. In Twin Rivers, this was obvious from the start and continues to the present day. The few give their time, their energy, and their passion, while the many remain free riders or passive consumers. This tendency, widely evident in the market society at large, is not conducive to community writ small.

It was volunteers who helped create the plethora of clubs and associations and kept them going. Without their contributions, the organizations would not have taken root. And for the lack of such volunteers, many a club and association died out in Twin Rivers. Others reappeared when the spark reignited. That spark is muted but still alive in the third decade of the life of Twin Rivers.

The last survey asked respondents to classify themselves according to their propensities to keep to themselves or seek to participate in organized social activities. The results show a striking tendency among residents to tend their own gardens.

Table 7.1
Self-Identification

Classify Self As:	1990s
More of a Joiner	34%
More of a Loner	66%
N = 500	

Table 7.2
Voted in Last Board Election: 1990s Respondents by Age

	Under 40	40+
Yes	34%	58%
No	66%	42%
	N = 102	N = 327

Chi Square = 0.001

Table 7.3
Twin Rivers Is "Worse" Re: "People Pulling Together When Needed"

	Under 40	40+
	18%	40%

Chi Square = 0.001

What is interesting here is the role of age, which in general was not found to significantly affect attitudes toward the community, the neighbors, or management, but as the data show, did affect activism, since older residents were far more likely to have voted in the last board election and to feel that the community was less cohesive than it should be. While the older residents were more active in the community, they were also more apprehensive about community spirit, with the not uncommon tendency to view the present less favorably than their memories of the good old days. On a few dimensions, the older residents were more negative. Differences are not always statistically significant but they do suggest a pattern. On nearly all the other items, there was strong agreement among older and younger residents, as the following table illustrates.

Table 7.4
1990s Residents: Reactions by Age

	Under 40	40+
Is there a Twin Rivers community spirit?: No	31%	39%
Family relationships more difficult: Yes	7%	16%
Make trust more responsive to residents?: Yes	48%	55%
Importance to you of Twin Rivers Day: Not important	38%	53%

Table 7.5
1990s Residents: Liking of Twin Rivers by Age

	Under 40	_40 +_
Do you like Twin Rivers?: Yes	72%	69%
I feel I belong to Twin Rivers	58%	60%
Plan to stay in Twin Rivers the rest of my life	22%	28%
In favor of townhouse communities	52%	60%

Organizations and associations are interesting not only for revealing the variety of interests in a community but also for their contribution to the "third" or civil sector of society. It is civil society that constitutes a counterforce to the state and to the market by expanding the range of people's concerns and their sense of the richness and wholeness of life. Civil society contrasts the public focus with the market's material and private focus, and helps generate a public conversation and a richer quality of life (Bellah 1985, p. 200).

While many residents said they moved to Twin Rivers for its promise of a rich and rewarding community life, getting them to participate in community affairs was a constant, uphill battle. Exhortations emphasizing that it was a resident's moral duty to volunteer time and energy to sundry projects appeared at every turn, but had little effect in the earliest years. A minority of perhaps 10 to 15 percent were active, while the majority were critics on the sidelines. By December 1973, 50 percent of the 1,200 residents were paid-up members of the homeowners association (_The Periscope_, December 1973, p. 2). Some residents considered this a fairly high percentage given the chaotic early conditions. Still, a teen basketball program died for lack of parent participation in 1975, leaving close to fifty youths in the lurch. "Not one parent was willing to give two lousy hours of their time to supervise!" (_The Periscope_, December 1975, p. 25). A similar situation in 1974 led to the warning that in five years there would be hundreds of teenagers in the community and parents would be demanding programs they would be unwilling to supervise (_The Periscope_, February 10, 1974).

Residents were equally reluctant to attend bi-monthly board meetings of the Twin Rivers Homeowners Association. The lack of participation led to the attachment of an announcement to the by-laws provided with each homeowner packet:

To All Residents in Quad IV, Welcome to Twin Rivers. Not only did you buy a home, but a community as well. . . . One of the most important things a new resident can do is to stay informed . . . and the easiest way is to attend Homeowners Association open board meetings." (*The Periscope*, January 1974, p. 4)

Residents were encouraged to "pitch in with friends and neighbors to build something which you can be proud of each time you pass, and which will stand out in the memory of your children as something 'my mommy and daddy helped build.' So . . . contribute something permanent" (*The Periscope*, September 1982, p. 7).

Throughout it was generally agreed that "If you want participation, you've got to hit them right between the eyes. . . . Subtlety doesn't work" (private communication from a supervisor).

For some projects—for example, the 1975 legal fund for the suit against the developer—participation was elicited by the promise of direct rewards. A $25 contribution to the legal fund entitled the donor to the completion of a personal income tax return, free of charge, by a TRHA board member and public accountant (*The Periscope*, March 1976, p. 2).

Difficult though it was to elicit public participation, a few were always willing to help. In 1974, when 52 percent of the 270 children in Twin Rivers were preschoolers and 25 percent were first- and second-graders, "a sizeable group of mothers" fought for more play space and equipment for Twin Rivers children.

The legal fund, discussed in chapter 11, enlisted residents for the exercise of "their community responsibilities" by having them make individual contributions. And by 1974, 750 residents had contributed $6,000, challenging the developer's claim that the lawsuit was the work of a small band of rabble-rousers. Eventually three-fourths of the homeowners contributed to the fund (*The Periscope*, March 1973, p. 1).

Thus, although there were never enough volunteers, there were always some. In the late 1970s, for example, the monthly newspaper, *The Periscope*, was put together by volunteers who wrote the articles, edited, did the layouts, typed the copy, and sold the advertisements. And all of the members of the TRHA were volunteers, as were the members of the fire company and the township rescue squad.

There were also many informal undertakings that depended on volunteer labor, as did help in emergencies. In the "Blizzard of '83," for example, residents cooperated by shoveling snow for neighbors or helping to remove cars so the roads could be plowed. In his reflections on that event, trust administrator Joseph Vuzzo reflected, "Cooperation like this during a time of emergency is what makes a group of homes and residents a community" (*The Periscope*, March 1983, p. 1).

Efforts on behalf of children generally roused some members of the community to action. Parent Watch, whose task it was to take turns making sure children were safe on the way to and from school, depended on people donating twenty-five minutes of their time one day a week. The parent volunteers were stationed at strategic spots throughout the community during the half hour before and after school, and reported suspicious activities to the police. The program was started by a group of mothers in Quad II and inspired similar groups in the three other quads.

"Project Helping Hand" likewise focused on children; participants displayed a picture of a hand in their windows to signal their availability.

"Parent Watch" received prominent publicity in 1984 when several attempted abductions of schoolchildren alarmed the community. The program, started by a group of mothers, received official sanction and CB radios from the police department. All four quads had Parent Watch groups. Parent volunteers were also solicited for a parent "hotline" that informed each family of their children's daily school attendance, and both programs focused the community's attention on an issue of shared concern.

Residents were called upon to participate in a wide variety of undertakings, from organizing transportation facilities for commuters to contributing to the construction of a new library building. Nineteen-eighty-two was christened the Year of the Library with appeals to community pride and practical benefits as follows:

> Remember all the things our library means to us — the special programs for everyone from toddler to senior citizen, the movies, the informative programs, the special way our librarians go out of their way to help everyone, the meeting room . . . sought after by all the organizations in the community. . . . It is truly the center of Twin Rivers in more ways than one. . . . We need the support of the entire community. This is your opportunity to show your community spirit. (*The Periscope*, September 1982, p. 10)

A Crime Watch program was begun in 1982. Here the public became the eyes and ears of the community by securing their own homes and identifying suspicious cars or persons for the police. "A group organized as a Community Watch can help by keeping an eye on each other's property while a neighbor is away on vacation or at work during the day." In addition to its contribution to the community's safety, an additional benefit of the program was that "it gets neighbors talking to each other and caring about each other and recreates the sense of community that has been lost with the growth of large cities (*The Periscope*, September 1982, p. 1, 16A).

The first lawsuit did much to energize the developing community for other projects, for it served as a model of what concerted action could achieve. Thus in 1979 local headlines read: "Twin Rivers residents force withdrawal of day care application." An ad hoc group of residents had fought the proposed facility on several grounds, fearing that the proposed center for 120 children would increase noise and flooding problems and so "result in a drop in property values." The planning board hearings were attended by an overflow crowd of "angry Twin Rivers residents" whose fervor carried the day by defeating the proposal (*Windsor-Heights Herald*, 15 March 1979, p. 1).

Throughout the years we find continual reminders that "there is a world of difference between a development and a community," and it is each individual's responsibility to "transform the former into the latter" (*The Periscope*, January 1974).

Along with community-wide projects and social events went the basic message: Help your community, help yourself, and become a part of what is going on.

Elections to local and township offices gradually brought out Twin Rivers residents as well. A resident was elected to the East Windsor school board in 1974. Those elected to the board of the homeowners association announced their gratitude to those "who came out on a cold and rainy night" to vote and pledged themselves to work for the community in various ways, from helping to organize the lawsuit to improving communications within and outside of Twin Rivers.

An early successful project that demonstrated the power of collective action was the campaign by the Twin Rivers Homeowners Association in favor of a new township ordinance that would require builders henceforth to use copper rather than aluminum wiring. The successful outcome was attributed to the "large number of people who conquered ignorance and apathy and acted on behalf of the greater community" (*The Periscope*, April 1973, p. 1). In the summer of 1985, a fiercely disputed proposal for a park-and-ride facility inspired active protest by the residents who feared its adverse effects on the environment.

Thus, by the 1980s, community projects, elections, and organized protests were embedded in the culture of Twin Rivers, much of which took shape around recreation and sports. The annual winter holidays event, teen pool parties, and athletic competitions such as the Twin Rivers tennis tournament, men's basketball league, and road races became standard fare and were well covered in local papers. Other projects had a more altruistic goal. In 1982, for example, one hundred parents built a tire playground for their children. Contributions of four dollars per person bought the equipment and paid the architect, while merchants donated food for the hard-working volunteers who constructed the playground. This successful self-help undertaking generated a sense of human fellowship and community bounty. Tree-planting projects, the creation of blood banks, and the organization of a rescue squad represented substantial victories over indifference or timidity, of which the residents could be proud.

Achievements of groups and individuals that exhibited team spirit and community power were lauded. Headlines such as "Twin Rivers Teams Prolong Win Streak," and "The Twin Rivers Torpedoes Swimming and Diving Team Caps Fine Season" proliferated, along with photos of victorious meets or outstanding winners. In fact, athletic competition was a major part of the community-building process throughout the decade.

The plethora of activities, projects, and social causes was inspired by local headlines and reportage in the local paper.

In his pioneering work on the community press, Morris Janowitz noted its key significance as a social indicator that "can only take on meaning with some degree of personal acquaintance with the area" (Janowitz 1967, p. 2).

The community press is not only an indispensable source of information about the local community but serves also as an integrative force, emphasizing common values and consensus. It thereby counteracts the "individuating tendencies and impersonality" of modern life" (ibid., p. 11).

By helping to orient people in local space, the community press is a source of psychic security for individuals. It also generates local pride, as "any slur on the local community is likely to bring forth responses . . . which act as the standard bearer of local pride (ibid., p. 91).

Contrasting three types of participants in the local community — those who are actively engaged in community organizations, those who are primarily active on projects and social exchange with neighbors, and those who are engaged in neither and are therefore labeled "isolates" — Greer (in Janowitz, 1967, p. 257) found no consistent dividing line among them that would help predict their participation in local life and their ideological stances on important issues.

The community press helps coalesce attitudes toward local issues as it serves as a commentator on public issues and as the public conscience of the local community. This underscores its integrative role. It speaks for the whole community (Greer, in Janowitz 1967, p. 264).

Elections also focused collective attention on shared objectives and common problems, even as they pitted candidates against one another. Barely a few months after the first residents moved in, in October 1970,

170 residents met to propose a slate of candidates for the homeowners association that was to advise the trust. In 1973 the voting power of Twin Rivers was publicly recognized for the first time. Reminded that they did their part in electing the total township team, the residents were informed of the township's interest in helping Twin Rivers with its problems, notably traffic issues and the hardships of commuting. With 42 percent of the township's population, Twin Rivers had become a political force to be reckoned with (*The Periscope*, June 1974, p. 15).

Other elections involved the homeowners in internal business. There was a 75 percent approval vote for the Twin Rivers Library. The high turnout was met with these appreciative comments by Roberta Hirshman, president of the Friends of the Library Committee: "Apathy move over — Twin Rivers cares about its library! . . . Thank you for showing us you care" (*The Periscope*, November 1981, p. 1). Another community vote was not so successful. A set of document changes that required approval of 75 percent of the beneficiaries was defeated largely because only 15 percent of the homeowners went to the polls. This caused the board and other concerned citizens great anguish, as two years of hard labor had gone down the drain.

A more encouraging response contributed to what came to be known as the Belz Mall Defeat. In 1982 a Memphis developer proposed to build a 410,000-square-foot factory outlet mall near the New Jersey Turnpike in East Windsor. The Twin Rivers residents became active, vocal opponents of this plan. Hundreds of them packed the township hearings in protest, warning of potentially horrendous traffic and crime problems if the mall were built.

The final public hearing took place at the Hightstown High School in August 1982. The meeting was unruly and turbulent. Loud outbursts from the audience, accompanied by hissing and booing, greeted the Belz Mall representatives when they rose to speak and show their slides of seven other malls their firm had constructed. In the ensuing three hours, fifty-two speakers from the audience took turns expressing their mostly negative views. Each member of the township council then rose to express an opinion, and the result was a vote of six to one against the proposal.

The key issues that had agitated the public were the potential traffic crunch and traffic accidents, personal safety from the criminal elements often attracted to such malls, air and noise pollution, and other quality-of-life issues. In addition, merchants were anxious about undesirable competition, and doubt was expressed about the financial benefit to the township. Indeed, the debate over potential benefits to the township split the council and eventually caused several favorably disposed council members to change their votes.

At the heart of the heated exchanges was a perspective on social change, dividing the residents between those who feared it and those who favored it. Notes made at the time reveal the following opinions: "East Windsor has been here since 1797, and change will come and it's something we have to deal with," especially since East Windsor needs new ratables in order to keep from raising taxes. Belz would have meant $100,000 in annual revenues, and "there aren't going to be any more developers" (groans from the audience). "When I knocked on your doors, you all said you wanted ratables; now you've changed your mind. . . . there have been a lot of misstatements—to be kind I'll call them that— tonight . . . I hope you all realize what you've done . . . but nothing is worth tearing the community apart" (from notes taken by Carol S. Stamets in 1982).

One member of the planning board had collected hundreds of signatures for a petition against the mall. At the hearings, posters opposing the mall were scattered throughout the room. Applause greeted the comments the audience wanted to hear. Anxiety was voiced in heated exchanges: "We're getting a low-class, low quality mall"; "Belz will make millions at our expense"; "We don't need tourism—we're not Orlando, Florida"; "Maybe we could have a sign, 'Please confine crime to the mall parking lot' and 'Children will be killed, pot will be sold.'" One man got up to spew forth the sentiments, "Goddamn mall, goddamn everything," to great applause (ibid.).

The next day's headlines proclaimed the defeat of the mall because town council members reversed their earlier decision and voted now to bow to the "will of the people." The one holdout, a woman, held fast to her original support of the proposal, but most of those who switched votes said they did so because of what they perceived as overwhelming opposition to the Belz proposal. The vote was greeted with wild enthusiasm by the audience and it was the topic of conversation for months afterward. In addition to defeating construction of the mall, it conveyed the strength that came from solidarity and concerted action. By all accounts, the sentiment in Twin Rivers was crucial in the defeat of the mall proposal, and this victory, controversial as it was, was accredited to the growing political strength of the community.

> This was a lesson in freedom and democracy. Use it or lose it. Eleventh hour participation increases your chances of losing it. Pay attention . . . to your community, your municipality, your country, your state, your nation. This was an effort involving cooperation among . . . residents in and outside of Twin Rivers, Hightstown residents, and merchants from both the Township

and Borough. For the first time in the eight years I'm living
here, I saw hatchets buried, hands joined. . . . Now it is up to
you to keep the ball rolling. Stay involved." (*The Periscope*,
September 1982, p. 4)

In this and similar messages, the residents are addressed directly as
"you," but in fact and of necessity, it is an impersonal communication.
One wonders about the impact of such impersonal directives on residents of a community that cannot draw on a fund of common memories or shared victories. Nor is the inclusive "you" anything but premature given the still segmented community. Nevertheless the message was
unrelenting in its insistence on participation and voting: "I urge others
to work for the community because it is personally rewarding to know
you've helped your community. Remember, there is always a need for
more hands" (*The Periscope*, December 1973). Appealing to Twin Rivers
"residents, investors and homeowners," the HOA pledged to "work for
you and with you and encourage your participation" (*The Periscope*,
January 1974).

By 1980, the end of its first decade, residents of Twin Rivers were
able to respond collectively to collective crises and could be moved to
action for the "right" cause. But while the collective pronoun united
many disparate individuals into a single voice on occasion, there was
still a "desperate" and continuous search for volunteers, especially as
women became employed outside the home in the 1980s. Gradually the
community became aware that its fantasy of a town-meeting, village-
green democracy rested on particular social, family, and gender arrangements that had all too readily been taken for granted. As these changed,
so did the reservoir of traditional resources.

The division within the community grew between those who gener-
ously devoted their time, energy, and effort and the many more who did
not. Apathy, indifference, and free riders were often deplored as major
afflictions. At times, neglect of signs and rules, disinterest in others, and
self-preoccupation were so widespread that the situation seemed hope-
less. "There are many residents in this community who apparently are
satisfied with *not* knowing what's going on around them" complained
The Periscope in January 1974 (p. 5).

It was a minority who made Twin Rivers go, a small minority devoted to service, who organized, supervised, spoke up, spoke out, created institutions, pitched in during hard times, worried, cared, and did
the hard work that gets a tremendous collective undertaking such as
Twin Rivers off the ground.

CHAPTER 8
SOCIABILITY IN A NEW COMMUNITY

Everything is united: good and evil, day and night, the sacred and the profane. Everything merges . . . the fiesta is a cosmic experiment, an experiment in disorder, reuniting contradictory elements and principles in order to bring about a renascence of life.

— Octavio Paz

The sociability of newcomers is, for many, used as proof that community exists. And in truth, adjusting to an unfinished site among unfamiliar but potentially like-minded others seems at the start to draw people together to exchange advice and information and provide steady boosts of morale. This seems to have happened in Twin Rivers where sociability was strikingly present from the earliest days. In fact, by the end of the first year of its existence, two-thirds of the residents could name more than fifty residents by name and two-fifths claimed to know more than a hundred. The easy informality and the need to share experiences in the new setting created an atmosphere of ready accessibility and mutual concern.

However, not all residents made friends or socialized easily. As many as one-third of them admitted to feeling acutely lonely in the first weeks and months after moving in, and a few never reached out to others. The social mix, instead of inspiring them, seemed to intimidate them.

This challenges one of the most widely accepted tenets of planning practice on the beneficial effects of social and economic heterogeneity. Planners typically aim at encouraging ethnic, income, and occupational diversity in a community. However, these goals are not easy to translate into practice and good intentions often founder on the realities of social distance and snobbery.

Twin Rivers was no exception. It aimed for a social and racial mix, which it did not achieve for many years.

But it could also be argued that there was a mix in regard to religious affiliation and occupation. In the first five years, Jews, who comprised around 3 percent of the U.S. population, made up 40 percent of the totality; Roman Catholics, 22 percent; and Protestants, 14 percent. However, formal labels are not enough. When we look at the degree of religiosity, the picture changes. Jews avowed the least (17%), Roman Catholics (47%), and Protestants, the highest religious commitment (56%).

Occupational characteristics, as gleaned from the husbands' occupations as chief breadwinners, exhibit an even wider range, from doctors and lawyers to salesmen and plumbers.

Like other privately developed communities, Twin Rivers attracted a young, well-educated, family-oriented population, economically comfortable, whose incomes were drawn from white-collar, sales, and technical occupations. Residents were largely white and native born, and some two-thirds were former residents of the eastern seaboard. So, on a very general level, we have a less heterogeneous community than originally envisaged. However, within that broad social spectrum, there was

Table 8.1
Husbands' Occupations, by Decade

Husband's Job	1970s	1990s
Salesman (real estate)	10%	9%
Independent professional	8%	6%
Salaried professional (technical)	24%	18%
Salaried professional (other)	14%	16%
Business manager	31%	15%
Skilled service (police, plumber, nurse)	5%	16%
Retired	2%	3%
Self-employed (not professional)	4%	15%
Other	2%	2%
Total	100%	100%
	N = 239	N = 540

considerable diversity as to specific birthplace, the precise jobs of husbands and wives, and the particular complexion of households, which varied in composition and styles of earning and spending.

Also, from the start, social and economic diversity was built into the master plan by the range — and prices — of the housing modules. Apartments would be rented by individuals earning a few hundred dollars a week while owners of single-family houses earned one thousand or more. Townhouses were in the majority but they were joined by adult condominiums, free-standing houses, and rental apartments, each representing a somewhat different economic niche.

There were also variations by density. The two nine-story apartment buildings with 117 apartments each were located in the high-density area. The single-family houses, at four dwelling units per acre, were in the low density area. The townhouses, at fifteen units per acre, represented the medium-density areas.

How narrowly one draws social boundaries to a large extent determines how much heterogeneity one will discover. This was certainly the case here, as more than half of the residents saw Twin Rivers as basically diverse, while the rest saw it as socially homogeneous.

The perceived diversity carried over into other assessments: There was unanimous agreement, for example, that Twin Rivers had numerous cliques (over 90% perceived cliques, 71% many cliques) based on interests (56%), on physical proximity (36%), and, far lower on the list, religion (24%) or family situation (16%). These cliques formed early in the life of the new community were the structure on which its future social life was built.

Another significant social division emphasized by the residents was that between owners and tenants. Two-fifths considered this a sharp divide. Renters were generally seen as more transient and less community minded, as well as less desirable as friends.

Asked how they felt about mixing different groups in the community, 100 percent of the residents declared themselves in favor of it, thereby endorsing a major tenet of the democratic creed. But they had very definite views as to the kind of social mix they favored. By and large, diversity was considered acceptable within definite economic boundaries. Two-thirds approved of mixing by income, which accounts for most of the homogeneity we actually find. The following is a typical comment:

> Important to be with your own "grade" of people. Can't live somewhere where people have furniture that costs much less than mine. Your children won't be accepted. Last thing I'd call

myself is a snob, but when you have children you learn that
you have to live with similar people.

The residents felt that the people were in fact cut from fairly similar
social cloth, not primarily because of income, race, or education, but
because of their regional origins. As proof, comments point to the large
contingent from New York City.

> Little New York City. People from New York have carried with
> them their habits and routines. We from the country are espe-
> cially aware of this. They carry on the "Sunday Stoop" customs
> for example.

> "Little Canarsie" — a small city in a small town. Translated
> Brooklyn. People wanted to get out of the city while still think-
> ing they live in a city. Clannishness, apathy, no overall view of
> Twin Rivers or East Windsor as a total community."

Cliques formed on the basis of interests, religious affiliation, social
and geographic antecedents; residential proximity also provided a basis
for social affinity, as the following comment makes explicit:

> Lifestyle starts it (cliques) and it goes from there. Street life
> people; coffee klatch, athletic people, and fighters for better-
> ment of community (against trust). They are very hard to break
> into.

Comparing views on social mixing with the actual extent of social
mix in Twin Rivers, the greatest actual similarity that most groups shared
was income; it was also the area where diversity was least welcome.
This view, which most of the residents in the 1970s held, remained constant through the years. Social diversity was more accepted if it rested
on an economic baseline. Racial mixing, though favored in principle,
was not realized in practice at first. Non-whites made up only a scant
percentage of those who moved into Twin Rivers in the 1970s. Decade
by decade, however, the racial and ethnic mix increased, so that by the
1990s the complexion of the community had changed substantially to
incorporate Asians, Latinos, and African-Americans, among others.
This was quite in accord with the professed wishes of nine-tenths of the
residents, who favored a mix of people by job, religion, age, and race in
that order (see table 8.2).

In general, then, Twin Rivers exhibited considerable homogeneity in
income, occupation, and age of residents, but if one looks closely at
specific occupations, consumption patterns, and ages, a more diversified
pattern is evident. Thus the desire for social similarity and the search

Table 8.2
Residents' Approval of Social Mix

	1970s
Type of job	100%
Religion	97%
Race	91%
Age	75%
Income	61%

Find it easy to meet people like myself:
  Yes = three-fifths
  No = two-fifths

for social diversification could both be satisfied in Twin Rivers. And depending on the criteria used to demarcate social distinctions, one could conclude that social mix both was and was not present in the community.

Given the diversity that did exist, most, but not all residents said it was easy to meet people like themselves. This suggests that their criteria for self-other identification were different from the criteria they gave for a desirable social mix.

Those who did not find it easy to meet people cited the existence of cliques and the difficulty of finding people with similar interests as the chief reasons for their sense of isolation. Heterogeneity, at least in regard to race and income, was favored more in the abstract than in actuality, and diversity of social background and lifestyles was widely perceived to exist, even garnering the judgment that Twin Rivers was clique-ridden. This indicates that internal social boundaries were drawn early — between pioneers and later residents, owners and renters — and reduced the sense of unity of the nascent community.

Interestingly, in every decade, sociability was more intense in the first three to four years after moving into the community. In the late 1990s, for example, here is a forty-seven-year-old man describing his family's first five years in the new community compared to subsequent ones, "We all knew one another at the start; it was a very nice feeling. Over the years, that has changed and we don't have that closeness now. As things got bigger, the closeness drifted off."

But while the original closeness may have diminished, specialized services and interests proliferated. As postulated by social research, a growth of population is accompanied by the growth of distinct subcultures. Hence with the passage of time, it was possible for growing numbers of residents to find like-minded others and satisfy specialized interests (Fischer 1976, pp. 60, 111).

Social Connectedness

For many residents, the intense sociability displayed by incoming residents of planned environments is seen as a harbinger of the community to come. The vivid social exchanges and informal socializing across front- and backyards make such a conclusion quite plausible. But closer examination suggests other motives at work.

There is first of all the paradox of loneliness, even if one is surrounded by people, that accompanies the move. The first days and nights are especially disconcerting. One has a house, often not functioning fully, but one is not yet at home. The new surroundings seem strange and unfamiliar. One is not sure about the routines one normally takes for granted. Everything has to be learned anew, a prospect both exciting and daunting.

The move itself has a powerful impact, positive and negative, depending on personal and social expectations. In Twin Rivers, the change seemed more drastic for women than for men. Most of the women had held jobs prior to the move and most stopped working outside the home, for family reasons, for as long as a decade thereafter. Their responses were divided, with one-half adjudging the changes in daily routines as positive, one-fourth mixed, and one-fourth as outright negative. The positive reactions came as a result of the joy of a new baby, a new house to be fixed up, and more socializing. The negative reactions reflected unfulfilled expectations, the stresses of settling in, and greater domestic responsibilities. Most wives saw the move as highly positive for their husbands, who spent more time than they had previously on home and family activities (15%), more on recreation and exercise (13%), and more on social activities with other men (13%). Many also had better jobs (15%) and a better commute (20%). But it was the move's perceived effects on the children, most of them infants and toddlers in the 1970s, that had the major impact. Nine-tenths of the women interviewed saw the move to Twin Rivers as overwhelmingly positive for their children, citing new and more playmates, a healthful environment, safety, and good schools as reasons for their optimism.

Thus, despite the stresses of the move into an unfinished environment with many strangers, the generally positive outlook helped the majority of residents make the transition into a new way of life successfully. The intense reaching out to strangers in the same boat is a way to assuage one's immediate — and temporary — distress. It helps to ventilate feelings about the trying process of settling in, as well as to obtain information and advice. Helpful as this often frantic socializing may be, it is too fragile and transient a base to carry the weight of community. And while residents came to know others in this preliminary way very quickly, such casual contacts did not forge the sustained links needed to build long-term relationships.

How to break the ice with proximate strangers is a question large numbers of Americans face repeatedly as they move from place to place in search of jobs, space, status, or new experiences. Not everyone was adept at this task — recall that two-fifths of Twin Rivers residents found it difficult to meet people — but the majority managed it, many very well, especially if they had children.

Children are great social magnets, and their playmates and friends often bring parents together. The seasons also play their part. The open, outdoor life, especially in warm weather, means daily trips to the pool or tennis court, work on lawns and patios, and pruning and planting gardens. These activities bring people into visual contact from which other contacts often follow.

Neighbors

One meaning of community is good fellowship and neighborliness. An atmosphere experienced as friendly and supportive enlists positive, ingroup feelings and loyalties; an environment that is deficient in these respects diminishes the sense of closeness and brings negative and uncooperative feelings to the fore.

All residents have neighbors, and in Twin Rivers, most were favorably disposed to each other in each decade. In the 1970s, more than half considered their neighbors friendly (6 percent "too friendly") and only 10 percent not friendly enough. These proportions remained constant throughout the years. Moreover, an analysis of time budgets showed that in that first decade, 60 percent of the residents mentioned visits to or from neighbors on the day prior to the interviews. These occurred virtually at any time of day, including the evening hours, often extending to an hour or two per visit.

For townhouse residents, neighbors are especially significant since one shares walls and outdoor spaces with them. In fact, neighbors rated highly in all three decades, were a definite source of comfort to the large majority of residents.

A comparison of the 1970s with the 1980s shows a spread of greater neutrality toward neighbors over time, but the basic pattern remained (table 8.3).

Neighbors were more highly evaluated than residents in general at both times (table 8.4) but especially in the later decade. And in the

Table 8.3
Views of Neighbors

Neighbors are:	1970s	1980s
Very friendly	57%	47%
Very unfriendly	3%	4%
Neither	22%	34%
Not friendly enough	4%	9%
Too friendly	8%	6%
Varies	6%	0%
	100%	100%
	N = 195	N = 71

Table 8.4
Percent Expressing Positive Feelings toward Other Residents

	1970s	1980s	1990s
Residents in general	53%	37%	54%
Toward neighbors	57%	62%	82%

1990s, the majority thought their neighbors friendly and two-thirds said that friendly neighbors were "very important" to them.

The presence of cliques was noted in all three decades, but the figures apply only for the 1970s and 1980s.

Cliques were taken for granted by the 1990s, the most important

Table 8.5
Basis for Cliques in Twin Rivers

	1970s	1980s
There are cliques	85%	72%
Basis for cliques:		
Special interests	35%	50%
Spatial proximity	15%	6%
Religion	16%	12%
Family situation	6%	10%
Age	6%	10%
Income	2%	7%
Pre–Twin Rivers background	9%	0%
Other	11%	5%
	N = 195	N = 71

determinant being interests in particular areas such as recreation, community service, hobbies, children, schools, and sports.

Friendships

In all three decades, close to one-half of the residents interviewed had made "best friends" in Twin Rivers. The large majority of these lived on the same block, though not next door, and were close in age. As table 8.6 shows, there was slightly less eco-centrism from decade to decade.

One other area of socializing concerns entertainment at home. Nearly all residents entertained informally, at least once every week or two in the 1970s, a trend that has sharply declined over the decades.

Table 8.7 shows there was a perceptible shift in the kind and amount of socializing that occurred in Twin Rivers. Over time, there were fewer block and pool parties and much less formal entertainment at home. In the 1990s fully one-fourth of the residents indicated that they entertained "less" than when they first moved into Twin Rivers, and of the remainder, the majority (62%) entertained informally and infrequently once every month or two.

Table 8.6
Spatial Location of Friends

	1970s	1980s	1990s
Have friends in Twin Rivers	47%	45%	53%
On the same block/quad	84%	73%	62%
Next door neighbors	0%	6%	—
	N = 195	N = 71	N = 450

Table 8.7
Extent of At-Home Entertainment

	1970s	1980s	1990s
Entertain informally			
Weekly	34%	33%	27%
Several times per month	50%	20%	42%
Less often	16%	47%	31%
What kind of entertainment			
Meals	59%	36%	40%
Snacks and drinks only	41%	61%	60%
	N = 195	N = 71	N = 450

Twin Rivers shares with other planned communities a certain set of priorities endorsed by the developers who create the physical shell first and let the community develop from there. The physical foundations are of course crucial, but, judging from the experience of Twin Rivers, there is no automatic unfolding of community sociability once they are built.

There is a proliferating, though still far from adequate, literature on the impact of physical design on social relationships. It includes the pioneering work of Festinger, Schachter, and Back (1950), which gave us the conceptual distinction between physical and functional distance; the study of Braydon Road by Kuper and his colleagues (1953); and specific research into human contacts in different kinds of settings ranging from college campuses to mental wards (Proshansky et al., 1970). The naive version of this view sees the arrangement of spaces and places as directly conducive to neighborliness or friendships. Sound physical arrangements, in this view, will contribute to the attainment of such values as cooperation, diversity, and sociability. More sophisticated discussions emphasize the complicated interplay between design and behavior, and, while they respect the significance of physical design, they insist on its dependence on social and cultural factors.

In the following pages we will consider the relative significance of physical versus social factors by examining friendships, socializing, range of acquaintances, and name recognition among Twin Rivers residents.

Studies of friendship patterns in new communities have shown that people will select their new friends from among those living near them. (Festinger et al., 1950; Whyte 1980; Kuper 1953). This is due in part to the fact that one is likely to become aware of the neighbors and co-residents with whom one shares facilities and pathways and in part to the fact that the new environment creates many questions and problems that others similarly situated may help resolve. In the formative phase of Twin Rivers, nearly one-half of the residents had made "best friends" in Twin Rivers and a much larger proportion (90%) had an extensive list of acquaintances. The role of spatial proximity was quite remarkable in this: Friends tended to be concentrated in areas close to home on the same block (47%) or in the same quad (39%).

This spatial centrism was supplemented by social factors. Three-fourths of their friends were of the same age, race, and religion. From the earliest period, homeowners confined their friendships mainly to other homeowners, and apartment dwellers to other apartment dwellers. This tendency of homophily increased with time.

As table 8.8 shows, dwelling type and quad location had a sizeable combined impact on the choice of acquaintances.

Physical proximity affects sociability also by the siting of houses. The fact that townhouse residents were more likely to know and inter-

Table 8.8
Dwelling Type and Acquaintanceship in Twin Rivers: 1970s
Percent Who Knew By Name

Dwelling type	Homeowners Only	Apartment Dwellers Only	Both
Homeowners	78%	—	22%
Apartment dwellers	—	44%	56%

act with neighbors suggests that visual contact precedes social contact —
if, that is, people like what they see. As Langdon (1994, p. 140) has
noted, people prefer to see houses that reflect their own aesthetic preferences. So, like wants to see like close to home.

Given the high population density in a townhouse community, reactions to one's neighbors are important for one's sense of well-being. As we
have seen, the large majority of residents gave their neighbors very positive
ratings in all three decades, much higher than those given to the community
overall. Asked about noise, that bane of modern life, eight-tenths acknowledged hearing sounds from their neighbors — including music playing (22%),
outdoor activities (13%), indoor activities (10%), as well as indoor conversations (9%). Side neighbors, of course, were more likely to be overheard
(58%), but noise did not turn out to be the irritant it is generally thought to
be, and noise was only rarely mentioned as a drawback to townhouse living.

The importance of the physical context and design is revealed also
in responses to a question, "Where do you meet new people in Twin
Rivers?" The central magnet, from the 1970s through the 1990s, was
the swimming pool.

If one looks at the overall pattern of sociability — whether considering friends, neighbors, or acquaintances — one notes a definite rhythm
or phasing over time. There is the intense, generally indiscriminate, of-

Table 8.9
Where Do You Meet New People?

	1970s	1980s
Swimming pools	68%	70%
Clubs, organizations	41%	30%
Other recreation areas	23%	22%
In parking areas	18%	3%
Homes, parties	26%	8%
Walking for pleasure	0%	3%
	N = 195	N = 71

ten frantic, socializing in the earliest months. Surrounded by strangers in unfamiliar territory and seeking to navigate around hurdles seen and unseen, residents seek out others in a bid for reassurance and comfort in their new homes.

Within the year, often within six months, the frenzy subsides. People settle in, shape up houses and lawns, arrange for schooling and health care, establish daily routines, and make houses into homes and strangers into co-residents. Numerous acquaintances, some close friends, and compatible neighbors help to anchor one's identity. Thereafter, feelings, activities, and patterns of work and leisure are sorted out and things fall into place for the majority who have committed themselves to living in the community.

At the start, the majority of residents of Twin Rivers intended to stay for some years, though not for life (only one-fourth had such long-term expectations). The main reasons for anticipating future moves were divided evenly between job relocation (39%) and the desire for a detached house (38%). The latter would diminish as experience with townhouse living increased. None of the other possible motives for leaving—conflict with neighbors, dislike of Twin Rivers, disappointment with the general conditions of life there—figured at all prominently. For the most part, residents came to stay for an indefinite future.

Physical proximity thus plays a varied role in sociability. It is moderately important for casual acquaintances, important for clique formation, and very significant for close friendships. To be sure, spatial closeness brings all groups into contact, but the quality and continuity of that contact depends on a number of additional factors. There must also be social and spiritual affinities if such contacts are to deepen in time. Design helps but it is not enough.

Privacy and Sociability

A common perception is that privacy vanishes in townhouse developments. However reasonable this may sound, it is not borne out in practice. In fact, in Twin Rivers, ratings of privacy improved over time. Interviews with residents that took place a decade apart showed this clearly. In the 1980s, 90 percent were satisfied with the privacy available, a considerable increase over the 57 percent who felt this way in the 1970s. In the 1990s privacy was both "very important" to residents (81%) and available to them.

Privacy is a function not only of densities but of visibility. For example, since the parking areas of Twin Rivers are located in front of the houses, residents could easily tell who was entering or leaving their houses, who had frequent visitors, who got what kinds of deliveries and so on. This made some people feel overexposed, but others took it in stride.

Privacy and sociability are hard to keep in balance, and the smaller a community, the more fluid the lines between them. Eighteenth-century New England towns, though smaller than Twin Rivers, faced some similar problems. Relationships were close, and church attendance, school activities, fairs, house-raisings, quilting bees, and births and deaths created an atmosphere of familiarity, mutual recognition, and mutual support. Anonymity was minimal. Gossip, propinquity, and encounters in shops and taverns effaced separation between public and private. Noise from close living arrangements was an irritant in the colonial period, with the courts called upon to settle disputes on occasion. Privacy, peace, and quiet were considered collective goods, an assumption that strikes us as novel. These could be preserved in a more deferential society that exhibited a "respect for other persons, particularly one's betters, and for privacy" (Flaherty 1972, pp. 93, 96).

Given the high density of people and houses, early settlers developed mechanisms for obtaining anonymity amid a bustling social life. Not everyone could be kept track of, even in such small communities, what with the constant arrivals and departures of migrants and strangers. Taverns, inns, and coffeehouses were centers of community life where people met, conversed, ate, and joked on a regular basis. There they developed "a collective sense of group privacy" as illustrated in the warning: "One must not tell tales out of the tavern." Moreover, suggests Flaherty, when neighbors know each other extremely well, they lose interest in one another and only dramatic events will rekindle interest. This suggests that the proverbial small-town curiosity about others may have more to do with boredom, loneliness, or the need for social contact than with a disregard for rights to privacy (ibid., pp. 105, 109).

To be sure, historically in the United States life was seen as "much more personalized, intimate, and communal than the fragmented and highly individualistic character of existence in industrial society," but "solitude" was apparently readily available when needed. Perhaps because society was then more interdependent and cooperative, privacy was less of a perceived need. Privacy was not "an absolute value" and had to be "balanced against other desirable goods," such as safety, security, and mutual fellowship.

Social life and social relationships are always important for a sense of well-being, most especially so in unfamiliar environs in the process of formation. And despite obvious shortcomings of house and landscape, facilities and services, Twin Rivers, from its inception, received a surprisingly good report card on neighboring, friendships, the range of acquaintances, and privacy. The physical layout helped bring people together at pools, schools, shops, playgrounds, and bus stops, and spatial connectedness advanced social connections. Best friends lived close by; the facing of houses and links to neighbors influenced social recognition and social exchanges. Proximity mattered in all these respects.

Hence, even in the pioneering phase, more than one-half of the residents liked Twin Rivers, with all its growing pains, "very much"; one-third, "pretty well"; and only 3 percent disliked it. There was a large reservoir of good will from the start.

However, we cannot ignore the minority, sometimes sizeable, who did not feel at home in Twin Rivers, found it hard to make friends, did not meet like-minded people, and suffered feelings of isolation and estrangement in the midst of vivid activity and movement. Those who did not move away created a negative undertow in the community.

Important as sociability is, moreover, it cannot substitute for a sense of community and community involvement. As the ratings of various facilities and services over the decades showed, community aspects fared poorly in comparison with physical and recreational amenities.

For example, fully two-fifths rated community participation in Twin Rivers as "poor" compared to, let us say, relations with neighbors, which barely 3 percent ranked as low. Asked what sorts of things they worried about from time to time in the 1970s, one-fifth mentioned the way the community was shaping up, a cause of concern that was second only to personal worries (36%). In part residents were worried because they had already grown fond of Twin Rivers, the majority (56%) liking it "very much," warts and all.

In the 1990s the majority (59%) indicated that community involvement was quite important to them; only 33 percent said it was not. A majority (56%) wished that Twin Rivers were more of a community. Most felt that community spirit was quite stable, but one-third thought it had weakened (34%). While the majority of residents are still not active participants in community affairs, two-fifths said they participated more in the 1990s than when they first arrived.

Sociability—having friends and acquaintances, good neighbors, and places for meeting new people—was strongly related to feelings about Twin Rivers. Those who had satisfying social relationships were satisfied with Twin Rivers (85%), while those who were disappointed with Twin Rivers (40%) were also disappointed with their relationships and social life, and described "most people here" as inconsiderate, selfish, or too competitive.

Community satisfaction was a key determinant in plans for leaving or staying. Of those who planned to stay in Twin Rivers for the rest of their lives, three-fourths cited their satisfaction with houses, neighbors, and social life, whereas those who planned to move within the coming year were unhappy with all three.

In sum, social gatherings, coffee breaks, talking in front- or back-yards are important for ventilating feelings about the stress of moving and adapting to new, idealized surroundings. However, such haphazard activities are too fragile a base to carry the weight of community. Physical proximity, while conducive to some initial and casual social contacts, is a precarious basis for further contact if residents do not share deeper values and worldviews. When, as in modern life, social diversity is the rule, neighbors may share a particular socioeconomic level but otherwise have little in common. In that case, physical proximity may become divisive and exacerbate personal differences. Proximity, then, is no guarantee of community, which requires a whole complement of values, interests, needs, and aspirations to take hold.

Collective Rites, Rituals, and Rewards

To build a community, even one less new and unsettled than Twin Rivers, people assume they should be able to count on the talents of the residents and their propensity for anonymous generosity, which are the earmarks of public service. But precisely because it is anonymous, such service is difficult to recompense and thus an individual's incentives to contribute are further reduced.

Gradually, therefore, the idea took hold in Twin Rivers that those "who have served the interests of Twin Rivers" and given their time and energy to it should be rewarded with "Certificates of Appreciation" (*The Periscope*, December 1981, p. 1). And in 1983 such certificates were presented to twenty-seven residents for their work as volunteers on committees, on the TRHA board, and as technical experts.

The first residents to be so honored were representative of both the social diversity of the residents and their individual talents. One man had been named an officer of the Order of the British Empire by Queen Elizabeth II for his work as a project engineer for the British nuclear submarine *Renown*. Others had won sports trophies, published poetry, and sailed the seven seas. There was John Woodruff, the only surviving gold medal winner of the 1936 track Olympics. He was the top half-miler of the country then. He and his wife purchased a lake condo apartment in 1971 and later they moved to Sacramento only to return to Twin Rivers in 1988. He was an enthusiastic returnee, reciting Twin

Rivers blessings as follows: great location, nearness to Turnpike, excellent maintenance and upkeep by the board. Often, he mused, "You know something is really good only after you leave it."

The Periscope had begun to feature one outstanding resident each month as early as 1974. The first was an attorney who had been elected to the TRHA board to fill a vacancy. The owner of an early patio-ranch model, he and his wife and two small children had lived in Twin Rivers for four years. He admitted to being a "little disappointed" in Twin Rivers, having hoped for more local employment opportunities, better landscaping, and a thriving shopping center. But he was also "proud to be a resident." By joining the TRHA board, he hoped "to bring back some of the enthusiasm of the earliest residents" by reviving the idea of block captains. He was concerned about vandalism and sought to have more voter participation in governance and better relations with the township (*The Periscope*, April 1974, p. 11).

The following month, the profile of the month featured the president of the TRHA, Dave Schwitzer. He was presented as "a hardworking person who is always trying to improve our way of life in Twin Rivers." A mechanical engineer with a wife and two young children, he commuted to New York daily, but nonetheless had been active in the community ever since he had moved there a year and a half earlier. He started as a block captain and was later elected to the board. Why did he become active? Because "he was dissatisfied with the way the internal affairs of the community were being handled." He sought to make the trust more responsive and Twin Rivers more cohesive. His keenest disappointment was the absence of a civic center in Twin Rivers, promised but not delivered by the builder. Such a central gathering place, like "an old-fashioned town meeting hall," would, he declared, counteract apathy and engender the community spirit needed for self-government (*The Periscope*, 10 May 1974, p. 11).

A third profile featured Neal Nevitt, chairman of the TAB, who was perturbed about the indifference of the residents to public issues. He had thought that "by moving into a newly developing community the residents would have been happy to seize the chance to shape and mold the community." Instead, he found that most people just sat back and watched "the community evolve." He targeted a more responsive trust, the lawsuit, and the absence of a civic building along with a recreation center as top priorities for Twin Rivers. A "many-faceted person" of wide interests — bike riding, theater, and gourmet cooking (his own) — he also managed a rock group on the side. He and his wife, then working toward her master's degree in special education, were both graduates of Brooklyn College. In the diversity of interests actively pursued and the commitment to working for the community, Nevitt typified the extraordinary qualities of the early leaders of the community (*The Periscope*, 15 November 1974, p. 17).

Other monthly profiles included Carolyn Hamilton, Twin Rivers librarian, "one of the people that makes Twin Rivers a successful community"; Marty Mark, "Fireman of the Year," who admitted to "an immense feeling of satisfaction when he has successfully helped to contain and extinguish a fire"; Marjorie Behrens, member of the board of directors of the TRHA and newest managing editor of *The Periscope*, who had been active in the community ever since moving there with her husband and two young children three years before. She felt very strongly "that people ought to do more than complain . . . and work constructively towards solving their problems" (*The Periscope*, 15 February 1975, p. 25).

And then there were Norma and Tony de Canzio, four-year residents of the community, "who devoted most of their spare time" working in the area of recreation. Responsible for the pools, swimming programs, and tennis lessons, they supervised a staff of thirty and served a population of 960 residents. This was in addition to their other community activities, such as membership on the Trust Advisory Board for Tony, and the League of Women voters for Norma.

The first board of directors of the Twin Rivers Homeowners Association consisted of eight men and one woman. The woman, a vice president for publications, had moved to Twin Rivers from nearby New Brunswick. The men included an architect, two engineers, a credit manager for a New York firm, an attorney in nearby Trenton, a Ph.D. in business administration, and a personnel manager in New York City. All were married with young children and all would leave their mark on the community.

A decade later, the residents featured were those who had lived in Twin Rivers for at least a decade and maintained high levels of service to the community. For example, Claudia Rosenberg founded the Parent Watch and the Crime Watch Program, actively lobbied for more police, was treasurer of the parent group at the school, and served on the TRHA (*The Periscope*, July 1985, p. 12).

She and other candidates for the TRHA board stressed familiar as well as novel themes. Familiar were the pledge to make a commitment to the community, to help solve the teen situation, and to increase police security. Novel was the concern for the physical plant and a capital reserve fund for emergencies. Property values, always of importance, became an even more salient concern as residents grew reluctant to pay for needed improvements, yet also wanted to secure their benefits.

In addition to local activists and volunteers, there were local heroes to point to with pride. Ten-year-old Mark Camiscioli saved the life of a friend who had fallen through the ice in Quad 4 lake (*West Windsor Heights Herald*, July 1983); a group of high school students helped residents exit from a burning building. Other honored local notables included Perry L. Drew, who had been physical plant manager of the township schools and for whom one of the two elementary schools in Twin Rivers was named. Still other residents were featured for being touched by tragedy (man drowns in Quad I pool) or triumph (student wins science prize). There were beauty contest winners and victorious baseball teams. Recent arrivals were welcomed with special mentions in *The Periscope* and departures were noted—residents whom "we will miss . . ." All of these contributed to the emerging collective profile of the admirable resident of Twin Rivers. Out of such images, sentiments, impressions, and events, a community grows its symbolic skin.

Twin Rivers well illustrates the operation of social incentives, such as prestige or respect, for the "achievement of group interest"; the social incentives may actually outweigh economic ones and "may be used to mobilize a latent group" (Olson 1965, pp. 60–61).

By the 1990s the theme of community as "home" became more salient. A newcomers night in February 1996 noted that several attendees had been raised in Twin Rivers, had left for school or jobs, and had "all grown up and decided to move 'home.'" Residents were frequently reminded: "Twin Rivers is our home. Take an interest in it" (*Twin Rivers Today*, March 1996, p. 2). Exhortations to build for the long term, "be part of planning the future," work "for the betterment of the community," repeat the earliest themes.

In January 1996 the TRHA board president focused his New Year's remarks on increasing resident participation, improving rule enforcement, identifying areas where service could be improved, and fostering better "communication in the community"—all traditional concerns of longstanding (*Twin Rivers Today*, January 1996, p. 2). These hopes were also included in a local variation of the Ten Commandments, offered by trust administrator Joseph Vuzzo as his New Year's resolutions:

Continue a high standard of maintenance and preventative maintenance programs.

Increase property values in the community. . . . promote and market the community.

Improve communications through mailings, flyers, *Twin Rivers Today*, and a computer bulletin board.

Continue public or resident forums at the regular meetings of the board of directors.

Accelerate our quest to make Twin Rivers the most desirable residential family community in the state.

Instruct children to pick up after themselves; no gum or candy wrappers on the ground.

Maintain our homes in a manner of which we all can be proud.

Respect and consider our neighbors in all of our actions.

Get involved in board committees to effect positive change in the community.

Accentuate the positives of living in Twin Rivers, not only within the community, but outside the community as well. (*Twin Rivers Today*, January 1996, pp. 1–2)

A similar New Year's reflection by TRHA board member and chair of the Community Awareness Committee, Evan Greenberg, sought practical advances such as a finished shopping center and continued better relations with the township and county, in part to "ensure that Twin Rivers gets the recognition it deserves." In that vein he reminded residents of the need to "stay focused on the goals that strengthen Twin Rivers, that build up its prestige, that improve the value of our homes, that break down barriers between neighbors and between courts." He urged that all residents work toward a community that "looks after itself, protects itself, keeps itself whole. . . . It's 1996 and Twin Rivers must focus" (*Twin Rivers Today*, January 1996, p. 4).

Ina Heiman moved into a three-bedroom townhouse in Twin Rivers with her husband in 1971. Active in the community throughout, she was a block captain who helped launch the library in 1973, while he served as a member of the board of trustees for over ten years. They raised two daughters and expressed their appreciation of Twin Rivers in countless ways. After her husband's death (a memorial park bears his name), Ina Heiman joined the board of trustees, while also working at the Twin Rivers library. These were her views on Twin Rivers in 1998:

> Over the years, Twin Rivers has definitely changed for the better. A large mix of cultures, religions, and ethnicities, it is a cosmos where everyone learns the "give and take" of living together. The children seem to benefit the most. I see many who leave, marry and then return to settle in Twin Rivers! . . . My suggestion to everyone is this: Be understanding and empathic in all of your . . . interactions. No one wants their lawn or flowers crushed by your child's bicycle. A pink house and a purple roof may help your individuality, but it destroys the harmony of our architecture. It helps greatly when living close together to . . . think "Golden Rule." Common courtesies become especially important. I love Twin Rivers. It's a great place to live! (*Twin Rivers Today*, March 1998, p. 14)

The 1997 candidates for the board of trustees made a varied group. Of these five volunteers, according to *Twin Rivers Today* (November 1997), one had lived in Twin Rivers since its inception. One had lived there for only two years. One was a retiree; several had raised children in Twin Rivers. And here is what each stressed as the problems to confront:

Hold on to what's wonderful about Twin Rivers and work on any lingering problems such as parking and the shopping center . . . and bring us all together in a still better tomorrow.

I feel that architectural controls should be revised to allow homeowners more choices . . . yet maintain the integrity of the design of the community.

Twin Rivers has given so much to our family; I feel it's time to give back to Twin Rivers. . . . I am dedicated to do what it takes to help Twin Rivers continually progress as a desired community.

Get an understanding of my neighbors' thoughts and needs. . . . I have ample time and desire to devote, to help improve the quality of life in Twin Rivers.

Twin Rivers is entering a new era. With a newly installed trust manager and with help from board members and residents alike, we can accomplish a great deal. (ibid.)

Early and later, candidates for the board of directors uttered similar themes and gave similar accounts of their hopes and dreams. They describe how they took years to make the move and how pleased they are, basically, with the house, the pool, and the mix of friendly people — their investments "in the totality of life."

One seriously considered proposal that surfaced several times during the 1980s was that of changing the name of Twin Rivers to something more glamorous. Ostensibly, this was to attract prime ratables and to improve resale value of the homes by appealing to the prestige and status interests of potential buyers, but it also reflected the aspirations of the residents. Nearby Princeton was the main inspiration for a new name; suggestions included Princeton Plains, Princeton Heights, and Princeton Lakes. The argument in favor was expressed in the following excerpt from an editorial:

[P]eople are always striving to better themselves, improve their self-image and public image. . . . Why can't a community do the same thing? If changing the name of the Township (which has no historical or sentimental value) can accomplish all this, why not do it? And, if having Princeton in the name is the golden ring, then go for it! (*The Periscope*, June 1982, p. 2)

But the township, finally, decided against it.

As time passed, there were more elaborate descriptions of Twin Rivers' qualities as a unique community and this helped improve its public image. Here is one couple's assessment:

We have the luxury of shopping in New York or Philadelphia. . . . We enjoy our leisure time in a quiet, rural setting. We are proud of that. The people who have moved here over the years have come mostly from urban areas to enjoy the less hectic and crowded lifestyle we enjoy. (*The Periscope*, August 1982, p. 6)

A resident of the condominiums stated:

What I find when I get off at night . . . fulfills me for the most part. There are things which interest me, even if I don't often take advantage of them: an attractive place to live in an area that offers opportunity to do many of the things right here in our own backyard. . . . we have swimming, tennis, and other sports, nice, flat, smooth country roads for bicycling, leisurely walks or dedicated jogging; privacy as well as sociability.

Shopping was praised, as was the fresh produce at local stands, and the restaurants nearby. The proximity of Princeton, only ten miles away, was considered a plus with its offerings of theater, art, and music. Enthused one resident: "[E]verywhere around here is history. . . . In the summer I feel I'm on vacation every weekend . . . and anything we might want to do is less than an hour away."

For some, relaxing with a book on one's private patio was always an option. So while the pace was demanding for those who commuted to jobs—rise at 5:30 A.M., board the commuter bus at 6:30, return home at 6:35 P.M. or later—the rewards were patent: nice neighbors, getting to know more and more residents each year, and "developing some roots" (*The Periscope*, March 1983, p. 4).

Upon his return from a National Condominium Association meeting in 1983, the trust administrator reported to the entire community that his exploration of two other large PUDs indicated that some of Twin Rivers' problems—rule enforcement, annual assessments, and collections—were universal, but that they were handled better by Twin Rivers. "I am more convinced than ever that our policy of uniform maintenance, preventative maintenance, capital improvement, and total community involvement is the most advantageous way to go," he stated (*The Periscope*, November 1983, p. 1).

Flattering portraits of residents, sports meets, and community service did much to publicize the community as a locus of desirable activities, as did the prizes given to the winners of contests for naming the local paper, *The Periscope*, in the early 1970s. There were community-wide celebrations and holidays that engendered a spirit of togetherness, and spontaneous social encounters. A big event was the annual Twin Rivers Day, launched in 1977. Every year thereafter the event was featured, embroidered with the diverse talents of the participants.

There were hot dogs and popcorn, of course, but also knishes and bagels, pony rides, Buffy the Ten-Foot Clown, games of chance and skill, booths displaying homemade cakes or pottery or knitted puppets, and representatives of civic, political, and service organizations (cancer care, MADD), veterans groups, and the National Organization for Women. Hundreds of balloons dotted the landscape, and demonstrations as well as rides by the fire company and the rescue squad gave eager children an opportunity to don helmets or climb up mobile fire ladders. From 10 A.M. to 5 P.M., hundreds of residents turned out to celebrate their community and each other. Free blood-pressure checks and demonstrations, make-up lessons, aerobic dancing, and clown make-up demonstrations were among the day's attractions. Athletic contests and talent shows revealed the feats of the young under the proud gaze of their parents. Sponsored by the Community Trust, the event became a kind of summer solstice. Later, *The Periscope* would relive the experience for its readers and enshrine the names of winners at baseball, basketball, and tennis as well as of the Little Miss Twin Rivers (Jessica, aged five) and Little Mr. Twin Rivers (Michael, aged four) contests. Coordinated by the recreation director, Clark R. Lissner, the event depended on the volunteer efforts of many people and generated wide community participation. The good weather (a rain date was always planned for), the excited children, the relaxed adults, the varied activities and tempting food and drink created a feeling of an old-time town fair or picnic in which the normal feuds and sparks were submerged in the surge of mirth and good will that buoys up the common life and the sense of belonging to a larger totality.

There were other annual events for particular segments or groups, such as the Christmas or Chanukah parties or the condominium picnics. In all of these activities, the efforts of the few benefited the many, for nearly always it was a minority who did the hard work — without direct compensation — of planning, organizing, and making the celebration possible.

The imprint of anonymous benefactors is especially poignant in a new community when people move away, leaving behind parts of themselves in iris beds, tire playgrounds, memories of cakes baked and cookies served at countless gatherings, projects initiated, and, even more difficult, carried through. In November 1981, *The Periscope* noted a couple whose flowers and plants helped beautify the community: "Every spring we will be reminded of the Blums, so a part of them does remain in Twin Rivers" (p. 6).

Gradually, then, the anonymous collective "you" becomes a symbol of countless contributions, large and small, of unknown individuals who have poured their portion of civic-mindedness into the common fund of stored memories and achievements. In this slow but steady way, a collective self-image and a legacy of sociability begins to take shape.

PART II
A COMMUNITY IS LAUNCHED

C. Building the Foundations

CHAPTER 9
SPACE, PLACE, AND DESIGN

A local area is not automatically a community.

— A Twin Rivers resident

Space, territory, turf belong to the domain where the social and the physical meet. They are simultaneously given and socially constructed.

College students have as their top priority upon arriving at the citadel the matter of space—that is, the room, and usually the roommates, that will house them. They spend countless hours thereafter maneuvering to get the space they desire or require.

This widely shared preoccupation with personal space extends throughout our society—from corporate managers' concerns about obtaining an office appropriate to their status to a couple's search for the house that will launch their life together. It is a critical issue and the source of anguish as well as delight, as one is reminded, often painfully, when neighbor strikes out at neighbor in long smoldering rancor over a boundary they may have uneasily shared for years. Space is always pregnant with meaning.

Planning environments for a contemporary population involves crucial spatial decisions about what to place where and why. Many elements have to be in place at the start. Satisfying aggregate demands is a challenge, especially under fluid social conditions as newcomers steadily add to the changing social mix. This differs from residential mobility due to job demands or the development of community over time, where people can shape their environs, step by step, through give and take. To construct a new town is enormously difficult. So many elements are involved in actually creating it, with political matters at least as important as economic and financial ones.

Typically, old building codes need revision, which brings in the local politicians, legislators, and lawyers; then there is fear of invasion of one's home turf by outsiders lacking the "right" values and manners. This is expressed not directly but by familiar euphemisms — the strain on existing facilities, excessive densities, traffic congestion, school overcrowding. Other fears concern demographic shifts — too many singles or elderly, too many children, or poor or immigrants — all threatening established traditions.

Newspapers also do their part in heating up the atmosphere. Hence, planned developments generally require extensive advance preparation, including public relations, cultivation of the media, paid advertising, and engaged citizens.

In all of this, and understandably, the chief targets of residents' frustrations — builders and developers — are significant risk takers. "They . . . have walked the rough, uneven, unpredictable path through planning boards, boards of adjustments, permits, approvals . . . lawsuits, appeals, affirmances, reversals, and in between all of these, changes in both statutory and decisional law. That can turn a case upside down" (Kirp et al., 1997, p. 139).

Traditional communities are planless "products of many past generations," their mores and beliefs having "grown slowly by innumerable additions and modifications without any regard for consistency, without any idea of subordinating them to some common and general aim" (Thomas and Znaniecki 1958, pp. 1423–24). The fit between social institutions and individual attitudes was not consciously planned but developed through long experience. New communities, by contrast, must create their institutions all at once. They are organized teleologically in terms of explicit goals, new values, and assessments of aggregate needs. Theirs is a task of a high order.

Another problem stems from the social assumptions inherent in the spatial design. One fact typically ignored in contemporary community plans is that the residents do not start out with a blank slate to be shaped by brick and mortar. Everyone brings ideas and aspirations of their own into the new setting. If the design does not readily accommodate these, it engenders almost immediate resistance that carries over into many areas. As residents attempt to bend the design of the nascent community to their wills, they often destroy it in frustration.

For example, from the start, the twelve tot lots were heavily criticized. Since their location was well concealed they proved tempting to teenagers for extracurricular activities, especially at night, which annoyed adult residents who had to clean up the broken glasses, beer bottles, and food remains the next day.

But while residents had their criticisms of design, they also had their favorite design features. Most appealing was the bridge over the quad I lake, which offered solace to many who responded to its beauty. "How can anyone not be satisfied" asked one Twin Rivers official, "when they have such a lovely sight available to them."

By tapping the responses of the Twin Rivers residents to their physical environment, as well as their modifications to it, it was possible to assess the fit between design and behavior, thereby helping to clarify the most elusive aspect of design, generally referred to as "the human factor."

Several design concepts structured the physical plan of Twin Rivers: the distinction between public and private spaces; the separation of vehicular from pedestrian movement; the walking distance ideal; the neighborhood (quad) idea; and the townhouse.

Several indicators were used to explore residents' uses and reactions. One was observation of strategic sites to tap aggregate uses. Another was residents' subjective reactions gleaned from the three large-scale attitude surveys and more than five-hundred face-to-face interviews. A third indicator tracked positive and negative modifications of the physical environment. *Positive* modifications include embellishments such as plantings, decorations, and signage. *Negative* modifications refer to defacements and destruction of buildings and sites. Finally, we also drew on "participant observation," whereby the investigator becomes part of the scene being studied and engages in certain typical activities — playing tennis, relaxing at the swimming pool, taking a child to school, or shopping at the convenience store — to experience these directly. Together, these various indicators provided critical information on how the design worked out in practice.

The good life includes good space, a space that is serviceable, accessible, and beautiful. And since our lives are spent in houses, work places, and communities, the built environment — its texture, appearance, and symbolic meaning — has substantial consequences. Indeed research has shown that housing, neighborhood, and the wider community play an important, even decisive, part in life satisfactions. Many subtle factors are at work here, involving rules of spatial behavior and conceptions of what constitutes attractive and reassuring surroundings. Spatial and territorial integrity contribute to one's sense of physical, psychological, and social self-preservation by giving one a sense of identity and security (Campbell et al., 1976, p. 174ff; Ittelson 1974, p. 129ff). Physical arrangements, location, centrality, and territoriality contribute to the creation of a sense of community and well-being. Design does not guarantee the attainment of these goals but it may facilitate or impede their realization. Good design, like a dress that fits well, enhances the self-satisfaction of those dependent on it.

Bettelheim has described an appropriate physical setting as the "safe center" from which life can go forward. And his own researches have shown how the built environment may influence the process of getting well, of gaining confidence, of trusting others (Bettelheim 1974). Indeed, the questions asked of an institutional therapeutic setting are not too different from the questions asked of environments generally:

> Will this place provide . . . safety . . .? Will it help create order out of my confusion? . . . Will it force me into a mold? Is the building attractive and reassuring enough to become the shell which will protect me . . .? (ibid., p. 103)

The issues of safety, protection, reassurance, coherence are of concern to everyone at some time. Newman has explored the significance of design for a feeling of safety in low-income residential environments (Newman 1972), and the desire for safety underlies the establishment of retirement communities as well as the move to new communities.

Indeed, one of the main goals of the New Towns movement has been its endeavor to achieve a better overall quality of life through design. It has stressed the creation of visual order, physical integrity, social balance, community participation, and ready accessibility to needed educational, health, and social services. That New Towns did not attain these to the extent hoped for should not detract from their considerable achievements, including the fact that they pioneered in the effort to include design as a way of improving the quality of life.

Thus design defines an environment, symbolizes the availability of resources, and expresses a plan for living. By shaping the spatial contexts in which life takes place, it also helps to maintain values to live by. Personal space, privacy, community, concern for others, opportunity for contact and movement — all are dependent on design. In this sense, the creation of desirable and workable physical settings is part of the pursuit — and the attainment — of human happiness.

The House: Property, Shelter, and Private Domain

The ownership of a townhouse is double-edged. As is true of home-ownership generally, it satisfies the need for a separate and private domain, but in being physically linked, it gives owners a financial and territorial stake in each other's lives and in the land they possess in

Table 9.1
What Is the Key Ingredient of an Ideal Community?

	1970s	*1980s*
"A detached house" (first response)	5%	27%
Did not mention a detached house	95%	73%
	N = 250	N = 71

The Twice-Interviewed Sample*

	1970s	*1980s*
"A detached house" (first response)	5%	21%
Did not mention a detached house	95%	79%
		N = 44

*These are residents interviewed both in 1973 and 1983.

common. The ideal of one's house as one's very own castle is hard to sustain under these conditions. Since the residents of Twin Rivers were traditional in their orientation to home ownership and all that implies for family, one would have expected the typical response to anything less than a single-family, freestanding house to be ambivalent. It thus came as a considerable surprise to see how positively residents reacted to the townhouses. Whichever indicator we examined — the reactions to the townhouse as a whole; the improvements sought; the responses to density, noise, or neighbors — the house came out as a plus. None of the anticipated fears — from invasions of privacy to intrusive neighbors — materialized for more than a small fraction of the population. On a fifteen-item index of housing satisfaction based on liking the townhouse overall and on specific ratings of various dimensions, two-thirds of Twin Rivers residents liked their houses, one-third were enthusiastic, and only a small minority had mixed feelings. A minuscule proportion (2% or less) said they disliked their townhouses. Townhouses, though sharing walls and common spaces, are connected in the minds of their owners, not with apartments, which they resemble somewhat, but with freestanding houses. Indeed, there is a rather consistent pattern of association between housing type and life satisfaction: Among apartment dwellers, it is noticeably low while among townhouse residents, it is high.

A house is seen not only as a haven and a shelter but also as a provider of outdoor play space for children with adult supervision nearby, and of space where adults may gather for gossip or social celebrations. On all these counts, the townhouse proved more than adequate. Even the high densities turned out to be acceptable provided that they also allowed for some private space and amenities close by. Contrary to much expert opinion, therefore, residents were most receptive to what was then considered a novel form of housing in suburbia.

Nonetheless, for some, ideals died hard. Despite the fact that they lived in attached housing and were even ready to acknowledge its advantages, a minority of residents remained faithful to the idea of a free-standing house. In fact, 5 to 10 percent knew almost immediately that a townhouse was not for them and left the community as soon as they could. A larger proportion stayed but may have clung to the ideal of a detached house.

Comparative data show that in the 1970s, in the flush of high expectations about the community, virtually none of the residents considered a detached house a key ingredient of an ideal community. By the 1980s, when problems had become evident, one-fourth regarded a detached house as the solution to their problems, and some would act on this conviction by moving away (table 9.1).

The comparison of homeowners interviewed twice, a decade apart, still occupying the same houses they had initially purchased, showed a similar pattern. Only 5 percent mentioned a detached house as a significant ingredient of an ideal community in the mid-1970s, but by the mid-1980s, 21 percent did so. But in both cases, the large majority were well satisfied and stuck with their townhouses.

Research has shown that residential satisfaction reflects four main land- and space-related factors: (1) maintenance and upkeep of property and grounds; (2) external appearance of the dwellings; (3) shape and layout of the buildings; and (4) landscaping (Becker 1977, p. 22).

The fact that the townhouses of Twin Rivers proved agreeable to most residents suggests that it is possible to find satisfaction in a housing type that may not be one's ultimate ideal. Indeed, the data suggest that most people don't hold on to one specific housing preference, but modify their ideas on the basis of experience.

A good deal seems to depend on skillful design that is flexible, and space that can be modified. Design can provide the illusion of spaciousness, thereby enlarging what Becker has called "the psychological size of the house" (ibid., p. 27). Design can make a small house appear spacious, even luxurious, by the use of skylights, high ceilings, windows above eye level, and mirrors. In our image-conscious culture, appearance is all, and the illusion of space is apparently as effective as the actual provision of space. By and large, the Twin Rivers townhouses seem to have provided both the space needed by the inhabitants and the spaciousness desired by them.

Townhouse Living and Privacy

There are many who believe that townhouse living cannot provide privacy, that coveted nugget of well-being in an individual-oriented society.

Table 9.2
Ratings of Privacy by Decade

	1970s	1980s
Privacy is		
Particularly good	32%	31%
Adequate	35%	45%
Bad	33%	24%
	N = 167*	N = 71*

*Totals include townhouse dwellers only.

High population densities, as well as the visual and auditory proximity of neighbors, it is feared, affect privacy adversely.

This study provides some interesting data about personal space in a dense settlement. Privacy fared well in Twin Rivers (table 9.2). In both the 1970s and the 1980s, the large majority of residents thought privacy was satisfactory, and one-third thought it especially so. The minority who gave it low marks decreased over the decade. This suggests that either people's need for privacy changed or that they became habituated to townhouse living. Privacy has been associated with user satisfaction in general, and this is true for Twin Rivers as well. There is a clear-cut relationship between high ratings on privacy and strong liking for the community (table 9.3).

Indeed, ratings on privacy improved with length of residence in the community. The twice-interviewed residents, for example, gave privacy higher ratings in the 1980s, when 90 percent were satisfied with it, than in the 1970s, when only 57 percent were satisfied. This again suggests

Table 9.3
Satisfaction with Twin Rivers Community by Rating of Privacy

Rating of privacy	1980s townhouse residents saying they like Twin Rivers very much
Particularly good	50%
Adequate	40%
Poor	10%
	100%

N = 71
X^2 = 10.17
df = 4
sig. = 0.031

that people adapt on the basis of experience and can learn to adjust their needs for privacy to new conditions.

Privacy is a function not only of density but of visibility and observability. For example, the parking areas in Twin Rivers are located in front of the houses, so it is easy to track the activities of other residents, and in the early years many were preoccupied with the activities of their neighbors. This made some feel as if they were living in a fishbowl (O'Toole 1971, p. 10). In time, however, people tended to lose interest in watching or ignored much of what they saw, spontaneously generating a privacy based on inattention.

However privacy was defined, it was not a problem at Twin Rivers. This further reinforced the acceptability of townhouse living for this contemporary population.

Neighbors in Townhouse Developments

One meaning of community is good fellowship and neighborliness. An environment that is perceived as friendly and supportive enlists positive in-group feelings and loyalties, whereas one experienced as deficient in these respects diminishes the sense of community by bringing negative and uncooperative feelings to the fore.

High densities, by increasing physical proximity, can promote either interpersonal friction or closeness. In Twin Rivers closeness was more common. The large majority of residents gave their neighbors very positive ratings in the 1970s, 1980s, and 1990s. Two determinants of neighborly feeling could be identified: (1) housing tenure and (2) spatial design.

The social division between those who own their own dwellings and those who rent them has often been noted. Such a division often creates disunity in an emerging community and reinforces social stereotypes. Homeowners tend to live in houses, renters in apartments.

Twin Rivers homeowners did tend to look down on apartment dwellers as being less desirable neighbors and less responsible citizens. In turn, apartment dwellers resented these slights and felt isolated and excluded from the incipient community. The social distance between owners and renters was vast from the earliest days. The two formed separate worlds and stayed within their borders. Adult homeowners in particular tended to confine their range of sociability to other homeowners, either within their own courts or outside them.

These patterns, once started, continued on their own momentum. Housing tenure was thus a significant determinant of patterns of sociability. Spatial design affected sociability in a somewhat different way. For the residents in general, and for ex–New Yorkers in particular, major sites for sociability were the common parking areas in front of the townhouses, a space where the neighbors' comings and goings could readily be observed, and where children played—the danger of cars notwithstanding. Above all, insiders could readily be distinguished from outsiders, as residents were able at a glance to determine who belonged and who did not.

Spatial visibility seems to have exercised a positive effect on sociability, as residents used the small front lawns for conviviality and gossip. That this was a reflection of siting rather than merely the availability of open space is indicated by the fact that the grassy common areas at the rear of the houses were not used for such socializing at all. Residents found them unsuitable or unappealing. They seemed to lack the necessary spatial ambiance for sociability.

Thus high densities made for high visibility, while the sharing of public spaces, parking areas, and services such as lawn maintenance and garbage disposal made for a high degree of interdependence. It was hard to avoid neighborly contact, and most residents desired not less but more such contact. The closed cul-de-sac arrangements also gave the housing courts a sense of spatial, if not always social, cohesion. The visual awareness generated there made for a gradual development of mutual recognition followed by verbal greetings, and these led to whatever further social contacts seemed agreeable.

In sum, house-related land and space were significantly related to privacy as well as to sociability. In addition to the spaces they shared, residents also cherished spaces of their own in the form of small patios fenced off at the rear of their townhouses. These small spaces, only between two hundred and four hundred square feet, were of great personal and symbolic significance. In addition to the outdoor space they provided, they distinguished the townhouse from the apartment, thereby bringing it closer to the traditional image of a detached house. Part of the charm of this space was that it permitted the residents to express themselves freely, without the social controls that operated throughout the community. And residents relished their little corners of solitude. Some created beautiful gardens, communed with nature, enjoyed barbecued dinners in good weather, or contemplated the eternal verities in private. It was a delicious taste of freedom in a community of shared spaces and ubiquitous architectural controls.

In conclusion, a major lesson gained from this close look at a community in the making is that a population wedded in principle to the single-family house can learn to appreciate, and even prefer, a form of shared housing in practice. This learning proceeded more rapidly than one would have thought and suggests that a well-designed townhouse can satisfy aspirations for privacy as well as for community. Given current U.S. economic and demographic trends toward smaller families, single-parent and two-job households, prolonged singlehood, high divorce rates, and an aging population, townhouse living may well become the housing ideal of the future.

The Walking Distance Ideal

An important planning principle in new communities is that of walking distance. It is based on the assumption that convenient access to desired facilities such as shops, schools, recreation, and friends would encourage people to walk to various destinations. How did this assumption fare in Twin Rivers?

From the start, virtually all residents in principle approved of walking but very few put principle into practice. Only one-fifth consistently resorted to walking for their visits and errands. The large majority relied on their cars and drove everywhere, even short distances. Were they simply children of their time or were there other reasons for not availing themselves of the opportunity to walk?

The research literature suggests that in modern times, the walking-distance principle works under certain conditions only. Distances between destinations should be short (two hundred to four hundred feet), and there should be attractive and appealing sights along the way so that walking becomes interesting and has elements of surprise (Langdon 1994, p. 131). This was not the case in Twin Rivers. Distances between homes and shopping, schools, or pools generally exceeded the maximum, and the typical half-a-mile distances proved discouraging to most residents, especially at the beginning when the landscape was bare, construction blight was everywhere, and neither public buildings nor private dwellings made the surroundings seem inviting.

For this community design, then, the walking-distance principle proved a mistake, a costly mistake, it turned out, because the developer's goal to minimize the car led to a serious parking crunch later. Already in the early 1970s, more than two-fifths of the households had at least two cars and two-thirds of the residents used these at least once each day.

By the early 1980s, all of these patterns had accelerated. More than one half (55%) of the households now had two cars, and 85 percent used these daily: 90 percent for shopping, to visit with friends, for chauffeuring their children to school (only 14% used the bus) and to extracurricular activities.

Given the pervasive use of the car, the planned-for pedestrian-vehicular division could not be maintained. This is the more surprising since this was to be a community dedicated to healthful activities in an environment of parks, playgrounds, walking paths, and open spaces. The 164 acres of open space boasted two lakes, four swimming clubs, twelve tennis courts, and many tot lots and children's playgrounds, along with the thirty acres reserved for parks, roadways, and parking areas. These were greatly appreciated but did not encourage more than a fraction of the residents to walk.

Parking Spaces: Mine, Thine, or Whose?

> Without doubt, one of the biggest problems in Twin Rivers today is the parking spaces. Two-car families have become three-, four-, and five-car families and parking spaces have become more and more difficult to find near our homes.
>
> —Colitsas, *The Periscope*

Since the builder originally envisioned a walking-distance community in which the car would be, if not superfluous, only minimally used, parking was not supposed to become a problem in Twin Rivers. However, as early as the mid-1970s, pedestrians were second to the car in their imprint on the community. The photographs taken in the early 1970s showed a striking predominance in the ratio of cars to people despite the fact that the prime objective was to photograph people in various activities. Of the 1,608 photographs taken in the years from 1972 through 1974, 1,316 showed people and 4,346, cars. Cars dominated the visual landscape, and were part of a three-way complex of house, car, and street. Indeed, a more detailed study of residents' reactions to a set of photographs of various sites and buildings of Twin Rivers showed that for the cross-section interviewed, the car and the townhouse together comprised the most frequently cited "typical" image of Twin Rivers (Wagner 1979).

In opting for the "walking-distance community," the developer had allotted only one and a half to two parking spaces per dwelling unit in the parking courts. This meant that more houses could be built but it also preordained huge problems in the future if his calculations proved incorrect, which they did. As the young families who first moved in became older and the children became teenagers, another car was often added. And as wives resumed employment, another car often proved necessary. By 1984 three cars per family was considered average, leading the trust administrator to request that third and fourth cars be parked at the end of the courts or in visitor parking lots. But requests are not laws and were frequently ignored, thereby exacerbating the parking problem in Twin Rivers. As parking violations increased, so did summonses and the irritations of residents. The new owner of the shopping center warned residents that those who parked at the shopping center would have to pay a monthly fee of thirty dollars per car. Those who ignored the warning signs suddenly found their cars towed. While signs and fines brought the problem under control for the shopping center, for the rest of the community parking became an ever sharper thorn in the side of civic order.

The parking of commercial vehicles in the courts and on private roadways likewise became an issue. "On one evening early in February 1985, the Physical Plants manager listed and tagged 27 non-conforming vehicles within townhouse parking lots." Some of these belonged to renters ignorant of the rules, for whom fines and towing were to provide costly lessons. "The Trust does not enjoy bothering or penalizing our residents," trust administrator Vuzzo announced. "Cooperation by conformance will eliminate that problem" (*The Periscope*, March 1985, p. 1). The problem persisted, however, and the board noted that "an increasing amount of time is being spent on the parking situation in Twin Rivers" (*The Periscope*, May 1985, p. 2).

In their distress, the residents called on the builder, the trust, and the township "to solve this problem before it is too late." They also spread the story, a myth according to some, that the developer had promised that he would tell prospective residents with two cars that Twin Rivers was not a place for them to buy, all to no avail (*The Periscope*, May 1973, p. 2). Three decades later, the problem has only become worse.

In an effort to deal with the situation, fines and summonses were formalized in public announcements:

> Please be advised unauthorized vehicles driving, parking, or standing in emergency lanes are now subject to either a fine, summons, or towing at the owner's expense. (*The Periscope*, May 1982)

Almost a year later, the tone became more urgent:

> Numerous residents have ignored [the] restrictions and have parked boats, campers, trailers, trucks, jeeps, and other unapproved vehicles within the PUD. Accordingly, as of October 15, 1979, violations will be punished by towing the offending vehicle at the owner's expense and may result in a lawsuit against the owner. Also, recreational privileges may be revoked for the owner and family members "until there is compliance with the parking rules." (The board of the TRHA, *The Periscope*, January 1983, p. 5)

These were desperate measures for a parking situation out of control and with no ready solution in sight. By 1987 a parking review committee was established by the TRHA Board. It reported the following as persistent and unresolved issues:

1. "Serious overcrowding" on many courts—so that residents cannot find parking spaces in their courts on a regular basis.
2. Parking of oversized vehicles in the courts creating safety hazards for pedestrians
3. "Abuses of parking privileges"—blocking spaces, parking in emergency vehicles spaces, leaving unused vehicles in crowded courts, parking before other residents' houses.

One suggestion that emerged from their deliberations was for the board and the trust to create up to eight additional spaces in the most seriously crowded courts. This helped somewhat. Other "solutions" were tried with some small success, but could not surmount the failure of the original design concept of the walking-distance community.

Obviously, the car culture permeated this new Eden. Ironically, a gas station was initially the gateway to the community. Still, as necessary as the car proved to be for the daily routines of the residents, it was often deplored in the interviews, not only as an aesthetic irritant to the tree-and-space-hungry settlers of Twin Rivers but to the turf battles over parking spaces that would come to put a heavy strain on human relationships.

The parking problem was a genuine test of the good will of Twin Rivers residents. Parking spaces close to home had been one of the attractive features offered to buyers, but such spaces were soon at a premium and became a huge bone of contention. Disputed claims to particular spaces became endemic. And so did the indignation over assaults to one's honor if one's turf was violated. Sometimes fisticuffs ensued followed by calls to the police. Rancor increased, as did spite, expressed in such behavior as explicitly taking another's parking space or taking up to two at once (*The Periscope*, June 1980, p. 7). For years, appeals to a sense of community proved ineffective. Fines, towing, and other suggested punitive measures proved unenforceable. Nor were parking problems confined to the lack of parking spaces. Illegal parking—for example, at the elementary school—and reckless driving by service vehicles and moving vans that crossed emergency lanes and ripped up common grounds, were deplored throughout the decades. Faulty communication between the township and Twin Rivers also created considerable tension, because residents were ignorant of township parking rules. Things came to a head when sixteen tickets were issued within one twenty-four-hour period to irate residents of Twin Rivers.

Quite a different, and unexpected, issue concerned the attractiveness of the parking areas as play spaces for the children. Although this was dangerous, it was also uncontrollable. Despite tot lots and playgrounds, "the children never play in their backyards or on their lawns. . . . At any time, including evenings, children of young age may be seen running or riding around, either daring drivers to hit them or unknowingly darting in front of the cars" (Irving Paris, "Letters to the Editor," *The Periscope*, September 1975).

Distance was once again the issue. While the parking courts were dangerous, they were close to home, and children were thus within the gaze of their caretakers. Also, cars were exciting. It took a great deal of effort, not always successful, to channel children — and parents — toward the formally designed play spaces.

The Neighborhood Idea

As a physical and social entity, the neighborhood is basic to the design of Twin Rivers. There are four neighborhoods called quads, each spatially marked off from the others and possessing local foci such as a convenience store, a swimming pool, and tennis courts. Characteristic housing mixes give each quad a special quality. Smaller families are concentrated in the first quad; larger families in quad 3; higher densities in the later quads, and so on.

The neighborhood idea and the walking distance concept were intended to result in the integration of housing, work, shopping, and recreation. Residents were expected to use local facilities and to walk to them whenever possible. These expectations were only partly met due to the initial lack of needed services and the aforementioned reliance on the car, even for short distances. Also, employment as well as shopping took residents away from Twin Rivers on a regular basis early on. The promised coordination and integration thus remained more concept than actuality.

The dispersive tendencies engendered by the unfinished nature of the community in its formative years were counteracted by the recreational facilities, especially the tennis courts and swimming pools, which engendered sociability and some sense of public activities.

Public Space: The Swimming Pools

The swimming pools of Twin Rivers, one to each quad, were heavily used from the first moment on. At a time when the community was still more dream than reality, the pools served a central social function for residents who came not only to swim but also to meet friends, make social contacts, and read, talk, sun, play cards, and *watch other people*. Eating at the pools was a source of contention and secret violations for years until 1982 when patios were explicitly added, which dispelled the animosity generated by the prohibition.

Pools were also among the first loci of territoriality. Originally, pools were to be accessible to residents in all quads, but when the quad 1 residents feared that their pool would be swamped by quad 2 residents, the move to confine pool usage by quad ensued. There were a variety of justifications: "the pools will become overcrowded;" "our children have the right of first access;" and "it is 'our pool,'" pure and simple. Somewhat later, as residents filled in quads 2 and 3, aspersions were cast on the recent arrivals. They were adjudged noisier, ruder, and not as deserving of whatever benefits the quad 1 residents sought to monopolize.

Over time, also, formal rules for pool usage became necessary because residents violated elementary codes of conduct for their own convenience. One of the most conspicuous was the consumption of food and drink at the pool without regard for cleanup. Others involved destruction of pool equipment, disregard of pool hours, and blatant disregard for other pool users. When persuasion to be considerate and mindful of civility proved ineffective, fines were introduced for specific violations. These worked to some extent but did not induce a philosophy of civic concern. Nonetheless, the extensive pool usage does generate a partial semblance of public life, where residents encounter one another and get a take on what is happening in the community.

Public space has long been considered an essential component of community. It is "the space . . . where public interaction occurs, where people can meet at their leisure, and where free and open discussion can take place." The absence of a public space is a symptom of the absence of community (Gottdiener 1997, p. 139). Even in urban settings, the preservation of public spaces is considered vital for social exchange and exposure to social diversity (Kayden 2000).

A Spatial Imago

To tap resident reactions to the physical characteristics of the nascent community in the period of its founding, photography proved a useful ally of research. To chart the community's changing appearance, a photographic record was kept from year one for more than two decades.

In addition to this longitudinal portrait, photographs were also used to explore the range of aesthetic and symbolic associations residents attached to the physical environment. Over time these crystallized into enduring collective perceptions of the community.

Such perceptions are an important component of people's orientation to a new environment. To grasp something of this process, a series of photos, depicting various sites and features of the built environment, were shown to a sample of seventy-one residents asking each to identify what was pictured, where it was located in the community, and how they reacted to each photo. This research, done in the mid-seventies when residents were largely recent arrivals, showed that the majority of the residents sampled were able to identify more than half of the seventeen photos after only a year or so in the community and had thus been able to familiarize themselves with its more obvious environmental features. (The photos depicted the bus stop, pizza shop, a set of townhouses, recycling bins, a school, a playground). But while residents could identify the *what*, they were far less able to identify the *where*. That demanded a larger grasp of the totality, which developed only gradually and piecemeal.

The cognitive and visual maps residents develop are greatly linked to the coherence of a community's design and the articulation of the built environment with cultural habits and preferences. In the initial years of disorder and unsettledness, many residents were disoriented and had difficulty in mapping the terrain to their satisfaction. Though the trying conditions of the first years were rectified after some time, the negative impressions lingered, constituting a permanent residue in the collective memory.

In the last survey (1999–2000), for example, when trees, landscaping, house façades, and plantings had provided an attractive second skin for the community, aesthetic flaws still rankled. Thus first impressions of the design proved to have a lasting impact and the earliest shared perceptions of the built environment became an enduring cultural legacy.

The Social Context of Design

One frequent assumption in planned residential environments is that the physical shell will engender community, and that community will follow from the sound arrangement of roads, houses, recreational nodes, and a complement of facilities and services. The results of the Twin Rivers experience suggest that there is no such ready coordination. A number of contradictions in the design actually impeded community formation. For example, the ostensible goal was to make Twin Rivers as self-contained as possible, but the majority of breadwinners had to commute to employment outside of the PUD. There was an inherent contradiction between the two objectives that existed in other areas as well.

As noted earlier, the absence of needed facilities at the start led residents to use the malls and supermarkets that were a short distance away by car. The shopping habits thus created were not easily changed, if at all. As a result, the shopping center within Twin Rivers could not thrive and even if the first settlers had patronized it exclusively, revenues would not have been sufficient to make it self-supporting. Hence outside shoppers were actually desirable from a commercial point of view. This created another contradictory pull. How could the shopping center become the collective focus of Twin Rivers yet also serve as a commercial magnet for outsiders? The clash between local and nonlocal shoppers was clearly in evidence.

In addition to problems of meshing macro and micro scales by design, other design issues stemmed from a lack of fit between planning concepts and human behavior. If it is important to them, people will impose their needs on a design and thus distort it. For example, neither the school nor the pool had adequate parking spaces. This was done quite deliberately to give residents an incentive to walk to these sites. However, the residents did not do so. Instead, they drove and parked wherever they pleased, creating a chaotic, and potentially dangerous situation for children and adults alike.

Design cannot compel behavior if it comes up against established habits or beliefs, and people will lash out against design features that attempt to do so. For example, residents ignored the carefully mapped footpaths in favor of paths they created by their own use. In this way residents literally voted with their feet.

These are among the issues that are difficult for architects and planners to resolve because they want to design places and spaces conducive to human comfort and joy while also serving matters of cost and efficiency. Planners and designers of space are not always cognizant of the fact that they pre-cast a collective life whether or not they are able to forecast it. This would not matter quite so much if buildings, roads, and open spaces were disposable or at least flexible. However, once physical boundaries have been drawn, roads laid out, infrastructures put in place, they define and constrain the framework in which human beings live.

Of course, the task of the architect, planner, and developer is rather formidable. New residents need something in place—houses, pathways, recreation, shopping, parking—and these must be provided early on. Many features eventually turned out to be quite satisfactory in Twin Rivers once the growing pains had eased. People will accommodate for the most part if they feel that there is good will and that the design is

not wholly insensitive to their needs and wishes. For planners and designers, progress rests on flexibility and the willingness to check out
expectations and build on experience. Above all they must be willing to
revise key assumptions.

Consider one quite typical assumption—that proximity (that is a
close, dense, physical texture) will generate the sociability conducive to
community. But what if proximity puts incompatible homeowners side
by side expecting them to share spaces—a townhouse, a front lawn, a
sidewalk? The result may then be enmity and conflict rather than neighborly connectedness. In short, by itself, spatial design decrees no single
outcome. It is a *potential*, a necessary but not a sufficient condition for
the community. Depending on how well the design fits the residents'
needs and priorities or is flexible enough for residents to modify it to
suit them, an ambience, positive or negative, is generated that may become embedded in the culture of place permanently.

Space and design are especially critical at the start because they
create the context for the first impressions of a new environment. And
first impressions shape subsequent reactions, often for the long term. In
Twin Rivers, the residents who said they were satisfied with the physical-spatial design tended also to be more positive toward other aspects
of the new community. Those disappointed were more negative in general. Space and design exerted a critical influence on residents' appraisals in the first two years. After that time, social factors became decisive—that is, whether one liked the other residents, had made friends,
and had worked out satisfactory arrangements for the family, the household, and the children. All of these significantly affected participation in
activities, organizations, social causes, and community-wide celebrations.

In Twin Rivers the design succeeded in some respects and failed in
others. Among the successful aspects were the character and location of
the townhouses. For most residents, these remained a positive element
in the ensuing decades. Less successful, as shown earlier, were the pathways and access roads, mainly because they show how ill advised are
attempts to force behavioral change through design. Less successful, for
similar reasons, was the movement to restrict car ownership to one per
household. With two-breadwinner families—and two cars—proliferating in the 1980s, the lack of parking space proved to be a source of
immense frustration.

Equally problematic was the physical demarcation of public and
private spaces, which led to persistent contentiousness among residents
as they competed for scarce space or ignored spatial rules. Often they
reinforced an adversarial stance toward the physical site and management dicta, and impeded cooperation, trust, and outreach.

A good example concerns the uses of grassy backyards compared with the uses of indoor patios. The differences were striking. The grassy backyards were anonymous, being neither public nor private, were rarely if ever used, and were in effect wasted space. Patios, by contrast, were extremely popular. They belonged to each house individually, providing outdoor privacy for barbecuing and relaxation, and they engaged great user interest and care. Hence spatial identity was significant for maintaining spatial integrity.

In sum, to help architects, planners, and developers improve their skills in designing for communities, it is important to assess, on a case-by-case basis, the fit between the social expectations that are built into design and actual social behavior. If done patiently and carefully, there is a chance to develop a rich compendium of principles for well-designed communities.

CHAPTER 10

PRIVATE AND PUBLIC:
WHOSE RIGHTS, WHOSE RESPONSIBILITIES?

There is always anarchy among the atoms.

— Nietzsche

In all communities, land, space, and place play an exceptionally dynamic role in generating questions about personal responsibility and the drawing of boundaries that set apart mine from yours and ours from theirs. Where space must be shared, conflicts are likely to multiply.

Even more than conventional communities, a planned unit development brings to the fore ancient questions about property rights and rightful claims in general. The prevalence of townhouses with their shared walls, services, and public spaces owned and administered by a community trust creates considerable ambiguities for residents as to the extent of their responsibilities and the limits of their powers.

Given the complex policy of shared ownership and the residents' backgrounds as renters, many from city apartments, one would have to expect some confusion about mine, thine, and ours. Add to this the lack of consensus about standards of cleanliness, property, and privacy and the confusion becomes endemic and unsolvable on an individual basis. Without an articulated social policy and a convincing rationale, dissonance and discord are likely to ensue.

Table 10.1
Residents'* Designations of Areas as Private or Public

	Private	Shared Private	Shared Public	Public	N
Sidewalk	5%	17%	21%	57%	71
Street/parking area	3%	36%	19%	42%	71
Front yard	35%	62%	2%	1%	71
Backyard	90%	—	—	—	71

Private Property: refers to a strong sense of ownership and for the use of the individual resident only.

Shared Private: refers to residents' and neighbors' joint use.

Shared Public: for the use of both residents and nonresidents; little sense of ownership.

Public Property: for anyone's use; no sense of ownership.

*Townhouse residents 1980.

A PUD incorporates a variety of spaces, from private townhouses and yards to public arenas. This introduces a considerable degree of indeterminacy into jurisdictions, from zones of privacy, where residents are held individually accountable, to public spaces, in whose upkeep everyone must share.

In an effort to explore this issue, residents were asked to designate each of the following according to whether they considered them private or public property: the front yards, the grassy backyards, the parking areas, and the sidewalks. Residents exhibited strong agreement on only two of these four areas. Asked whether they considered each of these private, public, or shared property, 90 percent agreed that the backyard is private, and 57 percent considered the front of the house as public property. The street in front of the house was seen as more public than private, whereas the front yard was seen as more private than public (Table 10.1). There was no uniform perspective. This challenges the findings of a comparative study of six townhouse developments that showed that 53 percent of residents regarded the outside of their homes (not otherwise specified) as essentially public and the responsibility of the home-owners association (Norcross 1973).

The absence of consensus on zones of responsibility is a source of strife in many a community and especially so in one that is new, rapidly changing, and based on a sharing of house, land, and space. The confusions and conflicts regarding one's proximate space are likely to carry over into the way more distant property is regarded, how well each person treats it, and who is seen to carry the primary responsibility for its appearance and upkeep.

Consider the case where one neighbor treats, and wants others to treat, the front yard as totally private property and hence his or her

Table 10.2
Responsibility for Maintenance of Property around the House

The responsibility is that of:	
Self alone	20%
The trust alone	13%
Shared	67%
Self and family	39%
Self and trust	6%
Family and trust	22%
N = 71 townhouse residents, 1980s	

own responsibility (35% in Twin Rivers agreed with that view), while another considers it shared private property (as did 62% of residents). These divergent perspectives may well create frictions and resentments as one neighbor maintains and the other neglects these proximate spaces. Judging from the residents' individual comments and the issues aired in the community paper, incompatible views about property created a perceptible climate of tension and grievances from the beginning. Disagreements might start with pairs of neighbors and from there fan out into the larger housing courts and eventually into the entire community, evolving into fixed attitudes of apathy and nonconcern.

A related area is that of maintenance of the physical site and the problem of litter. Asked whose responsibility it is to clean and maintain the property around the outside of their houses, residents were again divided, though two-thirds opted for shared upkeep (Table 10.2). As for litter, a pervasive issue gradually being brought under control, 94 percent of the residents considered it a definite problem for the community, and 25 percent considered it the number one problem. Here again, there were divergent degrees of concern.

For the one-fifth who "never" thought about the state of their neighbor's yard, three-tenths always did so. And for the 7 percent who never cleaned or swept the sidewalk in front of the house when it was littered, one-third always did. These are important differences in a small community. Even on the matter of the appearance of the front yard (which only one-third thought of as fully private property), three-fourths said they take pride in its appearance, whereas one-fifth admitted they do not. Presumably the first group expected a level of community cooperation that the second was unwilling or unable to provide.

Differing expectations about these mundane issues can lead to dramatic, even violent, altercations among aggrieved residents. Unaware that these individual attitudes reflect subcultural standards of conduct, most residents resort to vilification and blame of individuals as if incompatible norms of responsibility and pride are the outcome of willful antagonism and rancor. This then leads to attributions of ignoble intent to individuals and from there to profound grievances and misunderstandings among groups. If 38 percent of the residents feel the trust should take care of the community's litter, whereas 25 percent say it is the people's responsibility, where is there common ground? The allocation of parking spaces, for example, was a continuous irritant. Parking spaces readily became the focus of proprietary attitudes and an issue of serious contention among neighbors.

The delimitation of public versus private spaces with their attendant rights and duties is thus one of the most unsettling and enduring problems in Twin Rivers. Year after year, there have been explanations of what is considered the individual owner's domain and what belongs to the trust as caretaker of the common terrain. As late as 1983, a public communication from the trust administrator spelled out the details of this complex arrangement. "Twin Rivers," he declared, "is a very unique community, private yet quasi-public in nature" (*The Periscope*, June 1983, pp. 4–5), with the following areas of shared jurisdiction, liability, and responsibility among homeowners, the community trust, and the larger township in which Twin Rivers is located: sewer; street lighting; storm sewers; apartment complexes; undeveloped land; roads; garbage collection; parking; police enforcement; capital improvement expenditures; and industrial, commercial, and residential properties.

The details of these regulations were not widely understood by residents, even by the one-sixth who had lived in suburbs prior to moving to Twin Rivers. The multiplicity of rules bewildered them all. This is not surprising when one learns that the common areas are the responsibility of the trust but not so the trees planted by the developer on individually owned property. The trust takes care of the "common grassed grounds, open green areas, tennis courts, pools, parking lots, streets, emergency access, lawns, and lawn maintenance of front lawns." But, the "maintenance of backyards, fences, gates, trees and shrubs on the individual properties is the responsibility of the property owner" (*The Periscope*, June 1983, p. 4). In addition, the trust is responsible for some of the roads but not others, and for the storm sewer lines but not for the sanitary sewer lines. And then there is a whole set of rules that are enforceable only through the township. These include traffic regulations, building and construction ordinances, pooper-scooper ordinances, and maintenance of certain of the roads and the industrial and commercial properties.

Thus, the residents had to learn the extent and limits of each of three jurisdictions acting singly or jointly to maintain the aesthetic, spatial, and physical integrity of the developing community. A good many did not learn this easily, willingly, or reliably.

Territoriality

In their efforts to work out a common plan, residents often focused on physical and spatial features. As early as 1971, a year after Twin Rivers formally opened its doors, a group of residents opposed to the building of a service road in quad 2 became suspicious of the developer's intention and circulated a petition to rally others to their cause (O'Toole 1971, p. 18).

Also early on, there were numerous disputes over who could use the tennis courts and what activities besides swimming were acceptable at the pools — eating, for example, was prohibited. Hence the latter became the first act of public defiance of community rules. There were constant vociferous recriminations over spatial transgressions. Ex-urbanites turned homeowners, unfamiliar with the intricacies of lawn care, could work themselves into a frenzy over grass that took too long to grow, muddy playing fields, and all sorts of features of house or yard that failed to live up to expectations.

And sooner than one might have expected, proprietariness pushed aside democracy. When the developer of Twin Rivers sought to open the quad 1 and 2 pools to all residents, including renters, an indignant group of residents protested. They opposed the trust's policy of "swim where you want" and demanded a pool for every quad. As early as 1971, the pool in quad 1 had become "our own pool." A poll of eighty-six households showed that seventy-nine supported this stand, and the residents thus succeeded in securing their territorial exclusiveness.

Litter: Disregard of the Physical Environment

As early as 1973, an editorial in the Twin Rivers *Periscope* deplored the "increasing amount of litter," citing domestic castoffs, used Pampers, food wrappers, soda bottles, and other detritus spread across the community. The pools were particularly vulnerable since so many residents gathered there, and it was the site of a huge, and costly, cleanup problem. In the public commentary this was seen as proof of the lack of respect for property and pride in the community.

> Is there respect for private property? Apparently not. . . . Not when one's lawn becomes a playground for other people's children . . . and your house becomes a dumping ground for other

people's garbage, cigarette butts, half-eaten food. (*The Periscope*, September 1975, p. 32)

Ominous questions hung in the air: Do you supervise your children outdoors? Pick up garbage when you see it? Respect property other than your own? Do you want to live in a slum?

Garbage posed a serious problem, both as to its manner of disposal and residents' failures to abide by the scheduled pickups. Over and over, residents were chastised for throwing garbage into the lakes, allowing newspapers to be blown about, abandoning vehicles, and leaving dog waste in pool areas and grounds. Parents were urged to teach their children better community manners and to acquire some themselves — in the hope of getting residents to care more about the appearance of the community, *their* community.

> "Whose litter is it anyway?" asks a former New York City resident who remembers how litter decays. . . . "Please take a walking tour of your Quad. Notice ripped bags, can lids, fruit and vegetable peelings, glass, rotted wood, broken gates and fences. . . . Please take a few minutes to clean up around you on a regular basis . . . and let's teach our children to respect and care for the neighborhood." (*The Periscope*, vol. 4, no. 4, April 1985, p. 4)

Then there was the expense of the extra cleanup, funds for which could come only from increased fees for homeowners. Law-abiding citizens resented this, especially because everyone had to pay for the violators. Fines were instituted and the friendly local homeowners association took on the trappings of an exacting and punitive authority. But nothing seemed to turn the tide. In his desperation, the trust administrator urged the residents to try reprimanding violators and to join with neighbors to exert social pressure to bring nonconformists into line. Reminding the residents that compliance works on behalf of the entire community, he encouraged them to think in terms of interests they all shared: "The common ground is to be enjoyed, not misused" was the mantra.

Trying to capture the residents' attention on this matter proved difficult, since violations were not attributable to individuals but were anonymous acts. Without help from residents in identifying violators, the trust could not keep pace with the problem. This led the chairman of the Trust Advisory Board, Perry Shapiro, to offer to present "Pers" to the most outrageous offenders, among them: "Lenny the Torch," who uses the pool equipment as a cookout for his cousin's club; "Gloria La Feces," who uses pool containers for her diaper disposals; "Sidney Slickfinger," who unravels the webbing of six lounge chairs to make one large basket for sixteen pounds of cold cuts to be snuck into the quad 2 pool area; "Georgie the Pen," who signs up for six tennis courts and shows up for none; and "Shirley the Towel," who monopolizes eleven lounge chairs (*The Periscope*, March 15, 1975, p. 4).

Exactly a decade later, in September 1985, a "concerned resident" wrote a satirical letter to the editor of *The Periscope* about how some residents manifested their civic pride and concern. The points raised provide a convenient checklist of the continued unsolved problems of residents' indifference and abuse of the environment. The letter starts out by stating how much the writer enjoys Twin Rivers and what a concerned citizen she is.

- I leave my kids at the pool and go on my way knowing some-one else will watch them.
- I don't even worry about my dog or cat. . . . I just let them out to relieve themselves. . . .
- Occasionally . . . I will take the garbage from the backyard and put it behind my neighbor's fence or in the bulk area. . . .
- Parking is becoming a problem . . . and my neighbors are not too nice; they get upset because we take up two spaces for our new car and because we park our expensive pickup truck in the court.
- I like the idea of my being able to watch the kids and their friends play ball on the common area in front of the homes. Of course sometimes the trees or shrubs would be damaged and the grass would die but I could at least call the Trust and yell at them and get them to repair it, after all, I pay my fees. . . .
- My young teenagers can roam the community. . . . Admittedly, I don't know what they do or where the go, but I'm sure they don't get into trouble.
- I am concerned about the community. . . . I let my neighbors know I don't like their parking in front of my house. We don't talk to our next-door neighbor. If we change the oil in our car, we pour the old oil into the storm sewer.
- The only problem I see with Twin Rivers is that not every-body is as caring as we are. We love it here. (*The Periscope*, September 1985, p. 16)

Despite the community's dismal record on littering, the home-owners of Twin Rivers strongly rejected litter, considering it as an unde-sirable and unaesthetic feature of the community. Some waxed elo-quent, while others said it all in a single weary gesture of dismay and disapproval. No one seemed oblivious to the problem, no one had a good word to say about litter, no one admitted to littering, yet the litter did not go away. Asked what they would like to see done about litter, residents responded with very different opinions. Some thought there was "nothing to be done unless human nature changes"; others gave detailed prescriptions for punishing the offenders. Looking over the sum total of replies, it was possible to identify four types of responses:

- Those who put the onus on the Twin Rivers trust and the formal authorities (42%)
- Those who felt responsibility should be shared by the trust and the people (28%)
- Those who felt it was entirely the people's responsibility (25%)
- Those who had no solution or who saw no problem (4%)

Some representative replies were:

Litter Is the Trust's Responsibility (42%)

"Grounds need to be patrolled and maintained better by the maintenance people, not by the people who live here."
"More trash containers should be provided."
"More frequent garbage collection."
"Better control imposed on shop owners."
"Impose and enforce fines on litterers and dog owners."

Litter Is the People's Responsibility (28%)

"Everyone should chip in and pick up a little bit."
"People should clean up after dogs."
"People should be more proud of their community."
"People must train their children to be neater."
"It's up to the individual to do something about it."

Litter Is a Shared Responsibility (28%)

"Better garbage containers should be provided; and people have to learn to dispose of the trash properly."
"The trust should do a better job but people have to teach their children."
"People should be more aware; also better maintenance — both should put more effort into it."

Let us now examine what, if anything, differentiates these three groups.
Those who looked to the trust exclusively to solve the litter problem were likely the younger, better-educated, fully employed women.

Those who looked to the people to solve this problem were more likely older (age thirty-six or older), less well educated (high school or some college), and men. Those who felt it was a shared responsibility tended to be younger full-time housewives.

Residents in the earliest quads (1 and 2) were more likely to expect the trust to solve the litter problem. Residents in quads 3 and 4 (the more densely populated) were more likely to say people must solve the problem or make it a shared responsibility. The difference appears to be generational and temporal, and the two may be connected. The older residents were also the earliest settlers (in quads 1 and 2), who had more time to consider a "do-it-yourself" approach to community problems. The younger and more recent residents believe that the trust, the agency entrusted to take care of things such as snow removal, garbage collection, and recreation, should also handle litter. In contrast, the long-term residents tended to be more disenchanted with the trust's capacity to do so.

Experience in taking care of a house and a yard, especially during childhood, predisposes one to opt for self-reliance. People who had always lived in rented apartments tended to hold the trust more responsible, while those who had lived in a house owned by their parents tended to believe that responsibility for the grounds resided with the residents generally. Disappointment with Twin Rivers is also related to the allocation of responsibility. Those who are disappointed hold the trust more responsible; those who are not disappointed think that residents should assume more responsibility.

The problem of litter continued to be significant and resisted easy solutions. A 1980s follow-up survey yielded the following information:

How would you rank litter compared to other problems in this community?
Important   78%
Not important   22%

Do you feel you are doing your share in keeping the community clean?
Yes   81%

Police officers should give tickets to anyone they see littering.
Yes   62%

If people see litter, they should pick it up and put it in a trash-can (no matter whose litter is involved).
Yes   76%

It annoys me when my neighbor's yard is messy or dirty.
Always   31%
Often   21%

Wherever I go, I notice whether the ground is tidy or littered.
Often   42%
Always   24%

I always feel guilty when I litter.
Always   73%
Never   1%

I clean or sweep the sidewalk in front of my house when it is littered.
Always   34%
Often   37%
Never   11%

I litter.
Often   1.4%
Sometimes   9.9%
Rarely   43.7%
Never   45.1%

Each item on the scale, developed by researcher Steve Wenner, has a value of from one to five. Higher values denote higher litter consciousness. For purposes of analysis, the responses, whose actual values ranged from 19 to 44, were grouped into three categories as follows (Alpha reliability coefficient = .615 indicating a moderately reliable scale):

38–44 = High litter consciousness (n = 23)
34–37 = Moderate litter consciousness (n = 25)
19–33 = Low litter consciousness (n = 23)
N = 71

High litter consciousness was related to:

Low satisfaction with the community (44% vs. 26%)
Lower liking for current house (50% vs. 24%)
Relatively shorter residence in the community (41% vs. 26%)
Having had maintenance of property chores as a child (39% vs. 26%)
Taking pride in their current yard's appearance (80% vs. 11%)
Currently recycling garbage (42% vs. 26%)
Being disappointed with Twin Rivers (40% vs. 23%)

Although correlations do not permit one to infer a causal connection, it is clear that consciousness of litter is related to being disappointed with the community and the house. It is also interesting to note that childhood experience is strongly related to a concern with litter in adulthood. More recent residents who are coping with problems of adjusting their expectations to the actual conditions of house, community, and fellow residents are also most likely to be conscious of the litter about them. Above all, taking pride in the appearance of one's own property goes hand in hand with strong feelings about litter.

The majority noticed litter, felt guilty when they themselves engaged in littering, and took active steps to help in cleanup. Residents also agreed by and large as to the types of litter they found most problematic — dog mess and garbage headed the list. Asked if they themselves littered, nearly one-half said "never," and only 1 percent said "often." And this in a community where litter has been endemic and widespread since its inception. Residents did, however, admit to strong feelings about their occasional lapses into litter, three-quarters saying they "always" feel guilty when littering.

Children received top mention (38%) as the worst litter offenders; teenagers (17%) and dog owners (16%) were the runners-up. A sizeable number of residents (42%) also believed that renters had a greater propensity to litter than did owners. Renters were seen to care less about the community and to take less pride in property. These attitudes did not develop through experience within the community; rather, the residents brought them in with the move. Asked what should be done about the litter problem, two-thirds responded that police should issue tickets to offenders. Three-quarters felt that people should pick up any litter, even if it wasn't theirs. Clearly there is a gap here between attitudes and behavior. Offended by litter, eager to remedy the situation, and distressed by the pervasive presence of litter in the community, residents nonetheless disavowed any personal responsibility for it. But who was littering, if not the majority of residents?

To be sure, there was a solid group of concerned residents who not only disapproved of litter and wished it would go away, but who did their share to improve the situation. Recent surveys show that one-third of residents currently recycle newspapers, bottles, and the like, and 50 percent actively volunteer their time, working with community groups or keeping others aware of the issue. Indeed, 90 percent of the residents feel they are doing their share to preserve the appearance of Twin Rivers.

Here again there is a difference between the public and the private areas, and the responsibility people feel toward each. Residents are willing to take care of their own backyards (66%), and "always" or "often" sweep away litter on the sidewalk in front of their houses (71%), because they see the immediate area around their houses as their responsibility. But as regards general maintenance, 90 percent feel it is up to the trust to care for the community's upkeep and appearance, and they will not take part.

Responsibility is one thing. Feelings are another. Perhaps residents do not always act on what they believe, but it is striking how strongly they care about the issue.

In conclusion, litter is a problem that has beset the community from the beginning. It has troubled the authorities continuously, and they have used a variety of means to bring it to public attention. The information gathered in the interviews suggests that residents are as aware of litter as the trust is and deplore its effects on the community. Most blame children and teenagers as key culprits but it is clear that the adults do their share, even if they do not acknowledge it. Ideally, litter should be everyone's concern but in reality too many residents evade their responsibilities. And this is why, ultimately, such mundane problems of physical upkeep and maintenance, garbage disposal and litter, are "people problems" in the most basic sense. They reflect pride in self and in the common terrain, a respect for the property and well-being of all, and an awareness of the connection between the personal and the common good.

In time, fines and stricter regulations gradually helped bring litter under control. By comparison with the 1970s, when it was in the doldrums, Twin Rivers in the 1980s looked much cleaner and better cared for, and better still in the 1990s. Progress was evident but it was a continuous struggle, a never-ending process.

Crimes against Property and People

A settlement of ten thousand residents is likely to have its share of crime and assaults on property and persons. In a new community, the chances for antisocial behavior increase, as there is no traditional model to coalesce individual and collective self-interest. Then, too, the initial sense of uprootedness and transciency detracts from a public commitment, and the social diversity of a modern suburban population tends to dilute the basis for social consensus.

Also often noted is the fact that new developments are magnets for thieves and swindlers, since it is hard to distinguish rightful residents from devious strangers. The constant circulation of service personnel, moving vans, and visitors limits vigilance, and as the small-scale housing courts are still in process of formation, no one can watch more than their own small turf. Not to be ignored is normative violation from within the new community. In Twin Rivers this began with the first settlers in 1970 and continues in an unbroken progression to this day.

> In August 1972 six townhouses were destroyed by a fire believed to have been caused by arson.

In May 1972, 18 out of 1,260 households had been delinquent
   in their trust payments; and 13 were taken to small-claims
   court.
Traffic violations, such as disregarded stop signs, unsafe speeds,
   cars not stopping for school buses, and so on, were serious
   right from the start.
In 1974 a fire in the Village East apartments gutted several sec-
   ond-floor units. It, too, was attributed to arson.
The first drug arrests made the headlines in March 1974.

In April 1974 a twenty-three-year old housewife was raped, and
two composite sketches of the rapist were circulated. The event was
graphically depicted with the peculiar adviso that the rape was "the first
ever in a planned unit development." The police were checking out the
possibility that the rapist might have been one of the construction workers
nearby. By November the case was closed. Recalling three hundred
posters throughout the state, the police announced that the rape seemed
to have been invented by the woman and no further action was required. Nonetheless, inquiring about the residents' knowledge of the
incident indicated that the image had been fixed and formed part of the
evolving mythology of the community.
   Crimes are more disturbing in a new community not expecting them
and thus finding it difficult to take them in stride. Such crimes create an
undertone of fear that may erode the basis for the trust desired.
   Throughout the decades the weekly *Windsor-Heights Herald* (1984)
kept readers abreast of the crimes suffered or perpetrated by Twin Rivers
residents and outsiders. Burglaries led the list:

An Abbington Drive resident reported that his house had been
burglarized—a color television, a telephone answering machine, and a cassette stereo set were reported stolen.

Shoplifting, disorderly conduct, defacements of cars, robbery, muggings,
bicycle thefts, computer thefts, drugs, indecent exposure, ransacking of
houses whose owners were away at work, driving while intoxicated,
jewelry thefts, these were the most frequent crimes cited. A standard
design makes it easy to know just where entries and exits are located,
and the sliding glass doors of the houses were a favorite means of entry
for thieves.
   In the 1980s another sort of crime made its appearance, one that
both frightened and rallied the community. It concerned a series of attempted abductions of young children. Between January and May, 1984,
six such attempts were reported. In January a six-year-old boy walking
to school was accosted by a man in a car, and the boy fled. Later that

week a similar incident involved a twelve-year-old boy. In April of that year a seven-year-old girl was approached by a man in a car, who stopped her with the words, "Hi kid, come here, your mom is sick." As did the two boys, the little girl ran away. In May 1984 a sixth attempt involved a thirteen-year-old boy. The parents were said to be particularly worried because the community is so near the turnpike that an abductor and his victim could disappear very quickly. All incidents involved men in cars. All agitated the community and led the police to urge residents to teach their children self-protection.

By increasing the sense of vulnerability and interdependence, crimes may actually generate community feeling. A common danger, like a common enemy, mobilizes a sense of shared destiny. In addition, crimes motivate a population to devise institutions to protect the collective self. Rules and fines as well as penalties and legal actions multiply. In time one notes in Twin Rivers the issuance of "Ground Rules for Common Grounds"; traffic and speed limits; safety rules; criminal trespass complaints; and a Parent Responsibility Law, whereby the courts have the right to hold parents of a child adjudged delinquent subject to fines.

These, then, were among the recurrent problems of the community for which it had to find workable solutions. In the process of doing so, it became apparent that in order to defend and protect a community from danger, it was necessary to generate a vital sense of community. In turn, this was strengthened by the crimes and misdemeanors that confront a community.

Vandalism

If indifference to or violation of environmental rules is a personal expression of a lack of community feeling, vandalism is its collective expression. Like litter, vandalism is an indication of indifference to one's environment, an indifference likely to be greater when space is shared and when people have different codes and norms of civic pride and respect for appearances. Both have been true of Twin Rivers.

A community without established traditions lacks not only the institutions that will guide the common life but the normative consensus against which behavior will be consistently assessed and, if need be, punished. The extent to which social control rests on the anticipated reaction of others, as caught in numerous references to "they," "most people," "everyone around here," is the extent to which individuals can be said to have internalized a public perspective on normative preferences. Only when that happens can social conduct become self-regulating. In the absence of such collective standards, one can violate "the commons" with impunity and feel no moral pangs. Moral conformity "takes its peculiar coloration from the fact that the person feeling it has done or is about to do something through which he comes into contradiction with people to whom he is bound in one form or another" (Elias 1978, p. 292).

Twin Rivers did not, at the start, have even a modicum of consensus on community issues, hence no effective pressure could be brought to bear if residents neglected or abused the environment. Not surprisingly, neither shame nor embarrassment over environmental abuse were much in evidence.

There is also the fact that the inducements used to lure buyers into the community—such as "Here, everything will be done for homeowners," or "You can relax now, we will take care of you" may have lulled residents into inaction. Such slogans may set up expectations that are too great and sap personal initiative to address public concerns.

While vandalism is worrisome no matter where or when it occurs, it has a special meaning in new communities. Great expectations in new communities often become great disappointments. Prospective residents, starry eyed but apprehensive, look forward to more than new houses and safety for their children. They also secretly wish for their lives to be magically transformed, their marriages to be revitalized, their careers to bloom.

And when, after moving in, it becomes evident that the new community is also an unfinished community, the disappointment often knows no bounds. Most residents do manage to take it in their stride but a minority do not and they look for ways to even some secret score, to inflict the pain and resentment they have experienced, and to strike back anonymously through vandalism.

Vandalism has taken many forms in Twin Rivers. The following has occurred routinely: Public telephones have been dismembered, windows broken, the sprinkler system disrupted, playground or pool equipment broken; lounge chairs have gone missing; lumber has been pilfered from storage sheds; flower beds have been trampled and young trees broken; pets have gone on destructive rampages.

Frustration over a public telephone intentionally despoiled or pool equipment wantonly destroyed can create intense feelings of rage even among normally calm and reasonable people. At such moments, one experiences not only an inconvenience, no matter how stressful, but a deeper affront. It is an injury to one's sense that the world is reliable and safe and that the good forces will prevail. It is also a disturbing reminder that vengeance and destruction lurk close to the surface of organized social life.

Twin Rivers has responded to vandalism in a variety of ways: through indifference, denial, humor, and finally perplexed dismay. Some have tried to explain it away by blaming it all on children's high jinks, but this has provoked such comments as: "If enjoying their childhood means destroying property that we all pay for, then we will all pay for this abuse of freedom" (*Windsor-Heights Herald*, 23 October 1975, editorial page).

One leading citizen, then the president of the home-owners association considered the problem serious enough to invite the readers of *The Periscope* to share some wild speculations. He related a dream that featured "the ultimate act of swim-club vandalism." In the dream, he entered the pool area ready to dive into the water but he suddenly careened to a halt as he found himself "looking down into a deep dark ditch — [and realized that] the pool was gone" (*The Periscope*, October 1975, p. 6)

Over the decade of the 1980s there were many deliberations on this problem. To the extent that vandalism was acknowledged as a communal issue, the most frequently blamed were the children and the teenagers. The benign comments referred to their being carried away by the immediacy of the moment. The angry ones decried the intentional destruction of the environment as retaliation for missing facilities such as a teen center. At times it was not the community's own teenagers who were blamed, but outsiders who were seen to have lashed out against an environment they considered enviable, because it was new, and from which they felt excluded.

On a deeper level, however, mischievous or destructive youth was not, one felt, the primary cause. Had children been taught to respect the land and to revere the common grounds and facilities, they would not have been tempted to express their frustrations by assaulting the collective self. The children and teenagers did so because they were ignorant and often they simply carried out their parents' indifference. It was this indifference that needed to be dealt with. That was easier said than done, however, because indifference has deep cultural roots. Some attribute it to society's cavalier, not to say destructive, attitude to the environment and to the simultaneous worship of private property and indifference to that which is publicly shared: "There is a stark contrast between the American's attitude towards his private bubble of space and that toward all public spaces." The house receives the attention and care, as does the yard and garden, that public spaces are denied. "[S]idewalks, roadsides, public vehicles, parks, and many public buildings reveal a studied neglect and frequently such downright squalor that it is difficult to believe one is encountering a civilized community" (Zelinsky 1973, p. 93).

The long tradition of public indifference to the public domain has taken its toll in the characteristic profligacy with which Americans have regarded the land. Instead of communing with nature and revering this precious national resource, American society has stressed the need to subjugate nature and bring it under control. If, in the process, the land were destroyed, one would simply move on to exercise dominion over another untried space. This rapacity was not checked, as long as land seemed to be in limitless supply. Once that supply is questioned, as it is today, so are the cultural attitudes that sustained this self-serving ethos.

Of course, the sensitive observer of American mores did not need to wait until the twenty-first century to deplore this national myopia. As early as 1843, de Tocqueville, amazed at the facility with which Americans picked up their household goods to move on, described his disquiet at coming upon a spot in the forest with its makeshift dwelling and the traces of a hasty departure. "I stood for some time in silent admiration of the resources of nature and the littleness of man," he wrote, ". . . and when I was obliged to leave that enchanting solitude, I exclaimed with sadness: 'Are ruins, then, already here?'" (de Tocqueville 1990, p. 296).

It is not insignificant, then, that it is the public spaces that have been vandalized in Twin Rivers. These are the spaces that belong to all and, therefore, to no one. When "everything belongs to everybody . . . nothing belongs to or is enjoyed by anybody" (Chermayeff and Alexander 1965, p. 66).

Resentment about such environmental neglect and its possible detrimental effects on health, property values, and aesthetics was not long in coming and was the cause of the trials of the first decade. Major complaints included: distress over the "disgraceful" upkeep of the grounds, slow snow removal, unsightly garbage, the pollution of lakes, Pampers left at pools, pet violations, and lawns badly maintained (*The Periscope*, 15 March 1975, p. 32). In short, Twin Rivers had "bad community manners" to use a phrase coined by one of its leaders, Neil Nevitt (editor, and president of the Twin Rivers HOA [ibid.]).

The community did attempt to fight back, but the means used—contests for attractive landscaping, for example—did not work, mainly, one suspects, because there was no substantial community to be proud of in these early years.

The struggle to tame egocentricity and steer residents toward greater cooperation and respect for the public domain proved as intransigent as the problems of litter, vandalism, and, as we shall see, contention over pets, which continued to agitate the community.

Pets

"The rank smell of unneutered cat urine in my basement around my window wells," "on my storm door; in the shrubs in my backyard—

I'm tired of it! Tired of having my dog come in . . . smelling of it; tired of having my own cats get upset by the stench!" And then this warning—if this continues the cats will be brought to the pound and destroyed."

—*The Periscope*, March 1976, p. 22

I am certainly not a cat hater. . . . However, I firmly believe that in crowded Twin Rivers any owner of *any* pet must respect his neighbors by not allowing their cats and dogs to become a nuisance to the whole area.

—*The Periscope*, March 1976

Twin Rivers residents share the environment not only with one another, but with another category of living creatures, namely, pets. In the early 1970s, 46 percent of the households contained one pet or more, a figure that rose to 60 percent a decade later. They were thus in step with the national culture, when more than two-thirds of American households contained pets: 50 million dogs and 46 million cats for the country as a whole (Kanner 1985).

Pets are common in new communities for a number of reasons. There is more outdoor space for play and recreation, there is usually more domestic space within larger dwellings, and for many, images of suburban gentility go hand in hand with Spot the Dog or Felix the Cat. There is also the need for companionship in a strange environment until friendships are made and social life gets under way. Pets proliferate in such environments. Alas, they also get left behind when their owners move. The same is true on college campuses.

Pets, as the residents have been quick to point out, create friction among residents because of their toilet habits and their running wild over flowerbeds and lawns. This is a widespread complaint in new communities. Ex-urbanites, especially from apartments where pets are not allowed, notes Norcross in his survey of townhouse communities (1973, p. 36), rush out to buy a dog or a cat immediately upon moving in. Although loved by their owners, they are often resented by the neighbors whose lawns they despoil. Also, pets are not a part of formal plans, since "developers usually plan on adequate green areas for people, but fail to consider pets" (ibid.).

In Twin Rivers, the problem of stray pets surfaced after the first year, and a pet committee, formed in 1972, busied itself with devising pet regulations for this initial list of issues: dog-walking areas, waste disposal, unleashed pets, identification tags, vaccinations. The pet situation, it was said, created such "aggravation, harassment, and heated arguments" that "many a pet owner has been moved to consider selling their homes and leaving the Community." Common grounds, used as "giant doggy bathrooms," and barking dogs were loudly deplored. Foster parents were sought to take in lost pets for a brief period (*The Periscope*, December 1972). The problem did not stop at Twin Rivers boundaries, as indicated by pleas to the residents of the township to stop dropping their "homeless, sick, starving, and unwanted animals" in Twin Rivers (*Windsor-Heights Herald*, 24 August 1972, p. 4). The countless exhortations multiplied:

> To all pet owners: Please respect your neighbors' property and walk your animals only in the presented areas. Cat owners, do not let your cats out unleashed. (*The Periscope*, December 1974)

> If one chooses to own a dog, he must realize the responsibilities involved. . . . No reason why the rest of us should have to suffer the indignity of walking in someone else's dirt. . . . It's an eyesore, a health hazard. (*The Periscope*, November 1975, p. 22)

> I am tired of having my street look like a cow pasture. If the morons who walk their dogs where they please do not have enough common sense or decency to care about their neighbors, then by all means . . . some controls. (*The Periscope*, February 1976, p. 20)

Summonses were mentioned publicly for the first time in 1974, for dog owners charged with despoiling a particular area of Twin Rivers. There were sad tales of the inhuman treatment and dumping of unwanted pets into the wilderness of Twin Rivers, where starvation and a painful death could await them.

Also in 1974, a pet registry was begun. Descriptions and photos of existing pets were to be used to reunite lost pets with their owners (*The Periscope*, June 1974, p. 30). Other announcements thanked residents for agreeing to take abandoned pets into their homes permanently. Pets were often described in the terms one would use for human beings — lost and rejected, abandoned, grateful to be members of the family — and one feels that these terms reflect some of the feelings of aloneness and strangeness that beset the initial residents who likewise sought the warmth and comforts of a home. By January 1976 the Twin Rivers Pet Committee officially stopped functioning when the number of animals exceeded the number of volunteers willing to take them in. Residents were advised to take unwanted pets to the pound to be destroyed instead of exposing them to the elements.

Fines of ten to twenty-five dollars were imposed as early as 1975 (*The Windsor-Heights Herald*, 1 January 1976, p. 2A), and sanctions became more severe in time. Penalties came to include the loss of swimming pool privileges and a lien on one's property (*The Periscope*, March 1976, p. 11).

The rage of residents also accelerated:

> I'm tired of it. . . . I give this warning: to have stray cats picked up by the Dog Warden to be taken to the pound and be destroyed. (Letters to the Editor, *The Periscope*, March 1976, p. 22)

> Cats, as everyone knows, are the finest animals in creation, but they can dig up your flower beds and water the roses. (*The Periscope*, June 1983, p. 1)

And this ferocious rejoinder: "We have a dog to walk. . . . If anyone gives us any trouble then we're taking it out on their front lawn." A new resolution was adopted by the Twin Rivers board in 1979, regulating the conduct of pets on trust land and increasing fines to thirty-five dollars per violation (*The Periscope*, October 1984, p. 1).

By the 1990s pets were no longer the critical issue they had been in the first fifteen years of the community's life. The combined and sustained efforts of the trust, the township, and interested residents had succeeded in imposing some control through legal action and the mobilization of local public opinion.

Conclusion

The tension between individuals and the community is a familiar theme in American life, from the tightly ordered covenant communities of Puritan New England to the planned developments of our own day. In colonial times, land was critical for the opportunity to set oneself apart from community. It permitted individuals to give vent to their desires for elbowroom and to "live apart from the meeting house, religious ordinances, and pastoral care" (Stilgoe 1988, p. 7). While the original settlers of New England were content, according to Increase Mather, "with one acre per individual and twenty per family, in time, hundreds and thousands of acres were appropriated," and the ideal of houses clustered around the meeting house gave way to "scattered settlement patterns already common west of the Appalachians," revealing "a strong bias toward solitude" (Zelinsky 1973, p. 48). Still later, the desire for economic success propelled Americans to break their ties to the land, the hometown, the natal hearth and follow wherever opportunity took them.

Twin Rivers mirrors the national experience as it struggles with its problems. Taught to regard land as their natural right over which to assert their claims, residents now find themselves called upon to consider land a collective resource that they must help to preserve. The concept of land as a vehicle to maximize personal gain competes with the concept of land as a scarce resource requiring a new ethic of respect and consideration, which would have residents subordinate individual self-interest to the interests of the totality.

But residents of Twin Rivers were not prepared for the larger, long-term view. Neither by upbringing nor by experience were they ever made aware that the private interests they so assiduously pursued and defended actually required a supportive cultural environment, and that individual autonomy and private property always rest on collective permissions.

In the development of Twin Rivers, the realization that excessive individualism could destroy the nascent community first took hold among a minority of residents, those who chose to give their time, energy, faith, and imagination to help build the community they had, mistakenly, expected to come full-fledged with the purchase of their houses. It was this minority who kept sending the message: Care for your environment, worry about the landscape, love the terrain. The community may be an ugly duckling now but your loving attention will make it bloom. It is, after all, *your* community. True, "there are some people who don't care unless it comes to their front door. Now is the time for all of us to stop and think about these problems and show pride in *our* community" (*The Periscope*, September 1975, p. 32).

But it was not yet their community. That feeling had to be created, and it would be a long and arduous collective undertaking.

For the first five years of the community's life, there was a constant appeal to community pride obviously belied by litter, apathy, and vandalism. Since then, there have been considerable improvements, mainly as a result of the efforts of concerned residents and a hard-working board. They have waged a concerned campaign to solidify and beautify the community by assiduous plantings, careful maintenance, and the effective organization of services such as garbage collection and snow removal. The example set by their efforts seems to have kindled some bright sparks of community spirit that should eventually generate that pride in community that is essential for long-term survival.

Land-use planning and design are critical for the quality of life in all communities and this is even more true for townhouse developments where problems of "density, privacy, outdoor living, recreation space, and car parking" are of greater moment (Norcross 1973, p. 48).

One lesson to be learned from this examination of environmental concern for land and space is that the traditional reliance on the market as the yardstick for economic values does not extend to values regarding land and other collective resources. We are not dealing here with costs to be passed on to buyers with greater assets or greater desire for a product. We are talking about an exhaustible resource that may be destroyed forever, with no imaginary superbuyer to foot that bill.

Finally, there is the matter of the embellishment and defacement of the environment. Embellishments were limited because of the inhibiting architectural controls, and all were essentially focused on private property. Defacement of the environment, as in physical abuse and vandalism, involved, in the main, public areas and facilities, and they were the principal targets of the residents' disappointments and frustrations with the community.

Thus, the microscale of place, space, and territory obviously has large consequences for individual and collective life. Attitudes toward property, territorial responsibility, and sharing help determine ways of dealing with the larger questions of collective life. They are crucial ingredients for the creation of trust, cohesion, and accountability in a community, and they strongly affect the texture of day-to-day life and the promise of a long-term future.

If the land is abused and the environment neglected, the message conveyed to individuals is that no one cares and no one is in charge. To the aesthetic discomfort generated by the neglect of physical upkeep and appearance must be added a deeper discomfiture of abandonment and betrayal. The well-cared-for environment, like the well-cared-for person, inspires a confidence and pride beyond its more obvious manifestations. It seems to say to its inhabitants: Someone cares about how we live and therefore *we* care. The reverse is also true. In a profound sense, then, it is by learning how to share space and place that we become each other's keepers — and move one step closer to the desired and elusive goal of a humane life in common.

CHAPTER 11
GO FIGHT CITY HALL: THE FIRST LAWSUIT

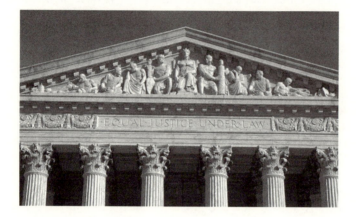

We are prepared to die for each other, but to live with each other is
much harder.

— Benjamin Zablocki

Those who expected instant community in Twin Rivers — and there
were many — were in for a surprise. Instead of community, they found
indifference and even disinterest, which kept residents focused on themselves and their families, on the houses they lived in, and on their jobs
outside the community. They might have been good citizens, paid their
bills, voted in national elections, but they did not respond to local community appeals, did not get involved in volunteer activities, did not concern themselves about the place in which they lived. Nor did they know
or care about those nameless others with whom their fate was intertwined. Such individuals were widely prevalent in Twin Rivers during
the early years, though only a fraction were free riders or actively antisocial. Many kept to themselves because they were ignorant as to how
to join with fellow residents to work on collective projects. No one had
alerted them to the necessity for community involvement, and there was
no guidance available to help them develop the skills needed for social
cooperation.

The feeling that the community was provisional and transient remained part of the ambience of Twin Rivers for the first decade of its

life. Gradually, however, a stable, involved core of active and concerned citizens did develop and these people helped dispel the tentativeness that had permeated the atmosphere. They developed the institutions for governance and control, for communication and participation that make for an ongoing collective life. Through their efforts, the community took hold.

The Skeleton of a Community

In the beginning, as the residents swarmed to their newly found utopia in the suburbs, the community existed mainly as a set of expectations and promises in the minds of the residents and the builder. The physical layout into four quadrangles and rows of townhouses was there of course and so were the developer, his staff, and the bank that acted as trustee. The physical center of the development was the sales office where a model of the completed community, along with maps and photos, greeted the prospective home buyer. Fantasies were played out there as resident after resident attempted to picture a completed community out of the isolated and fragmented portions that had been built and to imagine how the house they had just bought from plans would fit into it. Naturally, there was room for hyperbole.

Not surprisingly, once the residents did finally move into their houses, usually about six months after purchase, the discrepancy between their great expectations and the less exalted reality led to huge waves of disappointment. These soon expressed themselves in litanies of complaints. In part this was encouraged by the trust office, which allowed each resident a thirty-day period within which to register problems with the house and its surroundings.

However, the complaints contained from the beginning an element of righteousness and dismay that went far beyond legitimate queries and demands to repair drafty doors, faulty fixtures, or nonfunctioning heating systems. They had a special music and a tempo of compelling intensity. They hovered in the air as droplets of disappointment, stirred up by little breezes of discontent that created a permanent state of restlessness and blame. But curiously, in the bleak early days of transition and upheaval, it was the complaints that united these first settlers. They bonded instantly, although they knew nothing about one another or about what they had in common, except unfulfilled promises and dashed expectations.

"Let me tell you about our basement, or kitchen, or stairwell or wall-to-wall carpeting," became the currency of discourse. Residents, some bitter, some jovial, depending on their temperament and experience, took turns in describing the various degrees of imperfection they encountered in their new abodes. In the ensuing atmosphere of bewildered dismay, individuals naturally became keenly alert to other inadequacies of their Shangri-la, which added yet more fuel to the flames. On the surface, their disappointments, grievances, and righteous indignation cast a pall over these pioneers, but underneath they were actually forging the first bonds of community. In gathering to share complaints, they shared experiences, built up memories, and wove the filaments of a life in common.

Many residents, to judge from the interviews and the community newspaper, never stopped complaining or wanting to. It was as if their natures delighted in a daily dose of indignation and sought fresh sources to feed it. Others, however, took a more permanent step toward community by organizing to "do something about it." This usually meant a group going to the sales office and asking to speak to the developer, threatening dire action if things were not going to be fixed instantly, and otherwise harassing the developer who, not surprisingly, grew reluctant to meet with them. The residents responded with heightened resentment at what they considered his evasiveness. This would eventually result in the lawsuit that will be discussed in the next section.

For the time being, however, it led residents to look to themselves to deal with the growing pains of a new community. There were practical matters such as the hiring of subcontractors for physical maintenance, and garbage and snow removal, and the frustrations of waiting too long for needed repairs. An early lesson to be learned was that there was no single panacea for every ill and that the residents' support — either in the form of trust and patience or in terms of effort — was essential for eventual success. The mantra was: "Forget about the past. We are trying to establish an efficient and permanent crew, so we should be more than willing to tolerate the 'breaking-in period' " (*The Periscope*, 15 December 1974, p. 4). Residents learned, painfully, that tough bargaining might be necessary for sound results; for example, they threatened "withholding of payment from a landscaper" or other service agency.

Early on, also, the matter of trust dues assessments was a sore point, as residents did not understand why they were paying both the trust and the township for various services; or they protested the amounts levied, or resented the method of allocating each home owner's share. "On Wednesday, December 27, 1973 the Board of Directors of the Twin Rivers Home-Owners Association and members of the T.A.B. unanimously passed a joint resolution to inform the trustees of the dissatisfaction with the inequities of the trust payment increase" (*Windsor-Heights Herald*, 4 January 4 1973, p.1). Such reports became more frequent over time.

Teenagers were a source of problems, even when there were only a handful in the community. A teen center was one of the broken promises that would stir up the embers of discontent throughout the decade. The seemingly permanent state of construction of the community, with roads being surfaced and bulldozers plowing through space, or the sounds of moving vans disgorging yet another set of someone's possessions, was another constant irritant.

The question of a physical center for the development surfaced early. "Now that the pool is closed for the season there is no central meeting place and no place for messages and notices to be posted" (*Opus '70*, November–December, 1973, p. 12). A bulletin board in the administration building was promised.

The difficulty of getting the trustee or the developer to respond to queries was a sore point from the earliest years. "After numerous calls . . . we still have not received any answers. . . . we are still waiting" goes one report on the developer's lack of response to a list of forty items that needed repair or attention.

The continuous construction and the accompanying noise, dust, and physical disarray made it hard to distinguish the intact from the unfinished environment. In time, the early experience of disarray carried over into later behavior and the lessons of how to create and maintain an intact, well-manicured community were never fully learned. Note this description by a newly arrived resident in the last quad: "The conditions of life are 'ridiculous'; the parking lot is filled with mud; one can't walk anywhere; kids can't play anywhere; it is a time of 'mud and madness'" (*The Periscope*, 10 March 1973, p. 24).

Complaints about inadequate and unreliable lawn maintenance would reach a crescendo. The situation is "intolerable," "my front lawn has not been cut in weeks," were constant refrains, leading to an inevitable search for someone to blame, someone to hold accountable. "Perhaps" suggested one voice speaking for many, "if the trustee (the bank) would bother to supervise the contractor we would get the service we are paying for" (*The Periscope*, 15 June 1974, p. 3). Demands and outrage accelerated with reminders to the residents that it was, after all, *their* money that was being spent by the trust; therefore, the trust should be listening. Threats to put ads in the *New York Times* real estate section, which would expose the "poor performance of the developer," multiplied. The gathering storm eventually culminates in the famous lawsuit that pitted residents against the developer and the bank.

In addition to specific complaints and demands for better equipment and capital improvements, such as more outside street lighting, the question arose as to who had the right to choose the subcontractors—the trustee alone or the trustee and the citizen's advisory group (the Trust Advisory Board). What if the two disagreed? After all, such choices affected policies on which all the residents depended.

Parking problems and territorial violations of residents' parking spaces created much distress. "There are 20 families in our court and supposedly room for 40 cars to park . . . but there are 60 cars and no space for us" was another early refrain.

There were other, more complex questions. Who should foot the bill for sidewalks around the elementary school — only the residents whose children attend the school; all the residents; the developer; or the township, which is responsible for maintaining the schools? There were many who did not care about sidewalks at all and who did not want to pay for them.

Awareness of the human tendency to become habituated even to unsatisfactory conditions and to lose the momentum of outrage led to periodic warnings such as: "[K]eep those letters and calls coming. Don't become inured to poor performance" (*The Periscope*, 15 June 1974, p. 10).

There were unscrupulous merchants, shoddy work, and poor service. Initially, there was no collective experience, no cumulative resources to draw upon, making the residents easy prey to deceitful profiteers.

Safety was of great concern to the earliest residents because rules had yet to be worked out, and facilities and roads were still incomplete. Promises played an important role here too. The developer had promised residents that the schools would be within walking distance, but in fact by 1972 there still was no pedestrian route to the school, and parents were concerned for the safety of their children. And then there was the transportation issue. Residents expected an easy commute to jobs in New York City but had not been prepared for the twenty-minute walk "via a dangerous route across Route 33" or for the lack of parking near the bus stop. Instead of being pleased that the builder and the bus company were making plans to ameliorate the situation, residents were disgusted that this situation had not been anticipated before they arrived on the scene (*The Windsor-Heights Herald*, 22 June 1972).

There was a need for speed and safety rules within the local area because the roads had become more heavily traveled than expected. Problems of safety were accompanied by increasing noise and pollution levels for the homes near the roads. An early recommendation was to build a jug handle to divert traffic from the community, and to erect a traffic light. Added to these stresses were unforeseen disasters involving the houses, many incomplete but already in need of repair. Flooded basements in one quad were caused by a running water pocket under one of its courts. Residents complained about houses without screens or air-conditioning units. In the winter of 1971, a fire caused by faulty high-pressure valves raged through eight Lake Drive apartments and cut off heat and gas to sixteen more, leaving twenty-four families temporarily homeless. The disaster was featured in the state and local press and increased the residents' anxieties, as well as tarnishing the image of the community (*Trenton Times*, 10 November 1971, p. 2).

Another crisis stemmed from a break in a sewer pipe that sent raw sewage into eleven apartments. This led some to question the enforcement of building codes and fueled longstanding complaints about the poor quality of the construction generally.

All of these issues contributed to the blizzard of claims and counterclaims that confronted the developer, the bank, and the residents. Broken promises; unfinished and poorly constructed houses; inadequate facilities; incipient vandalism; an insensitive and often indifferent trust; and restless teenagers contributed to the conflict over turf and territory. Undoubtedly this first act set the tone for what was to follow by creating an alert, increasingly aggrieved and suspicious populace quick to demand its rights and primed to fight for them. At the same time, these very problems created an invisible reservoir of unity for the residents of this nascent community bound to the same space — concerned about the value of their economic investment and united by common grievances.

The early problems formed a leitmotif for the next decade centered on the basic ingredients of the common life.

In a curious way, also, grappling with the early problems in print, in face-to-face meetings, in confrontations with the trust, was more than the expression of discontent. In learning how construction flaws or unreliable subcontractors may be dealt with, members of the community acquired some basic insights into the business of living in this place at this time. Out of the trials and tribulations of this early shared experience the residents created the foundation for a common local culture that would be passed on to future generations. In the ensuing years, a newcomer would be able to turn to a long-term resident and get help with the problems specific to a particular house and/or issue. Early on, no one knew what to do or where to turn. The residents all learned together and this experience formed a part of the common culture that would make Twin Rivers a community.

It is not uncommon for residents of "new communities" to resort to legal means to wrest some measure of control from the authorities charged with management and oversight. In Twin Rivers these included the First Charter National Bank, which served as trustee (the trust); an administrator who set the monthly fees; and a Trust Advisory Board. The trust had decision-making power whereas the TAB acted primarily in an advisory capacity. Both were targets of resident dissatisfactions and frustrations. In fact, the first truly collective action taken by Twin Rivers residents was directed against the officials and agencies seen as responsible for the stresses experienced. Poliakoff (1980) describes as "endemic" residents' threats to kill official representatives of their community associations, their anger at the "authorities, and even, at times, vicious attacks on co-residents" (p. 756), attributing these extreme reactions to the great diversity of residents who may have shared a dream but not necessarily the values and norms needed to realize it.

Cultural clashes in such situations are frequent. In addition, there are contradictory expectations about individual rights and freedoms and the restrictions on freedom imposed by shared living conditions. Hence the open society becomes closed with the proliferation of such rules as: "no children; no pets; no playing of radio after 9 P.M.; no use of the pool after 8 P.M.; no sales or leases without approval" (ibid., 1980, p. 757).

Then, too, residents become disgruntled about a variety of unmet expectations, such as construction defects of the house, insufficient and inadequate services, rising costs, and, most significantly, experience a sense of powerlessness and dependence on what often seem to be high-handed authorities. Complaints, voiced individually at first, gradually took on a collective quality in Twin Rivers, fueled by a management perceived as insufficiently responsive to need. Grievances likewise took on a general character, shaped by an emerging rhetoric of grievances — "after years of aggravation, frustration, and conciliation . . . we demand" (*The Periscope*, 15 September 1974, p. 6).

In 1972 a list of demands, twenty in all, was presented to the developer by the board of the Twin Rivers Housing Association. His decision not to respond was the match that lit the flame. Impassioned residents and a few zealous board members sprang into action. After consultation, a lawyer was hired by the board to check on the validity of their claims, and a lawsuit was born. Its arrows were aimed at the developer, the trustee, and the township.

1. The developer was charged with failing to provide a community center as described in the sales brochure, insufficient open space as required by the state enabling legislation, and other deficiencies.

2. The bank trustee was charged with not acting in a proper fiduciary relationship toward the beneficiaries, that is, the residents. They resented the high fees paid to the trustee (3.5% of the annual budget) and were concerned about quality of construction limiting "the increase on the market value of our property" as well as arbitrary cost increases. The latter referred to the outrage engendered among residents by the 1973 increase in trust fees from $17 per month per dwelling unit to $18–$28 per month. Additional complaints centered on inadequate community facilities, defective roads, insufficient recreational areas, and misuse of the common open space.

A promised 20,000-square-foot civic center was a particular sore point. The residents insisted this had been part of the original contract, whereas the developer insisted that it had not. He said he had set aside some space for this or other possible buildings, such as churches and schools, in case the residents chose to build them. The residents believed otherwise. A survey of 182 households of all types of housing showed that 85 percent of Twin Rivers residents were in favor of a community civic center and that the residents felt betrayed and discounted. The builder-developer felt underappreciated for his good deeds and intentions and called the leaders of the resident protests paranoid rabblerousers.

3. East Windsor Township and the township planning board, the third target, were cited for their failure to maintain, control, and inspect the work of the developer in constructing Twin Rivers and for maintaining what residents considered an unconstitutional double standard of taxation: Twin Rivers homeowners paid property taxes to the township and monthly fees to the trust for garbage collection and snow removal. This, they argued, denied to the residents the equal protection under the law.

The strains between the township and the new development went far beyond specific issues and jurisdictional disputes, however. First of all, there was the rocky start. It would be an understatement to say that a welcome wagon awaited the newcomers. Their arrival generated much apprehension and unflattering attributions about the "pushy," "aggressive," noisy newcomers in the local press and informal commentary. Initially, too, given the early preponderance of Jews, some of these had anti-Semitic overtones. Hence there was a highly charged atmosphere of distrust and suspicion that caused the township-PUD relationship to be fraught with tension.

Such tensions are not unique. The Levittowners, studied by Gans, faced very similar reactions from their host community, though the particulars varied. Typically, the host community is more traditional, hence apprehensive and wary about the newcomers. In Twin Rivers, it targeted the initial preponderance of Jews, which brought forth stereotypes and prejudices from the Protestant majority in the township. In Levittown, Roman Catholic in-migrants were similarly singled out by the Protestant majority in that township (Gans 1967). The British experience offers numerous other examples (Ward 1993, p. 108).

To this must be added some institutional rivalries over taxes, police protection, and other services, which took at least a decade to be worked out and strained the adjustment process on both sides. Nor did these strains subside by themselves. It took years of hard work to achieve a good working relationship.

By the time the lawsuit was filed, trust and TRHA relations among the principals had deteriorated badly. Both sides felt misunderstood, frustrated, and mistreated. In letters to *The Windsor-Heights Herald* (1

February 1973), the two sides confronted one another. The president of
the TRHA restated the chief grievances, charged that the bank trustee
had failed to act in the best interests of its beneficiaries, and demanded
that control be turned over "to the residents, where it rightfully belongs." In response, the "builder's side," as stated by Herbert J. Kendall, "president" of Twin Rivers, declared these demands "half-baked"
and "immature," reflecting the destructive personal motives of a "group
of rabble rousers" and eliciting only "disgust with this childish tantrum-
like attitude." He saw the trust's mission as assisting "community groups
in creating at Twin Rivers a maturity which must precede the creation
of a real social community." He called the bank trustee "public-spir-
ited" and highly responsible by implicit comparison with the protesters,
about whose moral and financial acumen he had grave doubts. He concluded with the promise to continue to "work for the Twin Rivers community and make it a great place to live, work, and play."

In response, the chair of the Trust Advisory Board, calling Kendall's
letter "ridiculous" and "insulting," demanded a formal apology (*The
Windsor-Heights Herald*, 8 February 1973, p. 4). Tempers flared on
both sides, and the tempo of accusation and counteraccusation accelerated. "A Call for Revolution at Twin Rivers" blared the headlines.

It was an old battle in new dress between the people and the king,
for self-government versus control imposed from above. The campaign
pitted the residents against the bank-trustee. By assuming leadership
and control they would make it "our community." The control over
their own destiny was expressed in a form familiar to all Americans:
NO MORE TAXATION WITHOUT REPRESENTATION — in bold
block letters.

The lawsuit was filed in the New Jersey Superior Court in September 1973. Henceforth, the call to common action was a constant refrain. "Our (the TRHA's) fight is your (the residents') fight; "Stand up
and be counted"; "It is now in your hands"; "Remember your dreams
when you purchased here — support the battle" (*The Periscope*, 10 April
1974, p. 3). Money was both scarce and essential, and appeals for contributions were unrelenting. The slogan, KAG — Knock, Answer, Give —
met with considerable success. By December 1973, 70 percent of the
two thousand residents had sent in contributions amounting to $20,000.
Many donated their services.

The Twin Rivers attorney, for example, reduced his fees, and others
offered incentives to keep up morale and motivation. The public ac-
countant, a member of the TRHA board, promised a free income tax
return for anyone contributing $25 to the legal fund. And so another
$10,000 was raised.

The case never came to trial since the TRHA lost each trial round.

In October 1974 it lost its bid for residents' control of the PUD when it failed to obtain an injunction against the developer's move to transfer control to the First Charter Bank. It lost its final round when the judge ruled that the township PUD ordinance was valid and that decisions about open space and other standards should be left up to the township planning board, thus supporting local control and a flexible application of existing laws. On January 8, 1975, the lawsuit was effectively over. It had taken years of hard efforts, three fund-raising drives, and countless hours of volunteer labor to come to this conclusion. The effect was devastating, yet also strangely exhilarating.

Despite the keenly felt disappointment at the outcome, the process of organizing such a lawsuit by relative amateurs was highly significant for generating a fragile sense of community in Twin Rivers. In addition, the costs accrued, and greatly increased by the defendant's delaying tactics—"they're trying to motion us to death"—kept the sense of injured innocence alive and with it the desire for further action.

Volunteers kept collecting contributions, with appeals focusing on the residents' self-interest ("Our lawsuit can literally add thousands of dollars to the value of our homes") and on their sense of building a community ("Your support is desperately needed, don't let your community down," "The lawsuit is an investment in the future of Twin Rivers").

In February 1976 the TRHA board of directors voted to appeal the adverse decision of the court. The appeal was not successful, but it was important in generating the residents' resolve for yet another challenge — self-government—for 1976 was the year that a shift of power was in view if the residents would rally to the cause. Their votes would determine who would be entrusted with Twin Rivers' future: the TRHA or the bank trustee. The term of the bank trustee was to expire in November 1976, and the TRHA presented itself for election as the new trustee. This required a general turnout of the home owners, and an intensive campaign "to end the tyranny that has existed in Twin Rivers for seven years" was launched.

The rhetoric of the campaign had a familiar ring. It rallied "minutemen" to apprise their fellow residents of the need for their participation. It depicted the bank-trustee as arbitrary and unresponsive and demanded justice for the community. The analogy to the colonists' struggle against the crown in 1776 was drawn repeatedly and even inspired a poem, after Longfellow's "Paul Revere's Ride." The poem by Neal Nevitt, then president of the TRHA, is excerpted here.

. . . and then some neighbors standing there
And as he passed he heard them swear,

To end Trustee fees, three point five [referring to the bank trustee's
   3.5 administrative fee]
. . . Knowing a homeowner's vote was a must,
Who that day would rather be dead,
Than have no voice in running the Trust.
You know the rest, I need say no more.
Surely by now you're aware of the score —
The land is ours, as well as amenities,
. . . Responsibility brings with it fears,
But none of them worse than seven more years
Of having our dollars of Trustee taxation
Spent without right to representation
(*The Periscope*, February 1976, p. 14)

The people-against-the-tyrant theme injected a historic note into the
campaign and lifted it above the ordinary. It inspired intense effort and
lavish promises. As the new trustee, promised the TRHA, we will "give
our community a trustee who is directly answerable to the community"
(*The Periscope*, March 1976, p. 3).

The effort was crowned with success. The people had spoken. The
TRHA took control of the development's affairs and would bear sole
responsibility for the residents' common destiny.

Home-owner lawsuits against developers are extremely common in
PUDs and condominium associations. Twin Rivers was thus not unique.
What is unique is that it managed to sustain this effort for some four
years, surviving continuous changes in board membership and in residential turnover, and grievous setbacks in the lawsuit. Although residents did not gain the legal ends they sought, they made other gains
with long-term benefits. The momentum was maintained because the
disputed rights and claims generated intense feelings in support of the
beleaguered residents and united them against the powerful.

One of the axioms of contemporary sociology is that social conflict
"will strengthen the internal cohesion" of a group (Coser 1956, p. 88).
Conflict with outsiders, noted Simmel (1955), unites the group by sharp-
ening its boundaries and maintaining its identity. This benefits morale
but only if certain conditions are met: "[T]he group must have developed a minimum of consensus and must care about preserving the totality" (Williams 1947, p. 58).

The very expression of their grievances gave residents a lift, as their
shared reactions generated a sense of being connected to one another.
Also, until the final verdict, there was considerable optimism about the
outcome of the case. Gradually but unmistakably, after four major fund
drives, hundreds of hours of volunteer labor, and the continual coverage

in the local paper as well as in papers around the entire state, residents became self-conscious as a collectivity and ready to act on their own behalf. Thus the process of preparing the lawsuit mobilized community sentiment while also instructing the residents in the ways of organized cooperation, which did not come naturally to most of them.

From the perspective of how a sense of community is generated and secured, the lawsuit of 1973 constitutes a significant marker for Twin Rivers' identity and capacity for collective, that is, community-wide, action. With effort, interest, and commitment kept alive, community began, slowly, to take root.

The process of fighting city hall, in this case the developer and the trustee, took nearly five years. For a relatively small resident population it was a huge undertaking in uncharted territory. Not only were the residents inexperienced but they could not rely on legal precedents, because Twin Rivers was the first PUD in New Jersey. They found resources within the group. In addition to volunteer fund-raising, they could count on the accountants, lawyers, and real estate experts in their midst. Together, this small, devoted, hard-working group of residents helped secure an "investment in their future" (*The Periscope*, 15 January 1975, p. 7). It was a big test of collective will and a triumph of sorts. While the lawsuit definitely rallied community spirit, it also engendered quite opposite reactions. First of all, the lawsuit encouraged an adversarial posture as well as a cooperative one. There was an enemy, the trust and the developer, so that there was division within Twin Rivers as the board and the management clashed. Then, too, support for the lawsuit was not unanimous. A minority of the residents preferred a more conciliatory route. Condominium owners opposed the suit, perhaps because they already had a community center. Some residents approved of the lawsuit in principle but did not want to support it financially.

Levittown too—new, pioneering, idyllic though it aspired to be— "was continually wracked by power struggles." These were in part due to Levitt's desire for maximum control and residents' resistance to him. To his surprise, in fact, the residents "proved more unruly than he'd imagined" (Boxandall and Ewen 2000, p. 144).

Perhaps the most lasting legacy of the lawsuit concerned litigation as a means of settling disputes and the permanent residue of a distrust of authority this left behind. This would persist long after the lawsuit had been forgotten and self-government had been achieved. To their considerable dismay, moreover, many subsequent TRHA boards would learn that governments of the people can be just as heartily disliked as any other.

CHAPTER 12

LEADERS AS LIGHTNING RODS

Until philosophers are kings, or the kings and princes of this world have the spirit and power of philosophy, and political greatness and wisdom meet in one . . . then only will this our State have a possibility of life and behold the light of day.

—Plato, *The Republic*

If men were angels, no government would be necessary.

—James Madison, *Federalist*, No. 51

One of the surprises of this research into the makings of a community was the crucial role played by only a fraction of the residents in guiding the collectivity in myriad ways, from formal governance and legal transactions to the mobilization of the residents for community-wide projects and responsibility for the collective welfare.

It was their task, as representative figures or experts, to "create new schemes of behavior" as well as new institutions and forms of cooperation. This most difficult assignment, more than any other collective task, requires leadership (Thomas and Znaniecki 1958, p. 1303).

As exemplary individuals, leaders are "thought to embody communal values to an unusually high degree" and they can therefore channel collective energies to needed goals (Zablocki 1980, p. 295). Of course, principles are easier to state than to enact, and to discover and cultivate effective leaders is an uphill struggle in all social aggregates, from small, informal groups to "little" communities to large-scale social systems.

Twin Rivers was no exception. Leaders played a critical and often highly controversial role. But if early on it was difficult to attract residents to assume leadership positions, two or three decades later it would prove a source of fierce competition and contention among factions vying for "power," and those in power became key targets of vilification. This would have astonished the newcomers of the 1970s. They were well aware of—and grateful to—the few who volunteered their time to run for office, head crucial committees, attend board meetings, sponsor social and humanitarian projects, and, above all, care about their fellows and the fate of the commons.

The theme that "the community-minded are in the minority" was sounded early on and continues, unabated, into the present. Without these few doing the work for the many, as was pointed out repeatedly, none of the solid achievements would have been possible. And by the 1990s, that achievement was threatened by the actions of a fractious few, which greatly increased tensions within the community.

To learn about the motivations of those who chose to serve and make the sacrifices needed, one hundred leaders were interviewed during the three decades. The criteria for inclusion were serving on the TRHA governing board; chairing important committees to deal with such issues as parking, rule violations, recreation, and pets; and providing expertise for the entire community as tax advisors, pedagogues, architectural consultants, or reporters for the community paper. In the pages that follow, some of the general themes that seemed to engage members of this group, including their fears and hopes for the community in the making, will be drawn out.

From numerous past studies, one learns that leaders, to be effective, must not depart too sharply from those they seek to lead. In contrast to experts who are expected to excel their clients, leaders must be *with* their followers or lose them, and at Twin Rivers they were indeed with them. The family backgrounds, occupations, geographic origins, and religious affiliations of leaders matched those of the majority of the residents. Nor did their appraisals of the community depart significantly from those of most of the residents. They appreciated similar virtues—for the decade of the 1970s this included the quality of life and selected facilities and services—and they deplored similar inadequacies of parking and design.

Thus, in the founding decade, leaders were first among equals. One interesting difference was that the leader sample had more two-parent families (nine-tenths) than the residents generally (two-thirds). This

Table 12.1
Leaders' "Best and Worst" Features of Twin Rivers: 1970s

Best	Worst
Convenience	Scale too big for identity
Safety for self and children	Walking distance not working
Recreational facilities—pools, tennis courts	Poor shopping center
Good value for the money	Parking problems
Worry-free maintenance	No teen center
Children have many friends	Design monotonous
A good feeling overall	Insufficient social mix
	Neighborhood tensions
	"It's the little things that irk."

could mean that their lives had the stability needed to concern themselves with wider issues or that they had a more traditional division of labor, which freed up their time for the community.

In time, the concerns of leaders would change, but so did those of the residents generally. Most significantly, there was a shift from a concern about physical features—of house, open space, boundaries, and traffic—to such features as social relationships and social priorities. By the 1980s leaders frequently deplored the small degree of resident commitment to community issues and the absence of community spirit. By the 1990s the salience of the social dimension—factionalism, evasion of collective rules, lack of trust—had become more significant.

The potential for unity and cohesiveness, pretty much taken for granted in the first decade, now became a goal to be assiduously pursued lest it slip through the collective fingers. The spirit of goodwill, so evident in the 1970s, had begun to weaken as conflicts and frustrations multiplied. And when, by the second decade, the community had acquired two-thirds of its final population and had begun to assume its more permanent shape, there was a growing preoccupation with how to

Table 12.2
Goals Realized and Unrealized: Leaders' Views

Goals Realized	Goals Insufficiently Realized
Safety	Not enough ethnic, social mix
Good for the children	Aesthetic limitations
Worry-free daily life	Not enough caring for others
As much privacy as we want	Not enough trust
	Not enough cooperation

mobilize around common concerns and find ways to strengthen the social fabric.

The leaders, because of their greater responsibilities, were ahead of the rest of the population in identifying significant problems and in striving to address them. For example, they pointed to a problem with teenagers long before other residents did so, and they also articulated the tensions between the residents and the trust far earlier.

The leaders believed in the community and its future and thought that hard work, sacrifice, and goodwill would make for eventual success. Above all, they took the long view far more often than did other residents. And they were positive about the community in the making, even when they were critical of specifics.

Still, there was a characteristic inability — or reluctance perhaps — for both residents and leaders to spell out what they thought constituted a good, solid, desirable community. There were exceptions, of course, especially among board members and trust administrators, but in the main, the articulation of general ideas and abstractions proved difficult for leaders and residents alike. In addition, both found it easier to articulate negative criticism than positive appraisal, as complaints came more easily than encomiums.

This puzzled the pioneering visionary Gerald Finn, who had proposed the idea of such a community in the first place. It was his vision that spurred the transformation of a New Jersey potato field into a complex physical community. Gerald Finn, pursuing his "impossible dream," wanted to create "something great" that would make a big statement about community. A developer, he was moved by a romantic vision of a community where people would make a fresh start, lead happy, productive lives, and create a solid social mix to show democracy in action. He risked all of his own money and could have lost it all.

Eventually Finn would be disappointed, however, with what he found to be the lack of diversity and the architectural monotony of the final product, and he became increasingly concerned about Twin Rivers' course of development. By the mid-1980s, the residents' reluctance to participate in self-governance and involve themselves in important issues that would affect their joint future seemed self-defeating.

"Why is there so little commitment?" he was asked (interview, 1989). Here is his response in 1989: The residents, he said, seem to focus on the negatives too much, so that commitment is hard to develop. This leads to discouragement and then to apathy. Actually, this is not surprising, given the apathy that prevails throughout the society, since "America is not community-minded" and thus the self-preoccupation of the residents of Twin Rivers is a reflection of the general culture.

As to lessons for the future, Finn thought that key ingredients for a successful community required a great deal of money, a great deal of time, and total commitment by the developer to stay there and carry it through. "Do not impose your lifestyle on others but lead people to the new. And build on a scale you can manage."

But neither the visionary Gerald Finn nor the enterprising developer Herbert Kendall were present in Twin Rivers by then. Finn had been bought out by Kendall and the W. R. Grace Company, and Kendall, after some stormy years, bowed out to build other communities on the West Coast. He left disappointed in the way things had turned out, and he smarted under what he perceived to be the residents' ingratitude for the community he had brought into being for them.

After the departure of the principals, whose names are not familiar to the current residents, Twin Rivers struggled long and hard to win the right to govern itself (see chapter 6), and the effort, though victorious, left exhaustion in its wake. Henceforth, the lack of community participation became a recurrent theme. It burdened the minority of "community-minded" with excessive demands on their time and remains a recurrent complaint to this day.

Repeatedly, the residents were reminded that they had the power and right to affect decision-making. But a scant few (5%) took advantage of these rights in the 1970s, a figure that has increased somewhat by the 1990s (12%), but still remains a small minority.

Hence there are two questions to ponder: (1) Why are most residents reluctant to participate in creating a viable community, their own community? (2) What accounts for the minority who depart from the pack to do their part?

Resident Apathy

Two reasons for resident apathy emerge from the analysis of the responses of both residents and leaders. One has to do with the disturbing experiences of the residents in the formative years of the community's life, the other with a form of the "free rider" problem. In the formative 1970s, the builder-developer together with the bank trustee were blamed for most everything that went wrong or that failed to live up to residents' expectations. The developer became a special target of blame, accused of evading his responsibilities and of being indifferent to the needs of the residents. Instead of "dynamic leadership" we're getting "the royal run around" (*The Periscope*, May 1974, p. 4). The builder's presumed disinterest engendered cynicism and frustration. But resident apathy continued even with the departure of the builder and the transfer of governance to the homeowners association. Hence other explanations are needed. One was the "every man for himself" principle the first residents brought with them, which may have helped them navigate through New York City, from which many of them came, but was ill suited to a new community.

It did not take long before some people realized that something more was needed if Twin Rivers was to advance. Here is how Twin Rivers was portrayed in the first community paper in 1975: Twin Rivers consists of "2,500 disinterested families who happen to live in the same development." Its future "lies in the hands of these same residents but in the absence of strong leadership and an interested membership," Twin Rivers may not survive. The outgoing president of the Twin Rivers Homeowners Association (TRHA) board understood very clearly that without commitment and responsible leadership, the community would perish (*The Periscope*, December 1975, p. 16).

Even recreational pursuits, high on everyone's list of positives, were not immune. As late as 1985, the basketball league stood in danger of dissolution due to an absence of interested residents willing to volunteer as supervisors (*The Periscope*, March 1985, p. 10).

By the mid-1980s, the two-breadwinner family had become widespread as the tiny tots of the 1970s became teenagers eager to hang out with their own friends. Hence commuting time to jobs outside Twin Rivers took up a lot of adult energies and free time for community participation. But that could hardly be the principal reason — since there was no consistent pattern. Some employed parents always made time for the community, while many retirees and homemakers did not.

Lest we exaggerate the self-absorption of success-bent Americans in the late twentieth century, we should note that part of the reluctance to serve may have stemmed from feeling inadequate in knowledge and experience to serve in a public capacity. "Laymen are not professionals . . . [and] . . . this is not a job for laymen" (*The Periscope*, March 1973, p. 1).

Given the widespread reluctance to serve, whether for reasons of inexperience or self-preoccupation, the outstanding record of service by the committed few is remarkable indeed. They served long hours, without pay, perks, or even recognition. What made them assume such time-consuming, often thankless, and always demanding duties? How did they find the time to chair the committees, present themselves as candidates for the TRHA board, inform themselves about key issues and transcend personal preoccupations to take the long-range view? What propelled them to reach toward wider horizons? Each of the one hundred leaders was asked the same question and their replies are reassuring to those who believe that narcissism has become a permanent cultural condition.

Question: *You know the common complaint about how hard it is to find capable people willing to give their time to work on behalf of the community. What makes you different? Why do you work for the community?*

Replies:

- The excitement and challenge to make things better; "there's opportunity here to make a difference; I wanted to use my training and experience to build something fine" (M. J., age 36).
- "I believed in Twin Rivers. I came in very idealistic, very optimistic; there were lots of problems to solve; it gave *me* a purpose" (J. N., age 29).
- "I got involved six months after moving in — and one of the things that attracted me to Twin Rivers was that it had a plan and a purpose. It's good to reach beyond your own life" (R. T., age 30).
- "Ego. I wanted the recognition, the sense of power." "I could affect the direction the community would take." "If someone's going to make rules, it might as well be me." (L. H., age 33).
- "I had been critical enough of the powers that be and so I had to accept responsibility and try to add my own ideas. . . . If you want to change things, you've got to act, not just yell. . . . If I don't do something, who will?" (S. H., age 29).

Of all the reasons offered, however, one was endorsed virtually unanimously, though not with the same words.

- "If I expect something from society, I must give something back. That is what we were taught in my family."
- "My parents instilled certain values in me. I live these."
- "I can hear my mother now — 'Don't just be a taker. You've got to give back.'"
- "It's always a few who act for many. I'm one of the few."

The same idea again and again — my parents, mother, family told me, taught me, instilled in me — and I want to give something back.

More than most residents, leaders believed in the possibilities of the new community. A social experiment was under way and they sought to see the results. Above all, they felt a sense of responsibility toward the developing community; they owed something to it.

In their dedication to building a better community, they seemed to be able to work with others, inspire others, and care about the future they shared. "Some of us care about our fellow humans." Especially significant was the fact that they perceived a link between their participation and everyone's survival.

Psychic rewards operate as well—leaders feel useful and important and see themselves as effective actors—whereas nonparticipants seem to lack the confidence to get involved. Most people are reactive whereas leaders are proactive.

Because of their concern about the community, leaders also worried about the resident apathy that seemed to set in after the honeymoon of the first two to three years. Something intangible seems to have been at work here that no one could quite put a finger on, but it had as one unintended consequence the division of the population into a minority imbued with activist fervor and a majority sunk in passivity.

When the leaders were asked what could account for that division, they offered a number of plausible speculations.

- "I think people want to avoid conflict and keep their views to themselves."
- "Initially, there were 'terrible arguments' about property, parking, pets, signage—but that subsided and many withdrew into their cocoons."
- "Maybe it has something to do with the urban backgrounds of the first residents. They came here with a New York mentality, very self-oriented, demanding; they didn't want to cooperate."
- "People want others to do it all for them."
- "People care only about themselves; they don't know how to cooperate."

To avoid conflicts, to let those motivated and capable represent the group's interests are not unreasonable goals, of course. In a small community, the airing of differences on policies and priorities can produce lingering tensions as the political becomes the personal. And letting the motivated and capable minority act on behalf of the majority is, after all, the basis for representative government. But not to be ignored is the culturally encouraged preoccupation with personal success as against collective priorities. On the scale of preferred values, the public interest, the spirit of community, and cooperation rank low, often last, for these residents (table 12.3). Most importance was attached to safety, responsive management, the appearance of the community, and privacy. Least important to the latest group of residents were community-wide activities and the spirit of community. Another clue to residents' feelings stems from the appraisals of the importance "most residents" attribute to the values listed in table 12.4.

Table 12.3
Residents' Ratings of Community Features: 1990s

	Very Important	Moderately	Not Important
Appearance of the community	81%	18%	1%
Spirit of the community	34%	56%	10%
Friendly neighbors	64%	33%	1%
Privacy	81%	17%	2%
Safety	95%	3%	2%
Responsive management	85%	12%	3%
Community-wide activities	22%	54%	24%

N = 560

Note the features considered most important: Education (61%) and individual success (47%) top the list, followed by hard work (34%), material possessions (31%), and getting rich (28%). Least important are popularity (33% say not important), community involvement (33%), compassion for the less fortunate (28%), cooperation (18%), and good citizenship (17%).

These results denote the low standing of community involvement and activities in comparison with other desired goals such as educational attainment and personal success. Perhaps this helps explain the common, and widely noted, tendency to "let George do it." In the

Table 12.4
Priorities of 1990s Residents

	Very Important	Moderately Important	Not Important
Education	61%	30%	2%*
Individual success	47%	44%	1%
Hard work	34%	52%	5%
Material possessions	31%	52%	7%
Getting rich	28%	49%	15%
Voting, citizenship	25%	50%	17%
Cooperation	22%	53%	18%
Popularity	14%	45%	33%
Compassion for less fortunate	10%	54%	28%
Community involvement	9%	50%	33%

N = 500

*Totals under 100% exclude "Don't Knows" and "No Answers."

words of one candidate for the TRHA board in 1999, "Sometimes I think what the people really want is a Big Brother, one who will work on their behalf; articulate what they cannot express; anticipate what is needed; get things done. This may be effective and certainly is convenient but it threatens to diminish people's sense of responsibility to house, land, and community."

One conclusion underscored by these reactions is that community rests on the efforts, care, and visions of the few. If these meet with the approval of the majority, the leadership will be granted a continuing mandate to carry on. If not, dissent and protest will make themselves felt. Still, despite division, apathy, and criticisms leveled against the imperfections of the developing community, something akin to a sense of community began to coalesce by the 1980s. Fifteen years after the first residents bought into their piece of the American pie, the rudiments of an ongoing, organized community became visible. Aided and abetted by the nucleus of concerned leaders and a portion of the residents, the community had begun to take on a life of its own. There was growing participation in community elections, an extensive network of organizations and associations, the outlines of a public collective self-addressed in the community newspaper, and an identity recognized by others outside Twin Rivers.

- "Do I think Twin Rivers has a sense of community? Yes, I do believe so. Just look how people cooperate on projects more — the playgrounds, for example." (F. L., 1992).
- "There are a lot of community groups — Rescue Squad, Fire Squad, many others — and all voluntary" (A. R., 1985).
- "Yes, there's a tremendous sense of community. You face the same problems your neighbor faces" (C. B., 1987).
- "It's amazing how activism creates such a strong sense of community" (E. R., 1988).
- "Yes, there's pride in community. Sometimes it takes tragedy to bring it out — a fire, a loss, the fight against toxic waste. . . . Crisis brings out people and creates a sense of community because it forces people to move beyond self-interest" (O. R. 1988).
- "Yes, Twin Rivers holds together. They come out for an important moment or movement" (A. D., 1990).
- "Yes, because people remain in Twin Rivers; being born here and living here for a long time — all these create community. The children will forge community; their generation will create community" (C. H., 1990).

Some felt that community had not yet been achieved but would be in time.

- "I get the feeling that people want that sense of community and fight for it, but it's not yet achieved—that takes time. Twin Rivers is still proud of its newness" (R. E., 1986).
- "Twin Rivers has both apathy and community. During the week, there's no sense of community—as people are away at work; on weekends that changes" (F. P., 1989).

The less than one-sixth who said there would never be a sense of community cited the following:

- "There's no central place; Twin Rivers needs a spatial core" (B. I., 1976).
- "The population is part of modern America—restless, rootless, mobile, transient" (S. T., 1989).
- "Developer could have done more to set the right tone on behalf of community—with a teen center, movies" (L. N., 1997).

Time is a double-edged variable. On the one hand, the passage of time strengthens community identity, but on the other hand, time changes people's needs and preferences. Hence, a community center may have been important in the 1970s but not a decade later when adults no longer constituted a single, unified group. As diversity and the social mix increased, a single center could no longer serve everyone's interests. This confirms Joseph Vuzzo's observation, as trust administrator, that the phasing of facilities is very important and must be studied carefully so that timing is built into the process at appropriate points.

Over the three decades of its existence, therefore, both residents and leaders had learned important lessons. And despite a diversity of views and divisions of opinion within the leadership, residents increasingly perceived themselves as part of the same community. Much has been achieved by that devoted minority who were able to put the collective ahead of narrow self-interest. The following sentiments capture the feelings of a growing number of residents.

- "This is home where I come to at end of day; a sanctuary; it's not the house, it's the community that provides solace" (J. P., school principal,1989).
- "Being born here and living here for a long time, pride, all these create community. The children will forge community . . . their generation. It is for them" (T. N., editor, 1998).

The themes that leaders use to engage residents' interests are apparent in the speeches promoting candidacies to elective office. The most recent occasion for this was the 1999 election to the TRHA board. Here are the concerns and plans of the five candidates seeking three seats on the board (*Twin Rivers Today* September 1999):

Candidate Bernard Bush: "I see in Twin Rivers a pleasant and attractive place to live, with a fundamentally sound management, high-quality houses at affordable prices, well-maintained grounds and neighborly atmosphere." But there are problems, for instance: (1) "Piles of garbage of every description on our streets" — against the trust and municipal rules and ordinances. This is due to the "irresponsible behavior of a few of our neighbors." (2) The declining shopping center. (3) Danger from the heavy volume of truck traffic on the peripheral roads and worsening air pollution.

There are less practical but even more disturbing problems — such as "strident conflict" about public issues replete with insults and angry outbursts. This may destroy the community. "It creates hatred and mistrust, and is detrimental to the public health. . . . As a PUD, Twin Rivers is not simply a collection of individual householders. We are an organized community with a common purpose and with rules and regulations mutually agreed upon. We have a responsibility to work together to keep this a good place to live. That is my view of our community."

Candidate Evan Greenberg, a six-year member of the board seeking a second term, had served on many significant committees — the Architectural Design Review Committee, for one. He coordinated the Thirtieth Anniversary Concerts, negotiated for more reasonable cable rates, and obtained state and county financing for environmental projects.

The issues he considered essential for the future of Twin Rivers were a topnotch community center, thriving shopping center, the use of "our strength as a large community" to reduce costs for services such as home repairs, gas and electric rates, road repairs, and so on. He promised to "use . . . my skills and experience to continue what I call the Twin Rivers Renaissance. . . . This year's election will determine whether the Renaissance continues, or we lose our sense of community and stumble back into the dark ages."

Candidate Emily McDonald, an eleven-year resident, served on the Committee for a Better Twin Rivers, which was challenging the current board. If elected, she said she would seek the following changes: Create "open channels of communication between residents and the TRHA board; establish an ADR (alternative dispute resolution committee) to "mediate disputes, at no cost, between . . . residents and the board"; update architectural standards: "Twin Rivers is a great community . . .

by bringing our standards into the twenty-first century we can continue to enjoy our beautiful community . . ."; allow financial disclosure of expenditures to residents; . . . "as homeowners we have a legal right to know how our money is being spent. . . . I truly want Twin Rivers to be the best community it can be."

Scott Pohl, who was at the time of the election the board president, sought reelection to the TRHA board — "because of my commitment to the residents of our community." He had served on numerous committees, including Homeowner Services, parking, newspaper, public relations, and computers. If reelected, he said he would produce a recreation and fitness center for all residents, adults as well as children and teens. He would move to get the shopping center into shape and "continue the fight to keep our property values high." Also, he would work with real estate agents "to market our community properly." (Questionable real estate dealings had been exposed in 1999.) "I have a vision for our future which is bright and improves our quality of life," he said.

Candidate Donald Sharpe, a twenty-six-year resident of Twin Rivers and a mail carrier, stated: "I think this is a wonderful community and would like to see it stay that way. I normally do not get involved in the workings of the community. But there comes a time when everyone has to take a stand. I am a reasonable, fair, and rational person . . . and will use all of those qualities to do what is best for everyone in this community."

The December 1999 election was more critical than most others because a split had developed in the community that was threatening to foment disunity. On one side were the long-term reliables who had served for years and were in agreement on basic ideas and policies that had been developed, not without struggle, over a long period of time. On the other was a faction (members of the Committee for a Better Twin Rivers or CBTR) who challenged established practice and sought to put themselves in power as the true leaders of the community. Their dissatisfactions rested on two main sets of grievances. The first was the secrecy involved in the nature of the board expenditures and other types of information. This was considered a violation of the rights to privacy of information by representatives of the established groups. The second issue rallying this highly vociferous and agitated minority targeted those it considered to have held power too long. Its spokespeople decried "entrenched positions," high-handedness, and being "above the rules."

The countercharge was that this incendiary faction consisted of "reactionaries who wish to . . . undo our past"; they were characterized as "the irresponsible few" who were "a danger to a democratic Twin Rivers."

The schism revealed here was and continues to be serious and disturbing to many who deplore "the increasingly strident conflict, the shouting, the erroneous charges of misconduct," and the "mutual hatred and suspicion" these foster. Ultimately "such behavior will destroy our community and we must end this destructive conflict and find a way to reason together as good neighbors."

This was perhaps the most serious crisis Twin Rivers had confronted in its existence to date. One prior member of the board showed the depth of ill will fomented by the insurgents. "In the last two years," he said, "my family has been targeted for mischief by a group with no ideas, no morals, and no fortitude. They have resorted to harassing phone calls, groundless accusations, malicious photos and menacing letters. They do not care about the community or anyone else."

The die was cast — and the December 1999 election would tell which Twin Rivers would prevail. Three seats on the board could determine the future of the entire community.

The election of December 1999 was the most hotly contested in the history of Twin Rivers. One-third of the residential units (889 out of 2,400) were represented at the polls, and when the votes were counted, the incumbents "won handily over . . . the Board critics" (Toutant, *Windsor Heights Herald* 24 December 1999, pp. 1, 8A). Evan Greenberg, Scott Pohl, and first-time candidate Bernard Bush defeated Emily McDonald, Donald Sharpe, and Scott Matlovsky of the Committee for a Better Twin Rivers.

Not surprisingly, each winning candidate connected his success to his campaign message, but one letter to the editor by a current board member noted that the winners were elected by "the largest plurality in recent history" and saw this as "a mandate from the community." And all residents were enjoined to "be adult," put the past behind them, work together, and offer congratulations to the winners, condolences to the losers. The community was out of danger — for the moment.

In the election of 2000, the incumbents again defeated the CBTR candidates but now by an even larger margin of three to one. The board of directors thus had reason to feel reassured that the large majority of the community endorsed their performance.

Nonetheless, the challenging faction keeps to its agenda of high alert against the elected nine-member board. As an irritant to many, and a costly one judging from the group's penchant for legal action, it is also a manifestation of democracy in action. The majority prevails but dissenting minorities have the right to be heard. And heard they are.

Some of this can lead to lively exchanges in letters-to-the-editor columns of local papers but some of it sounds a discordant note of distrust and apprehension that detracts from the tasks at hand.

CHAPTER 13
UNITY AND DIVISION, CONFLICT AND CONSENSUS

Ours is a hugger-mugger unity.

— W. H. Auden

How to forge unity out of the many disparate elements of human aggregates is a question that has been asked for millennia. Always significant, it has become more urgent in a technically specialized civilization imbued with individualism and the competitive ethos. This creates a tension between two incompatible forces — between the cooperation needed for unity and culturally endorsed individualism — that is difficult, if not impossible, to resolve.

In the colonial American experience discussed earlier, we noted how hard the early colonies struggled to achieve unity in the face of strife and turmoil. The town meeting was crucial, for it provided a venue for a collective focus and the formation of a public consensus out of many competing views and voices. Town meetings were training grounds for democracy where community was put to the test as the one and the many confronted each other.

In her study of contemporary Selby, Vermont, population five hundred, Jane Mansbridge explored these questions for a modern population with diverse interests and lifestyles (Mansbridge 1983). In tracing the often tortuous paths for consensus on key decisions that affected the town as a whole, she noted the premium that residents put on conflict avoidance in order to achieve unity. The democracy they sought to further relied on consensus. Consensual democracy encouraged participants to identify with the town as a whole, which "in turn helps develop common interests." By contrast, there is "adversary democracy" which rests on acknowledging conflicting interests and their equal protection under the law (ibid., p. 5). Out of the clash of interests, policies take shape.

This distinction is critical, but it is rarely sufficiently heeded because of the mistaken view that consensus is the only legitimate basis of collective life. It was a persistent theme in the early American communities, though not always to the degree expressed in seventeenth-century Dedham in which every qualified male householder (restricted by race, age, and church membership) signed a covenant to bar from the town "all such as are contrary minded" and to admit only those who would "walk in peaceable conversation," give "mutual encouragement," and "seek the good of each other out of which may be derived true peace" (ibid., p. 134).

Conflict avoidance is likewise characteristic of communes, which often break asunder because of members' inability to cope with conflicts they cannot suppress. Yet conflict is endemic, and, given the insistence on consensus, it can be dealt with only by compelling the departure of the contentious faction or by resorting to coercive measures internal to the commune.

One mechanism to allow for the legitimate expression of conflict is that of majority rule. This is such a mainstay of contemporary political institutions that its problematic features for small communities are often overlooked. Experience has shown that majority rule leads to a festering resentment and frustration among those overruled by the majority, and this may poison the social climate.

To avoid this possibility, seventeenth-century citizens of New England confronted divisive issues by bringing them up "again and again rather than allowing a minority to impose its opinion on the majority" (ibid., p. 257), hoping thereby to achieve unanimity across division.

Fearful of strife and recriminations, citizens may prefer to withdraw from public participation. The fear of making enemies, along with the fear of public exposure and humiliation, was significant in Selby, where "your enemies are also your neighbors for life" (ibid., p. 64). We can conclude from this that withdrawal can be a protective device that avoids confrontation or ridicule and thereby preserves the ideal of community harmony in theory.

Nonparticipation in community affairs, greatly and widely deplored, thus seems to have roots in the social character of collective life and is not only, or even primarily, a matter of too little personal concern and commitment. What seems to be public indifference may protect the community by keeping disagreements with neighbors and friends at bay. "If my neighbor's for it and I'm against it, there'll be trouble," said one of Mansbridge's informants.

Still, conflict is unavoidable not only in a heterogeneous population with widely differing life experiences and aspirations, but also in the small, close-knit, homogeneous settlements characteristic of the early American colonial towns. Though united in their quest for a new life in an unsettled land, conflict was never absent. In Sudbury, for example (Powell 1965), the generations fought one another bitterly over property rights and privileges. This eventually led to the departure of the young to a new Sudbury adjacent to the old one. But here, too, despite the desire for harmony, conflicts and power struggles multiplied and laid bare the fissures beneath the façade of unity.

One way to cope with these realities is to recognize that two types of communities coexist within a common rubric. There is the "community of otherness" and the "community of affinity." The community of otherness rests on the realization that there are as many points of view as there are individuals but that people nonetheless have common concerns and goals. Thus, even when they clash, they affirm one another and hold in "creative tension the importance of self, others, and principles that ground the community" (Arnett 1986, pp. xv, 8).

In the "community of affinity," on the other hand, people often "huddle together for security and imagine they are safe and united because they use the same slogans even though they have no real relationship with one another." Although they eschew conflict and opposition, the result, often, is a "false community" (ibid., p. xv).

The larger and more diversified a community, the more diverse and potentially conflicting the interests of the members. The thrust of Mansbridge's argument is that communities must learn to use conflicts productively, yet many do not know how to do so.

Conflict may actually build community in the process of clash, debate, and compromise. When residents realize that conflicts can be expressed and resolved, they can begin to construct genuine community.

Of course, conflict may also find expression in symbolic form, for example in athletic contests and team competitions, which helps drain off some of the hostile energy (Mansbridge 1983; Gans 1967). Whatever the sources of conflict, and they range from mundane irritations to major ideological battles, the important lesson to heed is that community is built by conflict as well as by consensus. In the process of resolving power struggles and ideological confrontations, the outlines of community become visible above the lines of fissure and division. Successful communities must be able to integrate, within a single framework, the divisive along with the unifying forces.

In communal societies, "consensual rules" keep participants focused on what they have in common and on their aspirations toward harmony (Mansbridge 1983, p. 253), but in modern societies that rely on self-interest and an invisible hand to achieve the public good, such ideals are harder to find. Acknowledging one's dependence on others goes against the message absorbed in childhood, and individualism and self-reliance are at odds with an ethos of sharing and cooperation. At times, when individual interests clash with collective interests, the courts may have to resort to an ancient common-law doctrine of "necessity" that postulates that "there exists an implied agreement of every member of society that his own individual welfare shall, in cases of necessity, yield to that of the community, and that his property, life, and liberty shall, under certain circumstances, be placed in jeopardy or even sacrificed for the public good" (Poliakoff 1980, p. 760). Hence, even in traditional communities, individuation was frequently a source of tension and strife. The Polish villages described by Thomas and Znaniecki offer a rich compendium of examples. Historically, these villages owned pastures, forests, and water in common for centuries, with individually owned arable land distributed around a common belt of the village. But shared resources became violently contested as individuation increased with urban-industrial growth (Thomas and Znaniecki 1958, p. 1397).

The idea that one's personal fate is bound up with that of one's fellows was not at all self-evident to the residents of Twin Rivers. It had to be implanted in the residents bit by bit through the give and take of their joint existence. Internal cleavages surfaced early and many of these persist into the present.

Even in small, homogeneous settlements social divisions run deep. In Selby, for example, contention between the wealthier and the poorer citizens was a persistent source of strain, as the better-off had to pay higher taxes to provide the services, however minimal, for needier citizens (Mansbridge 1983, pp. 89–161).

In Twin Rivers, an interesting tension developed between early and later arrivals. Old-timers (sometimes with only one year's prior residence) and newcomers fought over taxes, zoning, schools, and services. Newcomers tended to feel that they were marginal, even excluded. This cleavage is historically familiar as natives oppose immigrants, or first families reject contacts with families of later vintage. Nonetheless, its tenacity in Twin Rivers was surprising in such a new settlement and under such fluid conditions, especially when amplified by the social distance between home owners and renters. Such divisions weakened the fragile unity initially forged and created long-lasting patterns of social mistrust.

In time, of course, the long-term residents outnumbered the new-comers and this diminished the tension between them. In the first five years of Twin Rivers' life, however, the proportions of early and later residents were roughly equal and this accentuated the strength of the division.

Why does this cleavage develop at all? Proprietary attitudes are part of the story. The first residents have struggled together and share the unique experiences of pioneers. Later arrivals miss not only these expe-riences but come into a situation in which the ground rules and all the early decisions have created a special culture to which they must adapt. Often this creates a permanent sense of marginality.

Mansbridge noted that even in very democratic organizations the old-timers distanced themselves from the newcomers, making them feel like outsiders. One issue had to do with basic information about past decisions. The old-timers did not want to rehash materials for the new-comers, and this left the newcomers at a considerable disadvantage (ibid., 1980, p. 181). Perhaps, for this reason, newcomers are frequently re-garded as less entitled to privilege or as somehow "inferior."

Another often-noted division is that between residents who own their dwellings, usually houses or condominiums, and those who rent them (usually apartments). One striking tendency in Twin Rivers, evi-dent virtually from year one, was that homeowners looked down on renters as less desirable neighbors and less responsible citizens who were less likely to contribute to the upkeep of the community. In turn, the renters resented such unwarranted aspersions on their motives and char-acter and felt isolated and excluded from the developing community. The two groups formed separate worlds and stayed well within their respective borders. Homeowners confined their range of sociability to other homeowners, especially in their own courts, and renters were rarely included.

Other divisions took on the more familiar form of the generational divide between teens and parents, and the gender divide between men and women, to be examined.

Men and Women React to the New Community

The move to Twin Rivers in the 1970s was a move for the family. Hus-bands and wives were united by their desire to make a fresh start in a new community along with other similarly situated couples. When they embarked on this venture, they did so as married couples (93%) and as parents of one (31%) or two (40%) children under five.

The majority of wives had held jobs before the move but only one-fourth continued to do so thereafter. Whatever plans they had for future employment, they put these on hold indefinitely.

The move accentuated the traditional family division of labor by gender, making the wives the primary homemakers, and the husbands the primary economic providers. Husbands commuted to jobs in New York City and Philadelphia, whereas wives remained within the boundaries of the unfinished community day after day.

This traditional division of labor seemed, initially at least, agreeable to both partners. The women chose to devote themselves to domestic priorities with considerable enthusiasm, while their husbands braved the daily commute without complaints. After all, both had thought long and hard about dislodging themselves from their urban nests to venture forth into suburbia. Couples told of the agonizing process of decision when the houses were as yet little more than tiny slots on a drawing board or map displayed in the sales room. Many described a process of indecision as they made a down payment, changed their minds and withdrew it, made a second down payment, changed their minds again, until a third time when they finally moved full speed ahead.

Given their lack of experience with home ownership, few of the residents knew what to expect or how to manage the small crises that cropped up. Used to landlords to complain to, they carried habits forged as tenants from city to suburb unaware that henceforth, new home owners that they were, they were on their own. Instead of the landlord, they turned to the sales office, the builder, the trust, and any and all who might serve as a sounding board for their bewilderment and frustrations as new suburbanites. In turn, their unwilling landlord substitutes tried, often in vain, to hide from the wrath of these often incensed, always intense, plaintiffs, leaving communications in a rather battered state.

Initially, however, couples held strongly together. They fixed up the house, ferried the children to school, invited the neighbors for coffee, and threw themselves into the hectic social life of new residents.

Gradually, however, within the year, the paths of husbands and wives began to diverge. The men rose early to catch the commuter bus to take them to their jobs outside the community, arriving back home twelve hours later when the children were asleep. By contrast, the daily routines of their homebound wives focused on cooking, cleaning, ironing, and child care, often with no one to talk to. Only 8% had paid household help and another 30% could count on sporadic help from their husbands on weekends.

Table 13.1
Ranking Dimensions of the Female Role: 1970s*

Ranked First in Importance (in percentages)	1970s, All Women	Women Under 29 Years Old with a College Degree
To be a good wife	44%	35%
To be a good mother	22%	22%
To be self-supporting	19%	16%
To be a success	10%	24%
Not sure	5%	3%
	100% (N = 195)	N = 54

*The question read: "One hears a lot about the changing role of women today. Please look at the list on this card and rank them in order of importance."

When interviewed in the 1970s and 1980s, eight-tenths of the 250 women interviewed described themselves as pressured for time, frazzled, and stressed out on a daily basis. Some sixty women kept logs for a month or more on the sources and frequencies of stressful periods. The pattern that emerged showed mealtimes, both breakfasts (36%) and supper time (40%) as the "worst" times of day for the majority. It was then that their feelings of being trapped in gilded cages was most pronounced.

We should keep in mind that the Women's Liberation Movement was launched in the 1970s and while most of the interviewed were not strongly supportive of the movement, all were aware of it. And a good many experienced some tension between traditional feminine goals and the new opportunities beckoning to women. This was especially the case for the younger women (table 13.1). Given the period's ferment around gender, the proportion of women who supported the Women's Liberation Movement did increase over time, from two-fifths who declared themselves supporters in the 1970s to more than two-thirds who did so a decade later. Favorable appraisals rested in the main on attaining equality in the workplace. This was also the basis for their support of the Equal Rights Amendment, which eight-tenths endorsed. The changing cultural environment obviously affected attitudes over time (table 13.2).

Although differences were slight, women were also more critical of the house and more detailed in their complaints than men, which may reflect the different symbolic meaning of the house for men and women. As the stage managers of the house, women are sensitive to interior layout, aesthetics, convenience, and comfort, whereas men, as the primary earners, are more concerned with maintenance and potential re-

Table 13.2
Perceived Gender Similarity: 1970s and 1980s

Twin Rivers Residents	1970s	1980s
Men and Women are:		
Basically similar	23%	45%
Basically different	52%	18%
Can't generalize	23%	37%
	N = 250	N = 71

sale value. Both liked the house, however, though the men somewhat more (87% vs. 75%).

In the years following the move, moreover, it was the women who carried the brunt of the transition. It was they who transformed the house into a home, and individual residents into more of a cooperative aggregate.

From the start, husbands spent far less time in the community during the week than did their wives. Their exposure to it was confined largely to weekends when they could take advantage of the pools, the tennis courts, and other sites for outdoor activities. By contrast, the women helped stitch together the collective fabric in their husbands' absences day by day. They spun the myriad networks of services and affection that create the invisible web of community. Given their greater exposure to the community, moreover, the women developed more extensive social relationships and met new people in more diverse settings — organizations, schools, recreational areas, and private homes. Husbands forged connection primarily with other commuters and users of parking lots and transportation loci.

Overall, in the founding decades, women effectively sustained the community and worried more about its course of development. And although the documented differences in men's and women's perspectives were not extensive, the strands of distinctive experiences drove a wedge between couples that would leave its mark.

Except for the longer commute — which the majority of men said they actually enjoyed — men did not, fundamentally, alter their daily routines after the move. The women by contrast confronted major disruptions in patterns of work and priorities, which made for substantial readjustments in their lives. This made the move and the settling-in process a very different experience for each partner and increased marital tensions and frictions for many. Most marriages survived intact but from one-fifth to one-sixth did not.

Thus, during the community's most formative period, wives and husbands lived in quite different versions of the same community. And while they literally looked out at the community through the same windows, they neither saw the same scene nor appraised it in identical ways. This weakened sense of their shared experience troubled the women. In their efforts to cope with the problems of an unfinished community and develop a viable pattern of life, they might blame their husbands for nonsupport or grow restive and distressed, increasing domestic tensions. Most couples managed to weather these storms reasonably well — in time men became more supportive in the home and women found ways to create more balance in their lives, which eased these strains.

In time, also, life took on more predictable routines, children made friends, and wives returned to part-time employment, so that the tensions and frustrations of the early years became but a dim memory. By the 1990s, gender differences were negligible and forgotten. Time, the great healer, had prevailed.

From the Children's Room

It has often been noted that preteens and adolescents are among the more disgruntled and least satisfied residents of new communities. This is due not only to the generally stressful nature of this particular stage of life but also because new communities tend to be oriented primarily to young adults and very young children, leaving the older child feeling neglected and deprived. The reasons for this are as yet obscure but each study adds another piece to the puzzle.

Of the more than three hundred lengthy interviews with individual residents in the 1970s and early 1980s, eighty involved children who were interviewed without a parent present. They ranged in age from 11 to 17 years but clustered in the 13–14 year category (specifically, 19% were 11–12 years old; 41% 13–14 years old; 20% 15 years old; and 20% 16 years and older).

Starting with the move itself, adults other than their own parents are not always aware of how wrenching it can be for a child of eight or ten to leave behind close friends and a familiar environment. But it clearly is. For these youngsters, for example, one-half said that leaving friends behind was the hardest part of the move and another one-fifth mourned the loss of a familiar environment. Despite this rupture, however, the move was seen as a positive experience for the large majority (85%), who thought that their lives had changed for the better with more activities, new friends, and more freedom and open space. And since, at that age, most readily made new friends, they began to feel at home within a fairly short time. In contrast to their parents, moreover, they turned out to be far less spaceocentric, the large majority (nine-tenths) drawing on the entire community for their social contacts. Their parents, on the other hand, confined their friendships to fairly close to home, one-half to the street and one-third to the quad in which they lived.

But while the youngsters appreciated the new setting for its openness and safety, they voiced strong complaints on other grounds. The lack of transportation facilities, not enough recreation, and inadequate shopping all loomed large in their minds, with the girls more dissatisfied with shopping and recreation, the boys stressed out about the absence of adequate space for sports and outdoor activities.

Both boys and girls complained about the absence of public transportation to get them to desired athletic, cultural, and social events outside the community. Many had come from urban settings with public transportation and activities within easy reach, and to which they could get on their own steam. In the present community they could walk and bicycle to various sites, which they did to some degree, but this proved inadequate for greater distances or if they had to carry cumbersome equipment or if the weather was inclement. On all such occasions, either mother (the chauffeur) was called upon, not without some resentment, or they simply did without, again, not without some resentment.

One facility that was keenly missed was a teen center of their own at which they would have been able to gather away from the watchful eyes of the adults. Given the skewed age distribution of the new community population, heavily weighted with young couples and toddlers, adolescents could not count on the critical mass necessary for their social life which seems to require both anonymity and visibility for maximum success. All in all then, not being very numerous in the first generation, older children and adolescents tended to feel shortchanged in a number of respects important to them.

In appraising this unfinished community basically designed for other age groups, they stressed feelings of relative deprivation not only in regard to the lack of special facilities but also in regard to community support.

One revealing question asked the youngsters to rank the groups listed in table 13.3 by how they felt toward teenagers.

The only group that the teenagers perceived as being very favorably disposed toward them were their own parents. And even there we see a sharp drop in their perception of how their parents responded to other teens. Adults in general were seen as less positive still. And police and shopkeepers were perceived as actively hostile.

A parallel question (table 13.4) asked the youngsters to state their feelings toward each of the same groups.

Table 13.3
Teenagers' Perceptions of How Others Feel about Them: 1970s and 1980s

Feelings of:	Strongly Positive	Anti-teen*
Your own parents about you	79%	2%
Your own parents about other teens	42%	9%
Other parents about teens	19%	13%
Adults in general about teens	10%	23%
Other teens about you	31%	3%
Children about teens	36%	7%
Teachers about teens	33%	10%
Police about teens	11%	30%
Store owners about teens	5%	55%
N = 80		

*Anti-teen includes strong and average dislike.

As was true for teenagers' perceptions of how others viewed them, they responded in kind. They were highly positive about their own parents but far less approving of other adults, the shopkeepers, and the police. A sex difference may be noted here, with the girls having perceived the shopkeepers as most hostile, and the boys perceiving the police, as such.

Also of interest was the focus of most youthful complaints on design aspects of the community, including its impact on their social and

Table 13.4
How Teenagers Feel about Others: 1970s and 1980s

How you Feel about:	Strongly Pro	Dislike*
Your own parents	85%	1%
Other parents	27%	8%
Adults in general	16%	11%
Other teens	35%	6%
Children in general	30%	9%
Teachers	35%	7%
Police	19%	16%
Store owners	5%	20%
N = 80		

*Dislike includes strong and average dislike.

recreational life. The adults were seen as reluctant and often hostile compatriots who tended to monopolize the desirable spaces for their own benefits. Hence the persistent refrain of the young that there was nothing to do and no place to go and no one who cared about them. Their complaints were exacerbated by bad weather and in the evening hours since the community was seen as basically designed for daytime and good weather.

Ironically, all that open space for which the parents left the crowded city was experienced, by their children, as too confining by its lack of activities, variety, and excitement. By contrast and in retrospect, the cities left behind may have seemed havens of freedom and mobility.

These findings are not confined to this one community. They are corroborated by a number of other studies both within and outside the American setting.

Burby et al. (1976), for example, in their comparison of thirty-six communities, of which seventeen were new communities, found that child-play areas were the most ubiquitous feature of new communities but that most children did not use them. As was true in Twin Rivers also, they preferred to play in their own or a neighbor's backyard or in the streets and parking areas.

A comparative study of a Swedish and an American suburb (Popenoe 1977) found complaints similar to those we have reported. Swedish youth complained that activities were too supervised, too hard to get to in the evenings, and the environment too unstimulating. Lack of transportation was also mentioned, as was monotony and boredom.

I agree with Dattner's observation that every environment is a learning experience, even a poorly designed one, though the lessons learned by the young are often negative ones. He mentions among the specific lessons the idea that the young do not matter as individuals but only as a category being forced to yield their individuality to uniformity and standardization. In addition, the young learn that they can have no constructive effect on the fixed and immobile environment because they seem to be able to change it "only in a destructive way" (Dattner 1969, p. 4).

Hence a wish list for the children in the initial decade would include the following:

1. To have a place of their own — away from adult supervision and interference where they could meet and be together
2. To have ready access to desired facilities and services, including public transportation so that they could get around on their own steam
3. To have facilities and services specifically geared to them that do not have to be shared with younger children

4. To have access to shopping, movies, and other diversions geared to their pocketbooks
5. To have more individual attention so as not to be reduced to a single uniform category called ten-year-olds or teenagers
6. To get respect from adults, a feeling of being wanted, and a positive attitude toward them in the community generally
7. To participate in design decisions affecting them

None of these are beyond reach, though some may involve additional costs but so does the abuse or neglect of facilities. The potential rewards are considerable too — improved morale, creativity, and a vital connectedness of children to the world they live in.

Time, which played a significant role in defusing tensions between husbands and wives, also helped children to settle in and settle down. Still, problems remain in the views of the adults. A question that addressed the problems of teenagers in the final survey in the late 1990s read as follows:

> In the first decade, Twin Rivers had a problem with teenagers complaining of "boredom" and "nothing much to do." Some residents feel that this problem has now been resolved and that teenagers are doing just fine. Other residents disagree. They believe that the teenager problem persists. Which best represents your own view?

In this survey, two-thirds of the interviewed thought that not much had changed for the young and that the problem had not been solved. Only one-fifth saw a definite change for the better. Still, as one who can assess both time periods, the environment for children and teens has been greatly transformed from the bleak unfinished site of the earliest years to what is now a thriving community. There are many programs and contests explicitly geared to teenagers and a critical mass of peers to be with. All this is dramatically different from the earliest years. What has evidently not changed are the strains of adolescence, which may well be a constant of modern life.

Sources of Cohesion and Unity

In historic communities of relatively long duration, cohesion is taken for granted and not remarked upon unless threatened by internal or external danger. In "new" communities, cohesion is problematic and its genesis not assured because the consensus on values and conduct remains to be developed. Consensus, cohesion, unity, sharing — each is a bit different from the others but together they point in the same direction.

Historically, coercive rule, though never unproblematic, might ensure survival, with the ruling group making key decisions for the aggregate who would go along for want of an alternative. Resistance could bring ostracism or worse. Equally powerful is religion and adherence to a common faith, used as a means to induce obedience, commitment, and guilt to keep the flock together. Not to be ignored is the fact that historically, the average citizen was bound to family and community by birth and thus lacked opportunity to escape. So place became destiny.

But the modern era wrought fundamental changes in this regard, both in social conditions and individual consciousness. Mobility became increasingly possible—even rewarded—and democracy altered power structures and power relations to reduce despotism and lock-step conformity. Individuals, increasingly expected to be in charge of their own successes and achievements, had to think for themselves and devise personal strategies to survive. Hence a division between private and public became ever more salient. Citizenship became not merely acquiescent but participatory. As consensus became more elusive and problematic, explicit societal mechanisms were needed to create and sustain it. Plato envisaged an ideal, small-scale polis whose unity came from virtuous and selfless guardians devoted to the public good and sustained by the citizens sharing a common mindset and outlook. Rousseau could no longer do so when he observed in *The Social Contract*: "It would be better before examining the act by which a people choose a King, to examine that by which it has a people; for this act, being necessarily prior to the other, is the true foundation of society" (Rousseau 1983, p. 45). This is certainly the case for community.

The striving for unity is universal but rests on a different foundation in aristocratic and democratic societies. In aristocratic regimes, where only a few run things, the people do not need to form alliances in order to act jointly, because "they are strongly held together" by other means. In democracies, by contrast, individual citizens are independent but "feeble" and so become powerless "if they do not learn voluntarily to help one another" (de Tocqueville 1990, ed., vol. 2, p. 107).

And when one endeavors to *create* community, instead of inheriting it, the clash of competing interests and interpretations is unavoidable. It involves a continuous sorting and weeding-out process between leavers and stayers. It involves deliberations as to which interests and goals are widely shared, who can be trusted, whom one can work with, talk with, plan with, and what are permissible—and taboo—topics for discussion. The search for consensus is "the primary aim" even in very small, communal groups and it is very hard to achieve (Zablocki 1980, p. 250). Zablocki proposes five distinct dimensions of consensus: the creation of common meanings, common goals, common strategies, common norms, and a sense of relative superiority to other ways of life.

Perhaps it should be underscored that neither consensus nor cooperative activity requires personal liking for those with whom one is joined in common enterprise. One can be greatly devoted to others without "real sympathies." Noble and serf had no "natural interest in each other's fate," yet "each had a sense of duty toward the other" (de Tocqueville 1990, vol. 2, p. 163).

Mansbridge posits a connection between the size of a community and the possibility for achieving consensus. "Small size promotes conformity," though we are not told how small is small (Mansbridge 1983, p. 283). Twin Rivers is small in comparison to a metropolis, but large in comparison to Plato's ideal polis.

The advantages attributed to small communities (Mansbridge 1983) are:

- A genuine common interest is easier to achieve.
- Opportunities for power and leadership are more widely and more equally distributed.
- Self-selection, hence social homogeneity, tends to be greater at smaller scales.
- Natural limits on the span of control keep things more cohesive
- More information is available to the members about each other, which may adversely affect privacy and anonymity but promote a sense of the whole.

Size alone is not sufficient, however. It must be supplemented by ideology and cultural affinities for the cooperative impulse to flower.

De Tocqueville, who saw Americans as cooperative and generous in the early nineteenth century, despite the intense emphasis on individualism, attributed this to the belief in equality which encourages a "reciprocal disposition" among individuals "to oblige each other." This obligation allows "the cooperative seed," triggered by mutual need, to become habitual. "What was intentional becomes instinct, and by dint of working for the good of one's fellow citizens, the habit and taste for serving them are at length acquired." Crucial here is that individuals think that it is to their interest to link themselves to others. But how to plant the same thought into a thousand minds at the same moment? De Tocqueville's answer points to the local press, without which there "would be no common activity" in democratic societies (de Tocqueville 1990, vol. 2, pp. 176, 105, 111).

In addition, there is participation in local affairs. This creates those steady ties of common purpose that bring people together in "spite of the propensities that sever them." It is attention to small affairs that helps people pursue "great undertakings in common." Equality helps develop the mutuality and reciprocity necessary for cooperation, and a common medium of communication helps to advance unity. In democracies, especially where people are scattered and separated from each other, means must be found "to converse every day without seeing one another, and to take steps in common without having met" (ibid., pp. 115, 112). The media — which in de Tocqueville's day meant the press — fulfill these aims. Whatever community is launched must be thought of not as a fixed entity but as "a flow of processes involving interaction, reciprocities, association, and interrelatedness." Community ranges from the most "fluid, fragmentary, and fortuitous to the most complex and stable" (Simmel 1971, p. 60). It is a process ever in process of becoming.

Has Twin Rivers achieved a balance between individual and collective priorities? Has it made room for the legitimate expression of conflict? Do positive feelings of care, support, and trust outweigh the negatives? On balance, though still a precarious one, I believe the answer is yes.

The residents' reported feelings about Twin Rivers are, in the majority, very positive. To be sure, their critical faculties are actively engaged throughout, though the specific targets vary, but these do not, apparently, erode the general appreciation of and commitment to the community as a whole.

As for coping with conflict and dissent, here too Twin Rivers has found ways to do so. One major means is its version of the historic town meeting, the open meetings of the board of the Twin Rivers Homeowners Association, where the residents, often vividly, present their views. But this was a relatively late development. In the first seven years, there was insufficient opportunity to air grievances legitimately, which led to tense, often hostile relations between homeowners and the bank trustee. After home rule was established, there still were years of floundering and attempts to hold conflict and disagreements at bay. After a decade, the current system evolved, in order to integrate the participatory, consensual propensities with the adversarial ones.

The reconciliation of major conflicts — over school budgets, monthly fee payments, a teen center, vandalism, and so on, and revealed in the clash of antagonistic views and values — did much to solidify the population as it sought solutions to common problems. In turn, this helped boost morale and confidence in the possibility of creating community.

Internal tensions existed from the start, pitting early arrivals against later ones, and homeowners against renters. From the perspective of the community as a whole, these group divisions were reflected in differing degrees of commitment and identification with Twin Rivers. Homeowners and long-term residents were generally more supportive of the community than their counterparts and were unified by their social distance from renters and more recent arrivals. This sense of unity spilled over into other aspects of life in Twin Rivers.

Another potential for unity in Twin Rivers was its small scale, spatially and demographically. It was easy to become familiar with every nook and cranny of Twin Rivers and to recognize hundreds of residents quickly. Social relations were accordingly direct and concrete, marked by a mutuality, empathy, and interconnectedness greater than that in urban and suburban settings. Not to be ignored are the many occasions for shared emotions of joy or grief that foster a sense of being united with one's fellow residents.

In addition, there were numerous opportunities to form or join many kinds of organizations. Twin Rivers had its own medium of communication, most recently *Twin Rivers Today*, which focused on events and provided information and advice to its readers. Finally, there was the relative equality of conditions, stressed by de Tocqueville, which reinforced awareness of interdependence and the desirability of cooperation.

Hence, in the latest survey, we noted the greatest support for townhouse communities in general and more residents feeling that Twin Rivers is providing roots for them. The basic parameters of community are thus in place. However, in 1995, after more than a decade of relative calm, a "small group of activists" began a write-in campaign challenging a "special assessment levied to cover additional costs," which "generated a bitter battle between two groups of residents: those on the homeowner board and the challengers." In 1995 the election supported the three incumbent candidates. By 1999 another crucial election loomed. In the meantime, the challengers had intensified their efforts to get into power, with house-to-house campaigns and strategies that many residents found objectionable. Voices grew louder and shriller, and the fragile community trembled, its precarious unity undermined, its good will strained.

SUMMARY OF KEY FINDINGS

Part I: Community as Image and Ideal

Chapter 1: Community: The Passionate Quest

This chapter reviews key concepts and theories of community and traces them through selected historic and sociological writings.

There are two major points made repeatedly by thinkers far apart in time and space. The first is that community, like politics, is always local, varying by the nature of its linkage to the wider society and the degree of its self-sufficiency.

The second is that an ongoing debate pits formalists, those who define community by institutional criteria such as governance and law, against humanists, who stress the emotional and spiritual aspects of community, including agapic attachment, sense of belonging, and empathic relatedness to others.

Plato and Aristotle are on the formal, institutional side, as are Cicero, Hobbes, and, in part, Rousseau. St. Augustine and Althusius belong to the emotional-spiritual camp. Clearly it is a matter of emphasis, since both are necessary, and different phases stress different priorities.

With the expansion of the scale of industrial society, the growth of a market economy, and the rise of the centralized nation-state, a far-flung society seemed to preempt the significance of local communities. The institutional nexus of work, family, education, and politics splinters. What the nineteenth century began, the twentieth century accelerated. For a time it seemed that the engines of progress were unstoppable and would devastate local communities. But time would show otherwise.

In Twin Rivers these processes were plainly in evidence as residents commuted to work or college, voted in national elections, and went outside the community for cultural activities. Yet equally clearly, the local community dominated their day-to-day lives and their horizons.

Chapter 2: Historic Models of Community

This chapter considers five historic types of communities to help delineate forces that build and forces that erode communities.

The ancient Greek polis provided a model of a civic community that tied all citizens (a highly select group) to common objectives. It pioneered a class-based form of democracy that appealed to thoughtful, concerned individuals to do their part for the common good. The small size and scale of the polis permitted citizens to experience the interconnectedness of their world directly and so nurture the spirit of community. As would happen two thousand years later, the polis succumbed to ailments familiar in modern times: the pursuit of individual glory, internal strife, and public indifference to collective obligations.

The monastic community is unique in the centrality of two important values: agapic love and disciplined freedom, although it experienced a perpetual struggle to attain these, tame egoism on behalf of the common good, and keep intrusion from the world outside within bounds.

The Puritan commonwealth pioneered the covenanted community on American soil. Its success inspired generations of followers, but in time, growth, internal division, and clashing perspectives undermined these communities, weakened their hard-won unity, and made economic individualism a supreme value. Utopian communities in the nineteenth century and urban communes in the twentieth underscore the need for institutional underpinnings and leadership structures along with idealism for survival.

Chapter 3: Key Theories and Concepts

This chapter reviews the writings of theorists from Plato and Aristotle through Althusius, Hobbes, and Rousseau to Tönnies and several contemporary thinkers. The lessons conveyed by them suggest that despite their varied social and historic circumstances, the struggle to achieve community seems to be constant.

Part II: A Community Is Launched

In Part II, selected themes are monitored for a single community followed from inception to maturity. Random sample surveys, interviews with residents and leaders, analysis of public records, photographic analysis, and participant observation were the techniques used to gather the desired information.

Chapter 4: Twin Rivers: The First Planned Unit Development in New Jersey

Twin Rivers is part of a tradition of a century-old process of building communities from blueprints. It also possessed what in the 1970s were unique features. It was not designed to be a conventional suburb with the proverbial picket fences setting apart single-family houses. Townhouses would link residents physically, visually, and aurally and make every home owner automatically a land sharer. Given this departure from the traditional suburban ideal, the big question from its inception was would it work? Would people purchase townhouses under conditions that limited their independence and control? Would they do so in sufficient numbers to make the effort viable? And, having bought into the arrangement, would they do their share in creating a satisfactory way of life? The answers to all four questions is yes, though not without many pitfalls along the way.

The residents, largely from modest middle-class backgrounds held high aspirations for themselves and the children they planned to raise there. Most couples purchased their first house in Twin Rivers. They had left urban apartments in Long Island and New York for this special suburban adventure. As the first planned unit development in the state of New Jersey, Twin Rivers was something of a social experiment. Further, it was unfinished when the first residents moved in, exacerbating the already difficult stresses and strains of moving.

Although the new home owners were resilient and filled with the spirit of enterprise, they were strikingly unprepared for the challenges that awaited them. They seemed to believe that the purchase of the townhouse was an automatic ticket to community. That this expectation was naive and doomed to failure would become painfully evident in time.

Chapter 5: The Residents Appraise Their Environs

How people feel about their houses and the community in which they live is decisive for the ambience they generate. Given their great expectations, disappointment about the imperfections of the unfinished site were inevitable. Most of the residents were unfazed, however, and worked hard to get their houses into shape and settle into life among strangers.

Despite the growing pains in the early months, there was much to appreciate. The majority of residents liked their houses, the recreational facilities, the safety for themselves and their children, their new friends, and the feeling of adventure.

The fact that there was some "community capital" to draw upon reflected the residents' willingness to give the new community a try. Fully 60 percent said they came for the community as compared to the 40 percent who came for the houses and cost advantages.

Stresses and strains abounded but the goodwill present at the start helped residents cope and eventually triumph. On a scale from 0 to 100, positive appraisals of life in the community always stayed above the 50 percent mark.

Chapter 6: Securing the Vox Populi: The Struggle for Self-Government

The first five years of Twin Rivers were characterized by an intricate minuet between the bank-trustee, the developer, and the Trust Advisory Board on the one hand, and a populace increasingly disgruntled about problems not attended to and arbitrary rules and regulations, on the other.

The struggle of the residents for self-determination triggered memories of the nation's historic struggles. Even the rhetoric reemerged— "No taxation without representation" echoed throughout the community as it struggled with the authorities. Charges and countercharges multiplied and, at times, paralyzed public life.

At last there came the day, in August 1976, when power passed from the bank trustee to the residents. The moment of triumph, however, was brief as the realization set in that responsibility now devolved only on "us." As was true for the citizens of the ancient Greek polis, Twin Rivers residents, while eager to air grievances and distribute blame, were less than eager to assume the obligations and responsibilities required. Fortunately, there were always a few who were willing to take on the burdens of civic duty for the many.

One persistent irritant had to do with the rules that maintained the aesthetic uniformity of the built environment. The residents resented these as invasions of their privacy, though they accepted sanctions in principle for others. When controls are invisible, it seems, people tend to regard them as in the nature of things. When controls are attributed to known persons acting for the totality, they come to be regarded as restrictions, and the people who enforce them become the enemy. After much strife and agitation, private tastes were forced to yield to public canons, but aesthetic restrictions proved a lasting irritant.

All told, in the first decade one-tenth of the residents volunteered for public service on a regular basis, a larger proportion (about one-half) participated only sporadically, and one-third stood permanently apart from the community.

Chapter 7: Joiners and Organizers: Community Participation

De Tocqueville would have said, "I told you so," had he been apprised of the extraordinary range of activities, associations, and programs that proliferated in Twin Rivers virtually from day one.

This seems to have had some contradictory implications, however.

On the one hand, these activities created a web of social interconnected-ness by joining together a great variety of residents. On the other, by coalescing groups according to separate interests, they accentuated frag-mentation, separate concerns, and private pursuits.

Moreover, the associational impulse was not constant. It was most intense in the first decade only to pale thereafter unless or until a com-pelling issue rekindled it. A minority of residents was always ready to contribute while many others were content to coast. There were a num-ber of reasons for this imbalance, among them, lack of time, heavy family obligations, inexperience, and the belief that one's contributions do not matter.

Although some residents were free riders, most were not. In fact, more than half responded to group appeals and were available some of the time. Even if volunteers were often in short supply, by the end of the first decade, the residents had created a library, a crime watch program, Project Helping Hand, chess clubs, reading groups, a speakers bureau, charity events, and an active social life. These were sources of great enjoyment and helped forge enduring friendships and group loyalties.

Chapter 8: Sociability in a New Community

Sociability was most intense but also least discriminating in the first decade. For the majority (three-fifths), it was "easy to meet people like myself," though that left two-fifths for whom this was not the case. By the end of the first decade, one-half of the residents said they had "best friends" in Twin Rivers, the majority of these living on the same block or in the same quad. Neighbors fared especially well in all three decades. In the 1990s more than four-fifths viewed their neighbors positively.

There were interesting changes over the decade in regard to home entertaining, which declined drastically. Formal dinners became more infrequent, and people became more selective, socialized with residents closer to home, and spent their time with a few like-minded others.

Both sociability and friendships came to reflect familiar sociological variables of age, income, race, and residence. Perceived social similar-ities increased the propensity for sociability, whereas perceived social differences tended to curtail it.

A collective rhythm of social life and sociability developed over time. This rhythm needs to be far better understood because it chal-lenges the widespread assumption that sociability reflects mainly per-sonal preferences and needs. In point of fact, friendships, neighborly relations, and more casual social ties depend on a complex cluster of spatial, temporal and social conditions and change as these do.

To build a collective identity from scratch, as was the case in Twin Rivers, takes many years. Such an identity is shaped by community-wide celebrations of holidays and special occasions, by public recognition of outstanding local figures, by residents featured in the local paper for special talents or achievements, and by those active on behalf of the community in the making. By celebrating one another, residents simultaneously celebrate the community as a whole. In this way, a collective persona takes form.

Chapter 9: Space, Place, and Design

A number of design concepts worked out as intended, but a number did not. The concept of keeping everything within walking distance, which was built into the spatial texture of Twin Rivers as it is into so many planned communities, ignored the necessity, hence prevalence, of the car for breadwinner commuters and shoppers. Ignoring these sociological realities was a recipe for frustration.

The neighborhood concept, expressed in the four quads of Twin Rivers, also proved problematic. Above all, it failed to provide the integration of housing, work, shopping, and recreation that it was intended to do. Both examples show that spatial design cannot achieve the ambitious agenda set for it if it does not fit the tastes and habits of its intended users.

Chapter 10: Private and Public: Whose Rights, Whose Responsibilities?

More than conventional communities, a PUD brings ancient questions about property rights and claims to the fore. Townhouses with shared walls and grounds create considerable ambiguities for residents about the extent of their responsibilities (as compared to the trust's, for example) and the limits of their powers. If, as in the case of Twin Rivers, there is an initial lack of standards of privacy, sociability, and proprietary claims, confusion often follows.

Residents varied greatly in how they delineated public and private domains. Possessive and proprietary attitudes surfaced early, as residents became attached to swimming pools, parking spaces, front lawns, and playgrounds.

Moreover, residents who make great efforts to embellish their private spaces of house, yard, and front lawn will often leave public spaces untended. Because common areas are everyone's space, they often becomes no one's space. Outreach and proprietary dispositions have deep cultural roots, and without explicit efforts to change these, cultural preferences will prevail.

Chapter 11: Go Fight City Hall: The First Lawsuit

It is not uncommon for residents to resort to legal means to wrest some measure of control from the authorities in charge of managing the aggregate in the first settling-in phase. It is a familiar drama of the people versus the king that has no easy solution. Residents resent the proliferating rules, and the management becomes a convenient target for a host of grievances and unmet expectations.

In Twin Rivers the familiar drama resulted in a lawsuit in 1973, only three years after the first residents had moved in. After three fundraising drives and years of volunteer efforts, the lawsuit was effectively dropped, having lost each trial round. The effect was a huge disappointment, though it also helped generate a sense of community. But it left Twin Rivers with a culture of distrust of authority that would reverberate over the decades.

Chapter 12: Leaders as Lightning Rods

As representative but ambivalent figures, leaders play a critical role in helping communities coalesce. In Twin Rivers, they were the minority who served on the governing board, chaired the major committees, and provided selective expertise for the entire community. One hundred leaders were interviewed to see what made them different from the majority.

This is a tough question and while there is no ready answer, several themes recur. For some, community service provided an ego boost: "I wanted the recognition and power." Others were protecting their interests and investments. More idealistic motives surfaced as well: "I wanted to build something fine"; "It gave me a purpose; it's good to reach beyond your own life."

Leaders saw themselves as effective problem solvers; they cared more; they liked feeling useful and important; and they believed in the community.

But the most frequent answer took them back to childhood: "My parents instilled certain values in me. I want to give something back. I live these values." Early on, they seem to have absorbed the message that one must do one's share, one had to be mindful of one's fellows.

Wanting to feel useful and important, most served without regard for personal gain. Above all, they were sensitive to the connection between their participation and everyone's survival.

Leaders were able to motivate and inspire residents, and, judging by the residents' reactions, they advanced the goals of first creating and later preserving the unity of the community.

Chapter 13: Unity and Division, Conflict and Consensus

In Twin Rivers, internal divisions emerged early. From the beginning, owners and renters regarded each other warily and negatively. Homeowners considered renters less responsible whereas renters saw homeowners as uppity and unfriendly. "Pioneers" were pitted against later arrivals. In both cases, the majority of homeowner-pioneers felt superior to the minority and more entitled to set the agenda for the community. The first group exemplifies what Martin Buber termed the "Community of Tribulation" as they had struggled with problems that later arrivals were spared.

Given the prevalence of Jewish residents at the start, some majority-minority tension was present in latent form, as Protestants and Roman Catholics had to come to terms with being in the minority, thus reversing their usual status. Eventually, these proportions would become more balanced, but in the first decade the imbalance was a source of bewilderment and tension.

Sociologically significant is the fact that the perception of being in the minority related to one's sense of belonging to the community. Those in the majority by age, family composition, religious affiliation, time of arrival, or housing tenure were more positive and optimistic about the community's future. Those numerically in the minority—no matter what the specific characteristics—were more critical of the community's failings, less supportive, and less satisfied with living there.

Also, in a small face-to-face community, one's enemies are also one's neighbors, whom one does not wish to confront. Nonparticipation in public life is thus rooted in the social character, more specifically the social scale, of a community and not only, or primarily, in individual predispositions. Since social conflict is endemic in social life, successful communities must be able to incorporate the divisive as well as the unifying forces.

Moving to a new community takes courage as well as imagination, for the community is not yet there. Instead, half-finished houses, unkempt spaces, limited facilities, and disoriented strangers are the sober reality. A host of problems looms as the community moves from site plan to living site.

After more than two decades, Twin Rivers has achieved many of the elements that define a community. It possesses organized patterns of conduct revolving around family, work, and social life. It is held together by institutions of governance and law and common concerns about house, children, recreation, and leisure.

Twin Rivers has also been the stage for universal life transitions that, though experienced by individuals, link and unify its members in powerful ways. From a child's first day of school to the senior prom, together with weddings, births, and funerals, shared events are etched into collective memories. Holidays, sacred occasions, seasonal rituals, and spontaneous responses to crises big and small create the backdrop for shared experiences. Together with the physical environment and the institutional structure, these are woven into a solid texture of human connectedness. Gradually a collective identity forms out of collective experiences — electoral victories and defeats, bitter winters and sweltering summers, and all the tragic and joyous occasions that make up human life.

To survive, a community must prevail over the ever-present corrosive forces that threaten to destroy its physical or moral integrity, and discourage the free riders and nonplayers who consume resources without contributing to them.

PART III
OLD IMPERATIVES, NEW DIRECTIONS

CHAPTER 14

THE CONTINUING SALIENCE
OF THE LOCAL COMMUNITY

All politics is local.

— Tip O'Neill

Life is local.

— Anonymous

Demographic, social, and cultural trends suggest that the need for community has not abated and that community will in fact emerge as more essential than ever in the future, if the four major trends discussed in this chapter persist, namely: the new immigration, an aging population, alternative sexualities, and communities by design.

The New Immigrants

Immigration has been a key source of America's economic progress and social diversity. The dynamism and cultural riches of the newcomers have invigorated the society by their labor, their creativity, and their dreams. What may surprise those who thought that massive immigration has ceased is that despite impressive technological change, the end

Table 14.1
Top Five Countries of Origin of Immigrants to the U.S. in 2000

Mexico	7,841,000
China	1,391,000
Philippines	1,222,000
India	1,007,000
Cuba	952,000

of the twentieth century resembled its beginnings in the waves of immigrants that came to these shores.

There are important differences nonetheless. The turn-of-the-nineteenth-century immigrants came mostly from Eastern and Southern Europe, whereas the origins of current immigrants span the globe. The older immigration featured peasants and unskilled laborers, whereas the more recent one has a sizeable component of skilled and professional persons. Both, however, spawned numerous immigrant settlements and altered the demographic complexion of the country irreversibly. According to the 2000 U.S. Census, 28.4 million U.S. residents were foreign born (see table 14.1). When one adds to these figures estimates of illegal immigration, it is clear that a huge process of cultural assimilation is under way.

From 1995 to 1996, in New York City, for example, more than 230,000 immigrants from more than twenty countries arrived and transformed neighborhoods and schools. Specifically, 20,000 came from the former Soviet Union; 19,000 from the Dominican Republic; 11,000 from China; and smaller numbers from Jamaica, Bangladesh, Haiti, Poland, Ghana, and Peru (Sachs 1999). They have left their imprint on the workforce, cuisine, and language.

Given the magnitude of this influx of newcomers, traditional views, in particular assimilation and melting-pot theories, are under review, especially for the second generation, which constitutes the transition between old and new worlds.

In the past, the brunt of generational conflict fell on the children of immigrants who jostled incompatible demands between parents and peers, old and new values. The process has often been described as a tragic conflict between the generations, of family betrayals and childrens' ingratitude. For children eager to succeed in the new society, the psychic costs are typically insecurity and anxiety as they learn that climbing the ladder of success exacts a price. The resultant psychic split and generational stress has long been a staple of drama and film, showing the young leaving the community their parents had struggled to preserve.

A focus on the second generation illumines different modes of immigrant adaptation to a new habitat and compels a reconsideration of traditional theories. For example, the 31 million Latinos in the United States in the 1990s who are expected, within the next decade or two, to surpass African-Americans as the largest minority group, reveal patterns of assimilation that do not require their cutting themselves off from their communities or becoming Americanized by sacrificing ethnic pride.

Although one must be cautious in generalizing about a group that represents twenty-two different countries of origin and great internal diversity in education, income, and ethnic traditions, research has revealed some significant patterns. Latinos currently comprise some 11 percent of the U.S. population. More than 60 percent come from Mexico. Contrary to the stereotype, more than one-half of these are economically middle class or higher. For the upwardly mobile among them, and in contrast to the patterns described for the late nineteenth century, community is not what they must leave behind but what they must build on to get ahead. Community has been the springboard for advancement for recent Latino immigrants and their children. These new developments challenge traditional theories of acculturation, as some immigrants appear to be explicitly enlisting their communities of origin for the upward climb in their new homelands. They draw on a variety of resources, either to facilitate their climb or as safety valves for the tough times. Thus, not only are immigrants likely to connect to different sectors within the host society but to diversify their connections within their own group. Diverse patterns of assimilation and channels for upward mobility have led Portes to propose a new concept of "segmented assimilation" (Portes 1996, p. 83).

"Segmented assimilation" refers to the different experiences of entering groups in their processes of accommodation to American society. There is "traditional assimilation and upward mobility, downward mobility by unsuccessfully competing in the mainstream economy, or upward mobility by living and working in ethnically homogeneous immigrant communities" (ibid.).

"Segmented assimilation" highlights a not uncommon division between rich and poor, stationary and mobile immigrants, so that one cannot expect a single outcome. There is a bottom and a top segment, the first are unskilled and poor and get stuck or trapped in their communities, whereas the second, skilled, well-educated individuals are bent on achieving professional status in the new country and eventually blend in with the rest of the middle class. Hence the major fault line for these immigrant groups is not race or ethnicity but education and social class. The millions of dollars spent from the 1960s on by the U.S. government to distribute Cuban immigrants across the United States in the belief that this would speed their cultural assimilation were thus misdirected. "Instead, Cubans gravitated back to Miami where their strength of numbers, connections and entrepreneurial know-how quickly translated into economic prosperity" (Fernandez-Kelly and Schauffler 1996, p. 52).

In other words, community and the concentration of cultural resources are valuable generators of "social capital." The term "social capital," christened by the French social theorist Pierre Bourdieu (1986) among others, refers to social networks and resources that help individuals advance economically even when they lack economic capital. Above all, "the entire community which forms the social context in which individual families function" is involved here, and this reinforces social solidarity and loyalty to kin and community. There is evidence that such community support has resulted in Vietnamese, Indochinese, and Punjabi students surpassing white students in school achievement (Zhou and Bankston III 1996, pp. 206, 201), despite poverty and residence in underserviced areas.

There is a similar force at work among ethnic networks and entrepreneurs. In Miami, for example, in the 1960s, Cuban businesses were supported by Cuban patronage and mutual assistance by cultural peers. By 1980 one-half of Cubans in the United States were either self-employed or employed by Cuban-owned firms (Portes and Stepick 1993, p. 137).

Thus the ethnic community offers significant benefits to individual aspirants. In particular it provides support in the form of "social belonging, trust, and reciprocity" that fosters cooperation and a sense of belonging that are helpful in the struggle to succeed. Presumably this is not every immigrant's pattern, but its prevalence for some suggests a new turn in the story of immigrant assimilation and success in the contemporary United States.

Community-based mobility has also been observed among Asian immigrants. Between 1990 and 1996, 46 percent of Asian immigrants settled directly in the suburbs (Chen 1999, p. A1), many of which became virtually exclusive provinces of particular ethnic groups. In some schools, as many as forty to fifty different languages are offered to meet the needs of immigrant children. As these newcomers moved in — creating Korean enclaves in one area, Indian enclaves in another, and Chinese, Thai, or Philippine concentrations in still others — they have often taken over middle-class white areas. The process does not proceed without tension but it creates a fascinating ethnic mosaic as people bring with them their specialty stores, food shops, music, places of worship, films, and feast days.

Immigrants have always tended to congregate with their own groups in ethnic subcommunities. An important difference between the immigration of the nineteenth and twentieth centuries, however, is the role of the community in the success of the individual. In the twentieth century, community was not what one left behind in the climb upward but what one used as a springboard to success. The concept of community as part of one's "social capital" challenges traditional theories—and policies—of acculturation and undergirds multiculturalism.

Multicultural trends are not peculiar to American society. In France "all minority languages," which were banned after the Revolution in the name of equality, "are getting a new lease on life." Gaelic has returned to Scotland and Basque to Spain (Simons 1999, p. 8). The Council of Europe, a forty-one-nation group, has developed a charter urging the use of indigenous languages in schools, media, and public life. There is now a bureau for lesser-used languages created by the European Union.

For most of the world, the local community continues to be the prime context for day-to-day life, and traditional communities persist for very traditional reasons that keep people together: historic loyalties; regional concentrations; and class, ethnic, racial, or religious affinities. But there are also new developments that reinforce community. For example, the global sweep of migrations with streams of migrants adrift in strange lands reinforces community for those who typically seek solace with "their own kind."

The fragmentation of modern life, which permits us to travel and connect across vast geographic distances, is the same force that paradoxically moves us back to roots and place. "The more global and uniform our civilization, the more people want to anchor themselves" (Enzensberger, in ibid., p. 8). Paradoxically, then, globalization engenders localism, each reinforcing the other. And localism may support immigrant advancement by fostering communal dependency and the maintenance of in-group attachments. Success then may depend on one's community.

Another Future Trend: Retirement Communities

In the next thirty years, the U.S. population is expected to increase by 80 million people—of which 70 million will be the elderly, variously defined by age (65 +) or by retirement status. To accommodate this sizable addition to the U.S. population, thousands of retirement communities will be needed, accelerating a trend that has grown cumulatively over the past quarter of a century.

The dramatic increase in life expectancy is only one source of this development. Another stems from changing patterns of family life, rising proportions of singles, childless, and divorced individuals, and declines in fertility rates. With the traditional family too small and fragile to provide shelter and care for its elderly members, the demand for alternative patterns of life is bound to increase. A prominent alternative is that of retirement communities, many of these already on the scene, currently accommodating 4 million largely affluent Americans. In 1790 less than 20 percent of the population reached age seventy. Two centuries later more than three-fourths do so. And since 1900, average life expectancy has increased from the forties to the seventies (for men) and eighties (for women). All of this suggests that retirement communities are likely to be high on any future agenda. In the last few decades, moreover, a good deal has been learned about what such communities require. Some may be adult playpens, as many have charged, but most are complex creations with a varied menu of social activities and projects. Although united by age, or rather by a given phase of the life cycle, retirement communities reveal a greater diversity than one might think. For students of community, they are an important source of information.

Turning to what they have in common, retirement communities are physically distinct, attached to warm climates, with a proper name and some form of governance either administered by the residents themselves or in conjunction with the developer or a bank trustee. Although age qualifications are variable, broadly speaking, age along with retirement status provides an important basis for a shared existence. The older the average age, however, the more imbalanced the sex ratio. For every widower, goes one estimate, there are five to six widows.

In the 1950s there was a small group of special communities targeted for older Americans; by the 1970s, some seventy retirement communities had been built along with hundreds of mobile-home parks, many of them by the Del E. Webb Development Corporation of Phoenix, Arizona, which pioneered the construction of sun cities and leisure worlds. By the 1990s, the number of retirement communities had substantially increased.

In contrast to earlier versions, however, such communities were organized not just around age, but around particular interests such as golf, tennis, or education, and most have a social life geared to a vast array of activities. In one of these communities studied in the late 1970s, the residents had spontaneously created 130 clubs ranging from stamp collecting to gardening, in addition to a constant round of dances, parties, and organized excursions. These helped residents attain their goals of security and safety along with friendships and social life. In Sun City, Arizona, the "most effective security system" was the neighbors who were active in Neighborhood Watch Committees. The author notes that this incorporation of "mutual concern" had "nothing to do with friendship," but constituted an impersonal resource widely recognized as a form of social insurance (Fitzgerald 1981, p. 215).

Other services and requirements stem from the age concentration in retirement communities. This includes medical services, health facilities, and assisted living arrangements. Meals on Wheels, a blood bank, strategically placed oxygen tanks, and home nursing care are also staples (ibid., 1981, p. 243).

The large majority of residents, as many studies have shown, prefer a community of peers their own age with whom they feel at ease. Age segregation seems to strengthen identification with peers and this develops a sense of confidence and trust that strengthens the emotional bonds that contribute to community.

In the wider society, the old often feel marginalized, whereas in retirement communities, they are in the mainstream majority. Lacking a status system based on wealth, power, or reputation, a powerful theme subscribed to in these communities is that everyone is equal. "When we come here we start all over again" (Osgood 1982, p. 107). However, despite the social homogeneity of retirement communities by age, race, or religious affiliation, they do develop their own forms of social hierarchy.

One source of hierarchical distinctions that has been noted by several researchers, myself included, is associated with time of arrival. This division, while not formally acknowledged, creates status divisions between first residents, considered somehow "better" for having arrived early, and the "lessers," that is, those who come later (Fitzgerald 1981, p. 222; Keller, chapter 13 in this book) As in high school, these can affect one's social life in the areas of invitations extended and respect garnered.

Sociability is another status marker. A generally admired trait, it differentiates outgoing residents from shy and retiring ones. And since not everyone is a joiner by nature, those who are not fade into the background. Hence there is loneliness and isolation amid all the activities. As people become widowed, their social life often dwindles. This is especially true for women (Osgood 1982; Fitzgerald 1981).

Nonparticipation in certain activities likewise divides those who fit into the admired mainstream and those who do not. Nongolfers in a golfing community, non–bridge players, nonclubbies — all are likely to be excluded from activities, parties, even from friendships in communities geared to these activities.

Yet another group facing negative judgments includes those who do not take pride in their homes and yards or are careless about their upkeep. And then there is a category of "older and sicker residents" who may be ostracized because "they represent everything the others fear such as getting old, getting sick, and yes . . . dying" (Osgood 1982, p. 120).

In addition to rankings of highs and lows, lessers and betters, there are schisms that frequently divide residents into opposed camps. In one retirement community of six thousand residents in Arizona, the question of whether or not to incorporate split the community in two. It pitted neighbor against neighbor and friend against friend. The president of the coordinating committee was "torn apart" by the battle and resigned, a "defeated" man. He withdrew completely from community life. "The lies they told, the personal damage they did. I'll never be the same person. I will never serve this community again and can never forgive my friends for the things they said and did to me" (Osgood, 1982, pp. 123, 124). Even after a decision had been reached, the "scars remained."

Some such schism erupts in a great many planned communities. In one Florida community, an equally vicious battle erupted over monetary allocations (ibid., p. 228). And in Ridgeview, Florida, the split occurred over the control of the clubhouse. In Twin Rivers, as described in chapter 13, the divisive issue concerned the board's making public the financial records of the community. The ensuing battles over such issues are fierce and unpredictable, often leaving ruins in their wake.

Most retirement communities, though diverse in social and demographic makeup, do manage to develop sources of unity. There is of course the rite of passage all share — the shift to retirement status. Both individually and together residents struggle to make the most of their later years. Living together in one place, they "share a common goal of succeeding in retirement" (ibid., p. 167). And then there is the fact that residents have a "similar future": They will stay together until they die. This will be their community for good, the last community in which they will ever live.

Given these special circumstances, retirement communities tend to develop special cultural styles and preoccupations. Key concerns include:

- Fear of inflation and worries about long-term finances
- Medical needs, illnesses, physical immobility
- Fear of getting sick
- Fear of dying

Then there is the typical attitude toward family. Most elderly residents do not want to turn to their children for help and be a burden on them. For many, in time, their new neighbors become their family. This is illustrated in a number of ways. In Sun City, for example, no cemetery had been constructed, and this accelerated the resort to cremation after death with the following justification: "We have no one," so who would keep up the grave? Having lost home towns and strong family ties, they have adjusted their funeral rituals accordingly (Fitzgerald 1981, p. 244). Often neighbors obtain burial sites next to each other with the result that they feel a greater sense of community with strangers than with kin back home (Osgood 1982, p. 228). Not wanting to burden children with demands for help has been documented for other groups and cultures. Lebanese Americans, for example, likewise desire to exercise control over their lives and not depend on relatives (Shenk 1991). And in one retirement community in Japan, residents moved there explicitly so as to not create problems for their children (Kinoshita and Kiefer 1992, p. 115).

While scale and age homogeneity facilitate the creation of social bonds, the truncated setting makes "even small differences in manners . . . assume great significance" (ibid., p. 177). The diversity of social backgrounds of the residents makes life more interesting but also less predictable since it is hard to validate individual self-presentations. This tends to create distrust and little self-disclosure (Kinoshita and Kiefer 1992). As the community grows demographically, moreover, its hard-won unity grows more fragile. "In the beginning, everybody knew everyone else, but now . . ." (Osgood 1982, p. 117) is a common refrain.

To understand the dynamics of retirement communities demands a careful assessment of their culture and goals to see how they fashion resources of time, skill, and scale into the web of community. Residents often enter such settings reluctantly only to become enthusiastic participants after a few weeks or months. This is where they experience caring for others and being cared for by them—essential for a feeling of community.

Communities by Design

Planning the physical layout of streets and playgrounds, houses and recreation, public facilities and private dwellings has been part and parcel of most Utopian writings on community since the sixteenth century, and became, in the twentieth, a staple of planning theory and practice.

Famous examples of communities by design include Levittown in its several versions for post–World War II veterans and their families. Its low-cost mortgages helped speed up the process of suburbanization in the United States and inspired model communities such as Reston, Virginia, and Columbia, Maryland. Sun cities and leisure worlds and many less familiar communities followed, leading more recently to a boom in building subdivisions for the middle class.

   The most famous current example of a designed community is that of Celebration, Florida, developed by the Walt Disney Company. Nearly all such efforts harbor an ideal of community, and Disney's Celebration had as one of its main goals to build in a "sense of community" by offering a well-defined town center with a set of public buildings such as a town hall, post office, library, restaurants, bookstore café, a public golf course, and 500-seat cinema, many of these designed by well-known architects such as Michael Graves (the post office), Robert A. M. Stern (the master plan), Cesar Pelli (the movie house), and Philip Johnson (the town hall).

   Celebration attempted to merge two worlds, one traditional and one contemporary, the latter focused on a state-of-the-art health-and-fitness center and a technically advanced educational system. Several goals inspired the plan, some of them contradictory: They hoped to create a sense of place that is lacking in today's soulless edge cities and to support social diversity by age, race, ethnicity, religion, and income. It was to be a place for "mingling and mixing," by creating the feeling of the traditional small town but with advanced high-tech facilities — "a modern, fiber-optically wired community with an old-fashioned center" (*The Economist*, 25 November 1995, pp. 27–28).

   Celebration took eight years to get off the drawing board. Focus groups became the basis for the tastes and decisions that shaped the final product as they did for James Rouse and Columbia, Maryland, in the 1960s. In the first year of operations, the demand to move in was so intense that the management team devised a lottery to select the initial residents. By November 18, 1995, 4,550 entries had been received, and of these, 350 would be the lucky winners.

   The 4,900 acres slated to contain a population of 20,000 within the next fifteen to twenty years, was part of a 30,000-acre tract that Disney had bought for a potential theme park in the 1960s. A greenbelt of 4,700 acres surrounds the town. The cost of building Celebration was $2.5 billion. As is true of planned communities generally, the framework and goals of the plan drew on the work of others for inspiration. Charles Fraser, famed for developing Hilton Head, among other sites, gave his protégé, Peter Rummell, then president of Disney Development Corporation, two central ideas for the community to be: a focus on education and a focus on health. Influential in the plans were the concepts of Andres Duany and Elizabeth Plater-Zyberg (2000), a husband-wife architectural team. They had created Seaside, Florida, which draws on the design principles of "the new urbanism," emphasizing spatial cohesiveness, higher densities, aesthetic design, and architectural controls. Robert A. M. Stern and Jacquelin Robertson prepared the master plan and saw the project through its critical phases to completion.

One constant of designed communities is the generation of extraordinary expectations in prospective buyers. These create an image that seeks to offer a balanced, harmonious way of life based on neighborliness, pedestrian access, public life, and sociability. Ideally, these would vanquish the isolation and fragmentation of suburban life. In Ebenezer Howard's Garden City model, developed in England at the turn of the last century, the neighborhood emphasized walking-distance access. A balance of activities amid a vital public life was the principle that Celebration was to advance.

The following design elements were to achieve a sense of place and community in Celebration:

1. Streets designed for pedestrian and bicycle locomotion and slow car travel.
2. A separation of leisurely, strolling paths from big arterial streets to carry heavy traffic.
3. Houses, placed close together, and front porches — all of these to promote neighborly contacts.
4. The initial batch of houses, ranging in price from $175,000 to $1 million or more, were to be within a five-minute walk from downtown.
5. Small lots — ten feet between houses on average — were to make for larger parks and public spaces.
6. Six basic house designs and a set number of colors were permitted under the strict design code for residents in the planned sites. All the externals must conform to code — such as signage, window treatments, plantings.

All told, Celebration rested on five cornerstones: education for young and old; health and well-being; the latest technology; a sense of place with easy accessibility, convenience, and attractive landscaping; and a sense of community, expressed in shared goals and responsibilities, a feeling of belonging, sound neighborly relationships, and a good quality of life.

To assess the viability of these promised benefits requires systematic exploration over at least a decade. Short of that, participatory observations, anecdotes, and impressionistic accounts must suffice. Of the latter, two books (Frantz and Collins 1999; and Ross 1999) contain elaborate descriptions of Celebration's infancy, and along with numerous articles, reviews, journalistic assessments and a personal visit, they form the bases for this summary evaluation.

The extent to which intended goals may be achieved depends, in part at least, on the assumptions underlying them. Let us examine some of the more prominent ones. Celebration ostensibly favored mixing people by income, ethnicity, age, and social class in the hope that this would advance community. But, as was true in Twin Rivers, the belief in diversity and pluralism was not always realized in practice. One reason for this was the cost of housing. In Celebration, prices were at least 25 percent higher than general market prices. This would obviously restrict buyers to higher income levels. In addition, residents put definite limits on the degree of social mixing they considered acceptable. Most did not want to lower income barriers because they wanted to maintain property values. When one lives in such close proximity, moreover, mixing by income, ethnicity, race, or religion needs careful preparation and monitoring so as to prevent the operation of exclusionary tendencies, conspicuous consumption, social envy, and value conflicts that haphazard mixing often entails.

The goal in Celebration, as in Twin Rivers, was to favor the pedestrian over the car. But in fact the "cul de sacs" broke up pedestrian circulation, and the large parking lots in the town center plus the lack of transportation made the car king (Nobel 1996).

There were a number of other contradictions to deal with. On the one hand, the high-tech focus accentuates the "home-based cyber-life," more solitary than participatory. Similarly, Disney's promotion of home shopping jibes poorly with its promotion of the traditional town center (ibid., 1996).

The residents of both Twin Rivers and Celebration were lured by a fantasy of community, of "spacious porches, wise and caring doctors" as well as the information highway (ibid.). "Disney's planners wanted to resurrect the porch, not just as an architectural element but as a mechanism for creating vigorous neighborhood life"; "front porches allow people to come out of their houses so they have an engagement with neighbors and the street" (Frantz and Collins 1999, p. 184). These dubious assumptions aside, the reality of the muggy summers and television defeated this goal.

Another decision that may have looked good on paper but did not work out in practice was to have residents live above shops in the town center. This was also to increase sociability. But, if an active town center does not shut down at night, it disturbs the peace and quiet, not to mention the sleep, of those who live above it. Such competing needs may defeat its primary social purpose.

In both Celebration and Twin Rivers, the residents resented the architectural controls and the Big Brother aspect of management. They understood the reasons for such controls but sought exemptions for themselves while holding others to the rules.

Another contradiction was the fact that planners intended to make Celebration closely knit and oriented to the residents who belonged there, but then proceeded to construct a million-square-foot shopping mall — "the largest open-air mall in central Florida" — designed to attract 10 million visitors a year. Then there was the walking distance ideal. The health center, situated beyond the golf course, was located beyond the comfortable quarter-mile walking-distance radius. The walking distance standard was further stretched by the two- to three-car garages attached to the townhouses. Just as in Twin Rivers, this assured the lack of public transportation, a frequently voiced complaint.

As might be expected, social issues surfaced early. The lack of racial and economic diversity was noted — with approval by some and dismay by others. "There is no room for the poor," said several residents. Celebration was settled by a middle-class population who sought the American Dream of mobility and success and a life away from the typical and unsolved urban problems of poverty, homelessness, and ethnic strife. Residents might be willing to help solve these but not to import them into the new community. Of course not all social problems could be held at bay. Time would bring several into view fairly quickly, petty crime, for example (Frantz and Collins 1999, pp. 320–22), and an internal status order of worth that irked many. The outlines of social marginality, economic hierarchy, and invidious distinctions according to house type, modes of dress, and other external insignias of rank were discernable by the end of the first year.

There was great distress also about promises unkept or postponed. Housing quality, for example, reflected the haste with which it was constructed. The poorly equipped school led to vociferous and intense complaints by the residents and defensive retorts by management from the first moments.

The hype of the Big Sell before houses were purchased imperceptibly gave way to modest disclaimers after residents had moved in. In the words of one architect: "The intention was to build a good place for people to live by providing architecture and planning that promoted social interaction and a sense of community" (ibid., p. 300). But, he concedes, it will be a better place in the future. It is up to the residents. That conclusion was not, however, stated up front, at the start, and thus it often came as an unwelcome afterthought.

The full evaluations of Celebration must await systematic investigation for at least the first decade, and probably more. Preliminary reactions as charted in the books by Frantz and Collins (1999) and Ross (1999) and many journalistic commentaries reveal several fault lines. Often mentioned is the Disney Company's penchant to respect its bottom line more than the residents' needs and the ensuing pressure on builders and architects to get out the product as fast as possible. The residents' irritation with the hype later was interpreted as deception, which would turn into cynicism. In part, this was associated with the departure of some of the original prime movers and their replacement by business types who favored the bottom line over the original vision.

Celebration and communities like it endeavor to meet the desire of middle-class Americans to replace the suburban mystique with the traditional, suitably updated, small town. And for all its lacks, Celebration *is* something of an alternative to sprawl and fragmentation. After all, Disney could have developed another "golf course community" but chose to do something more ambitious and difficult. And Celebration has already inspired a number of towns such as Newport Beach, California, and Fort Mill, South Carolina.

Not to be ignored, moreover, are the pioneering residents who had the courage and the willingness to brave an untried terrain. It was their determination to create community that made the plan a reality: "Nothing stopped them, not leaky roofs; not a Potemkin-village downtown without a supermarket, a hairdresser or a video store; not bad press or a carload of tourists" (Marling 1999, p. B9).

It is too soon to tell whether Celebration's design will eventually help remedy social ills such as urban sprawl, environmental neglect, and social isolation. Many have criticized it — prematurely — for not solving the problems of inner cities and, in fact, creating yet another suburb for the well-to-do. At the same time, one should note that Celebration has some impressive achievements to its credit. And whatever the final outcome, given its goal of going beyond suburban sprawl and disconnectedness, its ambitious agenda deserves attention. At this point, of course, all rests on faith. The full test of Celebration, requiring time and experience, will come too late to ameliorate the plan and the decisions that set it on its course. That loophole is to some degree helpful by giving Celebration time to grow but it also postpones effective action in the here and now. By projecting desired information into a distant future, its lessons can never be applied in the present. That absolves planners, designers, and architects from the full brunt of the critique that could improve their creations. Planned developments, designated "communities" long before they deserve the name, are proliferating across the land, indeed across the world. In the interpenetration of market strategies and cultural nostalgia, "community" often becomes little more than a sales pitch. Yet obviously it also touches a cultural nerve.

One frequent critique of the commercialization of community is that it loses the participatory, creative aspect and turns it into a commodity to be bought and sold. In turn, the consumer expects a product, an "instant community." When this proves a chimera, frustration, anger, and turmoil ensue.

Another rapidly growing trend is that toward "gated communities," organized for safety, exclusion, and top-down community rigidly regulated. Estimates put their number at twenty thousand with eight and a half million residents.

All of these developments have important implications for family, property arrangements, home ownership, and social cooperation. Whatever their limitations, they are a boon to young families eager for home ownership and middle-class lifestyles at prices they can afford. This has proved attractive in other countries as well. In the 1990s, for example, an American-style development featuring the "townkhaus" arose on the fringes of St. Petersburg in Russia. Safety and space drew young couples with small children who were willing to wait for shops, schools, and cultural activities not yet in place (Varoli, 2000). They, too, left the city to become home owners yet found that they had to pull together with others to achieve their goals. That process will surely take longer than they anticipated but at its best it will expand their connectedness to others.

Common Interest Developments (CIDs), including new towns, co-operative apartments, condominiums, and co-op housing, have increased from a bare 1,000 in the early 1960s to over 100,000 by the 1990s. These are expected to become the principal form of new home ownership in "most metropolitan areas" (Judd 1995, pp. 144–46, 155).

Gay Communities

The significance of community for a modern group has nowhere been more in evidence than in the transformation of homosexuality from a marginalized, "deviant" condition to an alternative and increasingly accepted form of sexual expression. The emergence of a homosexual subculture rooted in special communities was the most striking manifestation of this transformation.

Gay communities, as distinct from the underground gay nightlife that many cities harbored in the years between World Wars I and II, have existed in a number of cities for a century or more. In New York City, for example, the Bowery, Greenwich Village, and Harlem attracted large numbers of gays and were typically part of the bohemian underworld that had established itself in urban areas throughout the world. Although their growth and significance have not been sufficiently acknowledged by students of community, gay communities developed their own complement of institutions, values, and means of communication thereby providing a protective web for their members.

"A real gay community is more than bars, clubs, baths, and restaurants, important as these are. Nor is it simply an elaborate network of friendships, though these too are important." Rather, it is a set of institutions, including political and social clubs, "bookstores, church groups, community centers, theater groups . . . that represent both a sense of shared values and a willingness to assert one's homosexuality." The "greatest single victory of the gay movement" stemmed from shifting the public—and private—debate "from behavior to identity," notes Altman (1982, pp. 8, 9). And identity, being social in essence, derives from community. But where did this community—as distinct from the earlier homosexual districts—originate? The Civil Rights movement of the 1960s was one important source because it raised the consciousness of minorities. But perhaps an even more powerful force was commercialism seeking new markets.

By the 1980s a self-conscious, socially distinctive gay community offered a wide range of institutions for gays. This included "gay travel agencies, gay medical and legal services, gay bookstores, gay publishing houses," gay restaurants, hotels, sports arenas and media—newspapers, magazines, films. "No other minority has depended so heavily on commercial enterprises to define itself . . . especially for gay men" (ibid., p. 21).

Whatever the origins of the gay community, once gelled, institutions proliferated to solidify a way of life and a wide range of activities. There are gay pressure groups, political power blocs, resort areas, as well as gentrified neighborhoods and spatial enclaves. All of these increase group identity and cohesion. If some would call these ghettoes, then at least they are ghettos of "desire" whose separatism is "voluntary." From these newly forged communities, gay culture has extended its influence far out into the mainstream—via fashion, advertising, humor, and self-display (ibid., pp. 31ff.). "No longer sinners, criminals, perverts, neurotics, or deviants, homosexuals are slowly being redefined in less value-laden terms as practitioners of an alternative life-style, members of a *new community*" (ibid., p. 35, my emphasis). The gay community offers social status, a group identity, and support for overcoming "the alienation and impersonality of urban industrial society by stressing bonds of community" (ibid., p. 103).

Lest we exaggerate the positives of the gay community, we should also consider some of its negatives. As is true of all communities, once formed, there is pressure to conform to group norms and to a separatist ideology that segregates "us" from "them." Then there is the fact that while the gay community may display a unified front to the larger society, internally it may be sharply divided in regard to a variety of controversial issues, including adult-child sexual contacts, cross-dressing, public sex, and attitudes toward the straight world. The sense of community can help to gradually diffuse these internal battles. As the community coalesces and becomes more cohesive, it develops an ethical code geared to the needs and problems of the members. To do so effectively, gay communities will need to move from a commercial gay enclave to genuine community — a long and arduous task.

While one may generalize about gay communities, one should not exaggerate their uniformity. Gender, in particular, is an important source of distinction, as communities for gay men differ significantly from communities for gay women.

The general community attributes are similar for each: symbolic and spatial boundaries, a shared language, norms and social networks, and feelings of identity conducive to sociopsychological unity. These develop out of common projects and shared interests and in time give shape to distinctive cultural patterns and frames of reference that extend their reach across cities, countries, even continents (Wolf 1979, p. 73).

However, lesbian communities differ from male homosexual communities in numerous ways. They are less likely to be created by commercial forces seeking market niches. They tend to be poorer in economic resources, reflecting women's greater poverty in the society generally. And perhaps because of that, they emphasize equality and oppose social hierarchy and the need for formal leadership (ibid., p. 80). In addition, lesbians have a political mindset that seeks not only separatism from the wider society but from a male-dominated culture and patriarchal institutions that are seen to repress women.

Both communities also suffer from a certain transience and the fragility of romantic bonds, which, until recently, have lacked legal supports. Thus they must create traditions from scratch.

Like gay males, lesbians derive support from particular institutions. For lesbians, these include the Women's Switchboard, Women's Coffee Houses, lesbian bars, and media geared to their concerns. All of these help to cement identities and reinforce special bonds. Names are often taken not from fathers but from mothers' first names, from cities, or from nature (ibid., pp. 84–85).

A great deal of emphasis in the start-up phase of such communities is placed on creating unifying symbols (lavender stars), a mythology, historic antecedents, and rituals of group identity. Also, community cohesion and personal identity are enhanced by the group's hostility to the mainstream society that has long rejected them.

Sexuality also differentiates the two: For the male gay culture, casual and recreational sex, which the wider society often condemns as promiscuous and morally reprehensible, are more accepted, and this creates a special "communal eroticism" (Altman 1982, p. 35). By way of contrast, lesbians have typically been depicted as emphasizing long-term romance, tenderness, affection, and sentiment in their sexuality (Wolf 1979, p. 89).

The bathhouse is essentially a gay male institution. And while such places of assignation are not unknown in the lesbian community, they have far less centrality, as does anonymous, transient sex. At this point, it is not clear how to interpret this difference of emphasis since both gay males and lesbians seek that special partner and permanent unions, but for the males, anonymous, casual sex is a powerful countertheme. This could reflect differences in the socialization of men and women that carry over into gay communities or it may be a function of earlier generational attitudes toward sexual expression no longer prevalent in the sexually freer atmosphere of the 1990s. It may also, however, reflect differing value systems for the two types of gay communities with gay males tending to split off sexuality from other aspects of life while lesbians seek to incorporate it.

A common theme in both lesbian and male gay communities is that they are striving to create a more open, caring, and sharing world that will liberate humanity from old psychological and ideological shackles. Both also offer a group identity and social status to their members even if, as is true for other communities, these may be sharply divided internally on a variety of issues.

One interesting but as yet unanswerable question is whether, as gays cease to be a disdained minority, they will continue to need and support such communities and the solace they offer. There is reason to suppose that gay communities will change substantially once the basis for forming such communities has lost its driving force, but that remains a question for the future.

The four trends, and the communities they foster discussed in this chapter, are not likely to abate in the foreseeable future. Indeed they offer natural social laboratories for studying emerging community processes so as to deepen our understanding of them.

There is a further argument for the proliferation of spatial communities stoked by economic interests and technological advances. If this accelerates as most pundits assume, so will the need for rootedness, spatial identity, and belonging to smaller turfs as part of a compensatory dialectic linking global and local scales.

And if, as many have argued, the costs of modern, and postmodern, life will leave millions in psychic limbo, the desire for collective cushions will command public notice and political response in growing measure.

CHAPTER 15
CONCLUDING REFLECTIONS

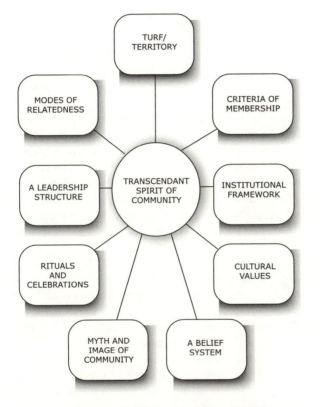

BUILDING BLOCKS OF COMMUNITY

[T]o feel much for others . . . to restrain our selfishness and to indulge our benevolent affections, constitutes the perfection of human nature.

— Adam Smith

Having come this far, I conclude with some general reflections on the possibility of the territorial community as an anchor of human existence. My reading of classic theory, historic experiences, and research on human behavior — including the in-depth case examined in this book — lead to a cautious optimism. Community clearly is not obsolescent or superfluous. In fact, the need for what William Faulkner called "a little postage stamp corner of the world" is greater than ever as humans enter the interplanetary era.

Constant Elements of Community

Many have lamented the multiplicity of terms — often contradictory and partial — used to denote community. But if one looks beneath the verbal pyrotechnics, there is considerable agreement on basic connotations and ideas.

Martin Buber defined community as "the overcoming of otherness in living unity (Arnett 1986, p. XII). Ferdinand Tönnies, the father of modern community studies, defined it as "a condition" in which individuals remain "attached despite all division, in contrast to society in which people remain separate despite all unifying forces" (Bender 1978, p. 17). Unity looms large in both definitions, but it is a multiple unity and one marked by a perpetual struggle to achieve "integration against difficulties" (Redfield 1960, p. 108). Most observers agree, moreover, that community is not defined by sociability but precedes it.

As is true of so much of social life, the fiction, the belief, indeed the myth of community may be more significant than the actuality. The ideal conception of community, where everything seems possible, often clashes with real-life communities in which nothing comes easily. This is true even in preliterate societies suffused by community ties and obligations. "The unity of the clan," notes Malinowski (1926, pp. 119, 121) "is a legal fiction in that it demands an absolute subordination of all other interests and ties to the claims of clan solidarity, while in fact, this solidarity is almost constantly sinned against and practically non-existent in the daily run of ordinary life."

Surprisingly, despite the vast technological and cultural differences that separate the electronic era from the stone age, the two share many essential features. In fact, a fairly limited set of attributes defines both. These range from physical properties, such as land and boundaries, to cultural and social properties.

The standard dimensions that form the bedrock of community are:

1. A bounded site of territory and turf.
2. Criteria of membership specifying who does and who does not belong. This provides a "consciousness of kind," a "we" versus "they" feeling to reinforce a sense of belonging.

3. An institutional framework of laws and rules, sanctions and rewards.

4. A set of values emphasizing cooperation, mutual responsibility, and sharing.

5. A belief system that validates a particular way of life and justifies its constraints and demands.

6. A myth of community embodied in images, ideals, aspirations, and goals.

7. Shared rituals and celebrations to give shape to a rhythm of collective life.

8. Leadership structure with leaders acting as guides, arbiters, and models.

9. Social relationships that are personal, direct, responsive, and trusting.

10. Transcendent purposes and goals—captured by "the spirit of community."

Each of these ten dimensions makes a distinctive contribution:

1. A bounded site demarcates a distinctive space and turf that helps generate a collective identity, a sense of closure, and safety. A name and certain landmarks offer a spatial signature.

2. Criteria of membership determine who belongs and who does not, providing access and privilege for insiders, exclusion for outsiders and nonmembers.

3. The institutional framework provides governance and rules to cope with routine circumstances as well as crises. Some communities find their genesis in a formal covenant while others focus on significant historic events or religious, racial, and ethnic solidarities.

4. A set of shared values shapes priorities and goals.

5. A belief system validates a common way of life and justifies the demands and costs required to realize desired goals.

6. A guiding image, often mythic, is linked to events prominently featured in the community. These may be natural disasters, historic triumphs, or notable trials. Myths are visions of the desired life or fictions of common origins and past events. They may bear little relation to reality. For example, Wylie (1974, p. 286) notes that the French village he studied clung to the illusion of changelessness despite the transient population's continuous mobility. Myths, images, sagas, and legends are symbolic modes solidifying community.

7. Collective rituals and celebrations generate a spirit of sharing and togetherness, as does any activity in common. An interesting example, culled from American history, concerns the debts owed by early settlers of New England to the sponsors of their newly established commu-

nities. All individuals in the community worked for seven years to pay off this debt, thus diffusing the collective burden (Demos 1970, p. 5). Collective rituals also enable communities to cope with the inevitable tensions and conflicts of collective life. Cultural meanings are thereby created "on a stage as wide as society itself" (Diamond 1981, p. 150).

Consider the aftermath of major national disasters with their prayer services and occasions for shared grief. In the TWA Flight 800 catastrophe of July 1996, for example, both the families directly affected by the loss of loved ones and a compassionate larger public were symbolically joined in a ritual of mourning. After a religious service on the shore near the crash site, TV viewers became part of a moving ritual of farewell. Roses placed in the ocean waters by the family members were carried out to the site of the fatal impact in a last gesture of grief. This simple public expression conveyed the deep feelings of the afflicted as well as the sympathies of a wider, empathic community of kindred spirits.

8. Leadership is crucial. Indifference or neglect by leaders generally spells a community's decline. Leaders are crucially important in times of emergency, of course, but also for the day-to-day routines of collective life. Leaders, no matter how indispensable, however, are typically viewed with ambivalence. In many a preliterate society, for example, public ceremonials may actually encourage the expression of ambivalence toward authority figures. Instead of denying such cultural contradictions and tensions, these are centrally featured, thus becoming part of the sacred drama of challenge and reconciliation in community life.

9. Social relationships — personal, direct, expressive — are significant building blocks of community. To be known or recognized in the public arena is reassuring, and the sense of trust and mutuality thereby generated gets funneled back into the community.

10. An investment of self — via time, energy, effort, and sacrifice — in community highlights the interdependence of members and their needs for one another. When one is able to identify one's own well-being with the common good, a major turning point has been reached — a point of transcendence. When one's plans and goals have been linked to a totality beyond one's self and one is willing to assume responsibility for its fate, community has happened.

In a charming account of a pet iguana that had to be given up for adoption, the owner weeps at her loss, exclaiming through her tears: "I can't believe I'm crying over an iguana!" . . . "She wasn't just an iguana to you" her husband said. "You took responsibility for her" (Greenhouse 2000, p. 94).

Clearly, then, community is a collective creation and some social conditions are more favorable for its emergence than others. Thus, the deeply ingrained conflict between individual and community of Western civilization "seems alien to Japan's social tradition." This is not due to a more intrinsic harmony in Japan, where conflict is endemic, but because of a certain "basic unity" that provides its cultural and institutional underpinnings (Gottmann 1981, p. 259).

An obvious question is whether each of the ten dimensions is equally significant and, if not, is there a way to prioritize them?

I would argue that for community to exist, all ten dimensions are essential, but their impact may vary according to the stages of community formation. Thus, the spatial aspects — turf, territory, site — are critical for launching the community, whereas transcendence, if achieved, marks the ultimate phase. In between, structures, values, rituals, and relationships take hold.

The case of Twin Rivers is illustrative here.

1. It starts with a bounded site and territory inspired by a set of practical aims of building a townhouse community.

2–4. It attracts homebuyers eager to claim their share of the American dream of house and, hopefully, community. They are imbued with a set of beliefs that feature home ownership, open spaces, safety, social opportunities for their children, material advancement, a sound family life, and, most notably, a flourishing community. These values reflect a historic model of community and its images of the good life, which provide the vision for the community to be.

5–8. Implementation occupies a prominent place during the first three to five years, when the institutional foundation, a leadership structure, and rules and sanctions are worked out. Slowly, as the edifice begins to take shape, leading personalities emerge, and collective rituals channel the practice of community.

9–10. By the end of the first decade a collective identity, a "we" feeling, and significant social bonding has taken hold. Many generous actions may now be identified and some melding of self-interest — "what is best for me and mine" — with the common good, "what is best for *us*," for the totality. A transcendent element of empathy and caring, a sense of wholeness and shared fate now beckons to the more community-minded who spread its spirit throughout the community. Henceforth the ship is seaworthy.

Of these essential dimensions, the two most difficult to achieve are: (1) care and empathy for one's fellow members, and (2) transcendence to a holistic spirit of community. Why should I care for the stranger who happens to dwell in my collective home? That is the fundamental question, especially in a culture that stresses the individual's responsibility primarily to self and family.

For Westerners, it has often been observed, "life means individuality. We know each other as individuals. . . . community is secondary."

But for most societies of the world, "it is the other way around. Individuals only exist because of the community . . . because *we* exist, I exist" (Sundermeier 1998).

This is at odds with a culture that views individuals biologically primed to be self-oriented. Elaborate theories and moral precepts are adduced to validate this article of faith. In a society that takes egoism for granted as innate and inescapable, it is hard to grant equal status to the contrary proposition, that altruism is equally a part of our biological endowment. Yet, such a case can indeed be made.

Altruism: The Exception or the Rule?

Consider the following dramatic and, to moderns, unimaginable true story of voluntary self-sacrifice. The story of Father Maximilian Kolbe is legendary. It takes us back to July 1941 in the death camp of Auschwitz where unspeakable horror encountered heroism.

One rule of the camp stipulated that any escape attempt by one inmate had to be atoned for by the death, through starvation, of ten men from the same bunker. And, upon the escape of one such man, ten men were selected at random to die in his place, among them Franciszek Gajowniczek, who cried out in despair to a wife and children he would never see again. It was then that the forty-seven-year-old priest, prisoner number 16670, stepped forth and said, "I am a Catholic priest and I wish to die for that man. He has young children. I am old." The guard, caring only to fill his quota of ten, accepted him without question. The ten would die harrowing deaths from starvation except for the last few, including Father Kolbe, who were later disposed of by lethal injection. According to an eyewitness, the priest ministered to the suffering men to the very end and died stoically, his body condemned to the crematorium along with countless others. The call for sainthood arose soon thereafter and he was eventually beatified by Pope Paul VI. The ceremony of October 17, 1971, was attended by Sergeant Franciszek Gajowniczek whose life Father Kolbe had saved.

The sacrifice of one's life, though rare, has countless historic precedents. There are legendary accounts of soldiers in wartime risking death to save a friend, mothers dying to save their children, firefighters turning back into the flames to rescue those trapped inside burning buildings. Clearly we see here an identification with those in need that transcends self-interest.

The propensity to respond to human need anonymously—as in donating blood to strangers—is also a "kind of altruism," which eventually comes "to advance the well-being of the whole community" (Titmus 1970, p. 213).

According to Titmus, blood donations can teach us something about reciprocity and social outreach. For, the "ways in which society organizes and structures its social institutions . . . can encourage or discourage the altruistic in man." And when part of the self is given away, "community appears" (ibid., pp. 225, 92).

Societies vary greatly in their receptivity to altruism as a principle of collective life. Modern societies, bent on self-interest, tend to undervalue it (Mansbridge 1990, pp. 135–36).

A striking example of altruism in recent history is that of "Holocaust altruism" in the Nazi period in Europe in the 1940s. Available estimates suggest that more than 50,000 non-Jews, at a minimum, risked their lives to help Jews, an action legally prohibited that could have resulted in the deaths of the rescuers (Oliner and Oliner 1988, p. 20). These risks were incurred on behalf of a despised, marginalized, minority group defined as alien and unworthy.

A study of 406 rescuers, 150 survivors, and 126 nonrescuers explored several key questions including whether rescue behavior was an attribute of personality or a response to a given situation of need, and whether it is a learned or innate characteristic of human beings. The findings suggest that rescue behavior reflects both personal qualities and values absorbed from parents early in life (ibid., p. 142).

In exploring the roots of such values, the researchers found that a key role was played by the nature of parental discipline in early childhood. Benevolent discipline and emphasis on reasoning and the consequences of one's actions for others create respect, trust, and a sense of warmth and concern for others. Particularly striking is the absence of physical punishment, often deemed to breed hostility and aggression, in the upbringing of rescuers (ibid., p. 179). This strengthened the conclusion that empathy, concern, inclusiveness, and responsibility for others are acquired, not innate, characteristics. Rescuers differed from nonrescuers in their degrees of empathy for suffering, in their feelings of connectedness to others, and in their strong sense of social responsibility (ibid., p. 175).

While this would lead us to consider parental values, modes of discipline, and personality as prime determinants of rescue behavior, one should not ignore the role of broader social factors. For example, several countries—Bulgaria, Denmark, and Italy—"managed to keep Jewish victimization to a relatively low level because of the cooperation of elite officials and local populations generally resistant to anti-Semitism" (ibid., p. 7). In fact, rescue operations were formally organized in, among other places, the Netherlands and parts of France, and among many religious groups. Not to be forgotten are the heroic achievements of extraordinary individuals such as Oskar Schindler, Raoul Wallenberg, and Chiune Sugihara (Levine 1997). The latter, as Japanese consul in

Lithuania in 1940, wrote exit visas for thousands of Polish Jews, saving their lives and eventually forfeiting his career.

The larger social environment is extremely important for encouraging or discouraging latent altruistic impulses. For lack of such support, many noble causes languish. What is often lacking is "direction for altruistic impulses at the highest levels of government," which undoubtedly has "an enervating, discouraging effect on many" (Frazier 1994, p. 128).

The kibbutz experience also suggests that a selfless devotion to others may be encouraged by social policies. It demonstrates "that those who view humanity as a species of predators are not entirely correct." Competitive impulses can be channeled into nonmaterialistic directions toward "spontaneous" social solidarity and voluntary sharing. In the kibbutz, no person's problem is his problem; every person is "our problem, even if he or she is a trouble maker and a burden" (Oz 1997, p. 46).

Altruism, in its concern for the totality, is a potential in all societies. It is a special form of gift exchange, which strengthens human bonds. It is practiced in preliterate as well as in technically advanced societies. When a gift is exchanged in a circular, rather than a one-on-one pattern it then becomes an "agent of social cohesion," which like a "faithful lover continues to grow through constancy" (Hyde 1983, p. 35). Gift exchange creates social connections and gratitude that may traverse an entire community. A circulation of gifts creates a community "out of individual expressions of good will" and the interest of the whole is thereby nourished (Hyde 1983).

It is like blood that "distributes the breath throughout the body . . . a substance that moves freely to every heart but is nonetheless contained, a healer that goes without restraint to any needy place in the body . . . and inside its vessels the blood, the gift is neither bought nor sold and it comes back forever" (ibid., p. 138).

Now back to our question about altruism. Is it as characteristic of human nature as is egoism and self-advancement? This is difficult to answer in a society heavily disposed to an individualistic life philosophy. Charles Darwin who shaped much of the thinking of the nineteenth century, definitely did not think so. In fact, it has been reported that he "once stated that if a single characteristic of a living thing existed for the sole benefit of another species, it would annihilate his theory of natural selection," usually summarized as the "survival of the fittest" (Frazier 1994, p. 129).

But an examination of the various cultures of the human species causes one to question the validity of Darwin's thesis. For there is now considerable evidence that self-denial, even self-sacrifice, in the interest of the group is not at all rare.

According to Kropotkin, mutual aid "represents an important and progressive element" in evolution. However, this element is generally underestimated because the competitive struggle for power is regarded as primary. Kropotkin goes on to delineate the manifestations of altruism as a kind of consciousness of human solidarity. "It is not love to my neighbor — whom I often do not know at all — which induces me to seize a pail of water and to rush towards his house when I see it on fire; it is a far wider feeling or instinct of human solidarity and sociability which moves me" (Kropotkin, 1955, pp. xii, xiii).

The practice of mutual aid derives its strength from "the unconscious recognition . . . of the close dependence of everyone's happiness upon the happiness of all." And, despite centuries of an individualistic ethos, "the nucleus of mutual aid institutions, habits, and contours, grown up in the tribe and the village community, remains" (ibid., pp. xix, 260).

Many other examples attest to the altruistic propensity of human beings. Miners working to rescue fellow miners trapped underground or members of "lifeboat associations" whose readiness to sacrifice their lives for the rescue of absolute strangers "is put to a severe test every year" (ibid., p. 275). In short, one could argue, as Kropotkin did, that mutual aid is the rule rather than the exception for "the vast majority of species" who stand to reap the high rewards of prosperity and survival.

"Kindness, caring and cooperation appear to be every bit as responsible for our survival as aggression, strength and dominance." And there is some research that links acts of altruism to longevity and improved immune responses. If confirmed and shared with the public, this might promote a trend toward "planned altruism" (Frazier 1994, pp. 129, 131).

Consider, for example, the village of Le Chambon where, during World War II, "goodness happened" (Hallie 1979, p. 269). Under the moral leadership of André Trocmé, the Protestant minister, the villagers voluntarily organized themselves into a collective lifesaver. The 3,000 inhabitants sheltered Jews at the risk of their own lives. To do so, they formed rescue networks of safe spaces to protect 2,500 refugees, most of them children, from Nazi persecution.

Heroic leadership, a genuine humanism, and spiritual commitment to help one's fellow humans, even against the opposition of the mayor and prefecture, helped Le Chambon achieve what no other villages had done.

It is a remarkable tale of courage and faith and proof that altruism and communal ethics are possible. "Under the moral leadership of André Trocmé and Edouard Theis, the people of Le Chambon would not give up a life for any price — for their own comfort, for their own safety, for patriotism, or for legality" (ibid., p. 274).

This is a stunning demonstration of the moving words of the poet Pablo Neruda:

> To feel the love of people whom we love is a fire that feeds our life. But to feel the affection that comes from those whom we do not know, from those unknown to us, who are watching over our sleep and solitude, over our dangers and our weaknesses—that is something still greater and more beautiful because it widens out the boundaries of our being and unites all living things.

Transcendence of self is the most difficult of all to achieve because it derives from the other nine dimensions. Many so-called communities falter here, resting mainly on structures and strictures. If transcendence is achieved, however, then both the form and spirit of community are in place. Community is above all "the consciousness of the whole," noted Emile Durkheim, the great nineteenth-century social theorist. It is that which links our individual existence to higher goals and sources of meaning. Its absence leaves egocentricity free reign.

Neither wealth, lofty credentials, nor fame are antidotes to the prevalent detachment from the public good experienced by many of the young today. To inspire their passions for a "commons" requires the smaller cells of community to catch fire. A concern for the public good stems from a sense of shared fate and an awareness that human beings are bound together and responsible for one another.

The great anthropologists have long told us that society, the impersonal social machinery of existence, becomes rigid and lifeless without smaller cells of community to keep it vital and humane. Lacking a sense of the whole and a common fund of understanding leaves many footloose and at sea. Most tend to blame this on individual failings but it is a collective disorder, an absence of binding ideals, that pulls a totality apart. Let me illustrate the distinction with two vignettes.

The first is a charming illustration of community in practice, especially as it relates to an empathic gesture to the proximate stranger. A ritual is practiced in certain modest restaurants in the south of France where patrons sit at a long table with a small bottle of wine by each plate. Before the meal begins, each diner will pour the wine not into her own glass but into that of her neighbor's. "In an economic sense nothing has happened"—no one has more or less wine than at the start—but community has appeared "where there was none before." In this small gesture, the soundings of community—of caring and sharing—are vividly present (Titmus 1970, p. 56).

The second story concerns a well-known car manufacturer and the debate as to whether a safety device should be added to its cars and trucks. Before putting the car on the market, the company tested three different devices that would tend to prevent the rupturing of a gas tank in a rear-end collision and a deadly fire. The costs ($1, $5, and $11) caused the company to decide that it would not add the safety device to the car. As a result, hundreds of people perished in rear-end crashes.

The first example treats the stranger as kindred spirit, as a member of my world. The second example treats all others as strangers, as ciphers, as "not us." If we would humanize the second example as a mode of calculating human worth, we must find ways to infuse it with the shared symbolic gestures of the first example.

I do not know if this is an age "longing for community," as some would have it. But I do believe it is an age that needs to understand community and its continued significance.

Many agree. Here is a young man reflecting on his life amid the lures of the technical civilization his generation takes for granted. He is dismayed that he and his peers seem "to lack any sense of necessary connection to anything larger than their own narrowly personal aims and preoccupations." The freedom from old constraints leaves him with a "weightless feeling," because his choices do not "connect to any larger narrative" in the "absence of the sense of common purpose" (Samuels 1999, pp. 124, 153).

This sentiment was echoed in a national survey of American life that found that 43 percent of Americans consider "selfishness and fakery" at the core of human nature, and greed and duplicity as pervasive. Confidence in business and business leadership, as well as trust in leaders generally, fell precipitously over the past decades—from 70 percent to 15 percent (Kanter and Mirvis 1989, pp. 5, 18).

We "lie in the lap of an immense intelligence" observed Ralph Waldo Emerson but it is inaccessible "until it possesses the local community as its medium." It is there that the emotional and moral foundations are laid down, because the local community, once established, contains "a settled people" who "understands its own habitat" and cares about its collective fate (Bellah 1991, pp. 267, 275).

Yet a typical current experience is to be unsettled, transient, as millions move across the face of the globe in search of food, safety, and shelter. This may make the local community superfluous. In the era of global interconnectedness and instant communication, it is easy for like-minded others to exchange information, rally to a cause, or find a sympathetic ear. However, electronically mediated social bonds are but pale precursors of community.

This impersonal bonding carries over into numerous arenas, as artists are invited to gather with other artists in a "community" of creative souls; chess players regularly meet in public squares to test their skills; single mothers are helped to find other single mothers to share their experiences; and the elderly venture into congregate housing. Ex-smokers, cancer survivors, victims of crime, all find their way to each other.

There are hot lines for the depressed, the suicidal, sinners seeking absolution, and "healing groups" sharing traumas and crises (McGuire 1989, p. 57). People are urged to adopt a needy neighbor or bring Christmas gifts to orphaned children. Though these hardly qualify as full communities, they endeavor to reclaim some measure of sharing and caring and some sense of responsibility for others.

Important as these efforts are, however, we should note that these islands of commonality are really specialized fragments of a larger, diversified whole and thus reinforce specialization. These subworlds of dance, the law, car racing, or computers may possess some attributes of community narrowly defined but by their partial focus they may simply be another form of privatism, a withdrawal from a wider social consciousness.

There is some controversy over nationalism as a modern form of community. The nation has often been described as the "largest effective community." Like other communities, it rests on locality and sentiments buttressed by shared values. "The lore of one's homeland, of the fatherland" can inspire patriotic and altruistic devotion notably in war (MacIver and Page 1949, pp. 296, 297). Of course, fierce nationalistic feelings may also precipitate wars and mutual distrust. Since nationalism links individuals to a political state and transforms them into citizens, it inspires modern forms of unity and legitimacy in terms taken directly from the language of community, thereby contributing to "the emotional unity of the nation" (Mosse 1983, p. 82).

But the nation is no substitute for the local community. To sustain emotional fervor for its projects and programs, it needs huge causes such as wars or economic crises. This is forcefully illustrated by the fate of Lyndon B. Johnson's Great Society program.

Johnson had a vision of the national community that would inspire Americans to compassion and sacrifice for the "War on Poverty" and so include the disadvantaged at society's table. His vision "was designed to lift Americans above material self-interest into a new realm of community consciousness" (Schambra 1986, p. 27).

Despite such noble goals, however, the movements for national unity are "extraordinarily difficult to sustain." And when the "community-mindedness of the nation begins to recede, such federal programs "lose their moral authority" and seem "intrusive, bureaucratic, alienating . . . and expendable" (ibid., p. 28).

The "fragility of the idea of national community" revived the "much older idea of community" — small, local, participatory, voluntary, empathic—that could inspire "citizenship, sacrifice, and public spiritness." The view of progressive liberalism that such communities had been doomed by twentieth-century industrialization and urbanization has not been confirmed. The "small republic" spirit has not perished and the "national community idea simply was not an adequate substitute" (ibid., p. 28).

Since the 1970s and Reagan's "New Federalism," the call has been sounded for decentralization, block-grant programs, volunteerism, and participatory democracy, featuring local communities, local government, voluntary associations, ethnic allegiances, and neighborhood cohesion.

But to argue for the critical significance of the local community is not to deny the reality of the mega-society. What is necessary is to link the two. Respect for this linkage expands our appreciation of each—the community to provide roots and identity, the wider society to expand our horizons and collective intelligence. To neglect that linkage—which modern societies with their elaborate lures make all too easy—is to risk succumbing either to Big Brother, who will assume the responsibilities the people abandon, or confront the destruction of the commons which is decimated by the relentless pursuit of individual gain.

The need for roots, wrote Simone Weil, is "the most important and least recognized need of the human soul" (Weil 1952, p. 43). And to be uprooted is a source of great anguish, robbing the afflicted of inner security and identity. "I have contracted the American disease of anomie, loneliness . . . and excessive self-consciousness," notes Eva Hoffman as she reflects on this loss as "a particular form of suffering" that thrives in the United States but is virtually unknown in her native Poland (Hoffman 1989, p. 22).

But while the need for roots and belonging is widespread, it is by no means uniform. At some stages of life, for some life experiences, at some ages, community may be more necessary than at others. The young, the upwardly mobile, and the voluntarily rootless cosmopolites may well disdain community for the wide-open electronic spaces, at least for a time. More settled or stable temperaments may avidly seek community. No single recipe will satisfy all tastes. Still, some base is required to fashion common ground. This is Bellah's argument for place loyalties, since those "closest to the situation can give it the best attention" (1991, p. 201). It echoes John Dewey's familiar warning that democracy is only a shell without this vital connection.

We might pause here to consider a frequently voiced concern about the penchant of local communities to become oppressive, intolerant, narrow-minded, and exclusionary. But are they unique in this respect? Authoritarianism, conformity, and exclusivity are a potential in all human aggregations—at mega-scales no less than at local scales. Hence the villain is not localism but close-mindedness, lack of public debate, and uniformity. That local communities may succumb to such tendencies is deplorable and eventually self-defeating, but the solution is not to be found by abandoning the local community for larger, technically more complex scales where intolerance and despotism can grow to huge dimensions. Community denied is as dangerous as community irrationally inflated.

At the local community level, a culture of care, respect, trust, and commitment may be cultivated not as noble abstraction but as lived experience. By humanizing social existence and fostering diversity, public dialogue, and empathy, a sense of community may be nurtured that can in turn nurture the general culture.

Like Rome, communities are not built in a day or even a year. But this truism is one often ignored. Whether we are trying to revitalize or enhance an existing community or create one from scratch, the process is long, slow, uneven, and often excruciating. It demands not only patience but a respect for the complex demands of collective behavior, theoretical and practical. Moreover, the culture of community takes time to gel and is fluid, while the physical setting of houses, schools, parks, and playgrounds is not. And beyond the institutional supports, the rules and the normative framework, community needs a special spirit—supportive, encouraging, watchful, and protective of the collective good.

To bring the planned unit development of Twin Rivers into existence required years of planning, political persuasion, legal maneuvers, and money. To bring the Twin Rivers *community* into being required that and much more.

One problem that surfaced early had to do with the extravagant fantasies residents harbored about the community to be. When these did not materialize, keen disappointment and disillusionment followed.

Visions of a potential Shangri-la were accompanied by the Big Brother syndrome, which encouraged a widespread belief that whatever might go wrong would somehow be taken care of. This abdication of personal responsibility, partly engendered by the hype of the sales pitch, resulted in a curious admixture of childlike dependency on the authorities on the one hand and keen resentment directed at the authorities, on the other. This ambivalent posture became part of the dominant cultural pattern of the developing community. Disappointments, complaints, and criticism notwithstanding, the majority of residents did manage to create a satisfactory way of life for themselves but they had to work hard for it.

The course of a community's development probably never runs smooth and that was certainly the case with Twin Rivers. Communities, like individuals, change over time and so do their priorities. In Twin

Rivers, the physical-spatial aspects were most significant in the first decade when the cultural climate was still quite raw, the site bleak, the landscape a bare shadow of what it was to become, facilities sparse, and the daily influx of newcomers inescapable.

The salience of physical-spatial features was striking at the start but receded over time because boundaries, pathways, and siting of facilities did not alter with the years or the seasons. The same cannot be said for social and family life, which changed substantially over the decades. Families were buffeted by strains amply documented for American society as a whole. The euphoria of newlyweds and young parents, who predominated among the original residents, gave way for at least one-third of them to divorce and complicated living arrangements. Ex-wives doubled up with other divorcees, or moved to cheaper quarters; many resumed employment while also raising children. Husbands frequently moved to apartments to be near their children and to remain in the community.

Social life also changed over the decades, becoming more selective and less spatially determined as personal tastes rather than physical proximity determined the range of one's social contacts. Neighbors became neighbors rather than friends, cliques diminished somewhat, and friendships were formed on a less casual basis. In contrast to "virtual communities" and their illusory social ties, moreover, here we see a shift from the superficial social ties of newcomers seeking any social contact to the more substantial, time-tested ties of a more settled population.

With time, also, two opposing stances toward authority became apparent. One group supported formal governance and resented the political in-fighting among contending factions they considered self-serving. The other was on principle opposed to any central authority and viewed politics as an age-old drama between the people and the king.

In Twin Rivers there were periodic clashes between these two factions followed by periods of conciliation and calm. In the 1990s hostilities between the two erupted with a vengeance, recalling the famous warning by James Madison in *The Federalist* that factions were a threat to national unity, or as in this case, to that of the local community.

In time, also, Twin Rivers would learn that a major drawback of majority rule, the mainstay of representative democracy, is minority resentment and frustration. At this writing, there is a strongly aggrieved minority in Twin Rivers. At the same time, a community image has jelled and its preservation now motivates growing numbers of residents. This is evident when we look at the issues that galvanize the community. Any perceived threat to the community's integrity and survival now resonates with a growing number of residents and propels them into action.

For the majority, the perceived benefits of Twin Rivers came to out-weigh the costs and disappointments. Safety, open space, comfortable and affordable houses with nearby tennis courts and swimming pools, new friends, and the adventure of joining with others to reach desired goals helped them rise above the difficulties. They were able to muster something of a frontier psychology and, despite the frontier anxieties that accompanied it, to brave a twentieth-century wilderness in order to lay the foundation for sustained community life.

As a pioneering social and architectural experiment of the 1970s, Twin Rivers has come a long way. Yet the coast is not yet clear. Many battles lie ahead—the battle for unity, for fuller civic participation, and for finding a balance between individual and collective goals, to name just a few.

Steps toward Community

If community was viewed as an inescapable necessity to the ancients, as the path to salvation for medieval sages, and as secondary to posten-lightenment thinkers, today it beckons to many as a cultural lifesaver. It represents the nucleus of human connectedness in a world of huge Kaf-kaesque institutions—megacorporations, malls, sports arenas, and con-vention centers. This is why many believe that local communities "are both the site of people's life gratifications and the only arena in which most citizens can take any meaningful action" (Logan and Molotch 1987, p. 15).

And while Americans tend to extol private over public life and self over community, a nagging reminder persists that individuals cannot go it alone. There is a longing for mutuality, sharing, and a commitment to larger goals that the culture does not sufficiently address. Even the most radical individualists do not, for the most part, "imagine that a good life can be lived alone" (Bellah 1985, p. 84). A satisfying private life, which everyone seems to want, is ultimately impossible without well-functioning communities. At a minimum, some degree of public order, public services, safety, and cooperation is necessary for individuals to pursue private goals and interests.

In this book, I chose to chart the course of how an aggregate of strangers goes about creating the basis for a common life, bounded by space, tied by shared interests, and making their way to a joint future. If their efforts bear fruit, they will have forged a common cultural identity of place and spirit.

In contrast to the community studies that focus on poor, minority, or immigrant populations, this study focused on middle-class Americans, largely native-born, well-educated young couples with young children who chose a then novel form of housing in the first planned unit development of New Jersey. The townhouses they purchased gave them a physical connection before they developed social, political, or emotional connections.

Townhouse ownership was still novel in the 1970s, though eventually it would become widespread. At the time it seemed an extraordinary opportunity to study the genesis (or stillbirth) of a community in the making with an upwardly mobile population imbued with traditional American values and a desire for a slice of the pie.

Great expectations, magnified by the lure of community (left largely undefined), were dashed, however, when residents, unprepared for such dense living arrangements, confronted an unfinished site filled with mud and unfamiliar neighbors.

This made the founding period stressful and frustrating and led to the kind of frantic socializing often confused with community. Along with the turmoil of the early days came a crescendo of grievances and resentments about unfulfilled promises on which a great deal of unproductive energy was expended. This suggests that excessive hype may lure buyers initially, but subsequently proves self-defeating; it leaves a cultural residue of distrust and wariness that may linger for many years.

The experience of Twin Rivers is astonishing in at least two respects:

1. It shows how difficult it is, especially in a culture of self-advancement, to become mindful of and foster social interdependence and a concern for the public good.

2. It reveals that tremendous lacunae exist in our general education for citizenship. This makes a collectivity extremely dependent on the active minority who devote themselves to building the rules and institutions needed and who, by their example, engender a conscience for community. At the same time, however, the active minority at the helm will arouse apprehension, resentment, and resistance to its power. It is an enduring tug of war, since community, if it is to be more than a rhetorical flourish, needs rules, sanctions, and leadership.

I would now like to touch on more general issues and questions about community. Many of these are age-old questions that perplexed the classic thinkers (see chapters 2 and 3) and that continue to be relevant.

The Passage of Time

A longitudinal perspective leaves no doubt that community develops by fits and starts and exhibits ups and downs that play a vital role in determining residents' satisfactions and optimism for the future. In short, time is an important dimension in community development. Time is rarely systematically dealt with in community studies, however. Notable exceptions, such as the Lynds' restudy of Middletown (1937) and Oscar Lewis's of Tepotzlan (1951) rest on comparisons at two points in time. This book tracks the development of a community over three decades. Over time, territoriality and exclusiveness increased in Twin Rivers as residents exerted claims over "their" pools, tennis courts, library, and other facilities.

Free riders multiplied also but so did the committed few working for the community. Associations of many kinds flourished virtually from the start. They brought residents together and helped to sort out the varied interests that appealed to a contemporary population. However, associations not only pull people together, but also increase fragmentation by channeling residents into separate domains.

This study also confirmed findings from other studies that having a stake in the community via home ownership and length of residence increased the residents' commitment and loyalty to the community.

The gap between private and public domains grew wider over time. Public consciousness of "the commons," it seems, is unlikely to develop unaided in a culture emphasizing individual over collective goals and private over public concerns.

Twin Rivers was especially interesting in this regard because as a townhouse development it was rooted in shared property arrangements and complex rules concerning mine, thine, and ours. Unfamiliar with these rules, residents needed instructions in how to sort out personal from collective obligations. Some residents, home owners in particular, were better prepared to do so than others, but for most residents it was a long and uneven process.

Highly significant here is the need to personalize public space so as to elicit care and concern for its preservation. Anonymous public space tends to become a no-man's-land, neglected and defaced. By contrast, the spaces people identified as their own—the house, the front sidewalk, the lawn, and the patio—typically received careful personal attention.

Interestingly, the second decade was the one fraught with most tensions and social conflicts. Midway between the euphoria and hope of the first decade and the relative stability of the third, the second most acutely manifested the imperfections and contradictions of the community-in-the making. Over time, one can observe the fluctuating rhythm of social life expressed in an ebb and flow of social participation, identity, and commitment until a stable plateau is attained.

Time plays a significant role in yet another way. While it strengthens the collective sinews, it also reinforces certain rigidities based on attitudes formed early on that become culturally entrenched. In Twin Rivers, the early disappointment with promises unfulfilled or broken, led to a distrust of authority and its pronouncements and rules that would last for a generation.

Citizenship and Leadership

One of the most consistent findings over the decades was the low level of participation in public life. This has long been noted as characteristic of communities with democratic political institutions. But the explanations for it have generally been couched in highly individualistic terms — of character, temperament, taste, selfishness, and the like.

But there are some alternative propositions, one of which I would strongly underscore. It has to do with the fact that in small, face-to-face communities such as eighteenth-century villages or the small towns of the nineteenth and twentieth centuries that have been described as the backbone of American society, one's neighbors and friends are the same people with whom one engages in political controversies and disagreements. Non-participation in public life may thus be rooted in the social scale of a community that does not permit the existence of an anonymous public to offer a neutral space for social and political debate.

How to carry on an ideological struggle without carrying it over into daily life is thus a central question. If people fear alienating a neighbor or a friend, they will avoid the cauldron of politics and public life.

Another factor was at work in Twin Rivers. Most residents started out with goodwill and seemed willing to do their share, but the demands of daily life — the commute to jobs, children's needs, and the upkeep of house and home — consumed most of the extra time available for public service.

Why did some residents find time for public service while others remained on the sidelines? Having watched this process over several decades, I suggest that both predispositions lead back to lessons absorbed in one's childhood. Most leaders attributed their public-mindedness and their labors on behalf of thousands of strangers to parents or other mentors who instilled in them the value of contributing one's share, of paying back to the community. Not all leaders, of course, were on such high moral ground. A few were arrogant and authoritarian, but the large majority were unsung heroes who helped forge community spirit and unity. Those who stayed in the background had no such childhood experiences or philosophy to draw on. They may also have been deflected by their awareness that the public is not always grateful to those who assume leadership positions.

It is no exaggeration to say that Twin Rivers would not have succeeded without some extraordinary leaders. In the years when conditions were still unsettled, these were the people who provided the concentrated energy and inspiration for collective survival. And over time, they pulled enough residents along for self-government to succeed.

Leaders continue to be indispensable — from the current trust administrator, Jennifer Ward, a most able manager, to the board members, committee heads, and countless volunteers who watch over schools, pools, services, and community needs. Critical though they continue to be, leaders have been ambivalently viewed from the start, and distrust of management has been pervasive. This may have begun as a healthy counterforce to excessive officialdom but it also proved an obstacle to harmonious relations between residents and leaders.

Nor did the ambivalence lessen after governance passed from the bank trustee to the residents themselves. Surprisingly, self-government proved no antidote. And by the third decade, a small group of malcontents fanned the flames of discord anew and threatened to undo the achievements of decades.

It seems that leadership accrues resentment no matter how small the scale. This has been documented in all sorts of community organizing efforts and suggests that we need to pay much more attention to it. Short of a charismatic leader who can often work wonders, governance, rule-making bodies, and managerial boards tend to be a perennial source of strife in new communities. Thus it is not only the faraway government in Washington, D.C., that is viewed with distrust and cynicism. The very same reactions were evident in Twin Rivers even though its "government" was democratically elected and highly accessible to its citizens.

Along with their ambivalence toward rules and quasi rulers goes the residents' tendency to complain and point fingers at those held responsible for presumed failings. An effective community organizer could be of great help here. Even more perhaps, the experience of building a community should be "a learning process," not an exercise in blame. Otherwise it is simply "the substitution of one power group for another" (Alinsky 1972, p. 125).

Social Differences and Division

How to cope with social diversity is a problem for all communities. And contrary to strongly held assumptions in architecture, planning, and community development, social diversity, though endorsed in principle, proves elusive in practice. Even in small and dense settings such as Twin

Rivers, perceived social similarity by income, age, housing tenure, ethnicity, and family arrangements was highly correlated with friendships,
social outreach, and sense of commitment to the community. Most important were income and economic parity, which overrode religion,
race, or ethnicity as criteria of affinity.

Religious differentiation took a fascinating turn in Twin Rivers. The
initial preponderance of Jewish settlers made Roman Catholics and
Protestants numerical minorities, thus reversing their typical status in
the wider society. What is striking is the impact of this reversal.

In the first survey (1970s), those who were in the numerical minority had more negative reactions to Twin Rivers than those in the majority. Minorities felt less a part of Twin Rivers, were more disappointed
with its offerings, less tolerant of its failings, and less satisfied with living there. No matter what the criterion for minority status, being different from the majority increased feelings of isolation and marginality.
Hence, the minority of apartment dwellers in a townhouse community,
the minority of Roman Catholics amid a plurality of Jews, the minority
of single parents where two-parent families are the community norm,
and the minority of renters among owners all felt less satisfied with the
community.

Even in small, accessible, interactive settings, to be in the minority
is psychologically uncomfortable. This challenges some of the basic assumptions held by planners, architects, financial institutions, and developers as to the desirability of social diversity close to home. A close,
dense, intermixture of people from different backgrounds is in their
view conducive to community. But what if proximity puts incompatible
families side by side, to share spaces, lawns, and gardens? Far from
amity, the result may then be enmity, and social conflict may impede
neighborly connectedness.

Given the ideological emphasis of American society on individual
achievement and independence, many people endorse the principle more
than the practice. Middle class in aspirations, most residents of Twin
Rivers preferred to live in close proximity to others who shared their
values, goals, styles of life, and income levels. This poses serious questions for practitioners and theorists alike, whose desire to advance democracy and equality leads them to advocate social mixing without regard to its unintended consequences.

To construct a social identity requires many years and depends on
many factors, including issues that mobilize public opinion, celebrations
that commemorate important events, athletic contests, essays by school
children rendering their experience of the community, in short, recognition of all the benign or destructive experiences that build collective
memories.

By the third decade, a collective identity had taken hold. More than one-half of the residents in the 1990s said Twin Rivers created roots for adults, and three-fifths credited it with creating roots for the children. More than one-half felt they "belonged" to Twin Rivers, and two-thirds felt committed to it. Three-fifths said they felt "proud" to be Twin Rivers residents.

Collective identity is a genuine achievement, captured in two simple words: *We* and *Us*. But that is only one-half of the story, for the achievement of a *We* and an *Us* goes hand in hand with the designation of a *They* and a *Them*. Hence collective identity rests on social exclusion to some degree, and while it strengthens the in-group vis-à-vis the outgroup it also engenders division. Outgroups — "adversaries and advocates" (Suttles 1972, p. 50) — define collectivities by means of labeling, media attention, and positive or negative prejudgments. In Twin Rivers, nearby Hightstown was the outside mirror. It played an important role from the start by its commentaries on the influx of residents, the idea of a PUD, and apprehensions about the future. The interior source of identity, stemming from attachments to others, shared experiences, and common goals took many years to coalesce, and was actually helped along by the rivalry between the PUD and the town.

Identity has long been problematic in American society. Unlike older, more traditional societies, here basic institutions have had to be invented. The continuous influx of immigrants has kept the problem of identity in full view. The emphasis on upward social mobility generally encouraged immigrants to abandon their roots in favor of some abstract and hard-to-attain American identity. This created a contradictory pull between claiming one's cultural roots and cutting one's ties to them for the larger objective of becoming American. The full costs of the abandonment will never be known, but an eloquent literature of internal exile captures some of its pathos.

The Conception of the Whole

To piece together an identity out of many disparate elements requires some sense of how the totality fits together and how deeply intertwined the diverse strands of collective life are. This is the most difficult dimension to grasp.

For the ancients, it was Plato, especially the older Plato, who drew our attention to the necessity of viewing the polis as a whole, since the "part can never be well unless the whole is well" (Gouldner 1965, p. 249).

In *The Laws*, consensus, shared values, and common standards were stressed far more than in *The Republic*, a work of Plato's youth.

And he came to put loyalty to the polis and priority to group goals above individual strivings for fame and glory. For Plato, virtue rather than happiness was the path to an integrated life and virtue was rooted in communal well-being.

One of the early modern prophets of holistic thinking was the Greek architect C. A. Doxiadis, who differed from most of his contemporaries by his persistent demand that architecture be comprehensive, not piecemeal, in its approach. We must, he said on countless occasions, deal with "one total overall program for human settlements" (C. A. Doxiadis 1974).

Both differ sharply from the philosophies of contemporary industrial societies, where individualism preempts community. But for most societies of the world, this has it all backward. Individualism can exist only because of community. As previously cited, "Because *we* exist, I exist" (Sundermeier 1998).

Twin Rivers, at best a pale shadow of the ancient polis, shares a number of features with it nonetheless. Its small scale makes it easy to become familiar with all of its dimensions. Residents can grasp the totality through daily encounters with other residents in shops, streets, pools and schools, shared rituals, problems to be solved collectively, and similar goals for the future.

For the ancients, life and the polis were profoundly intertwined. For the residents of Twin Rivers, though their horizons have been greatly expanded by modern technical modes of travel and communication, the center of day-to-day life continues to be the local community.

Despite great historic and cultural variations across the millennia, the forces undermining community appear to be remarkably constant. They include the free riders, factional disputes, inexperience, and lure of personal gain. But so are the forces that uphold it, such as people pulling together, awareness of the link between individual effort and the survival of the totality, and the ability to negotiate and compromise. A complex minuet binds the parts to the whole.

Through all of this, it is arguably people who matter most. In Twin Rivers, they cultivated a nourishing soil for community by their resilience and resourcefulness, their courage and goodwill. They remind us, once again, that people can accomplish great things if they are sufficiently determined or inspired. Residents may be disappointed when expectations exceed reality but they are not easily defeated. And they know things from their own experience that may elude the experts. How to tap that experience is the question. On the basis of this study, I would say: Do not ask people what they want. All too often, "people do not know" or cannot tell you (Alinsky 1972, p. 104). Instead, find ways to observe what it is that they do and how they react to the challenges before them. And take the long view.

In his comprehensive, indeed exhaustive, recent exploration of the decline of social capital, Putnam (2000), building on the work of de Tocqueville, Mill, Lippman, Dewey, Bellah, and others, issues a moral call for the resurrection of community. To recapture this, we need also to recapture the principle, accepted in earlier times, that the prosperity of the individual and of the community are intertwined. If a society is, ideally, a "community of communities" (MacIver 1920) then we cannot dispense with community even in the global era.

In conclusion I want to accentuate again how unprepared most residents of Twin Rivers were to create the promised community. Not only were they unprepared for what awaited them but for what was expected of them. Despite the alluring prospects proffered by salespeople and advertisements, once residents had purchased their townhouses, they were left pretty much to fend for themselves. This demanded not only patience and faith but a deeper knowledge of social behavior, both theoretical and practical, than most of them possessed.

To acquire that knowledge calls for an education in community living. Elements of this could be a formal part of everyone's school curriculum along with their informal learning from experience.

For "new communities" this could prod the human imagination, especially at the start, when fantasy can provide the needed emotional push to get them off the ground. Idealization can help residents focus on desired goals and keep them on course despite frustrations and problems. It is akin to courtship prior to marriage, a romantic glow that sustains continuity and identity.

But to survive, a community must prevail over the ever-present corrosive forces that threaten to destroy its physical or moral integrity, and it must discourage the free riders and nonplayers who consume resources without contributing to them.

The secret of enduring communities is to be mindful of corrosive forces and to keep them within bounds so that integration outpaces decline. Integration is key. It sustains the spirit of community.

What is the genesis of this spirit? Studies of preliterate societies at the heart of classic anthropological work provide clues. By comparison with industrial societies, preliterate societies are said to exhibit high degrees of integration. Institutions and sentiments coalesce so that religion, land tenure, subsistence activities, domestic arrangements, moral norms, and dominant ideological perspectives are reinforced and shaped into a balanced whole. Ordinary members engage regularly in common public events and ritual activities, a marked difference, in principle at least, from the vicarious participation that characterizes highly differentiated, large-scale modern societies.

I emphasize the words *in principle* because there is a danger of idealizing preliterate societies in order to reinforce our own romantic pre-conceptions. Preliterate societies may be conflict-ridden, noncoopera-tive, and imbalanced in crucial respects. However, the size and scale of these societies, and the necessity of members to hold together under the often treacherous conditions of life, reward those who tap and nurture the communal essence. Such societies are held together "socially, politi-cally, economically, and religiously by a system of mutual help"; a strong central core and deep points of connection bind the members of the community. Personal ailments and crises become transmuted elements in a shared existence. By projecting private pain onto shared symbolic screens, the community "takes over the burdens which, with us, fall entirely on the individual." Community that springs "from common origins," is composed of "reciprocating persons" and grows from within (Diamond, 1981, pp. 143, 159).

Preliterate individuals thus have a far greater chance to experience the world as integrated and whole than do members of so-called civi-lized societies. Not that those who live in preliterate societies are neces-sarily happy, contented, or untroubled. They have all the common hu-man problems — envy, jealousy, resentment, anxiety are ever present behind the culturally approved façades. But their social and cultural patterns help members externalize and express these so that personal crises are "woven into the outward and visible fabric of a community's social life." Also, despite technological underdevelopment and the often difficult struggle for survival, personal freedom and individual dignity are possible, even within a tight communal framework. The individual is no mere "reflex of the group," but an active agent and participant, in contrast to the familiar contemporary experience of "detached individ-uals losing themselves in some furious activity seeking anonymous union" (Diamond 1981, pp. 159, 167).

Amos Oz has noted that the prospects of human solidarity rest on "humor, relativism, patience, and the ability to live with the paradoxes of human nature" (1997, p. 46). To create a viable community is a triumph. It is not just the development and integration of social institu-tions, cooperative culture patterns, and an ethos of caring and sharing; it is a victory of human imagination, resilience, and hope.

I concluded these reflections on September 21, 2001, ten days after the slaughter of innocents following the terrorist attacks on the Twin Towers of New York City. Many have noted the extraordinary collec-tive response to this catastrophe along with the heroism of the mayor, the firemen, policemen, nurses, physicians, photographers, compassion-ate citizens, and many others who risked — and often lost — their lives to save strangers.

This showed to those who had viewed the grand city on the Hudson as hard-edged and imperious that community lay dormant beneath the glamour and the glitter when called forth by a wounded humanity.

Throngs of people came from near and far to stand as one before the devastation. Eloquent in their silence they reached out to console one another in a "community of tribulation."

In one second their — and our — lives had changed forever.

Stunned before this desecration, they recognized that life's meaning was anchored not only in personal ambition and projects but in human solidarity and the loving care of a community that nourishes and sustains us all.

EPILOGUE

IS THERE COMMUNITY IN CYBERSPACE?

"Is there anybody there?" said the Traveller,
Knocking on the moonlit door;

. . . .
. . . only a host of phantom listeners . . .

— Walter de la Mare

Shangri-la has long held an extraordinary fascination for human beings.
The oasis in the desert beckoning to the parched traveler, the golden
fleece sought by the doomed Jason, the land of Nod and the Edens of
childhood, all attest to the capacity of human beings to imagine ideal
worlds.

The Shangri-la of the twenty-first century would appear to be cyberspace — that magical realm on which hundreds of millions of earth-

lings project their longings for infinite possibilities of togetherness, harmony, and community. How easily we humans are seduced by utopian promises.

An interesting question for our time is whether electronic connectedness can create that community. The big debate focuses on whether community, if it is to exist in more than name only, does or does not require territory, space, or turf. The originators of cyberspace reflected the ideals of the 1960s counterculture in their endorsement of openness, freedom, nonconformity, and anti-establishmentarianism but with one big difference: their admiration of, and faith in, technology. Technology, in the 1990s view, would facilitate community in a new key. The precedents for such a community go back forty years to when "the farm" was launched, first in real life, and later in virtual form (Rheingold 1993). In its earthly version, "the farm" engaged the cooperation of more than one thousand individuals with the goal of building a self-sufficient community that would grow its own food and build the necessary institutions. Weariness and exhaustion put a stop to the earthly experiment but its lessons were carried over into the electronic "well" that attracted numerous groups from scientists to seers. Both farm and well were inspired by the desire to achieve direct democratic self-governance, freedom of expression, and open-endedness (ibid., p. 41), which in turn inspired later efforts.

These were impressive innovations to be sure, but did they deserve the designation "community"?

Writings on cyberspace generally refer to the rise of new kinds of communities by virtue of electronic connectedness, but to declare this is not to demonstrate it. The word "cyberspace" was coined by William Gibson in *Neuromancer* (1984) and continues to reflect its sci-fi parentage, as it lodges in the mystical web within which it was conceived and so prods the imagination but remains elusive.

"In cyberspace" writes Sherry Turkle, "we have the opportunity to build new kinds of communities, virtual communities, in which we participate with people from all over the world, people with whom we converse daily . . . but whom we may never physically meet" (Turkle 1995, pp. 9–10).

Cyberspace of course is fascinating as possibility but for all of its projected impact on identity, gender transformation, simulation, and mutuality at a distance, it tells us very little about community as structure, context, and stable reference point for life. It may well be that in this period of transition, of being between worlds, these forays into alternative selves and imagined connections may sketch in life for the mobile, transient multitudes and provide mirrors to anchor their floating, disembodied identities. But community requires more than mirrors.

Turkle discusses changing metaphors of emotional well-being as going from stable, linear, rooted modes to ones that are flexible, fluid, experimental. And she herself poses the key questions: How can multiplicity lead to a coherent identity? How can simulation preserve authenticity? To her questions may be added, when is multiple personality a creative enrichment, and when is it a psychic unraveling? As an adjunct to reality there is no problem with cyberspace; as a substitute, there is, even for Turkle, who sees its great possibilities for creativity and transcendence.

A comparison of virtual and "real" versions suggests that the word "community" is inappropriate, for cyberspace communities lack 90 percent of the defining criteria. Community has definite boundaries and is divided into central, public, and private spaces, whereas cyberspace is unbounded and limitless. Members of earthly communities, ideally, invest their time, effort, money, and commitment, whereas no such efforts are exacted in cyberspace. Not only is cyberspace voluntary but there is no entrance fee of any kind. Anyone may join and leave anytime.

1. Earthly communities are nurtured by trust, familiarity, and reciprocity, whereas cyberspace exalts anonymity and the freedom to sign on or off at will, making the collective experience transient and episodic.

2. Rules and norms, governing both admission and modes of coexistence are essential to actual communities but not to virtual ones.

3. Governance along with social institutions that maintain order and civility are indispensable for earthly communities but not as yet for virtual communities.

4. Earthly communities rest on the experience of sharing space, goals, traditions, and values. Cyberspace communities strive to keep their members connected more informally and loosely, and sharing is minimal.

Most writers stress the expansion of radii of connectedness for virtual communities. Communication is the key word, often allied with "open communication," "free communication," and even, or perhaps especially, anonymous communication. These are seen as panaceas, the solution to wars, the way to worldwide empathy. But what is the basis for such great expectations, especially when one can readily envisage quite opposite outcomes — that is, expanding radii of connectedness leading to greater misunderstanding, strife, and conflict?

Another projected benefit of virtual communities is a revitalization of democracy, with more discussion, exchange of ideas, and debate on serious issues. However, cyberspace could also deflect people's attention to mindless spectacles and escapism.

More abstract but suggestive is the possibility that cyberspace will advance democracy by the electronic creation of town hall meetings and, with these, strengthen the public sphere in which citizens can shape a collective outlook and devise solutions to common problems. This is the realm of civil society as the eighteenth century conceived it. True, technology permits the instantaneous communication of chat rooms and Multi User Dungeons (MUDs) but whether technology can effectively stimulate the loyalties and emotional cohesion of community is arguable.

What is clear is that Internet users have expanded at a staggering rate, the numbers growing exponentially from an initial 5 to 6 million in the mid-nineties to more than 100 million only five years later. No one disputes the growth of information highways and electronic malls, but how will this generate community? Are we dealing here with "imagined" communities as described by Benedict Anderson (1991), in which the space that unites them is symbolic? Or are virtual communities pretty much like real ones except for the swiftness of communications?

If we compare territorial and virtual communities more closely, we note important differences. Electronic connectedness links people by specialized interests, by chance, even by whim, but not by collective obligations. Cyberspace connectedness is marked more by fragmentation and splintering than by shared traditions and ideals. When people do not know each other and are able to take on identities at will, trust and caring, which generally rest on lengthy acquaintance, are unlikely to develop. The social networks that electronic linkages generate are transient, fluid, and abstract, hence not geared to provide strong ties with proximate, known others based on reciprocity, empathy, and responsibility. "Cyberspace is . . . full of electronic neighborhoods . . . where people mingle and pass each other without establishing significant connection. . . . electrons passing in the dark do not constitute a community" (Miller 1996, p. 334). Even traditional neighborhoods do not automatically advance community. They can be hostile jungles or isolated arenas or simply shared spaces in which people pursue private interests.

A common misperception about community is that it is defined by social interaction, hence anything that increases interaction would increase community. Esther Dyson, a leading voice in Internet circles, summarizes this common, if erroneous, view. The Internet "allows the formation of communities independent of geography . . . people need only share interests or goals to find one another" (Dyson 1998, p. 32). But there is a vast difference between social contacts and conversations, in this anonymous fashion, and communities, and Dyson gives no indication of how the first will lead to the second.

There is one development, however, that bears watching: community networks explicitly oriented to encourage locality-based on-line communication. In the 1980s and early 1990s, many of these went under, but some one hundred have survived and are currently thriving in Charlotte, North Carolina (Charlotte's Web); Philadelphia; and Seattle;

among others. The electronic village of Blacksburg, Virginia, encompasses 36,000 residents and their electronic exchanges are said to create "stronger ties among neighbors" (Shapiro 1999, pp. 12, 13), though this needs systematic exploration.

Thus, surfing globally may connect people locally, and one possible benefit for actual communities is greater awareness of one's proximate community and one's proximate neighbors (ibid., p. 14). In turn, this may advance knowledge of one's own community and interest in others. Also, more local dialogue may engender empathy and cooperation if mobilized for a shared cause. In this way, an on-line "commons could strengthen a public commons" or provide a neutral "third place" (Schuler 1996, p. 42), but this is as yet mere speculation. To date, electronic "communities" lack most attributes of real-world communities, namely, shared territory, identifiable boundaries, shared values and norms, central institutions, and the goal of collective and physical survival.

Electronic "communities" do have the shared medium of language, which permits the exchange of information, news, and opinions among interested participants. This may be exciting and stimulating, but it is insufficient. Experience has shown that for community to emerge, even minimally, virtual communities require some of the mainstays of territorial communities, such as "unwritten beliefs" about their collective survival, some moral precepts and civil codes, and at least a provisional ethics. As yet, no mechanism exists to enforce any of these. Above all, there is no way to create accountability in a virtual universe. If a MUD character sees fit to destroy some part of the setting in which people gather symbolically, this destroys it for all the participants.

Turkle (1995, p. 56) relates the problem of civil order in a short-lived MUD called "Habitat," which had managed to fashion a democratic voting process, a violence-free zone, and laws that would help discover the "proper balance between law and order and individual freedom," but it did not survive.

At this point, the Internet is an anarchic realm. Chat rooms are arenas without rules. They do offer contact for the bored, the lonely, the alienated, and social misfits but there is no unifying umbrella, no effective form of governance, to bring them into common endeavors. In fact, the connectedness featured on the Internet may offer a "false sense of belonging" (Miller 1996, p. 336).

Attempts to counter the anarchic potential of cyberspace have led at times to exiling — by electronic expulsion — a destructive or undesirable participant. In this way, cyberspace creeps toward conventional social procedures it had sought to leave behind.

Then there are new obsessions and addictions for cyber beings. The smitten may spend thousands of hours on chats, substituting cyberspace for real life. Computer addiction has been described as a "real and growing problem." Maressa Hecht Orzack, director of computer addiction services at McClean Hospital in Massachusetts, describes such addicts as suffering the ills of addicts generally, which may result in the sacrifice of family life, work, and social life to their computer life (1999, pp. 1–2).

Virtual communities seem to offer illusory identities to those lacking friends, family, and other human connections. As such they may assuage existential loneliness and social isolation, which can be a lifesaver for the needy. But this is not community in any serious sense of the term. Of course, even the illusion of community may be better than no community.

New terms such as "cyberanomie" "and cybermegalomania," suggest that illusory identities also have their costs (Klawans 1999, p. 11). As a "new home of the mind," separate from the physical world, we may be creating new forms of alienation in cyberspace, along with whatever on-line togetherness ensues (Dery 1997, p. 96).

Still, the struggle to devise rules of etiquette for behavior, and boundaries vis-à-vis the outside world, echo in symbolic form the experience of historic communities. Questions of privacy, property, and conformity are timeless for human aggregates and to see them played out on our computer screens strikes some familiar chords. In particular, there is the tension between individualism and collective control, the inevitability of authority, and the need for some kind of social order — all highly charged points of contention.

Hence even technocratic visionaries have been compelled to conclude that: "Like terrestrial communities, good on-line 'communities' require care and tending. Members need someone to resolve disputes, set the tone, find the sponsors . . . define the rules or modify them in accordance with community interests" (Dyson 1998, p. 46).

Observers of on-line gatherings have apprised us of other developments that are inimical to community formation even in the loose sense in which the term is used here. There are the shirkers or free riders who only "read or listen," do not make a contribution to the totality, and are not part of it (ibid., p. 48).

Most significant, in my view, is the fact that there is less at stake in electronic communities than in territorial communities. When real communities break down, real people suffer, environments get neglected, and institutions decay. When on-line communities fail, the consequences are far less momentous and people can turn to other symbolic settings instantaneously.

Some more disturbing negatives of virtual communities have also become apparent. By the late 1990s, more than 250 hate sites have been identified on-line, where they can spread their messages of racism, white supremacy, anti-Semitism, and ethnic exclusivity (Janovsky 1992, p. 24). Resistance, Inc., founded by George Burdi, has been described as sending the most powerful, hostile messages across the Internet as well as the radio, in videos, and publishing. The possibility to spread hate messages across the globe more swiftly than ever before leads some to worry that mass movements of hate could be created in an instant (Schneider 1995, p. A12). Hence, along with the vast storehouse of Web information that can be tapped on line to gather groups around art, theater, science, or popular culture is a destructive potential we cannot ignore. This prompts admonitions to proceed with caution and to not trust blindly in technology.

Misgivings also exist about the misuses of freedom in cyberspace. The freedom that was the insignia of cyberspace cannot exist without some controls, sanctions, and models for conduct. The current anarchy cannot become a permanent condition without serious costs. Lawlessness seems to be as destructive in cyberspace as in real life, as antisocial impulses destroy what benign, constructive impulses build. In short, cyberspace, too, is corruptible.

Other warnings focus on the role of powerful corporate forces and advertisers and the deflection of an authentic to an inauthentic public discourse by appeals to conspicuous consumption rather than to reasoned debate (Rheingold 1993, pp. 279, 282). "Infotainment" geared to market appeals and interests creates an arena of spectators and buyers rather than citizens that defeats the potential for civic debate in the electronic town hall.

The question of control of cyberspace looms increasingly significant. At a time when cyberspace still seems to belong to everyone, it appears to foster equality of rank, power, and status not available anywhere else. But apprehensions about global structures of control and monopolization cast a fearful dimension over the future, as global capital in alliance with global media come to prevail. When huge corporations possess an equal voice with single citizens, their huge powers buoyed by their limited economic liability are likely to drown out the views of ordinary people. This results in a dubious equality between corporate and individual clout. Indeed, the familiar indicators of an elite — as, for example, the hundred "Neterati," who meet annually at the PC Forum exclusively — and a nascent stratification hierarchy are already visible beneath the surface of openness and equality.

"Now that cyberspace is becoming an important arena for the major institutions of our society," writes Miller, it is likely "that the 'big guys' will impose law and bureaucratic order on cyberspace," or, more benignly, "manufacture consent" by creating a context within which a public opinion is shaped. An important source of power is "the ability to frame people's understanding of world events [and] to define the terms in which reality is discussed and options evaluated" (Miller 1996, pp. 325, 339). Already, globalization is a tremendous force feared by those who see their traditional cultures swamped by first-world wares. It has been calculated that "90 percent of the 6,000 languages currently spoken by the earth's inhabitants will disappear within the next century along with much of the culture that they express" (*Science News*, 25 February 1995, quoted in ibid., p. 339).

Virtual communities, as indicated by their name, are mirages. The absence of full sensory contact creates shadow communities at best. Solid communities provide "models of respect and assistance so we can learn empathy for others and the interdependence of our collective well-being" (ibid., p. 319). They teach us the necessity of caring and sharing, cooperation and loyalty. Cyberspace interaction, exciting, challenging, new though it be, has other aims and other horizons.

In one of the most stringent critiques of virtual communities, Doheny-Farina (1996) argues that we need communities of place to prevent the disintegration of the planet. He sees individuals increasingly isolated and cyberville as an escape from the world. The illusion of community may mask that isolation and eliminate the awareness of human interdependence. Whatever cyberville does offer — and there is as yet no consensus on what that is — it does not demand the investment in time, effort, and commitment to shared goals or the give and take of real communities.

"A community is bound by place [and] complex social and environmental necessities. It is not something you can easily join." One cannot subscribe to it. "It must be lived. It is entwined, contradictory, and involves all the senses — and long acquaintance" (ibid.). Communities need a center and a heart as well as a public arena where public discourse and actions can take place. To be "rooted in a community, one must spend a long time integrating one's life into a place." If collective sites serve special interests, they are not communities but private interests writ large (ibid., pp. 37, 93, 52). Electronic networks by their ready access to information can be used by place communities to have "meetings" and "discussions" via computer linkages — not as substitutes for town meetings or public forums, but as adjuncts to these.

It has been suggested that when community diminishes in real life, people turn to subtitutes and approximations. Coffee breaks, friendly exchanges around water coolers, conviviality in urban pocket parks all serve a purpose, but they are not of lasting consequence. Virtual communities are at present smoke and mirror communities. Whether this will change in the future, only time will tell. But *if* they are to become the real thing, they will need to take the lessons of "real" communities back into the future.

APPENDIX
OVERVIEW OF SURVEYS, 1975–1999

To obtain the desired information, representative samples of Twin Rivers residents were surveyed in every decade. The first survey, in 1975–76, was an elaborate survey of 250 women representing one thousand households. Its six sections consisted of forty-five open-ended questions on personal and family backgrounds, employment history, income, and educational attainments. This was followed by forty-two questions about their reactions to the move and ensuing changes for self and family members—reactions to house, neighbors, facilities, privacy, and services. A final section of fourteen questions focused on spare-time activities, chief moods and worries, and political participation. All told, the answers to these 101 questions, duly coded and processed, provided the baseline for subsequent analyses.

To round out the initial focus on the women of Twin Rivers, a special, if somewhat shorter, survey of men was added in the late 1970s. And in the mid-1970s, a youth survey (seventy-seven questions) focused on the teenagers to compare their reactions with those of their parents and other adults. This was duplicated in the mid-1980s.

The Gallup organization carried out a community-wide survey in the mid-1980s to parallel that of the 1970s. The thirty-three-item questionnaire used largely multiple-choice questions and probed changing requirements of residents and ongoing sources of satisfaction and dissatisfaction. The last community-wide survey was administered in the late 1990s and is reproduced below.

Several small-scale, intensive interview studies explored particular issues in depth. One of these tapped attitudes before and after the move for some forty residents to assess anticipations about the prospective community with direct experience. Another small-scale study consisted of interviews with forty-four residents at two points in time, a decade apart, for constancy and changes over time. In addition, one hundred civic and professional leaders offered their appraisals of the developing community in lengthy interviews.

The 1997 survey of one thousand Twin Rivers households had a general response rate above 50 percent (or five hundred residents). Of these, 10 percent (or fifty residents) agreed to lengthy follow-up interviews about Twin Rivers.

The random sample surveys, the interviews with particular groups, analyses of aggregate data, participant observation, photographic records and systematic tracking of collective events all contributed to the portrait of a community in the making.

TWIN RIVERS SURVEY 1997

1. As a result of living in Twin Rivers, how do you feel about townhouse communities?

    1. In favor
    2. Against
    3. Mixed feelings
    4. Not sure

2. Has Twin Rivers disappointed you in any way?

    —— Yes
    —— No

3. If yes, indicate reason:

    —— Too little community
    —— Not enough people mix
    —— Aesthetics, appearance
    —— Management
    —— Services provided
    —— Transportation
    —— Location
    —— Other

4. In general, do you like Twin Rivers?

    1. Like very much
    2. Like pretty well
    3. So-so
    4. Dislike
    5. Dislike very much

5. Twin Rivers is providing roots for

Me	—— Yes	—— No
For the children growing up here	—— Yes	—— No
For most of my friends	—— Yes	—— No

6. How much influence do you think people like you have over decisions made for Twin Rivers?

    —— A good deal
    —— Not much, but some
    —— None
    —— As much as I want

7. Compared to __ years ago when you first moved in, would you say Twin Rivers is worse, better, or the same in regard to:

Safety	__ Worse	__ Better	__ Same
Family life	__ Worse	__ Better	__ Same
Housing	__ Worse	__ Better	__ Same
Environmental quality	__ Worse	__ Better	__ Same
Appearance	__ Worse	__ Better	__ Same
Efficient management	__ Worse	__ Better	__ Same
Pulling together	__ Worse	__ Better	__ Same
Human relations	__ Worse	__ Better	__ Same
Community spirit	__ Worse	__ Better	__ Same

8. How would you rate Twin Rivers on each of the following from 1 (least) to 5 (most):

( ) Cooperation
( ) Social conflicts
( ) Friendliness

Tolerance to diversity
    ( ) of people
    ( ) of values
    ( ) of life styles

( ) Community-mindedness
( ) Individualism
( ) Civility, good manners

9. Twin Rivers in its first decade had a "teenage problem" with "boredom" and "nothing to do" being the teens' common complaints. Some residents feel this problem has by now been resolved and that teenagers are doing just fine. Other residents disagree. They believe that the "teenager problem" persists. Which best describes your own view?

__ Teenager problems persist, no change
__ Teenagers are doing just fine

10. In your view, how do most Twin Rivers residents rate each of the following:

Individual success	__ Very Important	__ Moderately Important	__ Not Important
Hard work	__ Very Important	__ Moderately Important	__ Not Important

Getting rich	__ Very Important	__ Moderately Important	__ Not Important
Athletic achievement	__ Very Important	__ Moderately Important	__ Not Important
Education	__ Very Important	__ Moderately Important	__ Not Important
Cooperation	__ Very Important	__ Moderately Important	__ Not Important
Popularity	__ Very Important	__ Moderately Important	__ Not Important
Consumer goods	__ Very Important	__ Moderately Important	__ Not Important
Voting	__ Very Important	__ Moderately Important	__ Not Important
Community Involvement	__ Very Important	__ Moderately Important	__ Not Important
Compassion for the less fortunate	__ Very Important	__ Moderately Important	__ Not Important

11. In recent years, this country has been debating whether the U.S. has changed from being a society of joiners to being a society of loners. Compared to 5 years ago (or when you first moved in) how would you classify yourself:

    __ More of a joiner
    __ More of a loner

12. How satisfied are you with each of the following:

The appearance of your house/apartment	__ Very satisfied	__ So-so	__ Dissatisfied
The amount of space	__ Very satisfied	__ So-so	__ Dissatisfied
The house/apartment overall	__ Very satisfied	__ So-so	__ Dissatisfied
Noise from neighbors	__ Very satisfied	__ So-so	__ Dissatisfied

13. Here is a list of activities. For each, indicate whether you engage in it more, less, some, not at all compared to 10 years ago (or since first moving in):

PTA	__ More	__ Less	__ Some	__ Not at all
Bridge	__ More	__ Less	__ Some	__ Not at all
Other games	__ More	__ Less	__ Some	__ Not at all
Team sports	__ More	__ Less	__ Some	__ Not at all

Individual sports

Golf	___ More	___ Less	___ Some	___ Not at all
Tennis	___ More	___ Less	___ Some	___ Not at all
Swimming	___ More	___ Less	___ Some	___ Not at all
Other	___ More	___ Less	___ Some	___ Not at all
An evening out with friends	___ More	___ Less	___ Some	___ Not at all
Dining out	___ More	___ Less	___ Some	___ Not at all
Go to Movies once a week	___ More	___ Less	___ Some	___ Not at all

14. Here is a list of characteristics about the residents of Twin Rivers. For each, please indicate whether it is more or less, or the same as it was 5 years ago (or when you first moved in):

Friendliness to strangers	___ More	___ Less	___ Same
Openness to diversity			
Of people	___ More	___ Less	___ Same
Of values	___ More	___ Less	___ Same
Of lifestyles	___ More	___ Less	___ Same
Individualism	___ More	___ Less	___ Same
Safety	___ More	___ Less	___ Same
General functioning	___ More	___ Less	___ Same
Management	___ More	___ Less	___ Same
Concern by the Twin Rivers Trust	___ More	___ Less	___ Same

15. Community mindedness   ___ More   ___ Less   ___ Same

16. Twin Rivers is a genuine community:

___ Yes   ___ No

17. Here is a list of activities. For each, indicate whether you engage in it more, less, some, or not at all compared to 5 years ago (or when you first moved in):

PTA	___ More	___ Less	___ Some	___ Not at all
Bridge (or other in-door games)	___ More	___ Less	___ Some	___ Not at all
Team sports	___ More	___ Less	___ Some	___ Not at all
Individual sports	___ More	___ Less	___ Some	___ Not at all
An evening with friends	___ More	___ Less	___ Some	___ Not at all
Dining out	___ More	___ Less	___ Some	___ Not at all
Evening TV-watching	___ More	___ Less	___ Some	___ Not at all
Weekly movies	___ More	___ Less	___ Some	___ Not at all

Twin River function	___ More	___ Less	___ Some	___ Not at all
Entertaining at home	___ More	___ Less	___ Some	___ Not at all
Engaging in community activities	___ More	___ Less	___ Some	___ Not at all
Engaging in political activities	___ More	___ Less	___ Some	___ Not at all

18. In your view, is there a Twin Rivers community spirit?

___ Yes ___ No ___ Sometimes

19. If yes, how is this spirit expressed?

___ People pull together when needed
___ People basically trust each other
___ People are active in different organizations
___ It feels like a community
___ I feel I belong to Twin Rivers

20. If no, because:

___ People don't cooperate
___ People can't be trusted
___ There is no sense of unity
___ There is no closeness
___ It doesn't feel like a community
___ I don't feel I belong to Twin Rivers
___ Other

21. Whom would you turn to for help with:

House repair

| _Friends in Twin Rivers | _Friends outside Twin Rivers | _Family members | _Professionals, (doctors, banks, counselors) | _My spouse only | _No one | _DK |

Child's sickness

| _Friends in Twin Rivers | _Friends outside Twin Rivers | _Family members | _Professionals, (doctors, banks, counselors) | _My spouse only | _No one | _DK |

To borrow money in an emergency

| _Friends in Twin Rivers | _Friends outside Twin Rivers | _Family members | _Professionals, (doctors, banks, counselors) | _My spouse only | _No one | _DK |

Job problems

—Friends   —Friends   —Family   —Professionals,   —My spouse —No one —DK
  in Twin   outside   members   (doctors, banks,   only
  Rivers   Twin   counselors)
             Rivers

Family problems

—Friends   —Friends   —Family   —Professionals,   —My spouse —No one —DK
  in Twin   outside   members   (doctors, banks,   only
  Rivers   Twin   counselors)
             Rivers

Marital problems

—Friends   —Friends   —Family   —Professionals,   —My spouse —No one —DK
  in Twin   outside   members   (doctors, banks,   only
  Rivers   Twin   counselors)
             Rivers

A serious illness

—Friends   —Friends   —Family   —Professionals,   —My spouse —No one —DK
  in Twin   outside   members   (doctors, banks,   only
  Rivers   Twin   counselors)
             Rivers

22. If you could have any two changes in Twin Rivers, what would they
be?

____ 1   Redesign the whole community
____ 2   Improve attractiveness and appearance
____ 3   Have a more varied mix of residents
____ 4   Make the trust more responsive to residents
____ 5   Have more facilities for teenagers
____ 6   Improve quality of construction
____ 7   Less density
____ 8   None, it's fine as it is

23. Do you wish Twin Rivers were more of a community?

____ Yes   ____ ·No

24. I am proud to be a resident of Twin Rivers:

____ Yes   ____ No

25. Do you feel committed to Twin Rivers?

____ Yes, a great deal
____ Yes, somewhat
____ No, not much
____ I plan to spend the rest of my life in Twin Rivers
____ I plan to move away within 1–2 years

26. What is your age?

    __ Under 25
    __ 26–30
    __ 31–35
    __ 36–40
    __ 41–50
    __ 46–50
    __ 51–55
    __ 56–60
    __ 61 or older

27. Total annual household income

    __ Under $25,000
    __ $26–49,000
    __ $50,000 or higher

28. Please check:

    __ Male   __ Female

29. In which Quad do you live?

    __ 1   Quad 1
    __ 2   Quad 2
    __ 3   Quad 3
    __ 4   Quad 4

30. Are you now employed?

    __ 1   Self-employed
    __ 2   Employed — full-time
    __ 3   Employed — part-time
    __ 4   Retired
    __ 5   Do organized, steady volunteer work
    __ 6   Looking for work
    __ 7   None of the above

31. If currently employed, please indicate what kind of work you do:

    __ 1   Salesperson (also real estate)
    __ 2   Independent professional
    __ 3   Salaried, tech, professional (engineer, accountant, chemical/research, etc.)
    __ 4   Salaried professional, other (teacher, librarian, insurance, banking)
    __ 5   Business management (executive, sales, personnel, retail, buyer, etc.)
    __ 6   Skilled service (nurse, secretary, sales, police)

___ 7   Other, please describe _____
         _____
         _____
         _____

32. What dwelling do you live in?

___ 1   Townhouse — rent
___ 2   Townhouse — owner
___ 3   Detached house
___ 4   Apartment
___ 5   Condominium

33. What is your marital status?

___ 1   Single
___ 2   Married
___ 3   Separated
___ 4   Divorced
___ 5   Widowed
___ 6   Cohabitation

BIBLIOGRAPHY

Adkins, Arthur. *Moral Values and Political Behavior in Ancient Greece: From Homer to the End of the Fifth Century*. New York: W. W. Norton, 1972.

Alexander, Jeffrey C., and Seidman, Steven. *Culture and Society: Contemporary Debates*. Cambridge, U.K.: Cambridge University Press, 1990.

Alinsky, Saul D. *Rules for Radicals: A Practical Primer for Realistic Radicals*. New York: Vintage Books, 1972.

Althusius, Johannes. *Politica Methodice Digesta*. Cambridge, MA: Harvard University Press, 1932.

Altman, Dennis. *The Homosexualization of America, the Americanization of the Homosexual*. New York: St. Martin's Press, 1982.

Anderson, Benedict R. *Imagined Communities: Reflections on the Origin and Spread of Nationalism*. London: New York, 1991.

Arnett, Ronald C. *Communication and Community: Implications of Martin Buber's Dialogue*. Carbondale: Southern Illinois University Press, 1986.

Aron, Raymond. *Sociologie des societes industrielles; esquisse d'une theorie des regimes politiques*. Paris: Centre de Documentation Universitaire, 1964.

Bailyn, Bernard. *Voyagers to the West: A Passage in the Peopling of America on the Eve of the Revolution*. New York: Random House, 1986.

Baldwin, Steve, and Lessard, Bill. *Net Slaves: True Tales of Working the Web*. New York: McGraw-Hill, 1999.

Barber, Benjamin R. *A Place for Us: How to Make Society Civil and Democracy Strong*. New York: Hill and Wang Publishers, 1998.

Bartkowski, Frances. *Feminist Utopias*. Lincoln: University of Nebraska Press, 1989.

Baxandall, Rosalyn, and Ewen, Elizabeth. *Picture Windows*. New York: Basic Books, 2000.

Becker, Franklin D. *Housing Messages*. Stroudsburg, PA: Dowden, Hutchinson & Ross, 1977.

Beiner, Ronald. *What's the Matter with Liberalism?* Berkeley: University of California Press, 1992

Bell, Daniel. *The Winding Passage*. New Brunswick: Transaction Publishers, 1991.

Bellah, Robert N. et al. *The Good Society*. New York: Knopf, 1991.

———. *Habits of the Heart: Individualism and Commitment in American Life*. New York: Harper & Row, 1985.

Bender, Thomas. *Community and Social Change in America*. Baltimore: Johns Hopkins Press, 1978.

Benett, Stephen Earl. *Apathy in America, 1960–1984*. New York: Transnational Publishing, Inc., 1986.

Benn, S. I. "Individuality, Autonomy and Community" in Eugene Kamenka (ed.). *City As a Social Ideal*. New York: St. Martin's Press, 1983. pp. 43–62.

Bennetts, Leslie. "Wired at Heart." *Vanity Fair*, November 1997, pp. 158–67.

Ben-Rafael, Eliezer. *Status, Power and Conflict in the Kibbutz*. Brookfield, VT: Gower Publishing Co., 1988.

Berman, Sheri. "Civil Society and the Collapse of the Weimar Republic." *World Politics* #49, April 1997, pp. 401–29.

Bernard, Jessie. *The Sociology of Community*. Glenview, IL: Scott, Foresman & Co., 1973.

Berthoff, Rowland. *An Unsettled People: Social Order and Disorder in American History*. New York: Harper & Row, 1971.

Bestor, Theodore C. *Neighborhood Tokyo*. Stanford, CA: Stanford University Press, 1989.

Bettelheim, Bruno. *A Home for the Heart*. New York: Knopf Publishing, 1974.

Black, Corinne M. *Utopia Lost: Aspects of Conflict in a New Planned Suburban Community*. University Microfilm International. Ann Arbor, MI, 1984.

Blair, Tony. "The Renewal of Community," June 2000 speech to the Women's Institute's Triennial General Meeting, London.

Boff, Leonardo. *Ecclesiogenesis: The Base Communities Reinvent the Church*. New York: Mary Knoll Orbis Books, 1986.

Bosanquet, Bernard. *A Companion to Plato's Republic for English Readers*. New York: Macmillan and Co., 1895.

Bourdieu, Pierre, and Richardson, John G. (eds.). "The Forms of Capital." *Handbook of Theory and Research for the Sociology of Education*. Westport, CT: Greenwood Press, 1986. pp. 241–58.

Breuer, S. "Von Tönnies zu Weber." *Berliner Journal Der Soziologie Heft* 2, 1996, pp. 227–45.

Briggs, Xavier de Souza. "Community Building: The New (and Old) Politics of Urban Problem Solving in the New Century." John F. Kennedy School of Government, Harvard University. Public Address on 27 September 2000.

Brubaker, Rogers. *Citizenship and Nationhood in France and Germany*. Cambridge, MA: Harvard University Press, 1992.

Bruchey, Stuart. *The Elderly in America*. New York: Garland Publishing, 1992.

Burby, III, Raymond J., et al. *New Communites, USA*. Lexington, MA: D. C. Heath, Lexington Books, 1976.

Burgess, Ernest W. *The Urban Community: Selected Papers from the Proceedings of the American Sociological Society, 1925*. Chicago, IL: University of Chicago Press, 1927.

Bushman, Richard L. *From Puritan to Yankee: Character and the Social Order in Connecticut, 1690–1765*. Cambridge, MA: Harvard University Press, 1967.

Cahnman, Werner J. *Weber and Tönnies: Comparative Sociology in Historical Perspective*. New Brunswick, NJ: Transaction Publishers, 1995.

Calhoun, Craig. "Nationalism and Civil Society: Democracy, Diversity and Self-Determination" in *Social Theory and the Politics of Identity*, Craig Calhoun. Oxford, UK: Blackwell, 1994. pp. 9–36, 304–335.

Campbell, Angus, et al. *The Quality of American Life: Perceptions, Evaluations, and Satisfactions*. New York: Russell Sage Foundation, 1976.

Caplovitz, David. *The Poor Pay More: Consumer Practices of Low-Income Families*. New York: Free Press of Glencoe, 1963.

Carr, Stephen, et al. *Public Space*. Cambridge, UK: Cambridge University Press, 1982.

Chen, David W. "Asian Middle Class Deter a Rural Enclave." *New York Times*, 27 December 1999, pp. A1, B9.

Chermayeff, Serge, and Alexander, Christopher. *Community and Privacy: Toward a New Architecture of Humanism*. Garden City, NY: Doubleday, 1965.

Clark, David B. "The Concept of Community: A Reexamination." *Sociological Review*, vol. 23, August 1973, pp. 397–415.

Clark, Terry Nichols, and Rempel, Michael. *Citizen Politics in Post-Industrial Societies*. Boulder, CO: Westview Press, 1997.

Cohen, Erik, and Rosner, Menachem. "Problems of Generations in the Israeli Kibbutz." *Journal of Contemporary History*, vol. 5, no. 1, 1970, pp. 73–86.

Cohen, Susan. "Missing Links." *Washington Post Magazine*, 31 July 1994, pp. 11–15; 24–31.

Coleman, James S. *Community Conflict*. New York: Free Press, 1957.

Colette. *My Mother's House*, and *Sido*. New York: Farrar, Straus and Young, 1953.

Cooley, Charles H. *Social Organization: A Study of the Larger Mind*. New York: Charles Scribner & Sons, 1925.

Coser, Lewis A. *The Functions of Social Conflict*. Glencoe, IL: The Free Press, 1956.

Crenson, Matthew A. *Neighborhood Politics*. Cambridge, MA: Harvard University Press, 1983.

Curtis, Michael, and Chertoff, Mordecai S. *Israel: Social Structure and Change*. New Brunswick, NJ: Transaction Books, 1973.

Dattner, Richard. *Design for Play*. New York: Van Nostrand Reinhold, Co., 1969.

De Grazia, Sebastian. *The Political Community: A Study of Anomie*. Chicago: University of Chicago Press, 1948.

De Tocqueville, Alexis. *Democracy in America*. vols. I, II. Bradley, Phillips (ed.). New York: Vintage Classics, 1990.

Demos, John. *A Little Commonwealth: Family Life in Plymouth Colony*. New York: Oxford Press, 1970.

Dery, Mark. "The Cult of the Mind." *New York Times Magazine*, 28 September 1997, pp. 94–96.

Dewey, John. *The Public and Its Problems*. Chicago: Swallow Press, 1954.

———. *The Search for the Great Community*. New York: Henry Holt Press, 1927.

Diamond, Stanley. *In Search of the Primitive*. New Brunswick, NJ: Transaction Books, 1981.

Doheny-Farina, Stephen. *The Wired Neighborhood*. New Haven: Yale University Press, 1996.

Doxiadis, C. A. *Anthropolis, City for Human Development*. Athens, Greece: Athens Publishing Company, 1974.

Duany, Andres, et al. *Suburban Nation: The Rise of Sprawl and the Decline of the American Dream*. New York: North Point Press, 2000.

Duany, Andres, and Plater-Zyberk, Elizabeth. "Their Town," *Historic Preservation* May/June 1992, pp. 57–61.

Dumont, Louis. *Essays of Individualism: Modern Ideology in Anthropological Perspective*. Chicago: University of Chicago Press, 1986.

Durkheim, Emile. *The Division of Labor in Society*. New York: Free Press, 1933.

———. "Review of Ferdinand Tönnies' Gemeinschaft und Gesellschaft." *Revue Philosophique*, vol. 27, 1889, pp. 416–22.

———. *Suicide, a Study in Sociology*. Glencoe, Ill., Free Press, 1951.

Elias, Norbert. *The Society of Individuals*. Translated by Edmund Jephcott. Oxford: Basil Blackwell, 1991.

Ellickson, Robert C. "Cities and Homeowners Associations." *University of Pennsylvania Law Review*, vol. 130, No. 6, June 1982, pp. 1519–1601.

Erikson, Kai T. *Everything in Its Path*. New York: Simon & Schuster, 1976.

———. *A New Species of Trouble: Explorations in Disaster, Trauma and Community*. New York: W. W. Norton & Co., 1994.

Etzioni, Amitai. "The Attack on Community: The Grooved Debate" from *Society*, vol. 32, no. 5, July/August 1995, pp. 12–17.

———. "E-Communities Build New Ties, but Ties That Bind." *New York Times*, 10 February 2000, p. E7.

———. *Rights and the Common Good*. New York: St. Martin's Press, 1995.

———. *The Spirit of Community: Rights, Responsibilities, and the Communitarian Agenda*. New York: Crown Publishers, Inc., 1993.

Feiss, Carl. "Early American Public Squares" in *Town and Square: From the Agora to the Village Square* by Paul Zucker. New York: Columbia University Press, 1959. pp. 237–55.

Fernandez-Kelly, M. Patricia, and Schauffler, Richard. "Divided Fates: Immigrant Children and the New Assimilation" in *The New Second Generation* by Alejandro Portes (ed.). New York: Russell Foundation, 1996.

Festinger, Leon, et al. *Social Pressures in Informal Groups: A Study of Human Factors in Housing*. New York: Harper Books, 1950.

Finley, M. I. *Ancient History*. New York: Penguin Books, 1985.

Fischer, Claude S. *The Urban Experience*. New York: Harcourt Brace Jovanovich, Inc. 1976.

Fisher, Robert. *Let the People Decide: Neighborhood Organizing in America*. New York: Twayne Publishers, 1994.

Fishman, Robert. *Urban Utopias in the Twentieth Century*. New York: Basic Books, 1977.

Fitzgerald, Frances. *Cities on a Hill*. New York: Simon and Schuster, 1981.

Flaherty, David H. *Privacy in Colonial New England*. Charlottesville: Virginia Press, 1972.

Follett, Mary Parker. *The New State: Group Organization, the Solution of Popular Government*. New York: Longmans, Green Press, 1918.

Fonseca, Isabel. *Bury Me Standing: The Gypsies and Their Journey*. New York: A. A. Knopf, 1995.

Foucault, Michel, and Gordon, Colin (ed.). *Power/Knowledge: Selected Interviews and Other Writings, 1972–1977*. New York: Pantheon Books, 1980.

Frantz, Douglas. "Living in Disney Town, with Big Brother at Bay." *New York Times Magazine*, 4 October 1998, p. 31.

Frantz, Douglas, and Collins, Catherine. *Celebration, U.S.A.: Living in Disney's Brave New World*. New York: Henry Holt, 1999.

Frazier, Shervert H. *Psychotrends*. New York: Simon and Schuster, 1994.

Friederich, Carl J. (ed.). *The Concept of Community in the History of Political and Legal Philosophy*. New York: Liberal Arts Press, 1959.

Fromm, Erich. *Escape from Freedom*. New York: Holt, Rinehart and Winston, 1969.

———. *The Sane Society*. London: Routledge Publishing, 1991.

Fulton, William. *The New Urbanism*. Cambridge, MA: Lincoln Institute of Land Policy, 1996.

Gallaher, Art Jr., and Padfield, Harland. *The Dying Community*. Albuquerque: University of New Mexico Press, 1980. pp. 1–21.

Gans, Herbert J. *The Levittowners*. New York: Pantheon, 1967.

Gibson, William. *Neuromancer*. London: Gollancz, 1984.

Gluck, Mary. *George Lukacs and His Generation, 1900–1918*. Cambridge, MA: Harvard University Press, 1985.

Goodman, Paul. *Growing Up Absurd: Problems of Youth in the Organized System*. New York: Random House, 1960.

Gottdiener, Mark. *The Social Production of Urban Space*. Austin: University of Texas Press, 1985.

———. *The Theming of America*. New York: Westview Press, 1997.

Gottmann, Jean. "Japan's Organization of Space: Fluidity and Stability in a Changing Habitat." *Ekistics*, vol. 48, no. 289, July/August 1981, pp. 258–65.

Gouldner, Alvin W. *Enter Plato*. New York: Basic Books, Inc., 1965.

Greenfeld, Liah. *Nationalism*. Cambridge, MA: Harvard University Press, 1992.

Greenfield, Meg. *Washington*. New York: Public Affairs BBS, 2001.

Greenhouse, Carol J., et al. *Law and Community*. Ithaca, NY: Cornell University Press, 1992.

Greenhouse, Linda. "The Long Tale of Madonna the Iguana." *New York Times Magazine*, 16 January 2000, p. 94.

Greer, Scott. "Postscript: Communication and Community" in *The Community Press in an Urban Setting* by Morris Janowitz. Chicago: University of Chicago Press, 1967.

Gusfield, Joseph R. "Utopian Myths and Movements in Modern Societies." General Learning Corporation, 1973. pp. 1–33.

Gutmann, Amy. "Communitarian Critics of Liberalism" in *Philosophy & Public Affairs*, Summer 1985, vol. 14, no. 3, pp. 308–322.

Haar, Charles M. *Suburbs Under Siege*. Princeton, NJ: Princeton University Press, 1996.

Hackney, Lucy D. "A Political Analysis of the Development Process in East Windsor Township." Senior Thesis, Politics Department. Princeton University, 1975.

Hall, John A. *Civil Society*. Cambridge, UK: Polity Press, 1995.

Hallie, Philip Paul. *Lest Innocent Blood Be Shed*. New York: Harper & Row, 1979.

Hardin, Garrett. "The Tragedy of the Commons." *Science*, vol. 162, no. 385a, Winter 1968. pp. 1243–48.

Hawley, Amos Henry. *Human Ecology: A Theory of Community Structure*. New York: Ronald Press Co., 1950.

Haworth, Lawrence. *The Good City*. Bloomington, IN: Indiana University Press, 1963.

Hearn, Frank. *Moral Order and Social Disorder: The American Search for Civil Society*. New York: Aldine de Gruyter Press, 1997.

Heintz, Katherine Macmillan. *Retirement Communities*. New Brunswick, NJ: The Center for Urban Policy Research—Rutgers, 1976.

Herberg, Will, (ed.). *The Writings of Martin Buber*. New York: Meridian, 1956.

Herrick, C. P. "Designing for Community" from *Modern Utopian*, vol. 1, no. 6, 1971.

Hillery, George A. Jr. "Definitions of Community: Areas of Agreement." *Rural Sociology*, vol. 20, no. 2, June 1955.

———. *The Monastery: A Study in Freedom, Love and Community*. Westport, CT: Praeger Inc., 1992.

———. *A Research Odyssey: Developing and Testing a Community Theory*. New Brunswick, NJ: Transaction Books, 1982.

Hobbes, Thomas. *Leviathan* [1651]. Oxford, UK: Clarendon Press, 1929.

Hoffman, Eva. *Lost in Translation: A Life in a New Language*. New York: E. P. Dutton, 1989.

Hondrich, Karl Otto. "Mensch Im Netz." *Der Spiegel*, 18/1999, pp. 131–45.

Hunter, Albert. "Local Knowledge and Local Power." *Journal of Contemporary Ethnography*, vol. 22, April 1993.

———. "Persistence of Local Sentiment in Mass Society" in *Handbook of Contemporary Urban Life* by David Street et al. (eds). San Francisco: Jossey-Bass, 1978, pp. 124–56.

———. *Symbolic Communities: The Persistence and Change of Chicago's Local Communities*. Chicago: University of Chicago Press, 1974.

Hunter, Albert J., and Gerald D. Suttles. "The Expanding Community of Limited Liability" in *The Social Construction of Communities* by Gerald Suttles. Chicago: University of Chicago Press, 1972.

Hyde, Lewis. *The Gift.* New York: Random House, 1983.

Infield, Henrik F. *Utopia and Experiment: Essays in the Sociology of Cooperation.* New York: Frederick A. Praeger, Inc., 1955.

Ittelson, William H., et al. (eds.). *An Introduction to Environmental Psychology.* New York: Holt, Rinehart and Winston, 1974.

Jameson, Frederic R. "On Habits of the Heart" in *Community in America: The Challenge of Habits of the Heart* by Charles H. Reynolds and Ralph V. Norman (eds.). Berkeley: University of California Press, 1988. pp. 97–112.

Janovsky, Michael. "Anti-Defamation League Warns of Web Hate Sites." *New York Times*, 22 October 1997.

Janowitz, Morris. *The Community Press in an Urban Setting.* Chicago: University of Chicago Press, 1967.

Jencks, Christopher. "Varieties of Altruism" in *Beyond Self-Interest* by Jane J. Mansbridge. Chicago: University of Chicago Press, 1990. pp. 53–67.

Joint Center of Housing Studies. "State of the Nation's Housing, 2001." Harvard University, Cambridge, MA, June, 2001.

Judd, Dennis R. "The Rise of New Walled Cities" in *Spatial Practices* by Helen Liggett and David C. Perry (eds.). Thousand Oaks, CA: Sage Publishing, 1995.

Kamenka, Eugene, ed. *Community As a Social Ideal.* New York: St. Martin's Press, 1983.

Kanner, Bernice. "Cat Theater." *New York Magazine*, 24 June 1985, pp. 22–25.

Kanter, Donald L., and Mirvis, Philip H. *The Cynical Americans.* San Francisco: Jossey-Bass, 1989.

Kanter, Rosabeth Moss. *Commitment and Community: Communes and Utopias in Sociological Perspective.* Cambridge, MA: Harvard University Press, 1972.

———. "Commitment and Social Organizations: A Study of Commitment Mechanisms in Utopian Communities." *American Sociological Review* 33, August 1968, pp. 499–517.

———. "Communes." *Psychology Today*, July 1970, no. 2, pp. 53–57, 78.

———. *Communes: Creating and Managing the Collective Life.* New York: Harper and Row, 1973.

Kaplan, Marshall, and Cuciti, Peggy L. (eds.). *The Great Society and Its Legacy.* Durham, NC: Duke University Press, 1986. pp. 24–31.

Kaufman, Harry. *Introduction to the Study of Human Behavior.* Philadelphia, PA: W. B. Saunders Co., 1968.

Kayden, Jerold S. *Privately Owned Public Space: The New York City Experience.* New York: John Wiley Press, 2000.

Keller, Suzanne. "The American Dream of Community: An Unfinished Agenda." *Sociological Forum*, vol. 2, no. 3, 1989.

Keller, Suzanne. "A Community in the Making." *Ekistics*, July–August 1987, pp. 271–78.

———. *Creating Community: The Role of Land, Space and Place.* Cambridge, MA: Lincoln Land Institute, 1986.

———. "Design and the Quality of Life" in *Major Social Issues* by J. Milton Yinger and Stephen J. Cutler (eds.). Glencoe, IL: The Free Press, 1978. pp. 277–89.

———. "Ecology and Community." *Environmental Affairs Law Journal*, vol. 19, 1992, pp. 623–33.

———. "The Family in the Kibbutz . . . What Lessons for Us?" in *Israel: Social Structure and Change* by Michael Curtis and M. S. Chertoff (eds.). New Brunswick, NJ: Transaction Books, 1973. pp. 115–44.

Kemmis, David. *The Good City and the Good Life*. Boston: Houghton-Mifflin Co., 1985.

Kinoshita, Yasuhito, and Kiefer, Christie W. *The Refuge of the Honored*. Berkeley: University of California, 1992.

Kirkpatrick, Frank G. *Community: A Trinity of Models*. Washington, D.C.: Georgetown University Press, 1986.

Kirp, David L., et al. *Our Town: Race, Housing, and the Soul of Suburbia*. New Brunswick, NJ: Rutgers University Press, 1997.

Kitto, H.D.F. *The Greeks*. New York: Penguin Books, 1959. pp. 65–76.

Klapp, Orrin E. *Collective Search for Identity*. New York: Holt, Rinehart and Winston, 1969.

Klawans, Stuart. "That Void in Cyberspace Looks a Lot Like Kansas." *New York Times*, 20 June 1999, pp. 11, 19.

Koenig, René. *The Community*. London: Routledge & K. Paul, 1968.

Kolbe, Maximilian M. *Encyclopedia Britannica*, 15th ed. 1974. Macropaedia, Britannica 3; Preece, Warren E. and Goetz, Philip W. (eds.)

Kropotkin, Peter. *Mutual Aid*. New York: Extending Horizons Books, 1955.

Kunstler, James Howard. *The Geography of Nowhere*. New York: Simon & Schuster, 1993.

———. "Home from Nowhere." *Atlantic Monthly*, September 1996. pp. 43–50.

Kuper, Leo (ed.). *Living in Towns*. London: Cresset Press, 1953.

Langdon, Philip. *A Better Place to Live: Reshaping the American Suburb*. Amherst: University of Massachusetts Press, 1994. pp. 107–147.

———. *Urban Excellence*. New York, NY: Van Nostrand Reinhold, 1990.

Lasch, Christopher. "The Communitarian Critique of Liberalism" in *Community in America: The Challenge of Habits of the Heart* by Charles H. Reynolds and Ralph V. Norman (eds.). Berkeley, CA: University of California Press, 1988.

———. *The Culture of Narcissism*. New York: Vintage Books, 1978.

———. *The True and Only Heaven*. New York: W. W. Norton, 1991.

Lasch, Edmund. "Communities." *New Society*, 15 May 1969, p. 19.

Laslett, Peter. *The World We Have Lost*. New York: Scribner, 1973.

Lears, Jackson. "The Mouse That Roared." *New Republic*, 15 June 1998, pp. 27–34.

Lenski, Gerhard E. *The Religious Factor: A Sociological Study of Religion's Impact on Politics, Economics, and Family Life*. Garden City, NY: Anchor Books, 1963.

Lerner, Max. *America As a Civilization*. New York: Simon and Schuster, 1957.

Lessard, Bill. *Net Slaves: Tales of Working the Web*. New York: McGraw-Hill, 1999.

Levine, Hille L. In Search of Sugihara. New York: The Free Press, 1996.

Lewis, Oscar. *Life in a Mexican Village: Tepoztlan Revisited*. Urbana: University of Illinois Press, 1951.

Lichterman, Paul. *The Search for Political Community*. Cambridge: Cambridge University Press, 1996.

Liell, John. *Levittown: A Study in Community Development*. Ph.D. diss., Yale University, 1952.

Liggett, Helen, and Perry, David C. *Spatial Practices: Critical Explorations in Social/Spatial Theory*. Thousand Oaks, CA: Sage Publications, 1995.

Logan, John R., and Molotch, Harvey L. *Urban Fortunes: The Political Economy of Place*. Berkeley: University of California Press, 1987.

Luckman, Benita. "The Small Life-Worlds of Modern Man." *Social Research*, December 1970, pp. 580–86.

Lynd, Helen M., and Robert S. *Middletown: A Study in Contemporary American Culture*. New York: Harcourt, Brace and Co., 1929.

———. *Middletown in Transition: A Study in Cultural Conflicts*. New York: Harcourt, Brace and Co., 1937.

Maccoby, Michael. "The Two Voices of Erich Fromm: Prophet and Analyst." *Society*, July/August 1995, pp. 72–82.

MacIntyre, Alasdair. *After Virtue: A Study in Moral Theory*. Notre Dame, IN: University of Notre Dame Press, 1980.

MacIver, Robert M. *Community, a Sociological Study*. London: Macmillan Press, 1920.

MacIver, Robert M., and Page, Charles H. *Society, an Introductory Analysis*. New York, Rinehart Publishing, 1949.

Maine, Henry. *Ancient Law*. New York: Charles Scribner, 1864.

Mansbridge, Jane J. *Beyond Adversary Democracy*. Chicago: University of Chicago Press, 1983.

———. *Beyond Self-Interest*. Chicago: University of Chicago Press, 1990. pp. 53–67.

Marans, Robert W., and Rodgers, Willard. "Toward an Understanding of Community Satisfaction" in *Metropolitan America in Contemporary Perspective* by Amos H. Hawley and Vincent P. Rock (eds.). New York: Sage Press, 1975. pp. 299–351.

Mardin, Russell. "Contested Community." *Society*, vol. 32, no. 5, July/August 1995. pp. 23–29.

Marling, Karal Ann. "Nice Front Porches, Along with the 'Porch Police'," *New York Times Book Review* 9 September 1999, p. E9.

McGuire, Meredith B. "Healing Rituals Hit the Suburbs." *Psychology Today*, Jan/Feb 1989, pp. 57–62.

McWilliams, Wilson Carey. *The Idea of Fraternity in America*. Berkeley, CA: University of California Press, 1957.

Meier, Christian. *Athens*. New York: Henry Holt and Co., 1993.

Miller, Steven E. *Civilizing Cyberspace*. Reading, MA: Addison-Wesley, 1996.

Minar, David, and Greer, Scott. *The Concept of Community*. Chicago: Aldine Press, 1969.

Moon, Donald J. *Constructing Community: Moral Pluralism and Tragic Conflicts*. Princeton, NJ: Princeton University Press, 1993.

More, Thomas. *Utopia* (1516). Boston: Bedford/St. Martin's Press, 1999.

Mosle, Sara. "The Vanity of Volunteerism." *New York Times Magazine*, 2 July 2000, pp. 22–27, 40–52, 55.

Mosse, George L. "Nationalism, Fascism, and the Radical Right" in *Community As a Social Ideal* by Eugene Kamenka (ed.). New York: St. Martin's Press, 1983.

Mumford, Lewis. *The Story of the Utopias*. New York: Bonit and Liveright, 1922.

Nelson, Benjamin. "Community—Dreams and Realities" in *The Concept of Community in the History of Political and Legal Philosophy* by Carl J. Friederich (ed.). New York: Liberal Arts Press, 1959. pp. 135–51.

Neruda, Pablo. "Childhood and Poetry" in *Elementary Odes* by Pablo Neruda. New York: G. Massa Publishing, 1961.

Newman, Oscar. *Community of Interest*. Garden City, NY: Anchor Press/Doubleday, 1980.

———. *Defensible Space: Crime Prevention through Urban Design*. New York: Collier Books, 1972.

Nisbet, Robert A. *Community and Power*. New York: Oxford University Press, 1962

———. "Moral Values and Community." *International Review of Community Development*, no. 5, 1960, p. 82.

———. *The Sociological Tradition*. New Brunswick, NJ: Transaction Publishers, 1993.

Nobel, Philip I. "Homesickness, Disney, the New Urbanism, and the Future of the American Suburbs." *Things 5*, Winter 1996, pp. 86–105.

Norcross, Carl. "Townhouses and Condominiums: Residents' Likes and Dislikes." Washington: Urban Land Institute, 1973, pp. 6–11, 101, 105.

Ober, Josiah. *Mass and Elite in Democratic Athens*. Princeton, NJ: Princeton University Press, 1989.

Oldenburg, Ray. *The Great Good Place*. New York: Paragon House, 1989.

Oldenquist, Andrew, and Rosner, Menachem. "Community and De-alienation" in *Alienation, Community and Work* by Andrew Oldenquist and Menachem Rosner. New York: Greenwood Press, 1978. pp. 92–107.

———. "Direct Democracy in the Kibbutz" in *Alienation, Community and Work* by Andrew Oldenquist and Menachem Rosner. New York: Greenwood Press, 1978. pp. 178–91.

Oliner, Paul M., and Samuel P. *The Altruistic Personality: Rescuers of Jews in Nazi Europe*. New York: MacMillan Free Press, 1988.

Olson, Mancur Jr. *The Logic of Collective Action*. Cambridge, MA: Harvard University Press, 1965.

Orzack, Maressa Hecht. "Computer Addiction Is Coming On-line." *Harvard University Gazette*, 21 January 1999, vol. XCIV, no. 14, pp. 1–2.

Osborn, Frederick J., and Whittick, Arnold. *The New Towns: The Answer to Megalopolis*. New York: McGraw-Hill, 1963.

Oser, Alan S. "In Planned Communities, Self-Rule Is by Association," *New York Times*, 6 November 1977.

Osgood, Nancy J. *Senior Settlers*. New York: Praeger, 1982.

O'Toole, Michael F. *Physical Features and Social Relations in a Planned Community*. Princeton University senior thesis, Sociology Department, 1971.

Oved, Yaacov. *Two Hundred Years of American Communes*. New Brunswick: Transaction Books, 1988.

Oz, Amos. "On Social Democracy and the Kibbutz." *Dissent*, Summer 1997, pp. 39–46.

Park, Robert E. *Human Communities: The City and Human Ecology*. Glencoe, IL: The Free Press Co., 1952.

Parsons, Talcott. "Beyond Coercion and Crisis: The Coming of an Era of Voluntary Community" in *Culture and Society: Contemporary Debates* by Jeffrey C. Alexander and Steven Seidman (eds.). New York: Cambridge University Press, 1990. pp. 298–305.

———. *Essays in Sociological Theory, Pure and Applied*. Glencoe, IL: The Free Press, 1954.

———. *Societies: Evolutionary and Comparative Perspectives*. Englewood Cliffs, NJ: Prentice-Hall, 1966.

Pocock, J.G.A. *The Machiavellian Moment: Florentine Political Thought and the Atlantic Republican Tradition*. Princeton, NJ: Princeton University Press, 1975.

Poliakoff, Gary A. "Conflicting Rights in Condominium Living." *Florida Bar Journal*, December 1980, pp. 756–61.

Pollan, Michael. "Town Building Is No Mickey Mouse Operation." *New York Times Magazine*, 14 December 1997, pp. 56–63, 76–81, 88.

Popenoe, David. *The Suburban Environment: Sweden and the United States*. Chicago: University of Chicago Press, 1977.

Poplin, Dennis E. *Communities: A Survey of Theories and Methods of Research*. New York: MacMillan, 1972.

Portes, Alejandro (ed.). *The New Second Generation*. New York: Russell Sage Foundation, 1996.

Portes, Alejandro, and Stepick, Alex. *City on the Edge: The Transformation of Miami*. Berkeley: University of California Press, 1993.

Powell, Sumner Chilton. *Puritan Village*. New York: Doubleday Anchor Books, 1965.

Proshansky, Harold M., et al. (eds.) *Environmental Psychology: Man and His Physical Setting*. New York: Holt, Rinehart and Winston, 1970.

Putnam, Robert D. *Bowling Alone*. New York: Simon and Schuster, 2000.

———. "The Strange Disappearance of Civic America." *American Prospect*, no. 24, Winter 1996, pp. 34–48.

Quinn, Arthur. *A New World*. New York: Berkeley Books, 1995.

Redfield, Robert. *The Little Community and Peasant Society and Culture*. Chicago: University of Chicago Press, 1960.

———. *Tepoztlan, a Mexican Village: A Study of Folklife*. Chicago: University of Chicago Press, 1930.

Reynolds, Charles H., and Norman, Ralph V. (eds.). *Community in America: The Challenge of Habits of the Heart*. Berkeley: University of California Press, 1988.

Rheingold, Howard. *The Virtual Community*. New York: Addison-Wesley, 1993.

Roberts, Ron E. *The New Communes*. Englewood Cliffs, NJ: Prentice-Hall, Inc., 1971.

Rohrich, Ruby, and Barach, Elaine Hoffman. *Women in Search of Utopia, Mavericks and Mythmakers*. New York: Schoerer Books, 1984.

Ross, Andrew. *The Celebration Chronicle*. New York: Ballantine Books, 1999.

Rouner, Leroy S. (ed.). *On Community*. Notre Dame, IN: University of Notre Dame Press, 1991.

Rousseau, Jean Jacques. *The Social Contract and Discourses* (1762). London: J. M. Dent & Sons, 1983.

Rousseau, Mary F. *Community: The Tie That Binds*. Lanham, MD: University Press of America, 1991.

Sachs, Susan. "As New York City Immigration Thrives, Diversity Broadens." *New York Times*, 9 November 1999, pp. B1, B5.

Sager, Anthony P. "Radical Law: Three Collectives in Cambridge" in *Co-ops, Communes and Collectives* by John Case and Rosemary Taylor. New York: Pantheon Books, 1979. pp. 136–50.

Samples, John. "Ferdinand Toennies: Dark Times for a Liberal Intellectual," *Society*, Vol. 24 No. 6, September–October 1987, pp. 65–68.

Samuels, David. "In the Age of Radical Selfishness." *New York Times Magazine*, 17 October 1999, pp. 120–26, 152–53.

Sandel, Michael J. *Democracy's Discontent: America in Search of a Public Philosophy*. Boston: Belknap Press of Harvard University, 1996.

———. *Liberalism and the Limits of Justice*. Cambridge, UK: Cambridge University Press, 1998.

Sanders, Irwin T. *The Community: An Introduction to a Social System*. New York: Ronald Press Co., 1958.

Schambra, William. "Is New Federalism the Wave of the Future?" in *The Great Society and Its Legacy: Twenty Years of U.S. Social Policy* by Marshall Kaplan and Peggy L. Cuciti (eds.). Durham, NC: Duke University Press, 1986.

Scherer, Jacqueline. *Contemporary Community*. London: Tavistock Publications, 1972.

Schnapper, Dominique. *Community of Citizens*. New Brunswick: Community of Citizens, 1994.

Schneider, Keith. "Hate Groups Use Tools of the Electronic Trade," *New York Times*, 13 March 1995, p. A12.

Schudson, Michael. "What If Civic Life Didn't Die?" *American Prospect*, no. 25, April 1996, pp. 17–20.

Schuler, Douglas. *New Community Networks*. New York: Addison-Wesley, 1996.

Schwartz, Barry. *Changing Face of the Suburbs*. Chicago: University of Chicago Press, 1976.

Sennett, Richard. *The Fall of Public Man*. New York: Vintage Press, 1974.

Shapiro, Andrew L. "The Net That Binds," *The Nation*, 21 June 1999, pp. 11–15.

Shapiro, Perry. *The Periscope*, April 1982.

Shenk, Donna. *Aging and Retirement in a Lebanese-American Community*. New York: AMS Press, Inc., 1991.

Shklar, Judith N. *Men and Citizens: A Study of Rousseau's Social Theory*. Cambridge: University Press, 1969.

Shutkin, William A. *The Land That Could Be: Environmentalism and Democracy in the Twenty-First Century*. Cambridge: Massachusetts Institute of Technology Press, 2000.

Simmel, Georg. *Conflict and the Web of Group Affiliation*. Glencoe, IL: The Free Press, 1955.

———. *On Individuality and Social Forms*. Chicago: University of Chicago Press, 1971.

Simons, Marlise. "In New Europe, a Lingual Hodge Podge." *New York Times*, 17 October 1999.

Singleton, E. Crichton. "Celebration: Disney's Experiment in New Urbanism" AIA On-line Convention 1998. http://www.e-architect.com/pia/rude/celebra.asp.

Salter, Philip E. *The Pursuit of Loneliness*. Boston: Beacon Press, 1970.

Small, Susan. *The Periscope*, March 1982.

Smith, Adam. *The Theory of Moral Sentiments*. London: Millar, Kincaid and Bell, 1759.

Smith, Page. *As a City upon a Hill*. New York: Knopf, 1966.

Smithers, Janice A. *Determined Survivors: Community Life among the Urban Elderly*. New Brunswick, NJ: Rutgers University Press, 1985.

Spencer, Herbert. *Evolution of Society: Selections from Herbert Spencer's Principles of Sociology*. Chicago: University of Chicago, 1967.

Stacey, Margaret. "The Myth of Community Studies." *British Journal of Sociology*, vol. 20, no. 2, June 1969, p. 134–47.

Stark, Andrew. "America the Gated?" *Wilson Quarterly*, Winter 1998, pp. 58–79.

Starr, Chester G. *The Origins of Greek Civilization, 1100–650 B.C.* New York: W. W. Norton, 1991.

Starr, Paul. "The Phantom Community" in *Co-ops, Communes and Collectives* by John Case and Rosemary Taylor. New York: Pantheon Books, 1979. pp. 246–73.

Stein, Robert B., et al. "Urban Communes" in *Old Family/New Family* by Robert B. Stein. New York: D. Van Nostrand, 1975. pp. 171–87.

Sternlieb, George. *Demographic Trends and Economic Reality: Planning and Markets in the* Eighties. New Brunswick, NJ: Center for Urban Policy Research at Rutgers University, 1982.

Stilgoe, John R. *Borderland: Origins of the American Suburb, 1920–1939*. New Haven, CT: Yale University Press, 1988.

Suarez, Roy. *The Old Neighborhood: What Was Lost in the Great Suburban Migration*. New York: Free Press, 1999.

Sullivan, William M. *Reconstructing Public Philosophy*. Berkeley: University of California Press, 1982.

Suttles, Gerald D. *The Social Construction of Communities*. Chicago: University of Chicago Press, 1972. pp. 50–64.

Suttles, Gerald D., and Zald, Mayer N. *The Challenge of Social Control: Citi-*

zenship and Institution Building in Modern Society. Norwood, NJ: Ablex Publishing, 1985.

Taubes, Jacob. "Community after the Apocalypse," in *The Concept of Community in the History of Political and Legal Philosophy* by Carl J. Friederich. New York: Liberal Arts Press, 1959. pp. 101–111.

Thomas, William I., et al. (ed.). *The Polish Peasant in Europe and America: A Classic Work in Immigration History.* Urbana: University of Illinois Press, 1996.

Thomas, William I., and Znaniecki, Florian. *The Polish Peasant in Europe and America.* New York: Dover Publications, Inc., 1958.

Thompson, E. P. "Rituals of Mutuality" from *Culture and Society: Contemporary Debates* by Jeffrey C. Alexander and Steven Seidman. Cambridge: Cambridge University Press, 1990.

Tilly, Charles. "Do Communities Act?" *Sociological Inquiry*, vol. 43, nos. 3–4, 1973, pp.198–240.

Titmus, Richard M. *The Gift Relationship: From Human Blood to Social Policy.* London: Allen and Unwin, Ltd., 1970.

Tönnies, Ferdinand. *Gemeinschaft und Gesellschaft: Abhandlung des Communismus und des Socialismus als empirischer Culturformen.* Leipzig: Fues, 1887.

Tönnies, Ferdinand, and Loomis, Charles A. (ed.). *Community and Society.* East Lansing: Michigan State University Press, 1957.

Toutant, Charles. "Board Members Win TR Election," Windsor Heights Herald, 24 December 1999.

———. "TR Pools to Stay Residents Only," Windsor Heights Herald, 27 March 1998, pp. 1, 10A.

Tuma, Thomas. "Am Anfang Ist Das Wort:-." *Der Spiegel*, 18/1999, pp. 102–107.

Turkle, Sherry. *Life on the Screen.* New York: Simon & Schuster, 1995.

Turner, Victor W. *The Ritual Process: Structure and Anti-Structure.* Chicago: Aldine Publishing Co., 1969.

Ungar, Sanford J. *Fresh Blood: The New American Immigrants.* New York: Simon and Schuster, 1995. pp. 195–217.

Valerio, Christy. *Elderly Americans: Where They Choose to Retire.* New York: Garland Publishing, 1997.

Varoli, John. "A Little Levittown on the Neva." *New York Times*, 13 July 2000. pp. F1, F8.

Vidich, Arthur J. "Revolutions in Community Structure" in *The Dying Community* by Art Gallaher Jr., and Harland Padfield. Albuquerque: New Mexico Press, 1980. pp. 109–132.

Viroli, Maurizio, et al. *Machiavelli and Republicanism.* Cambridge: Cambridge University Press, 1990. pp. 143–72.

Voegelin, Eric. *Order and History, Vol. 3: Plato and Aristotle.* Baton Rouge: Louisiana State University Press, 1967.

———. *The World of the Polis.* Baton Rouge: Louisiana State University Press, 1991.

Wagner, Jon. "Perceiving a Planned Community" in *Images of Information* by Jon Wagner. Beverly Hills, CA: Sage Publications, 1979.

Walzer, Michael. *Spheres of Justice: A Defense of Pluralism and Equality*. New York: Basic Books, 1983.

Ward, Colin. *New Town, Home Town*. London: Calouste Gulbenkian Foundation, 1993.

Warner, W. L., and Lunt, Paul S. *The Social Life of a Modern Community*. New Haven, CT: Yale University Press, 1941.

Warren, R. L. *The Community in America*. Chicago: Rand McNally, 1971.

Warren, Richard L., and Lyon, Larry. *New Perspectives on the American Community*. Homewood, IL: The Dorsey Press, 1983.

Warren, Roland L. "The Good Community — What Would It Be?" *Journal of the City Development Society*, no. 1, Spring 1970, pp. 14–23.

Webber, Melvin M. *Explorations into Urban Structure*. Philadelphia: University of Pennsylvania Press, 1964.

Weber, Max. *Economy and Society: An Outline of Interpretive Sociology*. London: G. Allen and Unwin, Ltd., 1978.

———. *The Protestant Ethic and the Spirit of Capitalism*. London: G. Allen & Unwin, Ltd., 1930.

Weinbaum, Batya. "Twin Oaks: A Feminist Looks at Indigenous Socialism in the United States" in *Women in Search of Utopia, Mavericks and Mythmakers* by Ruby Rohrlich and Elaine Hoffman Baruch. New York: Schocken Books, 1984. pp. 157–67.

Wellman, Barry. *Networks in the Global Village: Life in Contemporary Communities*. Boulder, CO: Westview Press, 1999.

Wellman, Barry, and Berkowitz, S. D. (eds.). *Social Structures: A Network Approach*. Cambridge, UK: Cambridge University Press, 1988.

Wesolowski, Wlodzimierz, et al. (eds.). *Postcommunist Elites and Democracy in Eastern Europe*. New York: St. Martin's Press, 1998.

White, David R. "In the New World of Euro Arts." *New York Times*, 30 October 1999, pp. 1, 32.

White, Merry I. "Global Japan: Internationalism in the Intimate Community" in *On Community* by Leroy S. Rouner. Notre Dame, IN: University of Notre Dame Press, 1991. pp. 91–104.

Whyte, William H. *City: Rediscovering the Center*. New York: Doubleday, 1988.

———. *The Social Life of Small Urban Spaces*. Washington, DC: Conservation Foundation, 1980.

Wiebe, Robert H. *The Opening of American Society: From the Adoption of the Constitution to the Eve of Disunion*. New York: Knopf, 1984. p. 42.

Williams, Robin M. Jr. "The Reduction of Intergroup Tensions." *SSRC Bulletin*, no. 57. New York, 1947.

Wilson, Edmund. *The Triple Thinkers: Ten Essays on Literature*. New York: Harcourt, Brace, 1938.

Wolf, Deborah Goleman. *The Lesbian Community*. Berkeley: University of California Press, 1979.

Wolin, Sheldon. *Politics and Vision: Continuity and Innovation in Western Political Thought*. Boston: Little, Brown, 1960.

Wright, Gwendolyn. *Building the Dream: A Social History of Housing in America*. New York: Pantheon Books, 1981.

Wright, James D. "Small Towns, Mass Society, and the Twenty-first Century." *Society*, vol. 38, no. 1, November/December 2000, pp. 3–10.

Wuthnow, Robert. *Learning to Care: Elementary Kindness in an Age of Indifference*. New York: Oxford University Press, 1995.

Wylie, Laurence William. *Village in the Vaucluse*. Cambridge, MA: Harvard University Press, 1974.

Yinger, John M., and Cutler, Stephen J. (eds.). *Major Social Issues*. Glencoe, IL: The Free Press, 1978.

Zablocki, Benjamin. *The Joyful Community: An Account of the Bruderhof, a Communal Movement* Now in Its Third Generation. Chicago: University of Chicago Press, 1980.

Zelinsky, Wilbur. *The Cultural Geography of the United States*. Englewood Cliffs, NJ: Prentice-Hall, 1973.

Zhou, Min, and Bankston, Carl, III. "Social Capital and the Adaptation of the Second Generation: The Case of Vietnamese Youth in New Orleans," from *The Second Generation* by Alejandro Portes. New York: Russell Sage Foundation, 1996, pp. 197–220.

Zimmern, Alfred. *The Greek Commonwealth: Politics and Economies in Fifth-Century Athens*. London: Oxford University Press, 1952.

The local media were monitored during the three decades and are selectively cited in the text. They include both newspapers from surrounding communities and the variety of Twin Rivers newsletters (sporadic and short-lived in the early decades) until a stable format was achieved. These include:

OPUS 1970–1973
The Periscope 1972–1985(?)
The Windsor Heights Herald 1972–1999
Trenton Times 1971
Twin Rivers Today 1982 to present

ACKNOWLEDGMENTS

No book is an island and every author is deeply indebted to those who gave of their time and talents to get a book into final shape. Hence it is with keen appreciation that I express my gratitude to the following:

The National Science Foundation, whose grant, under the guidance of H. Kenneth Gayer, helped launch the pilot study in the 1970s. The Guggenheim Foundation honored me with a coveted fellowship also in the 1970s; and the Rockefeller Foundation granted me a one month's stay in beautiful Bellagio, Italy, in the late 1980s. Princeton University proffered three summer grants for data analysis, and the DBH Foundation financed research assistance in the 1990s.

I am grateful to Gerald Finn, the visionary, and Herbert J. Kendall, the developer, of Twin Rivers. Each talked with me for extended periods in the early years and gave me the benefit of their considerable experience. Early on also, Attorney Leonard L. Wolffe gave me a remarkable overview of how the first PUD in the state came to see the light of day.

For the design and planning of the residents' survey in the 1980s, the contribution of Dr. Irving Crespi of the Gallup organization is gratefully acknowledged. For the 1990s residents' survey, I am similarly indebted to Dr. Edward Freeland of the Princeton University Research Center.

For in-depth interviews with large samples of Twin Rivers residents in the 1980s, I thank Carol S. Stamets and for those done in the 1990s, thanks go to Geraldine Harris. In distinctive ways, each established fine rapport with their informants and tapped their reactions and perspectives with commendable skill.

More generally, a word of appreciation for Robert L. Geddes, former dean of Princeton's School of Architecture, from whom I learned a great deal during the years of our collaboration as he strove to advance a rapprochement between architecture and the social sciences. And as always my gratitude to Robert K. Merton, master teacher and friend.

Daniel Bell read several early chapters and gave me the benefit of his vast knowledge and warm encouragement. And an anonymous reviewer's extraordinarily sensitive and detailed critique was a gift that I hereby acknowledge with anonymous gratitude.

A Fulbright grant in Greece gave me the opportunity to spend several years at the Athens Center of Ekistics under the impassioned leadership of the remarkable C. A. Doxiadis. As the creator of Ekistics, his pioneering efforts to devise a broadly conceived architectural education attracted students and practitioners from all over the world and created an extraordinary setting for his pioneering agenda.

Those years also started my lifelong friendship with Panaghis Psomopoulos, architect and Ekistician, who would carry the torch of Doxiadis forward into the future. I vividly recall our virtually daily conversations about architecture, sociology, the future of cities, and spatial planning. How young we were, and how passionately committed to improving the human condition.

Returning now to this side of the Atlantic, it was my good fortune to benefit from the keen editorial eye of Scotia MacCrea who not only made the manuscript more readable but became a friend in the process.

Thanks also go to Blanche Anderson for typing the final manuscript and readying it for publication with such assiduous care. Though she might well have groaned inwardly — "not another addition, excision, revision" — she never let on and was a marvel of goodwill throughout.

For bibliographical sleuthing and the 1990s photographs of Twin Rivers, Kevin Williams warrants appreciation and thanks.

I was also most fortunate that Laurel Cantor was able to give her time and artistry to the book.

My gratitude also to Marsha Kunin for excellent copyediting, and to Carolyn Sherayko for her splendid index. I thank Ian Malcolm, editor, for his wise counsel. I also thank Anne Reifsnyder, who guided the production of the book.

And of course, there are the residents of Twin Rivers, whom I came to admire and care about and whose acceptance of my long-term perusal of their lives and fortunes made the often arduous labors exciting and rewarding. Since we had agreed that the interviews were not for publication I cannot thank each personally but want to express my gratitude collectively.

A number of board members also spoke with me at length and I take this opportunity to underscore their devotion to their fellows and their voluntary contributions to the general welfare of Twin Rivers.

Special mention goes also to Joseph R. Vuzzo, Twin Rivers Trust Administrator, who served Twin Rivers for more than fifteen years with wholehearted dedication. He was unfailingly helpful in his readiness to share his insights and experience of this special community. His successor, Jennifer Ward, has likewise been most welcoming and accessible.

Special thanks go also to the Twin Rivers Community Trust Office, most especially to Lois Primer, for their unfailing kindness and responsiveness to my queries.

Finally, there is my gratitude to Charles M. Haar, who went way beyond the call of marital duty in his sustained encouragement and generosity of spirit. Ever ready to serve as sounding board, cheerleader, sensitive critic, and loving presence, his were the priceless gifts of time, genuine interest, good humor, and lots of take-out dinners.

INDEX

Page references in italics indicate tables.

PRINCETON STUDIES IN CULTURAL SOCIOLOGY